Drugs, Crime, and Social Isolation

**ADELE V. HARRELL AND
GEORGE E. PETERSON**
Editors

DRUGS, CRIME, AND SOCIAL ISOLATION

Barriers to Urban Opportunity

THE URBAN INSTITUTE PRESS
Washington, D.C.

THE URBAN INSTITUTE PRESS
2100 M Street, N.W.
Washington, D.C. 20037

Library of Congress Cataloging in Publication Data

Drugs, Crime, and Social Isolation: Barriers to Urban Opportunity/Adele V. Harrell and George E. Peterson, editors.

1. Inner cities—United States. 2. Afro-Americans—Social conditions. 3. Drug abuse—United States. 4. Social integration—United States. 5. Crime—United States. I. Harrell, Adele. II. Peterson, George E.

HN59.2.D78   1992   92-15121
307.3'362'0973—dc20   CIP

ISBN 0-87766-571-0 (alk. paper)
ISBN 0-87766-570-2 (alk. paper; casebound)

Urban Institute books are printed on acid-free paper whenever possible.

Printed in the United States of America.

Distributed by:
          University Press of America
4720 Boston Way   3 Henrietta Street
Lanham, MD 20706   London   WC2E 8LU   ENGLAND

THE URBAN INSTITUTE is a nonprofit policy research and educational organization established in Washington, D.C., in 1968. Its staff investigates the social and economic problems confronting the nation and government policies and programs designed to alleviate such problems. The Institute disseminates significant findings of its research through the publications program of its Press. The Institute has two goals for work in each of its research areas: to help shape thinking about societal problems and efforts to solve them, and to improve government decisions and performance by providing better information and analytic tools.

Through work that ranges from broad conceptual studies to administrative and technical assistance, Institute researchers contribute to the stock of knowledge available to public officials and private individuals and groups concerned with formulating and implementing more efficient and effective government policy.

Conclusions or opinions expressed in Institute publications are those of the authors and do not necessarily reflect the views of other staff members, officers or trustees of the Institute, advisory groups, or any organizations that provide financial support to the Institute.

URBAN OPPORTUNITY SERIES TITLES

Drugs, Crime, and Social Isolation:
Barriers to Urban Opportunity
Edited by *Adele V. Harrell* and *George E. Peterson*

Urban Labor Markets and Job Opportunity
Edited by *George E. Peterson* and *Wayne P. Vroman*

Big-City Politics, Governance, and Fiscal Constraints
Edited by *George E. Peterson*

Housing Markets and Residential Mobility
Edited by *G. Thomas Kingsley* and *Margery Austin Turner*

ACKNOWLEDGMENTS

We would like to thank all of those who contributed to the Conference on Drugs, Crime, and Social Isolation: Barriers to Urban Opportunity, and to the production of this volume. These include the many conference participants whose ideas and experiences helped to shape the contents of this volume; the Ford foundation staff who provided the support and vision for this project; Carlotta Molitor and James O'Connell who managed the logistics with ultimate skill; and especially the authors, reviewers, and editors for their concerted efforts to produce this work.

This work was funded by a grant from the Ford Foundation.

CONTENTS

Tables

Opportunity is a distinctively American value. Immigrants of all eras who have chosen to come to this country have been drawn to a place where those willing to work can find economic advancement and where groups of all kinds have the right of access to the institutions that support social mobility. For most of U.S. history, equal opportunity has been part of the basic consensus defining the goals of American society.

The city occupies a central role in this conception. The very notion of the city in the United States has been identified with accelerated opportunities that help to dismantle barriers confining people of a certain class, race, or ethnic group to permanent stations in life. Two trends now threaten the ideal of opportunity.

First, urban opportunities for advancement have narrowed. To a great extent, this is a result of the slowdown in aggregate economic growth. When average output per worker advances more slowly, fewer individuals are able to race ahead in their own lives. But this narrowing of opportunity also reflects the fact that institutions—particularly the urban institutions that historically have furthered economic and social opportunity for those not already in the middle class—seem to have failed these same individuals.

Second, the consensus surrounding equal opportunity has eroded. The term itself has become closely identified with a particular strategy of remedial action. As a result, the political debate over how, and to what extent, society should compensate for past unequal opportunity has tended to undermine agreement about the importance of an equal opportunity structure. The alternative to this structure might be labeled a competitive opportunity system, in which groups or individuals compete for access to the fewer opportunity routes now open, based on their own inherited endowments.

The Urban Opportunity Program, supported by The Ford Foundation, has the goal of reconsidering the last quarter century of changes in urban markets and institutions, from the perspective of the opportunity structure. Toward this goal, The Urban Institute sponsored a series of conferences on different aspects of urban opportunity. Four broad subjects were covered: drugs, crime, and social isolation; urban labor markets and barriers to job mobility; housing markets and residential mobility; and big city politics and fiscal choices. The papers in this volume grew out of or were inspired by one or more of these conferences.

The authors of this book assume the value of opportunity by focusing on its absence—on the conditions and circumstances that cut off or isolate city residents from the routes to upward advancement. In the process of responding to and analyzing what appear to be inequities in opportunity, they address many of the theories advanced to explain our current urban dilemma.

The movement of jobs to the suburbs and the sunbelt and the decline of the manufacturing sector have made entry-level, low-skill jobs harder to find in many cities. The growing concentration of urban poverty further reduces the resources available in inner-city neighborhoods and undermines schools and community vitality. In this environment, the social allure and economic incentives of the drug market have proved an attractive alternative for many inner-city residents, transforming their lives and further isolating them from mainstream opportunities.

To explore the processes that link these trends, this volume examines mobility into and out of poor neighborhoods, the impact of discrimination and labor market restructuring on job opportunities, and the effects of drugs and crime on families and careers in inner-city neighborhoods. Lest we be lured into policy prescriptions aimed only at remediating structural inequalities, the papers also delve into the meaning of these trends—from the perspective of those whose lives are shaped by the need to respond to these limitations in opportunity. These analyses reveal the difficulties inherent in policies based on single-cause assumptions, and the need for policies targeting both longer and shorter term objectives.

William Gorham
President

Chapter One

INTRODUCTION: INNER-CITY ISOLATION AND OPPORTUNITY

George E. Peterson and Adele V. Harrell

This volume addresses a troubling theme: the isolation of the inner city in America and the impact of that isolation on the opportunities of inner-city residents.

The concept of isolation has multiple dimensions. There is literal, physical separation, such as the distancing of inner-city residents from the suburban locations where jobs are being created and the racial isolation imposed by segregated housing patterns. There is social isolation resulting from class homogeneity of contacts and, according to some authors, weak participation of inner-city residents in social organizations. There is the isolation imposed by high rates of crime and drug activity, as well as the habits of inner-city street life, where acceptance of neighborhood behavioral norms can progressively cut off access to mainstream society.

These dimensions of isolation overlap with one another and profoundly affect opportunity patterns. Residential segregation implies segregated schooling, which, at least in urban America, means ineffective schooling. The chances that a child growing up in an inner-city neighborhood will become involved in crime and separated from society by being placed in jail are much greater than the chances that this will happen to a child living anywhere else. Incarceration has become one of society's most powerful signalling devices; even years later, the experience of having done jail time makes it far more difficult to find legitimate work. Whether inner-city isolation, except in the physical sense, is more than a metaphor for different life histories and unequal outcomes, however, is less clear. One purpose of the authors of this volume is to determine which dimensions of inner-city isolation are susceptible to empirical definition and testing, quantify these measures, and examine their consequences for lifetime opportunity.

There is irony in the concept of urban isolation. Historically, households have been attracted to cities because of the opportunities they afford for *connection*. Jobs traditionally were more concentrated and more abundant in the cities, and a wealth of workingmen's associations and, later, unions existed to support job mobility for workers. Social institutions—the product of what de Tocqueville called the American genius for civil association—flourished in the city, ranging from political clubs to parent-teacher associations and from self-help and cultural societies to immigrant associations. Nor were these organizations identified exclusively with the urban middle class. Following the Civil War, membership in the self-improvement, political, and social clubs, as well as churches of northern cities ran high among African-American workers and new immigrant groups.

Nonetheless, there long has been an alternative perception of life among the urban poor, which depicts the city's poverty areas as agglomerations of workers (or would-be workers) deprived of affiliation with the social and economic mainstream. The urban settlement-house movement of the early 20th century reflected this perspective. Its university founders believed that the "industrial classes" were so immersed in their daily labor that they lacked a sense of "citizenship" connecting them with the rest of the nation, or even with their working-class colleagues. To fill the void, the settlement reformers sought to create neighborhood centers that would serve as the hubs of a thick network of cultural, recreational, economic, and social institutions functioning amidst the slums. In the East End of London, for example, Toynbee Hall offered to the poor an astonishing variety of clubs and courses, from classical languages to botany and German literature, but also supported a children's country holiday program that in 1888 sent 17,000 children to the countryside, provided space for union meetings, and offered both moral and logistical support for rent strikes and the collective bargaining efforts of match girls and dockworkers (Himmelfarb 1991). In the United States, settlement houses sprang up on almost as large a scale in all the major cities, dedicated to the proposition that the urban poor needed to be reconnected with the rest of urban society. As Robert Woods (1923), head of South End House in Boston, wrote in defining the settlement idea: it started from the premise that "The great city . . . shows by multiple effects the danger of having people cut off from the better life of society," (p. 2) and sought to reconstruct the city by recreating neighborhood communities, with the settlement house becoming a neutral ground for contact between the classes.

In recent years, the conviction has intensified that the urban population is pulling apart. In its 1968 report the Kerner Commission offered its now-famous conclusion that America's cities were on the course of becoming two nations—separate but unequal (U.S. National

Advisory Commission on Civil Disorders 1968). The basis of this division was racial segregation, but separation of the races within urban areas had led to, and was reinforced by, a two-tier system of law enforcement, schooling, and income-earning opportunities that eventually would produce different aspirations and civic values among the segregated groups. Since the time of the Kerner Commission report, the nation has made progress in dismantling the legal supports of segregation and in removing several of the specific obstacles that the commission emphasized, such as barriers to minority housing purchases in the suburbs or the practice of having overwhelmingly white police forces patrol overwhelmingly black neighborhoods. Yet, there is widespread belief that, in practical terms, the two urban nations the Kerner Commission warned of are more a reality today than they were in 1968. As Edward Gramlich, Deborah Laren, and Naomi Sealand (chapter 8, this volume) have described the prevailing perception, there is a pool of mostly minority "poor people [living] in poor areas . . . . trapped both in poverty and in their poor neighborhoods, . . . suffer[ing] a lack of job opportunities, a lack of upper-class role models, excessive crime . . . . their children . . . condemned to substandard schooling." A special term—*the underclass*—has emerged to express this group's more or less permanent isolation from the urban mainstream.

This volume's authors explore several dimensions of the separation that has been hypothesized to isolate the inner city. Terms like *isolation* or *underclass* are freighted with many different connotations. Often they carry with them both an implicit diagnosis of what has produced the problem and an implied prescription as to the appropriate policy response. The result is a debate, heated at times, about solutions to the inequalities deriving from segmentation in urban areas. This debate is fueled by a lack of clarity, conceptually and empirically, about the relationship between nationwide and city-scale shifts in the opportunity structure, the adaptation to these shifts by people who organize their lives in response to opportunities as they see them, and the processes that link the two. Within the sociological community, the debate has crystallized between ecologically minded sociologists who emphasize the sorting and resorting of people and neighborhoods in response to economic restructuring or suburbanization and those who emphasize the specific policies, local institutions, and collective interests that lie behind reorganization of the city. (See Logan and Molotch, 1987; Gottdiener and Pickvance, 1991).

It therefore is important to endeavor to disentangle the empirical evidence in support of each part of the description of inner-city separation and to clarify along which dimensions urban neighborhoods are in fact becoming more differentiated. Where this differentiation appears in some cities but not in others, it is important to understand the local policies and local institutions, as well as market forces, that account for the different responses. Otherwise, analysis (and policy-making) can fall into generalizations about an isolated "underclass" whose exact features are left to each listener to fill in, according to his or her intuition and policy prejudice.

PHYSICAL ISOLATION

Physical isolation should be the least ambiguous index of separation. However, the recent record is not clear as to whether American cities are evolving in ways that reduce or exacerbate physical separation. By almost every measure, racial isolation in metropolitan areas declined in the 1980s. The proportion of blacks living in block groups in which at least 90 percent of the population is black, for example, fell in 36 of the 50 largest metropolitan areas. It rose in only 3, and was unchanged in 11 others. Alternative measures of racial segregation also fell (Farley 1992). However, the gains in integration in most urban areas were small, and racial isolation remains startlingly high in a number of large cities. In Chicago, St. Louis, Cleveland, and Detroit, for example, more than 60 percent of the African-Americans living anywhere in the entire metropolitan region live in block groups that are at least 90 percent black. Most of this concentration is found in the central city.

The concentration and separation of an "underclass" population can be viewed from the national perspective, by asking where the households defined as belonging to this class live. Although detailed data from the U.S. Bureau of the Census for 1990 are not yet available for analysis, earlier information reveals that by any of the usual definitions, poverty and "underclass" populations are highly concentrated in central cities. Moreover, at least in the largest cities the degree of concentration is rising. Half of the nation's poor lived in central cities in 1985 (Reischauer 1987), up from one-third in 1972. Although the total U.S. poverty population grew by only 8 percent between 1970 and 1980, the number of extreme poverty census tracts in central cities rose by two-thirds (Jargowsky and Bane 1990). Almost 70 percent of the residents of these extreme poverty tracts were black; another 20 percent were Hispanic. However, Jargowsky and Bane

(1991) have pointed out that the picture of rapidly intensifying poverty concentration drawn from comparisons like these is somewhat deceptive. When smaller metropolitan areas, especially in the South, are included in the comparison, the aggregate increase in concentrated poverty is much reduced, because of the reduction and dispersion of poverty occurring in these places. In fact, the overwhelming majority of central-city poverty growth has occurred in just a few cities, principally New York City, Chicago, Philadelphia, and Detroit.

Attempts to define and track underclass neighborhoods have reported greater concentration and more explosive growth. Mincy, Sawhill, and Wolf (1990) defined underclass census tracts as those that exceed the national averages by at least one standard deviation in all four of the following characteristics: high rates of school dropout, joblessness, female-headed families, and welfare dependency. The underclass neighborhoods that result from this definition are found to be located mostly in the central cities of the Northeast and Midwest. Between 1970 and 1980, the total number of people living in such underclass areas rose by 230 percent. This has suggested to some that a fundamental sorting out of the urban population is under way that could indeed lead to long-term physical separation, if not of races or ethnic groups, then of "classes" with a strong racial overlap.

Perhaps most striking from a national perspective is the degree of concentration of distressed households in just a few cities. As John D. Kasarda (chapter 3, this volume) demonstrates, 44 percent of the distressed households in the 95 largest cities (according to a household definition of *distress* similar to the census tract definition of *underclass* employed above) live in New York City, Chicago, Philadelphia, and Detroit alone—mostly in contiguous census tracts. Sixty-five percent of the severely distressed Hispanic households live in these same four cities. The size of the underclass ghettos means that most ghetto residents live surrounded by other neighborhoods of the same type. Their principal contact with the middle class may consist of uniformed, authority figures exercising control functions. From this perspective, the assertion that the United States has a de facto policy of relegating distressed, minority households to a few central city "reservations" may not seem so exaggerated. Why the experience of these four cities has been so distinctive, and what, in addition to size, sets them apart from the rest of the urban universe, remains a largely unanswered question. Is the isolation of inner-city Detroit principally the product of automobile companies that fled the city in the face of a racially changing workforce and plant environment, then failed to restructure to compete with foreign companies? Or would essentially the same outcomes have occurred, regardless of what the Big Three auto companies and the City of Detroit tried to do, because of de-industrialization forced on American companies by international competition?

Segregation indices measure where households of different types live in relation to one another. One can also measure physical separation in terms of where households live in relation to jobs. The extent and significance of the spatial mismatch between jobs that are being created in the suburbs and minority populations living in the central city are explored in another volume of this series (Peterson and Vroman 1992). However, some elements of the relationship help complete the picture of inner-city isolation. The differences in journey-to-work times for commutes within the city versus commutes from city to suburb, as examined by Kasarda for 1980 (chapter 3, this volume), are less than one might suspect. Black workers who cross-commuted spent two to six minutes more per trip than black workers who lived and worked in the central city. This amounts to an additional 4 percent to 20 percent in average travel time to get to suburban jobs, depending upon the metropolitan area. It is noteworthy that for commuting trips *within* the city, black workers have considerably greater travel-time differentials, suggesting that segregation of city residential neighborhoods, the distance between minority residential concentrations and job centers within the city, and the patterns of city transit routes may be as problematic for black households as the suburbanization of job creation.

In cases where the old industrial factories now being phased out were located immediately adjacent to low-income minority population neighborhoods, firms' moves to the suburbs can create far greater difficulties for minority workers. Fernandez (1991) reported that when a mid-sized manufacturing firm in Milwaukee recently moved to the suburbs, the black hourly workers in the labor force had to increase their commutes by an average of well over 100 percent, in both distance and time, to retain their jobs. Hispanic workers had to more than triple their commuting distances. However, it should be noted that the average commute for black workers prior to the move was far less than that for whites. Zax and Kain (1991) found that when a Detroit service-industry firm suburbanized, low-paid black workers tended to keep their central-city residences but to lengthen their commutes, whereas white workers at the same wage level were much more likely to quit their positions and take other jobs or move to housing closer to work. Black workers did not have the same options.

The evidence on physical isolation, then, is mixed. It seems to indicate that whereas overall racial segregation is declining—owing mostly to suburbanization of the middle-income black community—the geographical separation of distressed households from both middle-class neighborhoods and job centers is accelerating in the large metropolitan areas of the Northeast and Midwest, perhaps sharply. There is even evidence that distressed households are being separated from the governmental institutions intended to support them. Municipal budget cutbacks have brought, among other things, a recentralization of social services, which threatens to add "government" to the list of institutions no longer readily accessible in the inner city. Thus, at least for some urban residents, physical access to services, resources, and jobs is constrained and helps to limit the opportunity structure.

DRUGS, CRIME, AND UNDERCLASS BEHAVIORS

More important than physical distance in isolating the underclass is social distance, and more important than geographic location in setting apart a neighborhood is what might be called its behavioral norms. Contagion models (e.g., Crane 1991b; Montgomery 1991) hypothesize that socially deviant behaviors spread within neighborhoods by "infecting" healthy residents. The greater the number of disease carriers, the greater the probability that a healthy individual will be infected. To change metaphors, once a critical mass of a certain behavior has been reached (such as violent crime, welfare dependency, or drug use) the neighborhood is likely to "tip," so that such behavior becomes the local norm, accelerating its spread still further. These behavioral disparities themselves represent, at least in part, responses to the limited opportunities of advancement through conventional channels. Once in place, the local norms become powerful limitations on the choices seen as available or attractive to others.

Distressed neighborhoods are characterized by a number of deviant behaviors, but probably the most visible and most important involve drug use, drug selling, and violent crime. Spatial differentiation with respect to these behaviors has become acute in some cities, especially the largest cities where the other indices of inner-city separation are most pronounced. A study of 17 inner-city census tracts in Philadelphia tracked admissions to hospital emergency rooms for a year

(Wishner et al. 1991). The researchers found that "interpersonal violence-related injuries" serious enough to warrant emergency room treatment occurred annually in more than 8.5 percent of the males 20–24 years of age (almost all of whom were African-American). Even allowing for repeat injuries, this would imply that as many as one-third of the males in the sample area could end up in a hospital emergency room with this type of injury at some point between ages 20 and 24, while many others could visit the emergency room more than once. In all of the age brackets between 15 and 39 years of age the annual rate of emergency room injuries resulting from personal violence exceeded 6 percent for males (Wishner et al. 1991). Studies in Ohio have found that children born out of wedlock in black households have a 9 to 15 times greater risk of childhood homicide than the population at large. The odds go up further if the mother is a high school dropout, lives in a metropolitan area, or is a teenager at the time of birth (Winpisinger et al. 1991). This study did not examine the additional effects of inner-city residence, though the risks are known to be much higher in these neighborhoods.

Overlapping with patterns of crime has been the pattern of use and sale of illicit drugs. Since the 1970s, drug use has been more prevalent in large metropolitan areas than in small cities or rural areas—a relationship that has persisted across rising and falling trends in drug popularity (Miller et al. 1983; National Institute on Drug Abuse 1991a). Now in its third decade, the drug crisis has moved from marijuana smoking and cocaine snorting by young people in college and by professionals to the smoking of highly addictive crack cocaine among the poor. In 1982, past-month cocaine use was twice as common among whites as among blacks and other races (7 percent compared to 3 percent). By 1990, past cocaine use had dropped dramatically among whites (to 1.9 percent), but not among blacks and Hispanics. Indeed, drug historian David Musto (1988) warned of the emergence of a two-tiered drug culture in which inner-city ghetto use of the most addictive drugs sustains itself, while middle-class suburban use declines. There is, however, considerable evidence that in the last two years (1989–91) crack use among inner-city youth also has begun to decline. Eventually, this should translate into lower total usage, but in the meantime it has led to perverse situations in which inner-city youths make their living by selling crack to their elders.

The association between criminal activity and drug use is especially evident in cities suffering from high poverty concentrations. In 1990, over 60 percent of female arrestees tested positive for cocaine at police booking in Manhattan, Detroit, and Philadelphia, whereas over half of male arrestees tested cocaine positive in Manhattan, Philadelphia, and Chicago (National Institute of Justice 1991). Among children being held in New York State's youth detention system, cocaine use reached 26 percent, or a rate four and a half times that among children of the same age in school (New York State 1991).[1]

One of the important unanswered questions about underclass concentration has been whether neighborhood differentiation with respect to violent crime and drug use is increasing (Jencks 1991). At least within older cities, the answer seems to be that it is. Many poverty areas have in effect become "zoned" for risky behavior, leading to vast differences in the frequency of occurrence. In Washington, D.C., for example, arrests for drug use or possession in 1980 already were 6 times higher per capita in extreme poverty neighborhoods (those with more than 40 percent of residents below the poverty line) than in nonpoverty neighborhoods. However, between 1980 and 1988 the *increase* in drug arrest rates was 8 times greater in the extreme poverty census tracts. Violent crime rates started the decade more than 3 times higher in extreme poverty neighborhoods; the increase between 1980 and 1988 was almost 5 times greater. In Cleveland, drug arrest rates that started out 6 times higher in the extreme poverty tracts showed an increase that was 22 times larger between 1980 and 1988 (Wiener and Mincy 1991). Although police enforcement policies, especially toward drug use, may explain part of the extraordinary differences in neighborhood arrest rates, there seems little doubt that the underlying behaviors also have become more differentiated. In this respect, violent crimes and drug use differ from other behaviors sometimes ascribed to the "underclass." Wiener and Mincy found no overall neighborhood pattern to changes in teenage birth rates, for example, while robbery and burglary rates grew much faster in nonpoverty areas, as criminals apparently shifted their operations to neighborhoods where there was more to be stolen. This study also found that violent crime and drug arrest rates were more strongly linked to neighborhood *poverty* than to the combination of demographic and institutional proxies that have been used to define un-

---

1. Whether drug involvement *leads to (or independently predicts)* a higher probability of criminal involvement is unclear. It may be that those headed toward crime also engage in drug activity, and that, after adequate control for family, neighborhood and other influences, drug involvement adds little to the probability of criminal involvement. (See Goldkamp 1990). Even if this is true, the association between drugs and crime has changed neighborhood environments and added to the rewards of criminal behavior, as Fagan points out in chapter 4 of this volume.

derclass neighborhoods (such as high rates of single-parent families or welfare dependency).

Together with ethnographic and statistical evidence on the effects of criminal activity and cocaine use on lifetime opportunity, the evidence of intensifying stratification of urban neighborhoods by extent of socially deviant behavior suggests that more attention should be paid to these behaviors in defining functionally distressed neighborhoods. Drug use, drug selling, and violent crime are all behaviors with strong externalities that curtail others' ability to use a neighborhood. Moreover, Freeman (1992) shows how strongly a record of youthful criminal incarceration hampers long-term ability to earn income from legitimate work. Several chapters in this volume also provide ethnographic accounts of how drastically involvement in the inner-city drug world limits future opportunities.

SOCIAL ISOLATION

In William Julius Wilson's and Loic Wacquant's analysis of the underclass (Wilson 1987; Wacquant and Wilson 1989), the ultimate isolation of the inner city is its social isolation—that is, "the lack of contact or of sustained interaction with the individuals or institutions that represent mainstream society." Some of this isolation may result from physical separation or from levels of crime and drug use that drive out the institutions and people that normally would provide sources of interclass contact. But the concept of social isolation asserts furthermore that the lack of middle- or upper-class presence is crucial to neighborhood separation, and that inhabitants of underclass areas are unable to compensate in other parts of their lives for the estrangement that marks their residential neighborhoods.

Eloise Dunlap and Ansley Hamid, in chapters 6 and 7 of this volume, respectively, examine different aspects of social isolation, and in the process also consider how norms of drug use and crime are transmitted. Dunlap portrays inner-city families so wracked by drugs that they are unable to model any conventional values for their children or provide them with even the minimal connections to a stable outside world. In such families, the extended family provides its own, substitute universe filled with drug consumption and criminal activity, while interposing itself between individual family members and mainstream institutions. Hamid's account, which illustrates the ef-

fects of crack on middle-aged, formerly middle-class black males, emphasizes the precariousness of inner-city life. Even seemingly secure
jobs and good incomes are not enough to protect the men in his
account from the pressures of the street. Their descent into the all-
consuming world of cocaine dependence deprives the young people
in the community, especially young males, of the contacts they need
to help connect them to the world of conventional labor, thus com-
pounding their own isolation with community isolation.

Roberto M. Fernandez and David Harris (chapter 9, this volume)
construct a more formal test of Wilson's hypotheses of social isolation, using Wilson's sample of inner-city Chicago households. Along
some dimensions, they find alarming extremes of isolation from the
"mainstream," especially among nonworking poor women. For example, 17.6 percent of these women report having no friends that they
could turn to in an emergency. For those who do report having friends,
44.7 percent of the friends are on public aid and outside the labor
force, indicating a tendency toward a closed community. The nonworking poor as a group are significantly less likely to regularly attend
meetings of a wide variety of community, school, social, and church
organizations. By and large, however, Wilson's hypothesis that living
in poor neighborhoods substantially exacerbates the isolation of in-
dividually poor households is not borne out in this sample. Neighborhood effects on social participation, as measured by the influence
of the poverty and employment status of neighbors living in the same
census tract, were for the most part small, much smaller than the
effects of the household's own poverty and employment status. Ironically, some of the strongest neighborhood effects are found among
nonpoor "mainstream" households living in poor areas, who go to
considerable lengths to isolate themselves socially from their neighbors. This result would seem to weaken Wilson's argument that finding ways to retain a middle-class presence in underclass neighborhoods will by itself enhance social contacts. Some of the behavioral
norms in extreme poverty neighborhoods are likely to appear as
threatening to nonpoverty residents as they do to nonpoverty outsiders, with the consequence that mainstream households try to in-
sulate themselves from neighborhood contact rather than serve as
neighborhood resources. Fernandez's and Harris's findings, limited to
a single city, a relatively small sample, and a limited range of neighborhood influences on the individual, nonetheless highlight the dan-
gers of referring loosely to neighborhood effects. It is clear that there
is considerable heterogeneity across gender and income lines with

,pect to social connections within neighborhoods, and it is likely that the particular way that mediating institutions are organized has additional significance for household contacts.

ORGANIZATION OF THIS VOLUME

In his monumental study of poverty in London—arguably the first substantial product of "social science"—Charles Booth (1892) contended that the condition of the poor could be properly understood only through a combination of statistics and observation of individual lives. Individual observation was necessary, he said, to give specificity to studies and to capture the balance of influences on households as they appeared on the ground. Statistics, for their part, were necessary to preserve a sense of proportion, to avoid the fallacy of rushing to generalizations or policy conclusions from individual vignettes, however affecting. Booth and his colleagues lived and worked among the poor, recording their observations. They also canvassed, household by household, the entire population of the East End, producing a statistical picture of poverty and its gradations that was unique in its time.

This volume attempts to capture a similar mix of observation of individual lives—now called urban ethnography—and statistics, some drawn from original surveys conducted in specific cities, others from national data sources. We also endeavor to widen the historical lens a bit. Much of today's sense of loss of urban opportunity stems from the contrast, explicit or implicit, with the period beginning with World War II, when abundant industrial jobs were open to all. It is often forgotten how exceptional this era was in the longer-term development of American cities.

Roger Lane, in chapter 2, provides a historical backdrop for today's underclass debate. He examines the life of African-Americans in Philadelphia during the generation after the Civil War and contrasts it with recent black experience. The black middle class flowered during the earlier period, making vast strides in education and literacy, while opening up public employment to the point that by 1891 the proportion of African-Americans in Philadelphia's police force paralleled that in the city's total population. (This achievement had long since been lost when the Kerner Commission calculated the racial composition of city police forces in 1968.) The majority black population, though very poor, had almost none of the signs we have come to associate with an underclass. There was far less social and geographical separation than today. A rich network of clubs and associations linked black households together and to mainstream aspirations. Rates of violent crime, alcohol and drug use, and out-of-wedlock births were much more in line with the experience of the rest of the city population and, in some instances, were lower. Most fundamentally, Lane emphasizes, the black community aggressively embraced mainstream values, and pursued with great energy its efforts to move up the ladder of opportunity.

These efforts failed, not because of black indifference, but because of white racism that excluded African-Americans from jobs in the new industrial economy. Starting from a point of rough equality with immigrants in terms of labor skills after the Civil War, by 1900 fully 76 percent of African-Americans in Philadelphia were listed in the Census survey as either unskilled laborers or domestic and personal service workers, compared with just 28 percent of white immigrants and 12 percent of whites of native parentage. Only 8 percent of black workers held jobs in manufacturing, compared with 47 percent of white immigrants. Employers and unions were equally resolute in rejecting black industrial labor.

The origins of today's urban underclass are directly linked, in Lane's view, to this exclusion of African-Americans from what was then the modern economy, and to the inability of black households to reap the rewards of their investment in education. The black community steadily lost ground, relative to the rest of the urban population, in labor skills and social conditions. At all levels of black society, the conviction eroded that education and adherence to middle-class values would open up opportunity for advancement.

The pattern of relative decline was broken by World War II and the labor shortages it created. During the 1940s and 1950s factory jobs finally became available to blacks in great numbers. But, as Lane points out, black workers were being "piped aboard a sinking ship." The black share of industrial employment reached its zenith just as the long decline of America's industrial cities was about to begin. In the economic restructuring that followed, blacks again were excluded from the growth sector for good jobs, this time in the high-skill service economy. To look back at the 1940s to 1960s as a normative reference point for black involvement in the urban economy is to overlook the fact that this "golden age" was really the twilight of big-city manufacturing, and that when the industrial sector was the leading edge of the modern economy, blacks had almost no access to it.

John D. Kasarda, in chapter 3, examines the more recent period of cities' economic transformation and the impact this has had upon severely distressed urban households. In a departure from analyses that focus on neighborhood indicators, he first examines the location and growth of distressed households, defined as those combining less than high school education, single parenthood, poor work history, public assistance recipiency, and poverty. Such households are overwhelmingly located in the central areas of five metropolitan regions: New York, Chicago, Philadelphia, Detroit, and, to a lesser degree, Los Angeles. The first four cities are quintessential examples of the deindustrialization that has led to the loss of manufacturing jobs. Altogether between 1970 and 1987, these cities lost more than $17.0 billion (1980 dollars) in annual manufacturing earnings in their central counties.

Kasarda then considers the skill and spatial mismatches that have accompanied economic transformation. He argues that the average skill content of jobs has risen, and that as the overall metropolitan labor force has increased its educational level, those without modern skills and schooling have fallen farther back in the queue of employables. In New York City the number of jobs held by high school dropouts fell by 496,000 between 1970 and 1980, whereas the number of jobs held by college graduates increased by 307,000. Although the education level of the city workforce was also rising, it did not keep pace with the transformation of the job market. As a result, large numbers of city residents lost out in the job competition. The gap in employment rates between those with and without schooling widened.

A similar phenomenon occurred in other northern, industrial cities. In Detroit, in 1980 56.1 percent of black male residents with less than high school education were not working, compared to only 1.3 percent of black male college graduates. In Philadelphia, the same comparison showed a not-working rate of 60.1 percent for black high-school dropouts versus a 1.9 percent not-working rate for black college graduates.

With respect to the spatial mismatch, Kasarda demonstrates that suburban unemployment rates for blacks are substantially lower than central-city unemployment rates for those with comparable schooling. Moreover, the unemployment gap between the central city and the suburbs is greatest at the low end of the skill distribution, where it has risen steeply over time. These outcomes are consistent with the hypothesis that in the competition for formal-sector jobs, inner-city, minority workers without college preparation are disadvantaged by their residential location as well as by their skill levels.

Jeffrey Fagan (chapter 4) focuses his analysis on the functioning of the most significant *illegal* economic activity in the inner city, drug selling. He draws on interviews with more than 1,000 drug users and sellers in two New York City neighborhoods, Central Harlem and Washington Heights, to derive a picture of the social and economic organization of the drug market. Striking differences between the two neighborhoods were found. Central Harlem is the more isolated area, located at the center of a large black ghetto. There, the "crack" boom did not divert many residents from legitimate jobs to drug selling. Rather, most of the participants in the cocaine market had a long history of drug involvement and other criminal activity, and realistically saw very limited employment prospects in the formal economy. From their perspective, the alternatives to drug selling are public transfers or a haphazard collection of low-paying occasional jobs. Nor does the prospect of jail time serve as much of a deterrent; indeed for many youths jail tends to be viewed as a rite of passage. Against this background, the independent, entrepeneurial occupation of drug dealing has obvious appeal, both for income and prestige. Fagan shows that drug dealing substantially enhances dealers' net incomes (i.e., income from drug selling is not significantly offset by lost earnings from formal-sector work or public assistance).

Washington Heights is a neighborhood that, by most measures, is less distressed than Central Harlem. It is less isolated, with easy access by road and bridge to the "outside world." It has somewhat higher income levels, lower poverty rates, and greater racial diversity. Nonetheless, Washington Heights has been affected more by drug selling, has a more organized and violent drug market, and has higher overall levels of violent crime. Fagan attributes these differences to several factors. The ease of access creates a drive-in market for more affluent, white drug buyers who inject money into the local economy, stimulating supplier competition. The result is a higher level of drug income in Washington Heights, and more tightly organized distribution systems. It is the conflict between drug groups that triggers much of the underlying neighborhood violence.

There is also clearer evidence in Washington Heights of a trade-off between legitimate income and income from drug selling. Residents there have more job alternatives. At the same time, drug selling is a more organized and demanding occupation, requiring greater commitment to one's career choice and entailing greater risks of violence. Despite a clearer trade-off with legitimate work (as well as other forms of crime), the net economic gains from drug selling are considerably higher in Washington Heights. In effect, the greater human capital in Washington Heights, as well as the area's superior connections to middle-class buyers and international suppliers, combine to produce higher drug incomes but also higher risks of violence. Fagan notes that the neighborhood's commitment to illegal entrepreneurism is likely to survive a decline in crack demand, such as appears to have been under way since 1989. So long as well-paying formal-sector jobs are available only to those with skills and schooling, many Washington Heights residents will merely shift their efforts to other illegal markets where the same organizational energy and tolerance for risk can earn high returns.

In chapter 5, Elijah Anderson's ethnographic account of John Turner illustrates the social and economic choices at stake for young men entering their adult years with few job prospects, an early criminal record, and an understandable desire to maintain social standing with their peers. John Turner exemplifies in many respects a moderately motivated youth at the edge of the underclass. Despite receiving extensive personal assistance in dealing with his legal problems and in finding a job, John in the end drops those opportunities in favor of the faster money and riskier life of drug dealing. The reasons are complex—ranging from the rejection of his lifestyle by older black male co-workers to John's intuitive opposition to the rules of conventional society—and do not fit simple stereotypes of street youth without concern for family or future. Despite strains of idealism and ambition, John seems tied to the street even when offered a change. The account raises troubling questions about what types of intervention can reach youths like John Turner, who are unwilling or unable to take advantage of the mainstream opportunities offered them. Anderson concludes that intervention must come at a very early age before the oppositional culture has taken hold.

> [The] experience with John suggests that simply providing opportunities for members of the underclass is not enough; they must also be provided with an outlook that allows them to invest personal resources in those opportunities, thereby leaving behind the attitudes and behavior that block their advancement but that also give them security in their circumscribed world.

Eloise Dunlap (chapter 6) provides an ethnographic study of families—mothers and children—that live within the social and personal disorganization of drug dependence. Ironically, the very institution that provides the most support for households under stress—the African-American extended family—also serves as a vehicle for transmitting the drug culture. In the world Dunlap portrays, there is no stability. Relatives, friends, customers, and lovers appear and disappear in the home, along with possessions that are bartered or stolen and then vanish. One of Dunlap's subjects reports that, at one time or another, she has been the primary caregiver for 82 children—precisely because she is the least unstable member of the extended family and assumes responsibility for offspring when other family members are jailed, killed, or disappear. Amidst the tumult of adults and youths, and the regular incursion of street life into the home, children are introduced to drugs and violence at an exceptionally early age, while given multiple tryouts by siblings or relatives for criminal roles they can play.

Ansley Hamid (chapter 7) complements this sense of precariousness by presenting an ethnographic study of middle-aged males now living (or spending nights) in "freakhouses." The men in Hamid's study once held middle-class jobs, but lost them because of crack consumption. In case after case, Hamid documents the economic loss and degradation that decimated the ranks of adult black males, the "old heads" whose connections with the world of work were supposed to be models for today's youth. The process illustrates the other side of the ladder of opportunity, the downward mobility that can hurtle one-time solid wage earners onto the street. Even adult males established in the work force are constantly at risk, so long as they live in neighborhoods and frequent social settings where drugs are continually available and where they must come to terms with the "street" every day. Middle-class lives may unravel at any time—a fact that Anderson and others argue induces middle-class agents, like black probation officers and school teachers, to protectively distance themselves from the at-risk youths they should be influencing. Hamid concludes that the impact of crack on the inner city will be felt for a long time, even if youths turn away from its use, as now appears to be happening. The missing generation of older role models cannot be replaced. In many ways the middle-aged males living in freakhouses are more profoundly lost to today's adolescents than those who have migrated to the suburbs.

Probably the greatest obstacle to a better understanding of underclass dynamics has been the lack of longitudinal tracking of households. Underclass neighborhoods appear in a different light if they are constantly shifting collections of different households, from which individual families regularly escape via outmigration, than if they are the permanent homes of households trapped in the poorest sections of the inner city. The term *underclass* in fact implies a permanence of position that is even passed on from one generation to the next. Unfortunately, almost all that we know about the underclass comes from periodic snapshots of neighborhood areas, supplemented by interviewing of current residents. There have been no longitudinal studies of how households move into and out of underclass zones, or of what becomes of them when they leave. Edward Gramlich, Deborah Laren, and Naomi Sealand (chapter 8) take advantage of the recent addition of spatial identifiers to the Panel Study of Income Dynamics (PSID— University of Michigan, Ann Arbor, Institute for Social Research) to begin to fill this void by analyzing individual households' mobility into and out of poverty census tracts. They find that there is a large amount of movement among the poor, much of it from poverty zones to nonpoverty areas. For example, each year 27 percent of the poor white adults in families with children who live in urban poverty areas leave and move into nonpoverty areas. This remarkably high rate of emigration argues against the notion of permanent entrapment.

Gramlich and his coauthors show, however, that emigration rates from poverty areas are much lower for poor black households (10 percent per year). The probability of poor black households moving *into* urban poverty tracts from other locations, in contrast, is much higher. This process leads to a significant degree of sorting out. Urban poverty areas become poorer and more racially homogeneous over time, and the persistently poor become more likely to reside in them. The geographic isolation appears to have significant consequences. In this sample, the poor black households who move out of poverty zones enjoy greater subsequent income growth than the poor households who stay, whereas the poor black households who move into poverty areas experience less income growth than the poor households who remain in nonpoor areas. Most disturbing of all, the startling divergence by race of where children live becomes worse. Already, fewer than 1 percent of white children grow up in poor urban areas, and this share is falling rapidly. By contrast, 26 percent of black children live in urban poverty areas. Given households' current mobility patterns (and correcting for multiple movers), this share will keep rising until it reaches 32–35 percent. Given the evidence we have of inferior school quality in urban poverty zones (Orfield 1992), as well as the unequal rates of violent crime and drug activity, the sorting-out process appears to relegate black children to environments that markedly limit their lifetime opportunities.

In the final chapter, Roberto Fernandez and David Harris investigate William Julius Wilson's hypothesis of social isolation, drawing upon a household sample of friendship patterns and institutional affiliations for Chicago's poverty areas. They conclude that nonworking poor black men and women are consistently less likely to participate in local organizations than either the working poor or the nonpoor, and thus are cut off from institutional support for interclass contact. Most of this effect seems to be a consequence of the household's own class status, however, rather than of the type of neighborhood in which it resides. With respect to personal networks, the household responses indicate that both nonworking poor men and women tend to have friends of their own class—i.e., with fewer years of schooling and higher rates of nonemployment than the friends of those who are not poor. For women, but not for men, neighborhood poverty strongly reinforces personal isolation, further reducing the breadth and depth of personal networks. Overall, isolation from mainstream activities is more acute for poor women than for poor men, and more dependent upon the neighborhood environment. Thus, there is support in this sample for at least part of the isolation hypothesis. However, the role of neighborhood deprivation in intensifying isolation appears to be relatively small. If so, the authors conclude, it may be more effective to help poor people directly, regardless of where they live, than to try to reach the individual through collective neighborhood change.

POLICY ORIENTATION

For at least the last 150 years observers of poverty have attempted to classify the poor into different groups. One motivation has been to do justice to the manifest differences among those once lumped together under the heading, "lower classes." A parallel motivation, however, has been to guide public policy, so that remedial programs could be better targeted. For much of the 19th century the basic distinction drawn was that between the "deserving" poor and the undeserving— i.e., between those who were poor because of sloth or moral vice, toward whom society had no obligations beyond the poorhouse, and those who embraced the work ethic but were poor nonetheless. This latter group had a morally valid claim on society's succor, at least in finding work. The concept of the deserving poor has been resurrected in the last few years by public commentators and legislators, to try once again to focus public resources on those among the poor who are willing to work.

Charles Booth, in his *Life and Labour of the People in London*, introduced eight social classifications. The first two groups, A and B, correspond quite closely to what today is termed the underclass. Class A included "the lowest class of occasional labourers, loafers, and semi-criminals"; Class B, the "very poor . . . , dependent upon casual earnings." Except for its prose style, Booth's description of the members of Class B might be mistaken today for a contemporary ethnographic description, like Elijah Anderson's in this volume, of inner-city youth on the fringes of the formal sector: "They cannot stand the regularity and dulness of civilised existence, and find the excitement they need in the life of the streets . . . ." (See Himmelfarb, 1991: 107–110.) Above these groups Booth placed two classes of the working poor who rely, respectively, upon intermittent or small but regular earnings. Booth himself drew from these distinctions the policy conclusion that because the lowest classes, the extreme poor, exerted labor market pressure on the working poor, without committing themselves to the working life, society had to find a way to meet their basic needs while removing them from the free labor market. He suggested government-sponsored industrial farms. Even Booth's contemporaries did not take this particular recommendation very seriously, but it does call attention, as Booth desired, to the interaction among different segments of the poor or underclass population. Some youth and adults want to work but cannot find jobs. Others choose not to hold legitimate, low-paying jobs, because they find the alternatives of criminal or welfare income more attractive. Much of the recent poverty debate has been conducted on an ideological plane as if one, but not both, of these explanations must account for observed detachment from the labor force. In fact, both play a role. The practical question is how large the respective influences are, and, in cases where individuals have a reservation wage based on income alternatives from welfare or crime, how high this reservation wage is and what society can do to promote work as a legitimate option. More recent observers have emphasized other distinctions between the poorer sectors: between those who have temporary spells of poverty and the persistently poor, or between those who maintain ambitions of advancement and those who fall into a culture of poverty. The public policies advocated for assisting each class are quite different.

Discussions of the underclass likewise both introduce analytical distinctions and carry implications for policy targeting. At the broadest policy level, the underclass debate is consistent with a three-pronged approach to inner-city poverty. Some of the residents of inner-city ghettos possess labor skills but not jobs. For this group, targeted policies like transportation initiatives designed to convey workers to points of job creation (Hughes 1992) or downtown redevelopment efforts to create jobs are appropriate. A second group of residents want to work but lack job skills. For them, the policy priority is job and skill training. Some of this task may be accomplished through specialized training programs, but the most urgent priority is to provide better education in the inner city. For those who espouse oppositional cultural values or simply do not have the aspirations and expectations that would lead to labor market attachment, other policies may be required. These may be immediate and remedial, such as overhaul of the welfare system to reward work or alternative incarceration and probation programs designed to match youth offenders with work skills, discipline, and jobs, as well as long-term and preventive.

Some discussions—such as that by Dunlap in chapter 6, this volume—focus on the family or the extended family as the vector that transmits dysfunctional behavior to young children. This approach implies the need for very early intervention in children's lives, through such vehicles as Head Start, joint treatment of all family members for drug abuse, and mentoring programs that provide male role models for young boys. For some residents or in some areas, neighborhoods may, however, play a more crucial role, providing a social environment that is hostile to mainstream values and opportunities. In these cases, strategies to diversify youths' experience, so that they can choose their own role models, become critical.

The underclass analysis advanced by William Julius Wilson (1987) is distinguished by the importance it places upon the *neighborhood* in mediating individual experience. In his view, it is the neighborhood that "isolates" or "connects" the individual to mainstream opportunity. Other classes of society may have moved away from the literal, geographical neighborhood in their social orientation, in favor of a metaphorical neighborhood held together by job or professional networks and personal connections spread over the metropolitan area; but, lacking this variety of connections, the underclass is argued to be more dependent upon their immediate residential surroundings. Taken together, the chapters in this volume offer support for such a perspective, even though they also remind us that what may seem to be "neighborhood" effects, in the sense of neighborhood as a factor influencing the individual, are sometimes confounded with aggregation effects. A neighborhood may have some distinctive characteristics merely because it is an aggregation of poor or nonworking households, each of which would act similarly if placed in another environment.

So long as neighborhoods are a critical variable, the next logical question to ask, for both analysis and policy formulation, is How do neighborhoods exert their influence? The existing literature, though sometimes disappointingly imprecise on this point, emphasizes two broad, alternative lines of influence.

According to one interpretation, it is *who* lives in a neighborhood that matters. The social (and racial and income) homogeneity of underclass neighborhoods is viewed as their most confining characteristic. The absence of middle-class families is particularly crucial. In Wilson's writings, migration out of the ghetto by successful or aspiring black families is one of the main vehicles serving to intensify social stratification—even though the evidence that black outmigration by socioeconomic class is more selective than formerly is not very strong (Jencks 1991). Other mechanisms of city stratification are possible, such as de facto social zoning by governments, downward mobility among the middle-class households who remain in the ghetto, and higher rates of movement of minority poor *into* central-city poverty zones. Empirical support is beginning to accumulate for the view that physical isolation from the middle class is important. Crane (1991a, b), for example, reported that the presence of professional households in a neighborhood is an important factor in retarding the spread of teenage childbearing and high school dropouts among the poor. Although the mechanism of influence is not spelled out, presumably it involves embodiment within the community, including the schools, of mainstream norms that serve as a counterweight to acceptance of other behaviors. The statistical association between amelioration of unwanted effects and middle-class presence in neighborhoods must remain less than fully convincing, however, until the agency for transmitting and sustaining mainstream norms in this context can be better described.[2]

Taken at face value, this view of underclass isolation argues for diffusing poverty by placing poor families in middle-class communities, where they can come into contact with middle-class neighbors and institutions, or taking steps to reintroduce income and class diversity into the inner city through neighborhood redevelopment projects. Some of the policy experiments premised on this view of inner-city isolation do, in fact, show considerable promise—most notably, the Gautreaux experiment, in which black residents of Chicago's public housing projects have (under court order) been placed in the suburbs. The moves appear to have had a favorable impact on children's school achievements, adult earnings, and family aspirations (Rosenbaum 1991; Rosenbaum and Popkin 1990). Despite the promise of the Gautreaux experiment, however, it only partially supports the view that the class composition of neighborhoods is critical in spreading

---

2. As an example of how neighborhood agency can be spelled out, see Sullivan's (1989) contrast of the crime careers of youth in three different neighborhoods in New York City.

or retarding underclass behavior. The poverty families participating in the program tend to attribute their improved circumstances to the fact that there are better schools, more jobs, and less violence in the suburbs. These characteristics, of course, tend to be found in neighborhoods where middle-class and professional families live, but there are other, more direct ways of producing them.

A second line of argument emphasizes violent or disruptive *behavior* as the principal source of underclass neighborhood influence. Several chapters in this volume illustrate just how severely neighborhoods are set apart by their levels of violent crime and drug activity. Given such an environment, mothers frequently report that they are unwilling to accept the risks of working outside the home, either because it is dangerous to travel to and from work or out of fear of leaving their children alone. Several members of the Gautreaux sample who took jobs for the first time after moving to the suburbs reported that they previously had seen no point in working because it only made them more conspicuous targets for robbery or theft. Indeed, when residents of underclass neighborhoods are asked what they personally find most objectionable about their environment, they tend to place behavioral factors at the top of their list by a wide margin. An overwhelming 74.7 percent of a sample of residents of Atlanta's public housing projects listed drug use as the "most serious" problem in their area, followed by crime and violence. By contrast, only 2.3 percent listed housing conditions as their worst problem, and only 0.4 percent listed lack of jobs (City of Atlanta 1989). More than 80 percent of respondents indicated that they stayed inside at night as a matter of self-protection.

From this description and diagnosis of the underclass neighborhood problem, there has been deduced a quite different set of policy priorities. It becomes urgent to keep neighborhood disruptive behavior under control to the extent necessary to allow individuals to lead productive lives. New policing measures, such as community policing or attempts to establish neighborhood gun-free zones, community campaigns against drug dealing, and efforts to socialize or control youth gangs are examples of initiatives designed to counteract the street's control over a neighborhood, though systematic evidence of their success has yet to be assembled. Some of the most promising initiatives now being experimented with seek to create neighborhood institutions that give residents collectively a sense of control over their environment and empowerment in dealing with city agencies. For example, the Sandtown-Winchester community of inner-city Baltimore has received foundation support to go through a "visioning" process of how residents would like their neighborhood to change, and has been given discretion over refocusing and combining the local application of city government programs, from police protection to housing rehabilitation and health clinics, to help realize their vision.

Obviously, these different policies for dealing with inner-city neighborhoods are not incompatible with one another. All require a more reliable supply of job opportunities before they can become effective. However, in a time of acute budget constraints, there is bound to be competition for program funding at all levels of government. Analyses of *how* inner-city areas curtail the opportunities of individual households residing in them; assessments of how important these neighborhood influences are relative to other factors limiting individual development; and clarification of the extent to which the experience of New York City, Chicago, Philadelphia, Detroit, and Los Angeles has relevance for other cities will be critical in establishing the future antipoverty policy agenda.

References

Booth, Charles. 1892. *Life and Labour of the People in London*. London: Macmillan, 9 vols. (1892–97).

City of Atlanta, Department of Public Safety. 1989. *Illegal Drugs in Atlanta*. Atlanta: Author.

Crane, Jonathan. 1991a. "Effects of Neighborhoods on Dropping Out of School and Teenage Childbearing." In *The Urban Underclass*, edited by Christopher Jencks and Paul E. Peterson. Washington, D.C.: Brookings Institution.

————. 1991b. "The Epidemic Theory of Ghettos and Neighborhood Effects on Dropping Out and Teenage Childbearing." *American Journal of Sociology* 96 (Mar.)

————. Forthcoming. "The Pattern of Neighborhood Effects on Dropping Out and Teenage Childbearing." *American Journal of Sociology*.

Farley, Reynolds. 1992. "Neighborhood Preferences and Aspirations among Blacks and Whites." In *Housing Markets and Residential Mobility*, edited by G. Thomas Kingsley and Margery Turner. Washington, D.C.: Urban Institute.

Fernandez, Roberto M. 1991. *Race, Space, and Job Accessibility: Evidence from a Plant Re-Location*. Processed. Northwestern University, Evanston, Ill.

Freeman, Richard B. 1992. "Crime and the Employment of Disadvantaged Youth." In *Urban Labor Markets and Labor Mobility* edited by George E. Peterson and Wayne Vroman. Washington, D.C.: Urban Institute.

Goldkamp, John S., Michael R. Gottfredson, and Doris Weiland. 1990. "Pretrial Drug Testing and Defendant Risk." *The Journal of Criminal Law and Criminology*, 81 (Fall): 585–652.

Gottdiener, Mark, and Chris G. Pickvance (eds.), *Urban Life in Transition.* Newbury Park, Ca.: Sage.

Himmelfarb, Gertrude. 1991. *Poverty and Compassion: The Moral Imagination of the Late Victorians.* New York: Alfred A. Knopf.

Hughes, Mark Alan. 1992. "Transporting Workers to Jobs." In *Urban Labor Markets and Labor Mobility,* edited by George E. Peterson and Wayne Vroman. Washington, D.C.: Urban Institute.

Jargowsky, Paul A., and Mary Jo Bane. 1990. "Ghetto Poverty: Basic Questions." In *Inner-City Poverty in the United States,* edited by Laurence E. Lynn, Jr., and Michael G. H. McGeary. Washington, D.C.: National Academy Press.

—————. 1991. "Ghetto Poverty in the United States, 1970–80." In *The Urban Underclass,* edited by Christopher Jencks and Paul E. Peterson. Washington, D.C.: Brookings Institution.

Jencks, Christopher. 1991. "Is the American Underclass Growing?" In *The Urban Underclass,* edited by Christopher Jencks and Paul E. Peterson. Washington, D.C.: Brookings Institution.

Jencks, Christopher, and Susan E. Mayer. 1990. "The Social Consequences of Growing Up in a Poor Neighborhood." In *Inner-City Poverty in the United States,* edited by Laurence E. Lynn, Jr., and Michael G. H. McGeary. Washington, D.C.: National Academy Press.

Logan, John R., and Harvey L. Molotch. 1987. *Urban Fortunes: The Political Economy of Place.* Berkeley: University of California Press.

Miller, J. D., I. A. Cisin, H. Gardner-Keaton, A. V. Harrell, P. W. Wirtz, H. I. Abelson, and P. M. Fishburne. 1983. *National Survey on Drug Abuse: Main Findings 1982.* Rockville, Md.: U.S. Government Printing Office.

Mincy, Ronald B., Isabel V. Sawhill, and Douglas A. Wolf. 1990. "The Underclass: Definition and Measurement." *Science* 248 (Apr.): 450–53.

Montgomery, James. 1991. "Modeling Neighborhood Effects: Contagion versus Selective Deprivation." Paper prepared for Urban Opportunity Conference on Drugs, Crime, and Social Distress, Urban Institute, Washington, D.C. April.

Musto, David. 1988. *The American Disease: Origins of Narcotic Control.* New York: Oxford University Press.

National Institute of Justice. 1991. *Drugs and Crime, 1990: Annual Report.* Washington, D.C.: Author.

National Institute on Drug Abuse. 1991a. *National Household Survey on Drug Abuse: Main Findings, 1990.* Rockville, Md.: Author.

————. 1991b. *National Household Survey on Drug Abuse: Population Estimates, 1991.* Rockville, Md.: Author.

New York State, Division of Substance Abuse Services. 1991. *Drugs and Other Substance Use among School Children in New York State, 1990.* Albany: Author.

Orfield, Gary. 1992. "Urban Schooling and Metropolitan Job Inequality." In *Urban Labor Markets and Labor Mobility,* edited by George E. Peterson and Wayne Vroman. Washington, D.C.: Urban Institute.

Peterson, George E., and Wayne Vroman. 1992. *Urban Labor Markets and Labor Mobility.* Washington, D.C.: Urban Institute.

Reischauer, Robert. 1987. *The Geographic Concentration of Poverty: What Do We Know?* Washington, D.C.: Brookings Institution.

Rosenbaum, James E. 1991. "Black Pioneers—Do Their Moves to the Suburbs Increase Economic Opportunity for Mothers and Children?" *Housing Policy Debate* 2 (4):

Rosenbaum, James E., and Susan J. Popkin. 1990. "Employment and Earnings of Low-Income Blacks Who Move to Middle-Class Suburbs." In *The Urban Underclass,* edited by Christopher Jencks and Paul E. Peterson. Washington, D.C.: Brookings Institution.

Sullivan, Mercer. 1989. *"Getting Paid": Youth Crime and Work in the Inner City.* Ithaca, N.Y.: Cornell University Press.

U.S. National Advisory Commission on Civil Disorders [Kerner Commission]. 1968. *Report.* Washington, D.C.: Government Printing Office.

Wacquant, Loic J. D., and William Julius Wilson. 1989. "The Cost of Racial and Class Exclusion in the Inner City." *Annals of The American Academy of Political and Social Science* 105: 8–25.

Wiener, Susan J., and Ronald B. Mincy. 1991. "Social Distress in Urban Areas: Variations in Crime, Drugs, and Teen Births during the 1980s." Paper prepared for Urban Opportunity Conference on Drugs, Crime, and Social Distress, Urban Institute, Washington, D.C.

Wilson, William Julius. 1987. *The Truly Disadvantaged: The Inner City, The Underclass, and Public Policy.* Chicago: University of Chicago Press.

Winpisinger, Kim A., Richard S. Hopkins, Robert W. Indian, and Jeptha R. Hostetler. 1991. "Risk Factors for Childhood Homicides in Ohio: A Birth Certificate-Based Case-Control Study." *American Journal of Public Health* 81 (8, Aug.): 1052–54.

Wishner, Amy R., Donald F. Schwarz, Jeane Ane Grisso, John H. Holmes, and Rudolph L. Sutton. 1991. "Interpersonal Violence-Related Injuries in an African-American Community in Philadelphia." *American Journal of Public Health* 81 (11, Nov.): 1474–76.

Woods, Robert A. 1923. "The University Settlement Idea." In *The Neighborhood in Nation-Building,* ed. R. A. Woods. New York: Houghton Mifflin. [First published in 1892 in the *Andover Review.*]

Zax, Jeffrey S., and John F. Kain. 1991. "Commutes, Quits, and Moves." *Journal of Urban Economics* 29 (2, Mar.): 153–65.

Chapter Two

BLACK PHILADELPHIA THEN AND NOW: THE "UNDERCLASS" OF THE LATE 20TH CENTURY COMPARED WITH POORER AFRICAN-AMERICANS OF THE LATE 19TH CENTURY

Roger Lane

We are no longer sure what to call the African-American "underclass," but we know by any name that it exists. Its features are universally familiar: weak connections with the world of productive work, little education, social and geographic isolation, family instability, high rates of crime, drug addiction, and dependency. But if we can agree on these defining features—and that all have been worsening over the past generation—there is no such agreement about their causes. Some stress racial discrimination, others government policy, economic change, or a distinctive "culture of poverty." One of the few things common to the whole argument is a failure to begin at the beginning, to look at the history of urban black America for an explanation of its current situation and prospects. I hope here to clarify the debate through a look at that history, principally but not exclusively through the experience of a single city, Philadelphia.[1]

The relevant "beginning" is the time from 1865, the end of the Civil War and slavery, to about 1900. This was the period when black Americans, finally citizens in law if not yet fully in practice, began the long move off southern farms that would transform them from an overwhelmingly rural into an overwhelmingly urban people. Philadelphia was then metropolitan headquarters for urban black Americans, just as it is now painfully typical. A historian immersed in the earlier era

---

1. This chapter is based largely on information in my book, *William Dorsey's Philadelphia and Ours: On the History and Future of the Black City in America* (1991). William Henry Dorsey himself, an adviser to W.E.B. DuBois on the classic *Philadelphia Negro: A Social Study*, published in 1897, left a recently discovered trove of some 388 scrapbooks full of materials relating to African-Americana, notably but not exclusively dealing with the life of his native city, which enables a far fuller picture of urban black America than any previous source.

is struck continually by the fact that virtually all modern issues, and many modern experiences, were anticipated a century ago. During the 1890s W.E.B. DuBois listed the three main problems of Philadelphia's black community as, in order, crime, family life, and work habits. The leadership then stressed the need for a new black aesthetic to combat imposed "white" standards of beauty, debated the merits of integration versus separation, argued about the problem of dependence on a single political party, weighed the relative advantages of outside aid and self-help, and wondered whether to call themselves by the Spanish word for black, *Negro,* or to acknowledge a common ancestral homeland with the term *Afro-American.* But the most striking parallels—and differences—are economic.

PROGRESS OF THE BLACK MIDDLE CLASS FOLLOWING THE CIVIL WAR

The decades after the Civil War were a time of enormous black advancement, especially for the black middle class. But during this era of progress, like the more familiar one that followed World War II, the black middle class was undermined by weakness below them. In neither period—although for entirely different reasons—was the urban black majority able to participate, securely, in the dominant economic experience—then, the urban industrial revolution, and post–World War II, the service revolution. The most striking difference was that then, despite both an absolute level of poverty and a racism far worse than either of their late 20th-century equivalents, the black population suffered from relatively few of the structural and social handicaps that now define the underclass. But the biggest burden that blacks were made to bear then—an almost total exclusion from the dominant economy—did succeed, over time, in crushing too many, and led directly to the crisis we now face.

What made Philadelphia the metropolitan headquarters of 19th-century black America was first its size; the second biggest city in the nation had the biggest African-American population in the North.[2] Since roughly 90 percent of African-Americans still remained in the

2. Some places below the Mason-Dixon Line, such as Washington, D.C., did have larger black populations, but neither New York nor Chicago would catch up, absolutely or relatively, until the 20th century.

rural South, black Philadelphia was then small by modern standards. The official census showed an increase in the black population between 1870 and 1900 from about 20,000 to 65,000, the latter a little over 5 percent of the city's inhabitants. But this and other city populations made up in distinction what they lacked in numbers, and the direction and pace of migration were already making it clear that the future lay in the city. And The Philadelphia Story was then the urban black experience writ large.

Since the 18th century, the Quaker City had been headquarters of the A.M.E. (African Methodist Episcopal) Church, at that time the largest single black organization in the United States. As missionaries flooded South to harvest the freedmen during and just after the Civil War, membership in the A.M.E. soared twentyfold between 1860 and 1880, from perhaps 20,000 to 400,000. Philadelphia then and later was the A.M.E.'s Rome, "Mother Bethel," the place from which the best and brightest were given their marching orders, soldiers of Christ but also of secular deliverance, sent out nationwide as ministers and bishops to organize political parties and schools, as well as churches. During the same era the A.M.E. Book Concern, the only black publishing house in the world, produced not only religious tracts but books and journals of general political and cultural interest, written by men and women of all denominations.

The second biggest black organization, meanwhile, was centered only a few blocks away. The Grand and United Order of Odd Fellows was the most important of several fraternal organizations, such as the Masons, founded to provide modest sick and death benefits as well as social activities for initiates all over the country. The fact that headquarters and national conventions were located in the Quaker City meant that philanthropists and politicians looking for influential contacts from Tallahassee to San Francisco routinely called there for advice.

A third key institution, the Quaker-founded but black-run Institute for Colored Youth (ICY), was the newest, its rigorous academic program dating from just before the Civil War. The ICY was alma mater and/or employer of the first three black women college graduates in this country, the first black man to win an undergraduate degree from Harvard University, and the first black holder of a doctorate, a physicist from Yale University. The institute boasted that it sent more teachers to the South than any other school in the country. And like the A.M.E. and the Odd Fellows, it was one center of a network that linked urban black leaders across the country, as marriages, social excursions, common origins, institutions, and publications kept men and women from New Orleans, Chicago, and Boston in touch with each other and their common history.

All these institutions helped foster a lively intellectual life. The legendary black hunger for education following the Civil War was shown locally by the enthusiasm for graduation ceremonies at the Institute for Colored Youth. During the 1860s, although the graduates were still few and the entire African-American population of the city was officially no more than about 20,000, they had to hire the Academy of Music, then the largest hall in the country, to hold the huge crowds who wanted to see some eight or nine young people declaim their graduation orations and walk across the stage.[3] As black literacy in the city soared from roughly 20 percent to 80 percent over the final 30 years of the century, some 20 weekly newspapers and 1 short-lived daily fed the appetite for literate information and entertainment, and, equally important, served as publishing outlets for aspiring black writers of everything from feature articles to poetry.[4] By century's end, dozens of other black men and women worked for white journals and magazines, and Florence Lewis ran an entire department of the old *Philadelphia Bulletin*. Several black Philadelphians published volumes of poetry, Gertrude Mossell and John Durham wrote novels, Frances Harper a play, William Still a best-selling history, and others autobiographies, theological tracts, and appeals to racial pride.

Education also translated into professional gains. The local community had been served by just one educated black doctor in 1870. But the number of trained black physicians soared over the long generation that followed. The University of Pennsylvania's first black medical student, Nathan Mossell, was at first surrounded by a screen so that the sight of him would not disturb his white classmates. But Mossell, class of 1882, was not the first African-American doctor educated in the city. Reflecting the extraordinary role played by women in the community, Rachel Cole and Caroline Still Anderson had pre-

---

3. Although the number of graduates grew in later years, graduation was unnecessary for teachers. At a time when only about 1 percent of white Americans won high school diplomas, the equivalent of an eighth-grade education was more than enough to qualify teenagers to teach younger ones.

4. The "networking" among leading blacks was fostered by the contemporary newspaper habit of printing excerpts or indeed whole articles from other papers across the country. Dozens of black journals, many of which exist now only in William Dorsey's collection, also printed regular columns entitled "Letter from New Orleans," or wherever, keeping the readership informed of political, racial, religious, and social news throughout the country.

ceded him, at Women's Medical College. With the medical schools of the University of Pennsylvania, Temple University, Thomas Jefferson Hospital, and Women's Medical all now open, by 1900 the number of black doctors in Philadelphia reached over a dozen, enough to staff a separate Frederick Douglass Hospital and Nursing School. Far more were sent to other places, from California to Africa, including the first blacks and/or women to practice medicine in the states of Alabama, North Carolina and South Carolina and the cities of Chicago and Atlanta.

The situation of lawyers had been even bleaker than for doctors at the opening of the Civil War. At that time, outside of two New England states, even free blacks were denied the benefits of full citizenship. Pennsylvania, like most states in the North, grudgingly bowed to the Fifteenth Amendment in 1870 and granted blacks the vote. Two by-products of this advancement were the rights to serve on juries and to practice law. The city's first African-American attorney, John Lewis, arrived from Yale in 1876; as with doctors, Philadelphia boasted about a dozen more attorneys by 1900, not counting the others it exported, especially to the South.

African-Americans found many ways in this period to deal with discrimination in public facilities; one patron of a reluctant restaurant, who was charged the modern equivalent of $20 for a cup of coffee and a piece of pie, calmly finished his snack, threw a dime and several hundred toothpicks on the floor, and told the proprietor to sue him for the balance. But the law was more often ally than enemy in the North, and the new black attorneys joined others in taking advantage of a strong federal Civil Rights Act, passed in 1875, to mount a spate of suits that effectively desegregated much of Philadelphia.[5] More directly, of course, the power of the vote itself pushed politicians to desegregate all public facilities, culminating with the school system in 1881.[6]

The vote, too, slowly opened public office and, even more important, jobs in civil service. As with doctors, lawyers, and journalists,

---

5. The law made a genuine difference. However, the federal act was disallowed by the U.S. Supreme Court in 1883, and was succeeded only by a weaker state statute. Under this act, hard to enforce, Philadelphia, like many other northern cities, was effectively resegregated, and older blacks in the city today remember when they were confined, for example, to separate sections of movie theaters.

6. School desegregation, too, had its limits, and although the city's two high schools had to be open to all, and African-Americans such as Alain Locke and Jesse Faucett later led their respective classes at Central and Girls' High Schools, much of the system remained segregated de facto.

the starting point in the 1860s was effectively zero. But the number of black public school teachers in Philadelphia had reached over 30 by 1900, including several principals. The number of policemen was twice as great, and educated clerks, draftsmen, federal postmen, and customs officials added an important layer to the local middle class.[7] Although most of these jobholders had no hope of promotion, the city's black officeholders held out a solution. Because the city's blacks consistently outscored their white competitors on written tests of all kinds—Robert Abele, for instance, set a record on the Pennsylvania State Qualifying Examination for Physicians in 1897—the first distinctively black demand raised in local politics was that all offices be put under civil service and that all appointments be made in order of merit. Even the white press generally agreed that black civil servants—a historian would add, blacks as a group—were overqualified for their jobs in this era, as a result of a general refusal to promote them to positions where they might have authority of any kind over white workers.

Although the demand for civil service appointment by merit was never granted, all African-Americans could take pride in the recognition they won from whites in two other areas—sports and entertainment, especially music. Colleges such as the University of Pennsylvania and Harvard University first admitted blacks in this period, and then discovered that some of these student athletes could run track and play football as well as their young white gentlemen. By the late 1890s, too, as college sports became a business, athletic scholarships were born, and blacks as well as whites were recruited from such places as Philadelphia's manual training schools, miraculously hurdling the entrance examinations in Latin.

Although barred from many more openly professional sports, such as baseball, other African-Americans made enormous strides in arenas in which they were allowed to compete. For example, the jockey Isaac Murphy won the Kentucky Derby three times during the 1880s, earning the modern equivalent of several million dollars over his career. Three generations before Joe Louis, heavyweight Peter Jackson, a colorful poetry-writing international celebrity and favorite with the press, was "followed everywhere by huge black crowds, who regard

---

7. The earlier-mentioned Institute for Colored Youth was furthermore notable for the number of diplomats it produced in this era, beginning with Headmaster Ebenezer Bassett, the professor of Greek whom President Ulysses S. Grant appointed minister to Haiti in 1869, the highest government job to which any African-American could aspire for generations, with the exception of the equivalent posting to Liberia.

him as a modern Samson of their race and vindication of their claim as equal. . . ." (Dorsey Scrapbook, No. 44, page 17, *Philadelphia Item,* 2/2/90). When Jackson was denied a title shot by John L. Sullivan, who said that he didn't fight, "pigs, dogs, hogs or niggers," it was left then to a smaller man, Boston's lightweight George Dixon, "Little Chocolate," to open a long string of triumphs by winning, in 1890, the first African-American world crown in any sport. (Dorsey Scrapbook, No. 44, p 37, *Philadelphia Item,* 8/3/90).

In the same period, too, after a long era in which much American song had been borrowed, at one remove, from black music, the debt was openly acknowledged. Before the war the enormously popular minstrel stage had been reserved exclusively for pale performers in blackface. Afterwards, blacks were first allowed on stage and then conquered it—although by convention they still had to wear burnt cork, whatever their natural complexions, so that a form that had begun with whites imitating blacks ended with blacks imitating whites imitating blacks.[8] Europeans, meanwhile, were more open— serious African-American artists had long starred on the continent and earned powerful praise from such composers as Anton Dvorak.

WORKING CLASS—NOT UNDERCLASS

If growing white recognition and more tangible gains among the black middle class meant little directly to the black urban majority, that majority, too, was doing better than it had formerly. Most Americans then lived very simply; as of 1880 over half the white population of Philadelphia, and 90 percent of the black population, would by current standards be defined as living in poverty. But at the same time the post–Civil War decades witnessed the greatest economic expansion in our history, and as the urban industrial revolution took hold all citizens enjoyed higher real wages. If the black majority was both absolutely and relatively poor, even its bottom half was by no means an underclass.

To be more specific:

1. Proportionally more urban blacks than whites were then employed in the money economy, all across the country, in part because black women, unlike white women, had no tradition of quitting work

---

8. The phrase is Alain Locke's (1969: 45).

when married. They enjoyed, too, a proud reputation, at least in Philadelphia, of avoiding charity of all kinds, and were especially noted for the number and range of their mutual benefit or self-help organizations. The great majority of blacks, partly because they were denied commercial insurance, belonged to one or more of these associations, which paid sick benefits and funeral expenses for the members in return for small weekly or monthly fees. Many belonged to several such organizations.

2. Medical records involving deaths from alcohol-related diseases confirm the contemporary impression that blacks had less trouble with the dominant drug than did whites. And despite a few reports of cocaine use, toward century's end the most troublesome contemporary drug next to alcohol was morphine, the largest class of addicts being middle-class white women.[9]

3. Although black rates of violent crime were undeniably high, and rose over the period following the Civil War, they were far lower than today's. In the mid-century decades, their murder rates were lower than those of their immigrant Irish competitors, while the Italians, later, had rates that soared well above the black scale.

4. The majority of blacks not only believed in but practiced matrimony. Although their marriage rates were somewhat lower than the urban white average, and illegitimacy was higher, the figures have two easy explanations. The great majority of black city women worked as domestics, most of them living in, making marriage and children extremely hard to manage. Most black men, meanwhile, earned only about half of what it took to support a family of four.

5. Black birth rates in the city were substantially below those of whites. Most urban immigrants, whatever their color or ethnicity, had smaller families than they had been used to on the farm or in peasant households, for the classic reason that youngsters in the country were extra hands from a very early age, but long remained only extra mouths in the city. But most foreign immigrants were able to counter this, to some degree, by putting children to work in factories at 10 or 12 years of age; however much we now deplore child labor, they thought it essential to keep up the family income.

---

9. Smoking opium, generally associated in the late 19th century with Chinese immigrants and white gamblers and prostitutes, was the only one of the modern "drug uses" that was widely outlawed. Heroin was a rarely used headache powder, and cocaine a source of experiment among leading physicians such as Sigmund Freud and William Welch, as well as blacks in southern ports. The popularity of morphine, of course, was that in an age before doctors could generally cure anybody, they settled for making their patients—and themselves—feel good for a time, another practice that was still legal.

But African-Americans had no choices in Philadelphia; no one would hire their children. As a group, dominated by numbers from the rural South, black Americans had more than 50 percent more children than the national average. In Philadelphia, a typical city in that all groups tended to have smaller families, black women in 1890 had nearly 20 percent fewer children than white women. By 1900, the figure had dropped to nearly 30 percent fewer.

6. Urban African-Americans were neither geographically nor socially isolated. Doctors, lawyers, and laborers lived in the same neighborhoods, in part because of residential semi-segregation. Most lived toward the center of the city, close to the railroads and docks they served as laborers, or the rich they served as domestics. And they were joined together by an astonishingly thick network of associations, churches, and mutual benefit associations, bands, teams, and social and political clubs. The great majority belonged to one or more of these associations—there was in fact roughly one club officer to every black household in Philadelphia—and the biggest of them were interlinked across class lines.[10]

EXCLUSION OF THE MAJORITY FROM THE INDUSTRIAL AGE

It should be clear, then, as much recent scholarship on slavery has stressed, that African-Americans emerged from the Civil War without crippling handicaps, with reasonably strong family systems, work habits, and social institutions. Black Philadelphians—most of them migrants from the South—were not only willing but able to do the kind of employment offered by the great city, in many respects better able than the foreign immigrants who in fact soon bypassed them. The fact that they did not was simply because they were not allowed to—not only denied a place on the vaunted American "ladder of opportunity" but in some cases actively kicked off.

The fundamental reason was open racism.

---

10. Some organizations were intended to be exclusive to the elite, but few lacked some larger purpose beyond mutual entertainment. Their structure ensured that the elite had to appeal to others. Most of the bigger groups, notably the fraternal organizations, political clubs, and churches, put a high premium on the number of members, and the leaders had to be elected. Other associations went to the wider public to sell tickets to games, balls, or excursions, with tangible prizes and intangible prestige going to those who sold the most.

This is a word currently much used, but by historical standards much debased. In its late-19th-century heyday, when the authority of the pseudoscience of social Darwinism made it fashionable among the most educated, it implied that blacks and whites were so different as to be virtually separate species. And it generated an astonishing amount of nonsense.

Thus a professor at Johns Hopkins University, Baltimore, declared that blacks were dark because insufficient oxygen in the air of their native Africa had left them with unburnt carbon deposits in the skin. Physicians at an international conference in Paris discussed the significance of the "fact" that blacks do not sneeze. And doctors at Philadelphia's Hahnemann Hospital, called to deal with a policeman bitten during an arrest, confirmed folk fears of what on the street were called "blue-gum niggers" by solemnly declaring, more delicately, that "certain members of the Ethiopian Race," much like rattlesnakes, had poison sacs behind their gums. (Dorsey Scrapbook, No. 108, p 53, Philadelphia *Times*, 1/3/98).

The only saving grace in all this was said to be that, freed from the protection offered by slavery and thrown into competition with their white superiors, African-Americans would conveniently solve the race problem by dying out. Interbreeding had bought some of them a little time but weakened their constitutions, and mulattoes, much like mules, would prove sterile in four generations at most.

These beliefs were of course not universal, and there were always whites with enough common sense, or enough religious conviction about the brotherhood of man, to treat their fellow citizens with decency. The state of race relations defies easy summary, with many episodes of empathy and even love alternating with stories of insensitivity and violence. Northern papers, especially in their sports columns, routinely deplored racial prejudice, and so did most northern politicians. Reputable black leaders were treated with great respect— the state supreme court waived the residency requirements for the first lawyer, John Lewis, for example. And yet racism was powerful enough to cripple black attempts at advancement both by robbing them of traditional skills and by denying them the newer skills practiced in the newest, most vital, industrial sector of the economy.

Many African-Americans before the Civil War had practiced the best-paying blue-collar skills such as carpentry and masonry; after the war a combination of unions and employers, all over the country, combined to drive them out. The blame may be shared equally. National unions, still new in this period, generally proclaimed their willingness to welcome black members, but all-white locals, in an era when ethnic clan spirit ran high, were far more powerful, and the men often acted on their threats to walk off any job if blacks were put beside them. The few breakthroughs were encouraged from the top, but although some employers were genuinely sympathetic, most commonly they used black men and women as strikebreakers, and then abandoned them when their regular employees returned.

The exclusion of blacks from the blue-collar world can be seen in occupational counts of the time. In Philadelphia, the several prewar plumbers disappeared entirely from later censuses. Two counts of the community's carpenters and cabinetmakers, in 1861 and 1883, came up with precisely the same totals, five and one, despite an official population increase of roughly 50 percent and a booming economy. Apprenticeship was the best way to learn a trade, but for young black men the prospects were virtually nonexistent. Racism in the period's unions meant that, as the city's *Evening Telegraph* put it, blacks could "no more find entrance into the skilled handicrafts than they could fly into the upper air." (Dorsey Scrapbook, No. 73, p 13.5, *Evening Telegraph*, 8/27/90.) On the other hand, those African-American craftsmen who were able to carry on were not employed fully enough, it seems, to require regular help, and thus young apprentices, of any kind.

It was even easier to keep blacks out of the newer bureaucratic and factory jobs opened by the urban-industrial revolution. Outside of the civil service, despite their great gains in literacy, black Americans were almost wholly unable to ring their faces with white collars, as graduates of business colleges were unable to find work as secretaries. This was an era when a host of institutional and technological advances such as the typewriter, telephone, and department store created an army of new white-collar and bureaucratic jobs from which African-Americans were excluded. Most important—and hardest for modern observers to grasp—factory work, all across the country, was considered too good for black workers.

The significance of this cannot be overstressed. Virtually everywhere blacks were deliberately shut out of the modern sector of the economy. Although Philadelphia had perhaps the most varied manufacturing base in the world, the bottom line was that as of 1900 nearly 90 percent of those blacks who worked in the straight economy at all did so "below the collar line," with hands and backs, the great majority in just two census categories: "unskilled labor" or "personal and domestic service." That is, they were confined to jobs more characteristic of the middle ages than of the 19th century—let alone the 20th.

According to the 1900 census, fully 76 percent of African-Americans in Philadelphia were working in either "unskilled" labor or domestic and personal service jobs, compared with just 28 percent of white immigrants and 12 percent of whites of native parentage. Only 8 percent of black workers were employed in manufacturing of any kind—most of those in low-skill, preindustrial jobs such as brick-making—compared to 47 percent of white immigrants and 40 percent of native whites (Hershberg et al. 1981).

These results of racism combined with racism itself to undermine, over time, most of the strengths and advances of the black community. The poverty of the majority, first, undermined the position of professionals. Although black men and women could win degrees, that was no guarantee that they could make a living. As whites would not hire and blacks could not afford them, licensed physicians were found working as bellhops in downtown hotels, and in the early 20th century not one of Philadelphia's black attorneys could make a living through law practice alone.

As continued migration northward combined with racism to create ever-larger ghettos, black businesses lost fearful white customers, a patronage that could not be recovered by the impoverished black majority. The nettlesome problem of entrepreneurial history cannot be traced in this short space. But it was universally agreed that black businesses were in decline after the Civil War. The most successful, such as catering and restaurants, barbering and furniture moving, depended on white patronage that was lost when whites grew fearful of entering the ghettos to which the proprietors were confined. Those enterprises that were left were the type that actually thrived on segregation, such as undertaking or beauty parlors, and merely recirculated money within the black community instead of bringing it in from the white community.

The fact that many African-Americans fled to more secure employment in the public sector, as civil servants, proved an ambiguous benefit. The issue of jobs in government and related businesses was by far the most important political concern in late-19th-century black Philadelphia. With the partial exception of teaching school, government jobs ordinarily were restricted to loyal voters and party supporters. In Philadelphia, as across the nation, black voters newly enfranchised after the Civil War normally voted for the Republican Party, which they credited with winning the war, freeing the slaves, and granting the vote. To keep this sense of gratitude alive, as the urban black electorate swelled in the later 19th century, the GOP granted a number of political jobs to blacks, although sometimes grudgingly. Postal employees were the first appointments. Many members of the local black elite were employed by the post office, though following the rule that generally kept African-Americans out of jobs where they might have to deal with white citizens, especially from positions of authority, none of them was allowed during the 19th century actually to deliver the mail.

The symbolic issue of authority helped make the police department the focus of black demands. As the memory of the Civil War faded, it was not a Republican but a Democratic reform mayor, Samuel King, who as part of a bid for African-American votes in 1881 appointed the city's first four black policemen.[11] On August 22 some 2,000 people, or roughly one-third of the total number of African-American voters, crowded into Liberty Hall to celebrate the appointments, joined by leading white abolitionists. Despite considerable controversy—an ex-mayor declared that "darkies, uniformed as officers, and empowered to lay violent hands upon white men . . . is an insult too unpardonable to think of" (Dorsey Scrapbook, No 73, p 23, Philadelphia *Sunday Transcript,* 8/14/81.)—by the end of his term, Mayor King had appointed 35 African-American policemen, a number then far bigger than the total number of schoolteachers, messengers, janitors, or clerks employed by the city. By 1891, there were 60 African-Americans on the patrol force, a percentage reasonably close to the official black proportion of the city's population. But although much of this progress was due to Democratic efforts to win new voters, black leaders were largely unable to shake an almost monolithic dependence on the Republicans, or to make politics a route to genuine economic advancement.

One problem was that civil service jobs made many black leaders passively dependent on white politicians. The right to vote in the late 19th century was unquestionably a benefit to Philadelphia's blacks, but political activity was not as rewarding for them as for the Irish and others. The problem was that the unique economic situation of the African-American community—its exclusion from the wider rewards of the urban-industrial revolution—combined with racism and dependence on a single party to make it uniquely vulnerable to political exploitation. The legitimate rewards of politics—despite their great importance—were relatively few, and the illegitimate rewards were all too common. In general the jobs, when there were any for blacks, went directly to the elite. Large numbers of other blacks were

---

11. At a time when there were still no formal requirements of any kind for police officers, the black appointees stood out for their qualifications. All four were settled married men. One, a newspaperman, was an ex-slave, a graduate of Lincoln University, and a former law student at Howard University. Another was a Civil War veteran, secretary of the Equal Rights League, active Mason, music teacher, and longtime leader of his Presbyterian choir.

enrolled in political clubs simply to fight or cheat at the polls, and paid in the form of election-day bribes, lenient treatment from the magistrates when brought up for minor crimes, or quasi-official permission to run speakeasies and bawdy houses with little interference from the authorities. Neither the respectable nor the disreputable had power enough to combat political dependence.

The growing dependence on the Republican party cannot be blamed on the city's black leadership. First, there was the simple fact that the Democrats grew weaker in the city, state, and nation as the century progressed. In Philadelphia, during the 1870s and 1880s, the minority party could count on about 40 percent of the vote, enough in a decentralized system to win a number of offices; by the later 1890s, this percentage had sunk closer to 30 percent, and the party was generally shut out. The doubly paradoxical result was that although the black vote grew progressively bigger, it was progressively less crucial to the GOP, and still had nowhere else to go.

The other reason for dependence was the central fact of exclusion from industrial and other good jobs, and the failure to win them through legitimate politics. This was decidedly not the result of neglecting the issue. Politically articulate African-Americans of every persuasion continually stressed the need for better opportunities. Robert Jones in 1878 called for jobs not only in government but in the gas company, which was notoriously close to the city's Republican "Ring." Repeated calls were made, unsuccessfully, for a share of government contracting jobs. Many hoped the police appointments might help to conquer the wider prejudice against blacks in uniformed authority, the usual reason given for refusing to hire them as, for example, streetcar conductors. But the city's Republican employers did not respond by opening up jobs in the private sector, nor did local unions tolerate competition with white workers. In 1898, for example, white workers successfully struck against the hiring of two black motormen by the Philadelphia and Western Streetcar Company. The result of the failure to provide private-sector jobs, and the fact that the limited number of government jobs went mostly to members of the educated elite, was that there was nothing legitimate to offer the hundreds of black men who enrolled in all those political clubs to march, burn, and fight for the GOP.

The use of illegitimate political rewards was one of several factors that encouraged growing rates of crime. As the underside of the "entertainment" story, white politicians turned the nation's major black neighborhoods, from Beale Street to Harlem, into places semiofficially zoned, by white officials, as red-light or vice districts, places where crime and violence ruled, and where the most attractive role models available to the young were successful gamblers and prostitutes. The growth of black crime in general, and of murder rates in particular, is a complex story. Obviously the historically justified fear of white violence, and the tensions created by living, involuntarily, in districts full of wired-up strangers looking for action, helped encourage the habit of carrying weapons, which were then all too handy during routine arguments with family and acquaintances. But another social-psychological dimension resulted from black exclusion from the regimenting effects of industrial and bureaucratic work. These effects are shown in the relatively rapid decline in homicide rates for Irish and Italians, two other ethnic groups with high levels of preindustrial violence, as they were integrated into the urban work force.[12]

ORIGINS OF THE MODERN UNDERCLASS

The foregoing historical sketch makes it easier to trace the origins of the modern underclass. We cannot blame its condition on a handful of southern slave owners, in a society long gone with the wind. Its ultimate origins lie instead in racial discrimination that, well after the Civil War, denied economic opportunity to a black population that a century ago was ready, able, and eager to seize it. That denial, condoned if not supported by the majority of white Americans, doomed the great majority of urban blacks to poverty. This in turn crippled a once promising effort to build an independent professional and entrepreneurial middle class. And the effects of frustration were not merely long lasting, but cumulative, as the 19th century gave way to the 20th.

From the turn of the century to World War II, the urban black majority continued to make only slight gains in industrial employment. It continued to lose ground to white competitors in social conditions, as measured by growing gaps in two strong indicators: murder rates and the percentage of two-parent families. The proportion of black professionals, especially doctors, continued to decline across the country, as the failure to make significant gains in private white-collar employment killed the great faith in learning and bred instead a snowballing sense that education gets you nowhere—if you are black.

12. See Lane (1979) for the theoretical argument behind this analysis and Lane (1986) for the application of this argument to the black population, then and now.

This pattern was broken by the labor shortage of World War II, which, like the Civil War, ushered in a kind of second "golden age" for urban black America. This more familiar era brought important new gains in office and, most dramatically, in factory employment. By 1960, the census recorded that proportionally more blacks than whites were living in cities, and more blacks than whites, in Philadelphia as across the country, were working as operatives in factories. This second golden age, like the first, brought well-publicized breakthroughs in civil rights, middle-class occupational advancement, and higher education. Unlike the first, it also brought strong employment benefits to the working class majority and was accompanied for many years by, among other things, falling black murder rates.

But again, like the first golden age, this one was built on sand, although for different reasons. Direct racism was of waning importance. Nevertheless, if no longer shut out of the urban-industrial revolution, African-Americans were instead let in too late. During the 1940s and 1950s blacks in effect were piped aboard a sinking ship, welcomed into the urban industrial age just as that age was dying, with industrial cities losing population and jobs. As black unemployment, which hit a new low in the early 1950s, began to climb again into double digits, the indices of crime and family instability began again to climb as well.

The visible advances for the middle class continued for some years, and by the 1970s the proportion of educated professionals finally regained the levels reached three generations earlier. But once again, without strong support from below, these educational advances were undermined. Collegiate enrollment peaked in 1976, putting an end to the second golden age after a little more than 35 years—almost exactly the length of the first one. Here we have been ever since, with dying cities and industries not only spawning an underclass but threatening the hard-won gains of the black—and indeed the white—working and middle classes.

Although the public often focuses on crime and drugs in the cities, virtually all social scientists can agree that these are symptoms, rather than fundamental causes, of the black community's separation from the urban mainstream. From a historical perspective, four developments combined to kill the hopes and cripple the potential enjoyed by the black majority in the first decades after slavery.

The first of these developments, already sketched, was the long-standing economic discrimination that guaranteed poverty. Three secondary problems have resulted from this history. One of these problems is, for too many blacks, the development of a cluster of negative values and attitudes involving family and education, stemming from all those years when the pains of winning an education far outweighed the gains it might bring, and when it was nearly impossible for a man to earn enough to sustain a family. A historian hesitates to enter the fiercely ideological debate among sociologists that revolves around the phrase "culture of poverty." But without endorsing the views of the more ardent advocates of the concept, and without—the burden of this text should make clear—"blaming the victim," it is clear to a historian that some widely transmitted values, attitudes, or priorities now combine to keep many ghetto-dwellers from entering the economic mainstream. To deny that three or more generations of frustration and discrimination have had an effect is to deny the importance of history itself. And the fact that, for example, the number of black two-parent families declined, however marginally, even during the prosperous 1940s and 1950s, indicates one of the ways in which inherited experience may triumph over present circumstances. Similarly, the failure of many contemporary African-Americans on standard written examinations—a failure that stands in contrast to the successes of their post-Civil War ancestors, as well as to those of modern immigrants from Africa or the West Indies—suggests that the problem lies less with cultural bias in the tests themselves than with a long-standing and for many years legitimate suspicion of the benefits of standard education.

A second factor is the growth of huge segregated ghettos, which in time cut off many urban blacks from potential employers or customers—"geographical isolation"—and, once the middle class was able to escape, created large pockets of only the poor—"social isolation." Although the negative effects of social isolation, which rob whole neighborhoods of working role models, are real, so were the costs of the tight residential segregation that preceded it. The costs to the middle class of living in high crime districts, not the least of which was the problem of transmitting values to their children, were widely recognized in earlier years.

A third, more recent reason for the growth of the black underclass, more directly important now than a relatively faded white racism, is the shift from a manufacturing to a service economy. This new service economy demands levels of literacy and numeracy higher than the species has ever had to meet before—a problem that black Americans share with millions of white ones, and indeed with millions more in Europe and elsewhere—as those who are unable to meet the skill demands lose good jobs for bad ones, or none at all. For black Americans, the irony is that the manufacturing jobs now being lost were only recently won. A history stretching only as far as grandparental memories of the "good old days" of the 1940s and 1950s is not enough to place current experience in perspective. During periods of fundamental economic transition, black Americans always have been especially vulnerable to exclusion from the new economy.

Public policy, finally, did not directly cause either the racism or the economic shift that have created the underclass. But it has played a role, and may perhaps play another. Policymakers for generations failed to deal effectively with racism and more recently have failed to deal effectively with the differential impacts of economic change. Since the 1980s they have instead often implicitly encouraged the first and tolerated or aggravated the negative effects of the second. In many ways Philadelphia and the nation's other big cities have become monuments to the inability of public policy to work on behalf of the black community.

References

The *Dorsey Scrapbook*, The William Dorsey Collection at Cheyney State University, Cheyney, PA.

Hershberg, Theodore, Alan N. Burstein, Eugene P. Ericksen, Stephanie W. Greenberg, and William L. Yancy. 1981. "A Tale of Three Cities: Blacks, Immigrants, and Opportunity in Philadelphia, 1850–80, 1930, 1970." In *Philadelphia: Work Space, Family, and Group Experience in the Nineteenth Century*, edited by Theodore Hershberg. New York: Oxford University Press.

Lane, Roger. 1979. *Violent Death in the City: Suicide, Accident, and Murder in Nineteenth Century Philadelphia*. Cambridge, Mass.: Harvard University Press.

————. 1986. *Roots of Violence in Black Philadelphia, 1860–1900*. Cambridge, Mass.: Harvard University Press.

————. 1991. *William Dorsey's Philadelphia and Ours: On the History and Future of the Black City in America*. New York: Oxford University Press.

Locke, Alain, 1969. *The Negro and His Music: Past and Present*. New York: Arno Press, originally published, 1930.

Chapter Three

THE SEVERELY DISTRESSED IN ECONOMICALLY TRANSFORMING CITIES

John D. Kasarda

A rapidly expanding literature is targeting the impact of transforming urban economies on joblessness, poverty, and related social problems that are increasingly concentrated in our major cities (for comprehensive reviews, see Jencks and Peterson 1991; Moss and Tilly 1991). Underlying much of this research is the emergence of a large subgroup of inner-city residents who are detached from the formal labor market in far greater numbers and proportions than formerly documented. High rates of joblessness among this subgroup, in turn, have been associated with disproportionately high rates of poverty, school dropout, out-of-wedlock births, and welfare dependency.

When all of these attributes exist concurrently within households, they are purported to be mutually reinforcing, resulting in behavior that substantially diminishes the economic fortunes of affected members (Wilson 1987). Geographic concentration of such severely distressed households further magnifies these problems and accelerates their spread to nearby households through social isolation, peer pressure, and imitative behavior (Martinez-Vazquez and Saposnik 1990; Wilson 1987; Wacquant and Wilson 1989). The upshot is a spiral of negative economic outcomes for the households and their neighborhoods.

This chapter examines the scope and nature of severely distressed households in America's large cities and links their differential growth across cities to changes occurring in the structure of local economies. Severely distressed households are defined as those that simultaneously exhibit five attributes: low income, less than high school education, poor work history, single parenthood, and public assistance dependency. Public-Use Microdata Sample (PUMS) files from the 1970 and 1980 Census of Population and Housing are ana-

I wish to acknowledge the superior programming and research assistance of Edward Bachmann, Andrea Bohlig, and Kwok-Fai Ting.

lyzed to document the size and demographic composition of severely distressed residents in 95 of the largest metropolitan central cities. Utilizing microdata indicators that are analogous to behaviorally based census tract indicators of urban underclass populations (Ricketts and Sawhill 1988), comparisons are made in numbers and composition of this subgroup at the individual and spatially aggregated levels.

Following a discussion of hypothesized causal relations between urban industrial change and economic dislocation, cities with the largest concentrations of severely distressed residents and underclass populations are selected for detailed assessments of their transforming economies. These transformations are benchmarked against those occurring in other large cities where such disadvantaged subgroups have not experienced as much growth. A number of explanations drawing on both demand- and supply-side labor market factors are offered to account for observed differences across these cities in amounts of economic and social dislocation.

THE URBAN UNDERCLASS CONCEPT AND MEASURES

Perhaps no social science concept has generated more discussion and controversy in recent years than that of the urban underclass. Some argue that it is little more than new wine in old bottles—a pithy and stigmatizing term for poor or lower-class persons who have always existed in stratified societies (Gans 1990; Jencks 1989; Katz 1989). Others contend that the underclass is a distinct and recent phenomenon that reflects extreme marginalization from mainstream institutions and counterproductive behavior that reached catastrophic proportions in the inner cities by the mid-1970s (Auletta 1982; Glasgow 1980; Nathan 1987; Reischauer 1987; Wilson 1987). Despite the multifaceted and often ambiguous definitions of the urban underclass, almost all the definitions share the notions of weak labor force attachment and persistent low income (Jencks 1989; Ricketts 1990; Sjoquist 1990). Indeed, the first scholar to introduce the term *underclass* to the literature labeled its members as an emergent substratum of permanently unemployed, unemployables, and underemployed (Myrdal 1962).

Measurement of the size of the underclass is as varied as its definitions. A number of researchers have focused on individual-level indicators of persistent poverty, defined as those who are poor for spells from n to n + x years (Bane and Ellwood 1986; Duncan, Coe, and Hill 1984; Levy 1977) or long-term AFDC (Aid to Families with Dependent Children) recipients (Gottschalk and Danziger 1986). For example, Levy (1977), using the Panel Study of Income Dynamics (PSID, University of Michigan, Ann Arbor, Institute for Social Research) for the years 1967 to 1973, estimated that approximately 11 million Americans were persistently poor for at least five years. When belonging to the underclass is defined as being persistently poor for eight or more years, 6 million people were found to be members (Duncan et al. 1984). This represented approximately one-fifth of the 32 million Americans living in poor households in 1988 (Mincy, Sawhill, and Wolf 1990).

Another measurement strategy focuses upon the geographic concentration of the poor in urban areas. Using Bureau of the Census tract-level definitions of local poverty areas, Reischauer (1987) reported that, of the nation's population living in such poverty areas, central cities housed over half in 1985, up from just one-third in 1972. Bane and Jargowsky (1988) documented that the number of poor people living in extreme poverty tracts in cities (i.e., census tracts where more than 40 percent of the residents fall below the poverty line) expanded by 66 percent between 1970 and 1980, from 975,000 to 1,615,000. Moreover, just four northern cities (New York, Chicago, Philadelphia, and Detroit) accounted for two-thirds of this increase.

Using an identical definition of extreme poverty tracts, Green (1988) found that 30 large American cities added 527 such tracts between 1970 and 1980. Similarly to Bane and Jargowsky, he discovered that 492 (or 91 percent) of these additional extreme poverty tracts were located in his 15 sampled cities from the Northeast and Midwest. Whereas nearly half (N = 13) of the sampled large cities were in the South, they had a combined increase of only 36 extreme poverty tracts (17 percent), while the 2 large cities of the West, Los Angeles and Phoenix, together added only 9 extreme poverty tracts between 1970 and 1980. Clearly, then, the rise of concentrated poverty appears most severe in the older industrial cities of the North.

Mincy (1988) further documented that concentrated poverty is predominantly a minority problem. His analysis of extreme poverty tracts in the 100 largest central cities in 1980 showed that of the approximately 1.8 million poor people residing in these tracts, fewer than 10 percent were non-Hispanic white (175,178), while nearly 70 percent were black (1,248,151). Nearly all of the remainder were Hispanic.

As indicated at the beginning of this chapter, the concept of underclass is typically considered to entail more than poverty, however. It

is also posited to incorporate certain behavioral characteristics con-
flicting with mainstream values: joblessness, out-of-wedlock births,
welfare dependency, school dropout, and illicit activities. Attempts
have been made to measure the size of the underclass by using multiple "behavioral" indicators derived from census data. Ricketts and
Sawhill (1988) measured the underclass as people living in neighborhoods whose residents in 1980 simultaneously exhibited disproportionately high rates of school dropout, joblessness, female-headed families, and welfare dependency. Using a composite definition where
tracts must be at least one standard deviation above the national mean
on *all* four characteristics, they found that approximately 2.5 million
people lived in such tracts in 1980 and that these tracts were disproportionately located in major cities in the Northeast and Midwest.
They reported that in underclass tracts, on average, 63 percent of the
resident adults had less than a high school education, 60 percent of
the families with children were headed by women, 56 percent of the
adult men were not regularly employed, and 34 percent of the households were receiving public assistance. Ricketts and Sawhill's (1988)
research also revealed that, although the total poverty population only
grew by 8 percent between 1970 and 1980, the number of people living in the underclass areas grew by 230 percent, from 752,000 to
2,484,000.

Hughes (1988) showed an enormous increase between 1970 and
1980 in the isolation and deprivation of ghetto neighborhoods in eight
distressed cities. Hughes's mapping of the location and spread of
predominantly black census tracts in these cities revealed a substantial growth in the number of poor black neighborhoods that did not
border on integrated or nonblack neighborhoods. During the 1970s
many predominantly black census tracts became surrounded by other
overwhelmingly black census tracts, limiting the potential for contact
with nonblack residents by those who resided in increasingly isolated
tracts at the ghetto's core.

Hughes (1988) also compared absolute changes between 1970 and
1980 in the number of tracts with high coincident levels of adult male
joblessness, mother-only families, and welfare recipiency. He found
that these tracts, which he labeled "deprivation neighborhoods,"
mushroomed over the decade. In Chicago, for example, deprivation
neighborhoods increased by 150 percent, from 120 tracts to 299 tracts,
while the population living in these tracts expanded by 132 percent,
from 445,000 to 1,034,000. Similarly, in Detroit the number of deprivation tracts expanded from 60 to 197 (228 percent), and the population residing in these tracts increased from 193,880 to 708,593. Just

as remarkable, the ratio of black nondeprivation tracts to deprivation tracts completely reversed in both cities during the decade; in Chicago from three to two in 1970 to two to five in 1980, and in Detroit from five to two in 1970 to one to four in 1980.

Such location-based aggregate measures have been criticized on the grounds that, aside from race, most urban census tracts are quite heterogeneous along economic and social dimensions. Jencks (1989), for example, observed that, with the exception of tracts composed of public housing projects, there is considerable diversity in resident income, education levels, joblessness, and public assistance recipiency within urban neighborhoods. According to his calculations, even in extreme poverty tracts only about half of all families in 1980 had incomes below the poverty line, and some reported incomes up to four times the poverty level. "As a result, most poor families probably had next door neighbors who were not poor" (Jencks 1989: 15). He further noted Ricketts and Sawhill's (1988) findings that within the worst urban neighborhoods (those they defined as underclass areas) more than half the working-age adults held steady jobs, and only one-third of the households received public assistance. On the other hand, considerable numbers of urban residents who are poor, jobless, and dependent on public assistance live in census tracts where fewer than 20 percent of the families fall below the poverty line (Kasarda 1992).

THE SEVERELY DISTRESSED

Jencks (1989) argued that it is only attributes of individuals and not those of their addresses that should matter in measuring the urban underclass. Following this approach, I have utilized the 1970 and 1980 Public-Use Microdata Sample (PUMS) to identify severely distressed households and individuals in America's largest cities.

The 1980 PUMS file identifies metropolitan central cities and provides data for individual housing units and the persons living in them. Both the 5 percent (A file) and the 1 percent (B file) samples are used to obtain a sample of the 100 largest central cities based on their 1980 population. Of these 100 cities, only Amarillo, Corpus Christi, Lincoln, Lubbock, and Montgomery could not be identified. (For these five places, data are not provided for the central cities, only for their metropolitan areas as a whole; therefore, they were removed from the study.) The final sample thus consists of 95 of these cities. All sample counts (that is, households, persons, and children [under 18]) are weighted to the population size. This file excludes all persons living in group quarters.[1]

Five PUMS variables that are consistent with previous indicators are used to define underclass attributes of households and individuals. They are low education, single parenthood, poor work history, public assistance dependency, and poverty. Severely distressed households are those with *all* five of the following underclass attributes:

Low Education: Both the householder and spouse (if present) did not complete high school.

Single Parenthood: The householder is either single, divorced, widowed, or separated, and young persons under age 18 live in the householder's family.

Poor Work History: Both the householder and spouse (if present) worked less than 26 weeks or usually worked less than 20 hours a week in 1979.

Public Assistance Recipiency: At least one member of the household received public assistance income in 1979.

Poverty: The householder's family income was below poverty in 1979.

It may be argued that the requirement that all five attributes be present for severe distress, while conceptually appropriate, is too restrictive. For example, there may be distressed families or persons in households where children are not present or where the householder or spouse completed high school. For this reason, in the comparative analysis, I identify all households and persons in households with both poor work history and where the householder's family income was below poverty. (Recall that poor work history and poverty are the common threads to virtually all definitions of the urban underclass.)

---

1. Further details about the PUMS can be found in U.S. Bureau of the Census (1983).

SIZE AND RACIAL/ETHNIC COMPOSITION OF HOUSEHOLDS AND PERSONS

The first three columns of table 3.1 present, respectively, the number of severely distressed households and numbers of persons and children (under age 18) in these households for the 95 cities that could be identified in the 1980 PUMS files. Columns four and five show the percentage of severely distressed households that are non-Hispanic black and Hispanic, respectively, for each city, whereas columns six through eight describe the percentage of all severely distressed urban households by race/ethnicity found in each city (total households, black households, and Hispanic households, respectively). The cities are ranked by number of severely distressed residents (column 2).

The final row in table 3.1 shows that the 95 cities had a total of 305,480 severely distressed households in 1980. More than 1,250,000 persons resided in these households, including about 809,700 persons under age 18. Eighty-four percent of the households were black or Hispanic. Consistent with findings on the size and growth of extreme poverty tract and underclass area populations, four cities account for a disproportionate number and share of severely distressed households and residents—New York City, Chicago, Philadelphia, and Detroit.

These four cities contain 45 percent of the total severely distressed households, including 41 percent of the severely distressed black households and 65 percent of the severely distressed Hispanic households (table 3.1). New York City alone accounts for one-quarter of the total distressed households and 55 percent of all distressed Hispanic households (the latter living largely in the Puerto Rican community). When Los Angeles is included along with these four cities, the percentage of severely distressed households increases to nearly one-half of the 95-city total and nearly three-quarters of all severely distressed Hispanic households.

Hispanics comprise over one-half of the severely distressed households in New York City and over 40 percent of those in Los Angeles (table 3.1). In other large cities with more than 5,000 distressed households, blacks constitute the vast majority. Note, as well, that children constitute the majority of persons in the severely distressed households. For example, of the 293,540 persons in severely distressed households in New York City, 188,060 are persons under age 18.

Appendix table 3.A presents the racial and ethnic composition of severely distressed persons in each of the 95 cities. The racial and

Table 3.1 SEVERELY DISTRESSED HOUSEHOLDS(HH)/PERSONS/CHILDREN AMONG 95 MOST POPULATED CENTRAL CITIES: 1980

Central Cities	House-holds	Persons	Children Under Age 18	% Black House-holds	% Hispanic House-holds	% HH to 95 cities	% Black HH to 95 cities	% Hispanic HH to 95 cities
New York	76,780	293,540	188,060	35.5	56.8	25.1	15.3	55.2
Chicago	30,220	136,280	89,480	74.3	16.7	9.9	12.6	6.4
Philadelpia	16,300	69,620	42,720	73.5	12.4	5.3	6.7	2.6
Detroit	13,600	55,720	36,440	80.9	3.4	4.5	6.2	0.6
Los Angeles	11,020	45,240	28,500	50.6	40.5	3.6	3.1	5.6
Baltimore	9,680	42,420	25,780	82.6	2.1	3.2	4.5	0.3
Newark	6,760	28,760	19,620	64.2	32.0	2.2	2.4	2.7
New Orleans	6,060	27,420	18,160	94.7	2.0	2.0	3.2	0.2
Memphis	5,160	24,700	16,220	94.2	1.9	1.7	2.7	0.1
Cleveland	5,940	23,260	14,800	68.0	8.1	1.9	2.3	0.6
Washington, D.C.	4,660	20,700	13,020	96.1	2.1	1.5	2.5	0.1
Atlanta	4,660	20,020	12,820	91.4	2.6	1.5	2.4	0.2
Milwaukee	4,700	19,160	12,880	68.9	5.5	1.5	1.8	0.3
St. Louis	3,760	18,260	11,940	85.6	0.0	1.2	1.8	0.0
Boston	4,080	15,940	10,280	44.1	27.0	1.3	1.0	1.4
San Antonio	3,680	15,820	10,480	12.5	81.0	1.2	0.3	3.8
Columbus, Oh.	3,520	13,980	9,040	51.7	2.3	1.2	1.0	0.1
Houston	3,060	13,820	9,140	73.2	22.2	1.0	1.3	0.9
Dallas	2,600	13,200	8,700	69.2	7.7	0.9	1.0	0.3
Cincinnati	3,380	13,000	8,620	69.8	1.2	1.1	1.3	0.1
Jersey City	2,760	11,560	8,040	37.7	45.7	0.9	0.6	1.6
Indianapolis	2,900	11,400	7,400	79.3	3.4	0.9	1.3	0.1
Buffalo	2,980	11,140	7,440	67.8	8.7	1.0	1.1	0.3
Louisville	2,540	10,720	6,860	64.6	0.0	0.8	0.9	0.0
Pittsburgh	2,240	8,720	5,520	66.1	2.7	0.7	0.8	0.1

Jacksonville	2,100	8,400	5,700	85.7	0.0	0.7	1.0	0.0
Oakland	2,020	8,060	5,240	82.2	7.9	0.7	0.9	0.2
Dayton	2,060	8,000	5,260	59.2	1.0	0.7	0.7	0.0
Rochester	1,980	7,780	5,120	60.6	11.1	0.6	0.7	0.3
Norfolk	2,040	7,700	4,980	87.3	2.0	0.7	1.0	0.1
Richmond	1,900	7,660	4,840	90.5	0.0	0.6	1.0	0.0
Shreveport	1,600	7,500	4,400	81.3	12.5	0.5	0.7	0.3
Toledo	1,860	7,420	4,880	53.8	6.5	0.6	0.6	0.2
Birmingham	1,440	6,960	4,280	91.7	0.0	0.5	0.7	0.0
Miami	1,660	6,800	4,460	56.6	43.4	0.5	0.5	0.9
Gary	1,540	6,560	4,260	87.0	5.2	0.5	0.8	0.1
Kansas City	1,460	6,380	4,260	82.2	0.0	0.5	0.7	0.0
San Diego	1,720	6,240	4,020	30.2	51.2	0.6	0.3	1.1
Springfield, Mass.	1,620	6,240	4,160	23.5	45.7	0.5	0.2	0.9
Denver	1,660	6,180	4,080	26.5	59.0	0.5	0.2	1.2
Phoenix	1,380	6,140	4,100	27.5	47.8	0.5	0.2	0.8
Nashville	1,500	6,100	3,900	80.0	6.7	0.5	0.7	0.1
Tampa	1,420	5,960	4,100	74.6	7.0	0.5	0.6	0.1
Sacramento	1,580	5,780	3,520	31.6	25.3	0.5	0.3	0.5
Flint	1,540	5,680	3,660	66.2	1.3	0.5	0.6	0.0
Fresno	1,400	5,540	3,680	27.1	52.9	0.5	0.2	0.9
San Francisco	1,540	5,300	3,320	54.5	19.5	0.5	0.5	0.4
Minneapolis	1,380	5,220	3,240	34.8	2.9	0.5	0.3	0.1
San Jose	1,200	5,160	3,600	16.7	63.3	0.4	0.1	1.0
Syracuse	1,280	4,980	3,240	45.3	1.6	0.4	0.3	0.0
Long Beach	1,340	4,920	3,100	31.3	28.4	0.4	0.2	0.5
Akron	1,240	4,900	3,260	43.5	0.0	0.4	0.3	0.0
Providence	1,340	4,900	3,080	26.9	13.4	0.4	0.2	0.2
Charlotte	1,080	4,620	2,940	83.3	1.9	0.4	0.5	0.0
Chattanooga	940	4,520	2,900	78.7	0.0	0.3	0.4	0.0

continued

Table 3.1 SEVERELY DISTRESSED HOUSEHOLDS(HH)/PERSONS/CHILDREN AMONG 95 MOST POPULATED CENTRAL CITIES: 1980 (continued)

Central Cities	House-holds	Persons	Children Under Age 18	% Black House-holds	% Hispanic House-holds	% HH to 95 cities	% Black HH to 95 cities	% Hispanic HH to 95 cities
El Paso	1,200	4,500	2,700	0.0	83.3	0.4	0.0	1.3
Oklahoma City	1,080	4,360	2,880	55.6	9.3	0.4	0.3	0.1
Worcester	1,180	4,260	2,800	5.1	32.2	0.4	0.0	0.5
Grand Rapids	1,120	4,220	2,860	37.5	3.6	0.4	0.2	0.1
Albuquerque	1,000	3,820	2,440	6.0	86.0	0.3	0.0	1.1
Mobile	820	3,800	2,280	95.1	2.4	0.3	0.4	0.0
Jackson	800	3,700	2,600	100.0	0.0	0.3	0.4	0.0
Stockton	960	3,680	2,580	25.0	50.0	0.3	0.1	0.6
Columbus, Ga.	900	3,660	2,320	80.0	0.0	0.3	0.4	0.0
Lexington-Fayette	840	3,460	2,300	52.4	0.0	0.3	0.2	0.0
Fort Worth	760	3,420	2,320	65.8	26.3	0.2	0.3	0.3
Knoxville	800	3,400	2,160	42.5	0.0	0.3	0.2	0.0
Little Rock	660	3,140	2,160	81.8	3.0	0.2	0.3	0.0
St. Petersburg	720	3,060	1,940	72.2	2.8	0.2	0.3	0.0
Portland	800	3,040	1,860	45.0	10.0	0.3	0.2	0.1
Baton Rouge	700	3,020	2,040	88.6	0.0	0.2	0.3	0.0
Austin	700	2,900	2,200	28.6	71.4	0.2	0.1	0.6
Tulsa	740	2,860	1,860	51.4	2.7	0.2	0.2	0.0
Seattle	780	2,840	1,840	48.7	5.1	0.3	0.2	0.1
Wichita	700	2,800	2,000	28.6	0.0	0.2	0.1	0.0
Honolulu	760	2,780	1,700	0.0	36.8	0.2	0.0	0.4
St. Paul	800	2,780	1,880	20.0	10.0	0.3	0.1	0.1
Tacoma	820	2,780	1,660	22.0	4.9	0.3	0.1	0.1
Fort Wayne	600	2,540	1,760	50.0	3.3	0.2	0.2	0.0

Tucson	460	2,200	1,320	17.4	56.5	0.2	0.0	0.3
Greensboro	460	1,960	1,300	87.0	0.0	0.2	0.2	0.0
Des Moines	600	1,920	1,180	26.7	3.3	0.2	0.1	0.0
Omaha	700	1,900	1,300	57.1	0.0	0.2	0.2	0.0
Riverside	400	1,660	1,200	10.0	40.0	0.1	0.0	0.2
Fort Lauderdale	380	1,480	920	89.5	0.0	0.1	0.2	0.0
Las Vegas	320	1,420	800	81.3	6.3	0.1	0.1	0.0
Santa Ana	260	1,240	860	7.7	84.6	0.1	0.0	0.3
Virginia Beach	280	1,180	720	64.3	0.0	0.1	0.1	0.0
Spokane	340	1,040	580	5.9	0.0	0.1	0.0	0.0
Anchorage	300	1,020	600	13.3	6.7	0.1	0.0	0.0
Raleigh	220	1,020	600	72.7	9.1	0.1	0.1	0.0
Anaheim	260	960	600	0.0	61.5	0.1	0.0	0.2
Salt Lake City	220	900	580	18.2	45.5	0.1	0.0	0.1
Madison	180	760	460	33.3	33.3	0.1	0.0	0.1
Colorado Springs	0	0	0	.	.	0.0	0.0	0.0
Total (95 cities)	305,480	1,253,480	809,700	58.2	25.9	100.0	100.0	100.0

Source: U.S. Bureau of the Census, Census of Population and Housing, 1980, Public-Use Microdata Sample.

ethnic percentages vary substantially across cities, with non-Hispanic white proportions greatest in Spokane, Wichita, and Des Moines (no doubt reflecting the low percentages of nonwhites in these cities) and the non-Hispanic black percentage highest in Jackson, Mississippi, at 100 percent. Cities where blacks comprise over 90 percent of the severely distressed residents include Atlanta, Baton Rouge, Birmingham, Fort Lauderdale, Greensboro, Jackson, Memphis, Mobile, New Orleans, Richmond, and Washington, D.C. Hispanics comprise over 80 percent of severely distressed residents in Albuquerque, El Paso, San Antonio, and Santa Ana. In general, only small numbers of Asians, Pacific Islanders, and American Indians are found in severely distressed urban households, constituting but 1 percent of the severely distressed residents in the 95 cities.

AGGREGATE VERSUS INDIVIDUAL INDICATORS OF DISTRESS

It is informative to compare the counts of severely distressed households and residents that are tabulated using the Ricketts-Sawhill (1988) census tract measures and those generated for the same cities using individual-level PUMS indicators that are roughly analogous. Ricketts-Sawhill defined underclass areas as those census tracts for which the value of each of four underclass indicators is greater than or equal to one standard deviation above the 1980 mean. These indicators are:

Female-Headed Families: The proportion of families with children under age 18 that are headed by a woman.

Low Education: The proportion of young persons (ages 16 to 19) not enrolled in school and not high school graduates.

Poor Work History: The proportion of males aged 16 and older who worked less than 26 weeks a year.

Public Assistance Recipiency: The proportion of households or families with public assistance income.

The PUMS indicators used for comparison are the same as those used for severely distressed households, excluding poverty. Thus, to be counted as underclass, the household must simultaneously exhibit the following four characteristics: low education, single parenthood, poor work history, and public assistance dependency, as described previously. Table 3.2 illustrates that in the largest cities the Ricketts-Sawhill (1988) underclass measure generates consistently higher numbers of households and persons than the PUMS measure. Differences are greater for household counts than for person counts, with Detroit exhibiting particularly large differentials. Further analysis revealed that the average size of households in cities qualifying as underclass using the PUMS measure was considerably larger than the average household size in the Ricketts-Sawhill underclass areas. The fact that Ricketts-Sawhill counts of households and persons in underclass areas are greater than the PUMS measures may reflect the social and economic heterogeneity of the underclass areas in these cities.

Appendix table 3.B presents the racial/ethnic comparison of underclass population counts using the Ricketts-Sawhill (1988) and PUMS measures for all 95 cities. With a handful of exceptions, the counts by race and ethnicity generated by Ricketts-Sawhill at the tract level and PUMS at the individual level parallel one another. Not all Ricketts-Sawhill counts are greater than the PUMS counts. Substantial differences are found for Boston, where PUMS generates nearly 20,000 underclass residents compared to less than 10,000 with census tract measures, as well as for Memphis (10,466 Ricketts-Sawhill versus 28,920 PUMS), Pittsburgh (3,194 Ricketts-Sawhill versus 11,400 PUMS), and Washington, D.C. (18,775 Ricketts-Sawhill versus 29,300 PUMS). Observe that differences in the tabulation of blacks account for most of the discrepancies between the Ricketts-Sawhill and PUMS measures.

Table 3.2 COMPARISON OF HOUSEHOLDS AND POPULATION ACCORDING TO RICKETTS-SAWHILL (R&S) AND PUMS MEASURES OF UNDERCLASS, 1980

Central Cities	Number of Households		Number of Persons	
	R&S	PUMS	R&S	PUMS
New York	149,698	90,720	420,722	348,540
Chicago	60,895	36,080	189,853	165,840
Philadelphia	36,779	20,260	113,845	88,860
Detroit	57,165	18,540	159,804	78,200
Los Angeles	28,112	14,760	93,894	62,320

Sources: U.S. Bureau of the Census, Census of Population and Housing, 1980: Summary Tape File 3A and Public-Use Microdata Samples (PUMS).
Note: See text for explanation of Ricketts-Sawhill (1988) census tract measures and PUMS measures.

To assess the dynamics of severely distressed household and population changes in the five largest cities, the county group sample (5 percent data) of the 1970 PUMS is used to facilitate the comparison of severely distressed households between 1970 and 1980. Since in the 1970 PUMS, central cities cannot be identified, central counties are used as a basis for comparison (for New York City and Philadelphia, city and county boundaries are identical). In addition, poor work history is redefined as both the householder and spouse (if present) working less than 27 weeks in 1979, so that this characteristic is comparable between the 1970 and 1980 PUMS.

Table 3.3 presents the change in the numbers of households, persons, and children under age 18 by race for New York, Chicago, Philadelphia, Detroit, and Los Angeles. New York City exhibited by far the largest growth of severely distressed households, persons, and children, with Hispanics constituting over two-thirds of the increase in that city's severely distressed households and persons and over 90 percent of the increase in children under age 18 in severely distressed households. For Chicago, Philadelphia, and Detroit, blacks constituted the vast majority of increase in severely distressed households, persons, and children. Los Angeles experienced relatively little growth in severely distressed households and persons. Indeed, this city had a net decline in children in severely distressed households, due largely to sharp declines in the number of non-Hispanic white households that are severely distressed. Conversely, there was a considerable rise in the number of Hispanic households, persons, and children in severe distress.

These results on the growth of severely distressed households and individuals are consistent with findings on the dynamics of population growth in extreme poverty and underclass areas, as shown in table 3.4. Jargowsky and Bane (1991) found that two-thirds of the growth of population in extreme poverty tracts in major cities was accounted for by New York, Chicago, Philadelphia, and Detroit. Likewise, a number of analyses by Urban Institute researchers have shown that these same four cities contributed the largest percentage of population growth in underclass areas.

Table 3.4 reveals that the number of extreme poverty tracts increased in New York City between 1970 and 1980 from 73 to 311, in Chicago from 47 to 132, in Philadelphia from 23 to 51, and in Detroit from 23 to 45. Underclass tracts (classified by the Ricketts-Sawhill

Table 3.3 NET CHANGE OF THE SEVERELY DISTRESSED POPULATION BETWEEN 1970 AND 1980

Central Counties	Units	All Races	White	Black	Hispanic	Others
New York	Households	31,740	1,720	8,120	21,660	240
	Persons	90,540	4,520	18,820	66,100	1,100
	Children	39,920	1,660	1,900	35,500	860
Chicago	Households	11,780	1,380	7,160	3,140	100
	Persons	40,820	3,760	24,460	11,980	620
	Children	17,620	1,720	8,060	7,420	420
Philadelphia	Households	7,060	1,140	4,600	1,200	120
	Persons	26,200	2,900	18,700	4,140	460
	Children	11,540	1,080	7,880	2,340	240
Detroit	Households	6,600	740	5,460	420	−20
	Persons	19,600	140	17,780	1,540	140
	Children	9,200	−680	8,860	860	160
Los Angeles	Households	3,660	−2,620	560	5,640	80
	Persons	7,240	−12,980	−2,260	22,220	260
	Children	−940	−9,720	−4,740	13,660	−140

Sources: U.S. Bureau of the Census, Census of Population and Housing, 1970 and 1980, Public-Use Microdata Samples.
Notes: White refers to non-Hispanic white; black refers to non-Hispanic black.

Table 3.4 NUMBER AND DISTRIBUTION OF DISADVANTAGED POPULATION, 1970 AND 1980, BY SUBAREA

City/Characteristics	Areas with 20 Percent Below Poverty 1970	Areas with 20 Percent Below Poverty 1980	Areas with 40 Percent Below Poverty 1970	Areas with 40 Percent Below Poverty 1980	Underclass Areas 1970	Underclass Areas 1980
New York						
Number of tracts	457	791	73	311	27	140
Number of residents	2,111,486	2,773,520	299,961	997,654	94,866	420,722
Percentage of city population	26.8	39.2	3.8	14.1	1.2	6.0
Chicago						
Number of tracts	231	380	47	132	17	62
Number of residents	828,661	1,189,110	156,175	367,801	72,491	189,853
Percentage of city population	24.3	39.6	4.6	12.2	2.1	6.3
Philadelphia						
Number of tracts	101	146	23	51	12	26
Number of residents	505,837	731,487	105,035	219,124	74,229	113,845
Percentage of city population	26.0	43.4	5.4	13.0	3.8	6.7
Detroit						
Number of tracts	146	179	23	45	7	53
Number of residents	438,227	582,316	55,251	114,225	29,786	159,804
Percentage of city population	29.0	48.4	3.7	9.5	2.0	13.3
Los Angeles						
Number of tracts	162	234	25	30	10	19
Number of residents	577,180	992,663	82,123	95,906	36,074	93,894
Percentage of city population	20.4	33.5	2.9	3.2	1.3	3.2

Source: U.S. Bureau of the Census, Census of Population and Housing, 1980, Summary Tape File 3A.

[1988] indicators) increased in even greater proportions, with huge swells in the population in the extreme poverty and underclass areas of these four cities. In New York City, for example, population in extreme poverty areas rose from just under 300,000 to nearly 1 million between 1970 and 1980 (from 3.8 percent of the city's population to 14.1 percent), and its underclass area population rose from about 95,000 in 1970 to about 421,000 in 1980 (from 1.2 percent of the city's population to 6.0 percent).

Los Angeles, on the other hand, exhibited much lower growth in its extreme poverty areas than the four major frostbelt cities (table 3.4). It did add nine underclass area tracts between 1970 and 1980, contributing an additional 58,000 residents to its underclass total. Still, by 1980 only 3.2 percent of Los Angeles's residents were classified as either residing in extreme poverty areas or underclass areas, compared to Detroit, whose underclass population expanded from 2 percent of the city's total population in 1970 to 13.3 percent in 1980.

Differential changes in the size and racial/ethnic mix of a city (or central county) can heavily influence changes in the number and city percentage of severely distressed households tabulated for each racial/ethnic subgroup. New York City, for instance, declined by 823,000 residents between 1970 and 1980, but actually lost 1.4 million non-Hispanic whites while adding 176,000 blacks, 204,000 Hispanics, and 190,000 Asians and others. Los Angeles City alone added nearly 400,000 Hispanics during the decade. It is therefore important to control for racial/ethnic change when assessing differential growth rates of severely distressed residents by race and ethnicity. Table 3.5 does this by presenting for the five central counties the percentage of members of each racial/ethnic group that had (1) no distress attributes, (2) poor work history and poverty, and (3) all five distress attributes (severely distressed) in 1970 and in 1980.

For all five central counties, the percentage of total population with no distress attributes declined (table 3.5). This was largely due to a shift in the demographic composition of the cities to those racial/ethnic subgroups that had smaller proportions of their membership with no distress attributes. In three of the four northern cities, the "other" (predominantly Asian) subgroup showed rising proportions with no distress attributes, whereas the fourth city (Philadelphia) exhibited a decrease. With the exception of New York City, the percentage of blacks with no distress attributes in the largest northern cities declined between 1970 and 1980. The percentage of whites with no distress attributes remained nearly constant in New York and Philadelphia and rose slightly in Chicago and Detroit. In Los Angeles, the

Table 3.5 PERCENTAGE OF POPULATION WITH DISTRESS ATTRIBUTES, 1970–1980, BY RACE/ETHNICITY

Central Counties	Race	No Distress Attributes		Poor Work History and Poverty		All Five Distress Attributes	
		1970	1980	1970	1980	1970	1980
New York	Total	45.6	43.8	10.7	15.4	2.6	4.1
	White	53.8	54.1	6.3	7.1	0.3	0.5
	Black	34.4	34.6	17.8	23.1	6.1	6.4
	Hispanic	25.6	26.1	19.6	29.1	7.9	11.5
	Other	49.0	54.0	9.6	8.4	0.6	0.6
Chicago	Total	55.5	53.2	7.1	10.2	1.9	2.7
	White	63.2	64.9	3.9	3.9	0.2	0.3
	Black	34.8	31.6	17.7	24.5	7.4	8.1
	Hispanic	31.9	30.1	8.1	14.6	3.1	4.2
	Other	64.2	70.7	9.3	6.7	0.7	0.7
Philadelphia	Total	41.0	39.5	10.9	16.2	2.2	4.1
	White	48.7	49.1	6.7	8.2	0.4	0.8
	Black	27.8	26.5	18.0	26.0	5.2	8.1
	Hispanic	21.9	22.2	23.2	38.2	9.3	13.4
	Other	43.9	41.0	8.2	21.7	.	.
Detroit	Total	51.8	49.1	7.5	11.5	1.7	2.7
	White	58.2	59.1	4.4	5.5	0.6	0.8
	Black	35.6	31.8	15.6	21.8	4.6	6.0
	Hispanic	39.8	39.7	9.8	15.2	1.4	5.3
	Other	45.8	57.8	10.1	9.9	1.1	1.4
Los Angeles	Total	57.9	51.9	7.2	8.0	1.2	1.2
	White	64.8	63.6	5.2	4.7	0.5	0.3
	Black	39.4	39.7	17.3	17.3	5.2	3.8
	Hispanic	36.5	31.7	9.7	9.8	2.1	2.2
	Other	67.1	62.7	7.1	9.4	0.7	0.3

Sources: U.S. Bureau of the Census, Census of Population and Housing, 1970 and 1980, Public-Use Microdata Samples.
Note: White refers to non-Hispanic white; black refers to non-Hispanic black.

proportion of Hispanics and Asians (other) with no distress attributes declined while for non-Hispanic whites and blacks the proportions were fairly stable.

The second set of percentages in table 3.5 describes the change in distribution between 1970 and 1980 of residents by race/ethnicity in each city who had both a poor work history and were in poverty households. All cities exhibited rises in the percentage of persons in households with poor work history and poverty during this period, with sharp increases in all four northern cities. Most of this rise in the northern cities can be accounted for by substantial increases in black and Hispanic households with these characteristics.

In 1980, almost 30 percent of the Hispanic residents in New York City were in households with a poor work history and poverty, and 38 percent of Hispanic residents in Philadelphia lived in such households (table 3.5). Note that there was little increase in the percentages of Los Angeles's Hispanic and black populations residing in households with poor work history and poverty. Los Angeles experienced a decline in the proportion of its white households with these characteristics, while the percentages of this city's black and Hispanic residents who resided in households with poor work history and poverty were stable between 1970 and 1980. The percentage of Los Angeles's Asian (other) residents in households with poor work history and in poverty rose slightly.

The third set of columns in table 3.5 provides the percentage of city residents in each racial and ethnic group who reside in households with all five distress attributes (denoted earlier as the severely distressed). These percentages rose for the total population and for white, black, and Hispanic subgroups within the four northern cities. In Los Angeles, which also had the smallest proportion of residents in households with all five distress attributes in 1970, only the percentage of its Hispanic residents with all five distress attributes increased.

Table 3.6 provides data on the absolute change, percentage change, and percentage distribution shift of residents residing in households with poor work history and poverty between 1970 and 1980 for the five central counties. Despite losing over 800,000 residents during the 1970s, New York City actually added 266,800 people in households with both poor work history and poverty. Almost all of this increase was due to substantial increments in blacks and Hispanics who were poor and not working regularly. This trend is mirrored in the three other large central metropolitan counties in the North. Chicago had a 63 percent increase in the number of blacks who were in households with poor work history and poverty and a more than 200 percent increase in Hispanic residents in such households. Detroit also experienced a substantial percentage increase (71 percent) in its black population residing in households with these characteristics.

The third row of figures in table 3.6 for each city (which also can be calculated from table 3.5) reveals the substantial incremental shift during the 1970s in the percentage of black and Hispanic residents living in households with both poor work history and poverty in the major northern cities. Philadelphia also experienced a large upward shift in its Asian population who were in households with both poor

Table 3.6 CHANGE IN POPULATION WITH BOTH POOR WORK HISTORY AND IN POVERTY 1970–1980, BY RACE

Central Counties	Change 1970–80	All Races	White	Black	Hispanic	Others
New York	Net change (in thousands)	266.8	−47.8	128.6	173.2	12.8
	Percentage change 1970–80	32.3	−15.3	48.7	72.1	125.3
	Percentage distribution shift	4.7	0.8	5.3	9.5	−1.2
Chicago	Net change (in thousands)	159.0	−23.5	127.8	50.3	4.4
	Percentage change 1970–80	41.6	−15.6	63.1	210.5	105.7
	Percentage distribution shift	3.1	0.0	6.8	6.5	−2.6
Philadelphia	Net change (in thousands)	68.0	−1.3	51.7	13.4	4.3
	Percentage change 1970–80	32.8	−1.7	45.1	121.8	532.5
	Percentage distribution shift	5.3	1.5	8.0	15.0	13.5
Detroit	Net change (in thousands)	70.1	−3.9	71.8	1.6	0.6
	Percentage change 1970–80	35.4	−4.7	66.1	32.9	35.6
	Percentage distribution shift	4.0	1.1	6.2	5.4	−0.2
Los Angeles	Net change (in thousands)	97.9	−68.0	35.3	99.3	31.3
	Percentage change 1970–80	19.7	−26.5	27.7	99.2	213.2
	Percentage distribution shift	0.8	−0.5	0.0	0.1	2.3

Sources: U.S. Bureau of the Census, Census of Population and Housing, 1970 and 1980, Public-Use Microdata Samples.
Note: White refers to non-Hispanic white; black refers to non-Hispanic black.

work history and in poverty. Los Angeles, on the other hand, experienced virtually no increase in its minority proportions who were in such households.

ECONOMICS IN TRANSITION

In examining the hypothesized causes of the differential rise of joblessness, poverty, and related problems of the inner city, much attention has been given to changing urban labor markets. Efforts to model and assess the implications of these labor market changes have taken both labor demand and labor supply approaches. Moss and Tilly (1991) have provided a thorough literature review and appraisal of the evidence and issues raised by these studies; I only note the highlights here, emphasizing changing labor demands.

The basic argument on the demand side is that there has been a dramatic decline in the demand for lower-skilled labor in particular industries, occupations, and locations. As a result, both skill and spatial mismatches have emerged between urban resident groups and job opportunity structures. Blacks and Hispanics have educational distributions skewed toward the bottom end, whereas demand for poorly educated residents has been slackening in recent decades. These minorities have very low proportions who have the higher educations that are increasingly required for employment in new urban growth industries. Not only have industries with higher education hiring requirements been replacing those with low education requirements in the central cities, but even within traditional urban industries there has been a shift away from the less educated (Katz and Murphy 1990). As a result, jobless rates of poorly educated inner-city residents have skyrocketed since 1970, regardless of race (Kasarda 1989, 1990).

At the same time that poorly educated people have remained confined in the central city, jobs appropriate to their skill levels have dispersed to the suburbs. Farley (1987), Hughes (1989), Price and Mills (1985), Vrooman and Greenfield (1980), and Welch (1990) document the negative earnings and employment consequences that lower-skilled job dispersion has had for inner-city minorities.

Wilson (1987) provided a cogent description of the impact of urban economic transformations on black male joblessness and its relationship to a range of other problems that characterize the ghetto poor. He focused on the loss of manufacturing and other low-skill jobs from the central cities and the resulting economic and social dislocations. Modeling the precise effects of urban industrial shifts during the 1970s and 1980s on wages and employment of black and white males, Bound and Holzer (1991) found that one-third to one-half of the employment decline of less-educated young blacks in the 1970s can be accounted for by these shifts, especially manufacturing job loss.

As observed earlier in this chapter, four cities (New York, Chicago, Detroit, and Philadelphia) had particularly large increases in their severely distressed populations and residents of extreme poverty tracts and underclass areas between 1970 and 1980. This increase is consistent with prior studies cited (Ricketts and Sawhill 1988; Bane and Jargowsky 1988) that showed that the bulk of increases in extreme poverty and underclass area populations were in the largest industrial cities of the Northeast and Midwest. In this section, I examine industrial transformations and other economic base changes in these cities and compare them to changes occurring in four of the largest cities in the South and West (Atlanta, Dallas, Los Angeles, and Phoenix).

Table 3.7 provides an overall comparison of change in economic activity within the four frostbelt and four sunbelt cities (central counties) between 1970 and 1980 and between 1980 and 1987, based on changes in jobholder earnings (in constant dollars) by place of work. It should be reiterated that these data are for central counties that—as in the case of Chicago (Cook County)—are substantially larger than the central cities. Nevertheless, the devastation of the economies of

Table 3.7 CHANGE IN PLACE-OF-WORK EARNINGS (IN MILLIONS OF CONSTANT 1980 DOLLARS) AND PERCENTAGE CHANGE, 1970–87

Central County	Change, 1970–80 ($ millions)	Change, 1980–87 ($ millions)	Percentage Change, 1970–80	Percentage Change, 1980–87
Chicago	662	4,045	1.3	7.6
Detroit	− 1,885	− 1,487	− 7.8	− 6.7
New York	− 11,925	21,601	− 14.4	30.5
Philadelphia	− 3,310	1,232	− 18.3	8.4
Atlanta	1,929	3,008	24.5	30.7
Dallas	6,803	6,668	56.5	35.4
Los Angeles	12,270	19,039	19.5	25.4
Phoenix	5,039	5,381	76.3	46.2

Source: U.S. Department of Commerce, Bureau of Economic Analysis, 1987 Regional Economic Information System, machine-readable file.
Note: All earnings figures reported in this and subsequent tables in this chapter are for place of work and are adjusted to 1980 dollars utilizing the Consumer Price Index.

the major northern cities during the 1970s and (with the exception of Detroit) their recovery in the 1980s may be observed in the top panel of table 3.7. Earnings in New York City alone declined by nearly $12 billion between 1970 and 1980 and rose by nearly $22 billion during the 1980–87 upswing in that city's economy. The four sunbelt cities did not experience these dramatic swings in economic activity, with fairly stable growth throughout the 1970s and 1980s. Note, in particular, the significant percentage growths in their economies during the 1970s.

Table 3.8 illustrates how the changes in jobholders' total earnings were distributed among eight industrial sectors. Manufacturing earnings were particularly hard hit in the four largest northern central counties during the 1970s and continued to spiral downward during the 1980s. Construction earnings and retail trade earnings were also substantially diminished between 1970 and 1980 in the northern cities. Only service sector earnings were robust in these cities during the 1970s, led by substantial increases in earnings in business, legal, and health services. The fiscal crisis of New York City may also be observed with its nearly $2 billion drop in earnings in government between 1970 and 1980.

The recovery of the economies of major cities of the North in the 1980s was led by strong growth in their financial, real estate, and service sectors. New York City alone experienced a $19 billion increase in earnings of workers in finance, insurance, real estate, and other service industries (table 3.8).

The four sunbelt cities were resilient in their earnings across industries during the 1970s. Los Angeles, especially, experienced powerful growth in manufacturing earnings between 1970 and 1980, in contrast to the cities of the North. Table 3.9 further highlights the robustness of the sunbelt cities compared to the frostbelt cities by presenting percentage changes in earnings for the central counties by industry. Whereas New York City and Philadelphia each lost approximately 40 percent of their jobholder earnings base in manufacturing industries during the 1970s, jobholder earnings in these same industries increased by 33 percent in Dallas and 62 percent in Phoenix. Clearly, there were sharp contrasts between the economies of the frostbelt and sunbelt cities throughout the 1970s, when severely distressed populations differentially expanded in the frostbelt cities.

Table 3.10 depicts the changing industrial composition of the cities, as evidenced by the percentage distributions of workers' earnings by industry, for 1970, 1980, and 1987. Whereas manufacturing and trade showed considerable proportional declines in frostbelt cities, finance,

Table 3.8 CHANGE IN PLACE-OF-WORK EARNINGS (IN MILLIONS OF CONSTANT 1980 DOLLARS) BY INDUSTRY, 1970–1987

Central County	Time Period	Construction	Manufacturing	Transportation/ Utilities	Wholesale	Retail	F.I.R.E.[a]	Service	Government
Chicago	1970–80	-167	-2,433	114	255	-538	796	1,866	614
	1980–87	185	-3,048	153	138	213	1,926	4,394	209
Detroit	1970–80	-457	-263	-69	-507	-692	-219	230	64
	1980–87	-14	-1,819	-16	-12	-201	130	668	-190
New York	1970–80	-1,150	-5,778	-831	-1,216	-2,117	297	531	-1,866
	1980–87	1,592	-1,474	-864	81	775	9,161	9,750	2,703
Philadelphia	1970–80	-424	-1,846	-40	-369	-478	-45	261	-392
	1980–87	-57	-599	-240	-14	16	442	1,471	230
Atlanta	1970–80	29	-19	327	336	50	171	616	392
	1980–87	127	198	321	121	118	535	1,399	195
Dallas	1970–80	599	941	550	925	577	716	1,434	522
	1980–87	173	583	599	375	570	1,169	2,656	510
Los Angeles	1970–80	567	1,537	1,059	1,723	364	1,283	5,373	-34
	1980–87	736	1,268	386	798	980	3,048	10,163	1,895
Phoenix	1970–80	684	909	361	365	522	409	1,138	553
	1980–87	252	678	251	287	513	699	1,959	710

Source: Bureau of Economic Analysis, 1987 Regional Economic Information System, machine-readable file.
a. F.I.R.E.—finance, insurance, and real estate.

Table 3.9 PERCENTAGE CHANGE IN PLACE-OF-WORK EARNINGS BY INDUSTRY, 1970–87

Central County	Time Period	% Change Construction	% Change Manufacturing	% Change Transportation/ Utilities	% Change Wholesale	% Change Retail	% Change F.I.R.E.[a]	% Change Service	% Change Government
Chicago	1970–80	-5.7	-14.7	2.6	5.1	-10.3	22.0	20.9	11.1
	1980–87	6.7	-21.5	3.5	2.6	4.5	43.6	40.7	3.4
Detroit	1970–80	-39.9	-2.6	-4.2	-28.5	-28.5	-17.3	7.0	2.5
	1980–87	-2.0	-18.7	-1.0	-1.0	-11.6	12.4	19.0	-7.1
New York	1970–80	-36.2	-37.3	-9.9	-15.3	-31.6	2.7	2.8	-16.9
	1980–87	78.6	-15.2	-11.4	1.2	16.9	80.0	50.6	29.5
Philadelphia	1970–80	-43.9	-40.5	-2.6	-25.7	-29.5	-3.2	7.7	-12.5
	1980–87	-10.5	-22.1	-16.2	-1.4	1.4	32.9	40.3	8.3
Atlanta	1970–80	7.1	-1.7	29.9	29.5	5.5	22.4	46.7	36.2
	1980–87	28.6	17.7	22.6	8.2	12.4	57.3	72.2	13.2
Dallas	1970–80	65.7	32.7	49.4	65.4	42.9	69.3	71.7	48.3
	1980–87	11.4	15.3	36.0	16.0	29.6	66.8	77.3	31.8
Los Angeles	1970–80	17.3	8.7	24.7	37.0	5.2	33.5	41.4	-0.4
	1980–87	19.1	6.6	7.2	12.5	13.4	59.6	55.4	22.4
Phoenix	1970–80	118.3	62.1	84.9	87.5	60.7	88.9	99.6	53.4
	1980–87	20.0	28.6	31.9	36.7	37.1	80.5	85.9	44.7

Source: Bureau of Economic Analysis, 1987 Regional Economic Information System, machine-readable file.
a. F.I.R.E.—finance, insurance, and real estate.

Table 3.10 DISTRIBUTION OF PLACE-OF-WORK EARNINGS BY INDUSTRY: 1970, 1980, AND 1987

Central County	Year	Construction %	Manufacturing %	Transportation/ Utilities %	Wholesale %	Retail %	F.I.R.E. %	Service %	Government %
Chicago	1970	5.6	31.8	8.2	9.5	10.0	6.9	17.1	10.5
	1980	5.2	26.8	8.4	9.9	8.8	8.3	20.4	11.6
	1987	5.2	19.5	8.0	9.4	8.6	11.1	26.6	11.1
Detroit	1970	4.7	41.3	6.7	7.3	10.0	5.2	13.6	10.8
	1980	3.1	43.6	7.0	5.7	7.8	4.7	15.8	12.0
	1987	3.2	38.0	7.4	6.0	7.4	5.7	20.1	12.0
New York	1970	3.8	18.7	10.1	9.6	8.1	13.5	22.6	13.3
	1980	2.9	13.7	10.7	9.5	6.5	16.2	27.2	12.9
	1987	3.9	8.9	7.2	7.4	5.8	22.3	31.4	12.8
Philadelphia	1970	5.4	25.3	8.4	8.0	9.0	7.7	18.8	17.5
	1980	3.7	18.4	10.1	7.2	7.7	9.1	24.8	18.7
	1987	3.0	13.2	7.8	6.6	7.2	11.2	32.1	18.7
Atlanta	1970	5.3	14.4	13.9	14.5	11.4	9.7	16.8	13.8
	1980	4.5	11.4	14.5	15.0	9.7	9.5	19.8	15.1
	1987	4.5	10.2	13.6	12.4	8.3	11.5	26.0	13.0
Dallas	1970	7.6	23.9	9.3	11.8	11.2	8.6	16.6	9.0
	1980	8.0	20.3	8.8	12.4	10.2	9.3	18.2	8.5
	1987	6.6	17.3	8.9	10.6	9.8	11.4	23.9	8.3
Los Angeles	1970	5.2	28.3	6.8	7.4	11.0	6.1	20.6	13.5
	1980	5.1	25.7	7.1	8.5	9.7	6.8	24.4	11.3
	1987	4.9	21.8	6.1	7.6	8.8	8.7	30.3	11.0
Phoenix	1970	8.8	22.2	6.4	6.3	13.0	7.0	17.3	15.7
	1980	10.8	20.4	6.8	6.7	11.9	7.5	19.6	13.6
	1987	8.9	17.9	6.1	6.3	11.1	9.2	24.9	13.5

Source: Bureau of Economic Analysis, 1987 Regional Economic Information System, machine-readable file.

insurance, and real estate (F.I.R.E.) and services expanded. By 1987, 54 percent of all earnings in New York City were accounted for by jobholders in the F.I.R.E. and service sectors. In Philadelphia, 43 percent of all earnings were in these two predominantly white-collar sectors. In contrast, declines in manufacturing earnings proportions did not tend to be as large in the sunbelt cities and the overall transition of these cities to service sector industries not so marked. That is, by 1987 none of the four sunbelt cities had 40 percent or more of their earnings accounted for by jobholders in the F.I.R.E. and service sectors.

Table 3.11, parts A and B (the frostbelt and sunbelt cities, respectively) highlight the industry-selective nature of employment change in the central cities and the suburban rings of the four frostbelt and four sunbelt metropolitan areas for the periods 1967–77 and 1977–87. Between 1967 and 1987, Chicago lost 60 percent of its manufacturing jobs, Detroit 51 percent, New York City 58 percent, and Philadelphia 64 percent. In absolute numbers, New York City's manufacturing employment declined by 520,000 jobs and Chicago's by 226,000 jobs. During this same period, New York City added over 110,000 manufacturing jobs in suburban rings and Chicago 34,000, all between 1967 and 1977. Retail trade was also hard hit in northern cities between 1967 and 1977 and only modestly recovered in the following 10 years. The big burst of employment in the northern cities was in their service sectors, with New York City adding 286,000 such jobs between 1977 and 1987. (Some of this increase is artificial, owing to definitional changes in the industries included in the Census of Selected Services for those two dates.)

Suburban ring employment growth in northern metropolitan areas was very strong, with the exception of manufacturing in Detroit and Philadelphia. Trade and services in the suburbs added hundreds of thousands of jobs in each of the four northern major metropolitan areas.

Turning to the sunbelt cities, table 3.11, part B, reveals that their central cities did not suffer nearly so severely with manufacturing and trade job losses during the 1967–77 period; in fact, all four cities added manufacturing jobs between 1977 and 1987, along with experiencing growth in their trade and service sectors. In Dallas-Fort Worth, Los Angeles, and Phoenix, central-city growth in trade and services was substantial. The suburban rings of all sunbelt cities continued to blossom, with accelerated job growth in the 1980s compared to the 1970s. The main difference between frostbelt and sunbelt metropolitan areas in terms of employment change, then, involves the

Table 3.11 CHANGE IN EMPLOYMENT (IN THOUSANDS) BY INDUSTRY FOR
SELECTED METROPOLITAN AREAS, 1967–1987

A. Frostbelt Cities

Metropolitan Area/ Industry	1967–77	1977–87	Percentage Change, 1967–87
Chicago			
Central city			
Manufacturing	−180.9	−145.4	−59.7
Trade	−79.1	−45.0	−35.6
Service	19.9	83.6	74.9
Combined	−240.1	−106.8	−33.6
Suburban ring			
Manufacturing	71.1	−37.1	10.5
Trade	148.3	122.0	141.4
Service	55.9	170.7	560.7
Combined	275.3	255.6	95.3
Detroit			
Central city			
Manufacturing	−56.4	−51.1	−51.3
Trade	−46.9	−17.0	−53.2
Service	−10.1	10.7	1.1
Combined	−113.4	−57.4	−44.6
Suburban ring			
Manufacturing	23.5	−44.1	−5.2
Trade	97.5	104.8	121.0
Service	53.5	161.9	585.5
Combined	174.5	222.6	66.1
New York			
Central city			
Manufacturing	−285.6	−234.7	−58.1
Trade	−140.6	34.5	−15.2
Service	16.1	286.2	83.8
Combined	−410.1	86.0	−16.6
Suburban ring			
Manufacturing	84.8	28.4	33.5
Trade	118.3	172.5	85.9
Service	69.0	270.6	365.4
Combined	272.0	471.6	96.7
Philadelphia			
Central city			
Manufacturing	−106.4	−61.6	−63.7
Trade	−33.7	1.6	−19.9
Service	7.2	48.7	97.8
Combined	−132.8	−11.3	−29.9
Suburban ring			
Manufacturing	−15.7	−14.9	−9.9
Trade	82.8	102.3	111.0
Service	56.6	161.2	615.0
Combined	123.8	248.6	72.7

Source: U.S. Bureau of the Census, Economic Censuses, 1967, 1977, 1987.

Table 3.11 CHANGE IN EMPLOYMENT (IN THOUSANDS) BY INDUSTRY FOR
SELECTED METROPOLITAN AREAS, 1967–1987 (continued)

B. Sunbelt Cities

Metropolitan Area/ Industry	1967–77	1977–87	Percentage Change 1967–87
Atlanta			
Central city			
Manufacturing	−14.1	0.4	−25.4
Trade	−16.1	3.7	−14.6
Service	13.1	46.7	191.9
Combined	−17.0	50.8	19.9
Suburban ring			
Manufacturing	42.8	54.0	156.9
Trade	80.0	163.0	465.4
Service	28.3	137.1	1,497.8
Combined	151.1	354.1	404.3
Dallas/Fort Worth			
Central city			
Manufacturing	−6.5	8.8	1.3
Trade	28.6	40.8	49.1
Service	34.5	101.6	289.5
Combined	56.6	151.2	57.1
Suburban ring			
Manufacturing	49.8	−55.3	−10.9
Trade	62.5	130.0	470.1
Service	19.7	112.7	1,436.6
Combined	132.0	187.4	317.2
Los Angeles			
Central city			
Manufacturing	−21.6	2.6	−5.3
Trade	28.8	74.5	39.1
Service	44.5	214.2	180.3
Combined	51.7	291.3	44.6
Suburban ring			
Manufacturing	−8.3	52.9	9.0
Trade	83.5	137.1	81.6
Service	79.1	250.5	363.3
Combined	154.3	440.5	69.5
Phoenix			
Central city			
Manufacturing	16.0	17.5	79.4
Trade	28.8	43.7	163.2
Service	18.4	68.6	515.2
Combined	63.3	129.8	186.5
Suburban ring			
Manufacturing	9.3	33.7	251.5
Trade	31.5	48.4	496.3
Service	9.6	50.8	940.0
Combined	50.4	132.9	462.6

Source: U.S. Bureau of the Census, Economic Censuses, 1967, 1977, 1987.

dramatically divergent employment opportunities in the central cities, especially in manufacturing.

I now turn to characteristics of the subareas of the eight central cities. Selected data are presented for these cities' low poverty areas (where less than 20 percent of the households fall below poverty) as contrasted with areas within each city where 20 percent or more and 40 percent or more of the households fall below poverty. Table 3.12, part A, illustrates subarea characteristics within the four northern cities; part B presents the same data for the four sunbelt cities. Observe in part A the sharp declines in the ratios of employed persons aged 16 and older per 100 persons in the subareas who are unemployed or out of the labor force (OLF, over age 16) as one moves from nonpoverty subareas to increasingly intense poverty subareas. Note also the high percentage of poverty-area workers who were still employed in manufacturing as late as 1980. Of those jobholders in extreme poverty areas, 27 percent were employed in manufacturing in both Chicago and Detroit, 24 percent in New York City, and 22 percent in Philadelphia. Note that the percentage residing in extreme poverty areas who are employed in manufacturing is greater than the percentage both for the city total and in nonpoverty areas of cities for all northern cities with the exception of Detroit, which is approximately equal. Two other important factors should be noted: the high percentage of persons in the poverty areas who have not completed high school and the similarly large percentage who reside in households with no vehicle available. As jobs with lower education requirements have dispersed from the central cities to the suburbs, many of these people have been left behind without transportation to these jobs.

Although poverty and extreme poverty areas are not as substantial in the sunbelt cities, table 3.12, part B, shows that many of their residents experience somewhat similar plights. Poverty areas in these cities do, however, tend to have lower percentages of workers employed in manufacturing and higher percentages who have worked in the previous year. They also tend to have more households with automobiles available.

DOCUMENTING SKILL AND SPATIAL MISMATCHES

The importance of skills mismatches and, to a lesser extent, spatial mismatches in major cities of the Northeast and Midwest is highlighted in tables 3.13 and 3.14. Table 3.13 presents changes between

Table 3.12 CITY AND SUBAREA POPULATION CHARACTERISTICS, 1980

A. Frostbelt Cities

City/Characteristics	City Total	Nonpoverty Areas	Areas with 20% Below Poverty	Areas with 40% Below Poverty
Chicago				
Ratio employed persons aged 16+/100 persons unempl or OLF[a]	121.00	153.00	80.00	48.00
% Workers aged 16+: Employed in manufacturing	26.62	24.84	30.96	27.43
% Males aged 16+: No work in previous year	27.33	21.51	37.92	50.70
% Persons aged 25+: Completed less than high school	43.75	37.31	56.52	61.89
% Households with no vehicle present	37.20	29.16	51.97	66.79
Detroit				
Ratio employed persons aged 16+/100 persons unempl or OLF	81.00	110.00	58.00	41.00
% Workers aged 16+: Employed in manufacturing	28.65	28.43	28.99	27.47
% Males aged 16+: No work in previous year	33.46	25.89	41.85	49.62
% Persons aged 25+: Completed less than high school	45.80	37.47	55.38	62.16
% Households with no vehicle present	27.44	14.51	41.31	58.32
New York				
Ratio employed persons aged 16+/100 persons unempl or OLF	112.00	134.00	81.00	58.00
% Workers aged 16+: Employed in manufacturing	17.38	15.38	21.92	23.97
% Males aged 16+: No work in previous year	29.69	24.88	38.58	45.95
% Persons aged 25+: Completed less than high school	39.83	32.53	54.00	62.94
% Households with no vehicle present	58.61	48.69	76.19	82.26
Philadelphia				
Ratio employed persons aged 16+/100 persons unempl or OLF	92.00	113.00	68.00	45.00
% Workers aged 16+: Employed in manufacturing	20.87	20.41	21.72	21.89
% Males aged 16+: No work in previous year	32.74	26.17	42.25	50.20
% Persons aged 25+: Completed less than high school	45.74	39.05	55.95	64.28
% Households with no vehicle present	38.41	27.21	54.48	66.82

Source: U.S. Bureau of the Census, Census of Population and Housing, 1980, Summary Tape File 3A.
a. OLF—out of the labor force.

Table 3.12 CITY AND SUBAREA POPULATION CHARACTERISTICS, 1980 (continued)

B. Sunbelt Cities

City/Characteristics	City Total	Nonpoverty Areas	Areas with 20% Below Poverty	Areas with 40% Below Poverty
Atlanta				
Ratio employed persons aged 16+/100 persons unempl or OLF[a]	116.00	164.00	91.00	54.00
% Workers aged 16+: Employed in manufacturing	13.17	11.54	14.78	14.57
% Males aged 16+: No work in previous year	27.82	20.02	33.86	46.37
% Persons aged 25+: Completed less than high school	39.80	22.33	54.87	68.33
% Households with no vehicle present	30.40	13.91	44.08	64.51
Dallas/Fort Worth				
Ratio employed persons aged 16+/100 persons unempl or OLF	206.00	233.00	141.00	89.00
% Workers aged 16+: Employed in manufacturing	18.74	18.28	20.62	18.29
% Males aged 16+: No work in previous year	16.04	13.16	25.92	34.93
% Persons aged 25+: Completed less than high school	31.50	24.96	55.05	58.60
% Households with no vehicle present	10.79	6.04	28.30	49.30
Los Angeles				
Ratio employed persons aged 16+/100 persons unempl or OLF	151.00	177.00	109.00	54.00
% Workers aged 16+: Employed in manufacturing	23.05	20.72	29.33	27.76
% Males aged 16+: No work in previous year	22.35	18.33	30.95	39.94
% Persons aged 25+: Completed less than high school	31.40	22.97	51.65	57.55
% Households with no vehicle present	17.21	10.09	33.84	50.58
Phoenix				
Ratio employed persons aged 16+/100 persons unempl or OLF	166.00	181.00	91.00	70.00
% Workers aged 16+: Employed in manufacturing	18.00	17.64	21.41	17.87
% Males aged 16+: No work in previous year	18.02	16.13	31.04	36.93
% Persons aged 25+: Completed less than high school	26.65	22.29	60.24	67.07
% Households with no vehicle present	7.31	5.17	23.52	34.11

Source: U.S. Bureau of the Census, Census of Population and Housing, 1980, Summary Tape File 3A.
a. OLF—out of the labor force.

Table 3.13 EDUCATIONAL DISTRIBUTION OF CITY JOB CHANGE, JOBHOLDERS, AND OUT-OF-SCHOOL BLACK MALE RESIDENTS, AGED 16–64, 1980

Central City	Less Than High School	High School Only	Some College	College Graduate
Chicago				
Change in city jobholders, 1970–80	− 210,499	− 22,863	51,481	117,462
Distribution of city jobholders, 1980	23.4	28.2	23.8	24.7
Black male residents aged 16–64, 1980	43.2	34.0	16.0	6.9
Black male residents not working, 1980	58.1	26.6	12.8	2.5
Detroit				
Change in city jobholders, 1970–80	− 112,321	− 55,906	35,739	22,609
Distribution of city jobholders, 1980	21.1	32.8	25.8	20.3
Black male residents aged 16–64 1980	41.6	36.2	16.2	5.9
Black male residents not working, 1980	56.1	28.9	13.6	1.3
New York				
Change in city jobholders, 1970–80	− 496,229	− 99,874	164,640	307,201
Distribution of city jobholders, 1980	22.0	28.8	21.2	28.0
Black male residents aged 16–64, 1980	39.8	39.1	13.4	7.6
Black male residents not working, 1980	52.5	28.3	14.9	4.4
Philadelphia				
Change in city jobholders, 1970–80	− 143,440	− 7,529	30,744	57,834
Distribution of city jobholders, 1980	23.2	36.3	18.4	22.0
Black male residents aged 16–64, 1980	44.5	40.6	9.5	9.5
Black male residents not working, 1980	60.1	28.8	9.2	1.9

Sources: U.S. Bureau of the Census, machine-readable Public-Use Microdata Sample Files: 5 percent A Sample, 1980; 15 percent County Group Sample, 1970.

1970 and 1980 in the number of jobs held in the four largest northern cities in terms of the actual educational level of city jobholders. Most striking is the fact that northern cities experienced not only substan-

Table 3.14 PERCENT OF NOT WORKING, OUT-OF-SCHOOL MALES AGED 16–64 BY RACE, EDUCATION, REGION, AND CENTRAL CITY-SUBURBAN RESIDENCE FOR SELECTED METROPOLITAN AREAS: 1968–70 TO 1986–88

Region, Race, and Education	1986–88		1980–82		1976–78		1968–70	
	Central City	Suburbs	Central City	Suburbs	Central City	Suburbs	Central City	Suburbs
Northeast:[a]								
White								
Less than high school	35.5	27.5	32.4	27.9	27.8	23.9	15.1	11.3
High school graduate	16.7	13.4	18.0	13.0	17.3	12.6	6.6	4.6
Some college	10.2	8.6	11.3	9.0	13.4	9.1	7.4	4.6
College graduate	6.0	4.7	6.2	3.9	8.8	5.4	5.6	2.2
Black								
Less than high school	44.3	32.5	45.4	40.7	43.9	36.8	18.8	14.0
High school graduate	25.8	26.3	30.2	24.8	28.2	22.5	10.8	6.5
Some college	15.4	13.0	25.1	N/A	29.5	N/A	11.2	N/A
College graduate	14.7	N/A	15.4	N/A	11.8	N/A	8.7	N/A
Midwest:[b]								
White								
Less than high school	38.9	24.7	32.8	25.5	23.8	17.5	11.5	8.2
High school graduate	21.7	14.1	20.7	13.2	17.6	7.9	5.1	3.9
Some college	16.6	9.3	14.1	10.7	7.7	5.1	3.8	3.0
College graduate	5.3	5.7	7.1	3.8	4.0	2.5	2.6	2.5
Black								
Less than high school	58.0	30.5	51.5	42.2	42.4	29.0	23.5	10.8
High school graduate	36.4	24.7	35.3	26.8	29.1	13.6	9.8	10.7
Some college	27.3	12.2	26.8	N/A	18.7	N/A	6.9	N/A
College graduate	10.4	N/A	11.0	N/A	4.5	N/A	N/A	N/A

Sources: U.S. Bureau of the Census, Current Population Survey, March (Annual Demographic) machine readable files, 1968 to 1988.
a. Metropolitan areas include Boston, Newark, New York City, Philadelphia, and Pittsburgh.
b. Metropolitan areas include Cleveland, Chicago, Detroit, Milwaukee, and St. Louis.

tial declines in jobs held by those who did not complete high school but also considerable declines in jobs held by those with only a high school degree. At the same time, the number of city jobs held by those with higher education mushroomed.

The four cities that accounted for the lion's share of the increases in concentrated poverty populations during the 1970s (New York, Chicago, Detroit, and Philadelphia) also experienced the lion's share of declines in jobs held by high school dropouts and by those with only high school degrees. In 1980 there were 496,229 fewer workers in New York City who did not have a high school degree than there were in 1970 (table 3.13). The number of workers holding only a high school degree (12 years of schooling completed) also decreased by 99,874 during the decade, while the number of city jobholders with some college attendance or a college degree increased by 164,640 and 307,201, respectively. Similar patterns were exhibited by the other large northern cities, with major increases in jobs held by those with education beyond high school and even greater declines in employment by those with a high school degree or less.

Portions of the decrease in city jobs occupied by those without high school degrees and growth in number of jobs held by those with higher education reflect improvements in the overall educational attainment of the city labor force, including blacks, during the 1970s. These improvements, however, were not nearly so great as the concurrent upward shifts in the educational levels of city jobholders. As a result, much of the job increase in the "some college" or "college-graduate" categories for each city was absorbed by suburban commuters, while many job losses in the "less-than-high-school-completed" or "high-school-only" categories were absorbed by city residents. Moreover, general improvements in city residents' educational levels meant that less-educated jobless blacks fell further behind in the hiring queue (Lieberson 1980). Particularly affected were those large numbers of urban blacks who had not completed high school, especially younger ones. For city black youth, school dropout rates ranged from 30 percent to 50 percent during the 1970s and early 1980s, with case studies of underclass neighborhoods and schools suggesting even higher dropout rates among the most impoverished (Hess 1986; Kornblum 1985).

Table 3.13 also illustrates the structural dilemma facing sizable portions of the black urban labor force. It compares the 1980 educational distributions of those employed by city industries, including the self-employed, with the educational distributions of all out-of-school black males aged 16–64 and out-of-school black males aged 16–64 who are not working. The educational disparities between black residents and jobs are dramatic. Despite educational gains, black urban labor remains highly concentrated in the education category where city employment has rapidly declined since 1970—the category in which people have not completed high school—and is greatly underrepresented in the educational attainment categories where city employment is rapidly rising, especially the category of "college graduate." As late as 1980, the modal education-completed category for out-of-school black male residents in the four cities was less than 12 years.

Those out-of-school black males who are jobless display an even more mismatched educational distribution in relation to the city job structures. For example, in Philadelphia, whereas 44.5 percent of all black males who were out of school had fewer than 12 years of education in 1980, 60.1 percent of black males out of school and jobless had not completed high school (table 3.13). More than 50 percent of jobless black males in all cities had completed less than 12 years of schooling. Comparing these figures with the percentage of city jobs filled in 1980 by those with less than a high school degree and with changes in city jobs occupied by the poorly educated between 1970 and 1980 reveals the substantial educational disparity faced by urban blacks in general and blacks not at work in particular.

This educational disparity between city jobs and black residents poses a serious structural impediment to major improvements in urban black employment prospects. It may be that any individual black male who has not completed high school can secure employment in the city—some vacancies almost always exist, even in declining employment sectors. But, given the demographic-employment distributions shown, if large portions of out-of-work urban blacks all sought the jobs available, they would simply overwhelm vacancies at the lower end of the educational continuum.

The structural mismatch between city jobs and black labor that is displayed at the higher-education end of the continuum helps explain why policies based primarily on urban economic development have had limited success in reducing urban black joblessness. Most blacks simply lack the education that would enable them to participate in the new growth sectors of the urban economy. Whereas city jobs taken by college graduates have skyrocketed, the percentage of urban black males who have completed college remains extremely small. For those who are out of work, the disparity at the higher-education end is even greater.

If a skills mismatch is at the heart of the joblessness problem, we should see corresponding rises in the unemployment rates of poorly educated white city residents as well as blacks over the last decades.

Table 3.14 documents that this is indeed the case. The jobless rates by education levels of out-of-school black and white males (aged 16–64) for the largest central cities and suburban rings in the Northeast and Midwest were constructed by pooling their data within four separate three-year time periods between 1968 and 1988. Pooling of the within-region city and suburban data for three-year time intervals (1968–70, 1976–78, 1980–82, and 1986–88) enabled the generation of sufficient sample sizes to obtain more reliable estimates of jobless rates by race, education, and intrametropolitan residential location.

Results show that for every time period and residential location, blacks have higher rates of joblessness than whites. This supports long-standing arguments that race is a critical variable in accounting for joblessness (Ellwood 1986; Holzer 1989). Results also show that, for both whites and blacks, there is a strong relationship during each time period between education completed and joblessness. For the 1986–88 period, the lowest percentage of central-city residents not working who had not completed 12 years of education was 35.5 for whites in the Northeast, and the lowest percentage for suburban-ring residents was 24.7 for whites in the Midwest (table 3.14). This confirms the instrumental role of human capital factors in metropolitan employment and the serious handicap of a limited education, regardless of race and residential location.

Apropos the skills mismatch thesis, jobless rates of central-city whites who have not completed high school have monotonically risen during the 1968–88 pooled time periods (table 3.14). In fact, increases in white male joblessness since 1976 among the least educated are greater than those for their black male counterparts in both north-eastern and midwestern central cities. These results were replicated for non-Hispanic whites, with sharp increases in city jobless rates of those without a high-school degree during the past decade. The post-1982 economic recovery experienced by most of the cities in table 3.8 thus bypassed both poorly educated blacks and whites, lending empirical credence to the skills mismatch argument.

Apropos the spatial mismatch thesis, note that jobless rates for white and black males who did not complete 12 years of education and who resided in the suburban rings declined after 1982, although only among blacks are the declines substantial (from 40.7 to 32.5 between the 1980–82 and 1986–88 intervals—table 3.14). During the same period, jobless rates for the least-education black males in mid-western suburbs declined from 42.2 to 30.5.

Whereas suburban residential selectivity may account for some of the decline in joblessness among poorly educated suburban black males during the 1980s, such declines are consistent with the contention that less-skilled blacks have better employment prospects in the suburbs than in the central cities. In this regard, not only are jobless rates among the least-educated blacks and whites consistently lower in the suburban rings than in the central cities, but also the absolute gap in the percentage of jobless people between the least educated central-city residents has widened during the past two decades. Since residential segregation in these suburbs tends to be nearly as great as in the central cities, especially for the least educated blacks, segregation per se would not appear to be the pivotal factor explaining city-suburban jobless differences (Jencks and Mayer 1990; Massey and Denton 1987). Growth in low-skill job opportunities in closer proximity to poorly educated black suburban residents would seem to be a more plausible explanation of the somewhat lower suburban rates.

This relative accessibility explanation is supported by comparative journey-to-work times of poorly educated black and white jobholders residing and working in the central cities and suburbs of major metropolitan areas in 1980. Table 3.15 shows these commuting times, by means of transport, for black and white workers without a high school degree for three residence-workplace categories—live in the city and work in the city; live in the suburbs and work in the suburbs; and commuters between cities and suburbs. (Commuting times are shown for the largest metropolitan area in each of the four census regions for which suburban boundaries could be determined from the PUMS.)

Poorly educated black workers who live and work in the city or who commute across city-suburb boundaries have consistently higher one-way journey-to-work times than those who live and work in the suburbs, regardless of means of transport. In the northern metropolitan areas of Chicago and Philadelphia, the accessibility advantage of poorly educated blacks living and working in the suburbs is particularly striking, compared to living and working in the city.

Table 3.15 also highlights the greater accessibility poorly educated whites have to their workplaces compared to poorly educated blacks. For almost all residence-workplace categories across the four metropolitan areas, blacks have longer journey-to-work times than whites. Again, the black accessibility disadvantage is especially acute in the two major northern metro areas.

POLICY COMMENTARY

Today's inner-city economies may be considered to comprise three components: (1) the mainstream economy, consisting of traditional

Table 3.15   MEAN COMMUTING TIMES TO WORK (ONE-WAY, IN MINUTES) OF EMPLOYED PERSONS BY RESIDENCE AND WORKPLACE, MEANS OF TRANSPORT, AND RACE, 1980

Metropolitan Area and Race	Private Transportation			Public Transportation		
	Live in City Work in City	Live in Suburbs Work in Suburbs	Cross-Commute	Live in City Work in City	Live in Suburbs Work in Suburbs	Cross-Commute
Atlanta						
Black	24.8	21.7	28.2	42.4	38.3	48.4
White	17.6	21.4	30.4	41.6	26.2	46.4
Chicago						
Black	33.7	21.8	38.1	46.1	23.9	48.1
White	24.0	18.0	31.0	38.1	27.1	48.1
Los Angeles						
Black	25.6	23.2	31.1	42.0	34.3	47.7
White	19.9	18.9	26.8	40.4	33.3	44.8
Philadelphia						
Black	29.3	21.0	33.1	42.0	34.3	48.5
White	22.8	17.9	30.2	40.4	29.7	46.8

Source: U.S. Bureau of the Census, Public-Use Microdata Sample files, 1980.
Note: Data are for workers without a high school degree.

and newer-employing institutions ranging from manufacturing and trade to the full complement of blue- and white-collar service industries; (2) the underground economy, composed of drug trade, prostitution, and other illicit activities; and (3) the welfare economy, based on a variety of cash and in-kind public assistance transfers.

Within the mainstream economy, the functional transformation of cities from centers of goods processing to centers of information processing and the suburbanization of lower-skill jobs resulted in both skill and spatial mismatches for large numbers of inner-city minorities lacking the education to take advantage of new urban growth industries or unable to relocate near appropriate suburban jobs. These minorities, especially blacks and certain Hispanic groups such as Puerto Ricans, also appear to lack the social networks and familial and economic solidarity to overcome their structurally disadvantaged positions in transforming urban economies. As a result, with the deterioration of their traditional blue-collar employing bases in the inner cities, they have increasingly relied on the two surrogate economies (the underground and the welfare economies) to stay afloat.

Given rising formal-sector skills limiting their employment in new growth sectors as well as low hourly wages for jobs for which they are qualified, many of the disadvantaged see themselves better off in the underground economy where incomes are actually or perceived to be higher. The underground economy also provides substantially more temporal flexibility and personal autonomy than working in mainstream institutions. This may be particularly important to lifestyle choices of teenagers and young adults.

Partly in response to, but also reenforcing, inner-city joblessness and poverty were certain public assistance programs introduced in the 1970s. These programs were guided by the reasonable principle that public assistance should be targeted to areas where the needs are the greatest as measured by such factors as job loss, poverty rate, and persistence of unemployment. The idea was that the most distressed areas should receive the largest allocation of government funds for subsistence and local support services for the economically displaced. Although these policies unquestionably helped relieve pressing problems such as the inability of the unemployed to afford private-sector housing or to obtain adequate nutrition and health care, they did nothing to reduce the skills or spatial mismatch between the resident labor force and available urban jobs. In fact, spatially concentrated assistance may have inadvertently increased the mismatch and the plight of educationally disadvantaged residents by binding them to inner-city areas of severe blue-collar job decline and to areas that, by program definition, are the most distressed.

For those individuals with some resources and for the fortunate proportion whose efforts to break the bonds of poverty succeed, spatially concentrated public assistance will not impede their mobility. But for many inner-city poor without skills and few economic options, local concentrations of public assistance and community services can be "sticking" forces. Given the lack of skills of these individuals, the opportunity cost of giving up their in-place assistance if they were to move would be too high. They may see themselves as better off with their marginal but secure in-place government assistance than taking a chance and moving in search of a minimum wage, entry-level job, often in an unknown environment.

The spatial confluence of blue-collar job decline in the 1970s and 1980s with rising illicit activities and welfare dependency in the inner cities has generated a powerful spatial interaction of the three. Associated with this interaction, a plethora of concentrated social problems has further aggravated the predicament of people and neighborhoods in distress, such as high rates of family dissolution, out-of-wedlock births, school dropout, joblessness, and violent crime. Negative stereotyping and distancing by outsiders (often with racial connotations) has resulted in further spatial and social isolation of the severely distressed from mainstream institutions, magnifiying their dilemma.

No straightforward policy prescriptions exist for ameliorating this predicament. In previous papers (Kasarda 1985, 1989, 1990), I have outlined a variety of proposals that, in combination, would help to reduce the skill and spatial mismatches documented in this chapter. These include (1) educational upgrading and vocational training programs in the inner city; (2) computerized job-opportunity information networks; (3) partial underwriting of more distant job searches by the ghetto unemployed; (4) tax incentives to promote affordable housing construction in the suburbs by the private sector; (5) need-based temporary relocation assistance for ghetto unemployed once a job has been secured; (6) housing vouchers as opposed to additional spatially fixed public housing complexes in the inner city; (7) stricter enforcement of fair housing and fair hiring laws; (8) public-private cooperative efforts to van-pool unemployed inner-city residents to suburban businesses facing labor shortages; and (9) a thorough review of all spatially targeted low-income public assistance programs to ensure that they are not inadvertently anchoring the ghetto poor in areas where there are few prospects for permanent or meaningful employment.

I am not as sanguine as I once was of the prospects of such policies *significantly* reducing inner-city joblessness and revitalizing the ghettos. I am far less sanguine about the prospects for more radical prescriptions—such as a Marshall Plan to rebuild the ghettos—since political and economic realities, in all likelihood, preclude such massive government intervention. Simply put, the will of most Americans for such major intervention does not exist.

I am further tempered by the limits of government to affect what many believe to be at the root of the urban underclass dilemma—*attitudes*, of those outside as well as within the ghettos. Government cannot legislate away discriminatory stereotyping and other racist views held by many outsiders. Positive attitudinal changes will likely occur only as outsiders come to believe through actions of the ghetto poor that, despite their social and economic disadvantages, they subscribe to traditional American values of strong families, individual initiative, self-sufficiency, responsibility, discipline, and normative order, and that they eschew self-destructive behaviors.

Government cannot weave such values back into ghetto communities nor dictate behavior of their residents. Almost by definition, the moral authority for these tasks must come from within the community, from charismatic leadership and voluntary and religious organizations like the traditional black Protestant church or the Nation of Islam, with its emphasis on the family, disciplined economic self-support, and antidrug, anticrime programs. In the end, restoring strong internal normative order, responsibility, family cohesiveness, and racial/ethnic economic solidarity may be the only real option for the ghetto poor to break out of the cycle of poverty, revitalize their neighborhoods, and enjoy the benefits heretofore restricted to the social and economic mainstream.

Appendix Table 3.A DISTRIBUTION OF SEVERELY DISTRESSED POPULATION BY RACE, 1980

Central Cities	Total	White	Black	Hispanic	Others	% White	% Black	% Hispanic	% Others
Akron	4,900	2,480	2,420	0	0	50.6	49.4	0.0	0.0
Albuquerque	3,820	220	200	3,320	80	5.8	5.2	86.9	2.1
Anaheim	960	320	0	640	0	33.3	0.0	66.7	0.0
Anchorage	1,020	440	100	140	340	43.1	9.8	13.7	33.3
Atlanta	20,020	1,000	18,440	360	220	5.0	92.1	1.8	1.1
Austin	2,900	0	700	2,200	0	0.0	24.1	75.9	0.0
Baltimore	42,420	4,800	36,160	1,100	360	11.3	85.2	2.6	0.8
Baton Rouge	3,020	280	2,740	0	0	9.3	90.7	0.0	0.0
Birmingham	6,960	440	6,520	0	0	6.3	93.7	0.0	0.0
Boston	15,940	3,840	7,300	4,620	180	24.1	45.8	29.0	1.1
Buffalo	11,140	2,560	7,400	1,080	100	23.0	66.4	9.7	0.9
Charlotte	4,620	600	3,940	80	0	13.0	85.3	1.7	0.0
Chattanooga	4,520	940	3,580	0	0	20.8	79.2	0.0	0.0
Chicago	136,280	8,940	106,020	20,520	800	6.6	77.8	15.1	0.6
Cincinnati	13,000	3,260	9,460	180	100	25.1	72.8	1.4	0.8
Cleveland	23,260	4,800	16,280	2,140	40	20.6	70.0	9.2	0.2
Colorado Springs	0	0	0	0	0	NA	NA	NA	NA
Columbus, Ga.	3,660	620	3,040	0	0	16.9	83.1	0.0	0.0
Columbus, Oh.	13,980	6,160	7,440	260	120	44.1	53.2	1.9	0.9
Dallas	13,200	2,300	10,000	900	0	17.4	75.8	6.8	0.0
Dayton	8,000	2,640	5,220	80	60	33.0	65.3	1.0	0.8
Denver	6,180	580	1,720	3,660	220	9.4	27.8	59.2	3.6
Des Moines	1,920	1,160	520	100	140	60.4	27.1	5.2	7.3
Detroit	55,720	7,000	46,380	2,000	340	12.6	83.2	3.6	0.6
El Paso	4,500	500	0	4,000	0	11.1	0.0	88.9	0.0
Flint	5,680	1,640	3,940	40	60	28.9	69.4	0.7	1.1
Fort Lauderdale	1,480	100	1,380	0	0	6.8	93.2	0.0	0.0

continued

Appendix Table 3.A DISTRIBUTION OF SEVERELY DISTRESSED POPULATION BY RACE, 1980 (continued)

Central Cities	Total	White	Black	Hispanic	Others	% White	% Black	% Hispanic	% Others
Fort Wayne	2,540	1,040	1,400	60	40	40.9	55.1	2.4	1.6
Fort Worth	3,420	320	2,140	960	0	9.4	62.6	28.1	0.0
Fresno	5,540	880	1,420	3,140	100	15.9	25.6	56.7	1.8
Gary	6,560	580	5,700	280	0	8.8	86.9	4.3	0.0
Grand Rapids	4,220	2,100	1,640	260	220	49.8	38.9	6.2	5.2
Greensboro	1,960	160	1,800	0	0	8.2	91.8	0.0	0.0
Honolulu	2,780	420	0	1,160	1,200	15.1	0.0	41.7	43.2
Houston	13,820	500	10,360	2,900	60	3.6	75.0	21.0	0.4
Indianapolis	11,400	1,600	9,400	400	0	14.0	82.5	3.5	0.0
Jackson	3,700	0	3,700	0	0	0.0	100.0	0.0	0.0
Jacksonville	8,400	700	7,700	0	0	8.3	91.7	0.0	0.0
Jersey City	11,560	1,560	5,080	4,920	0	13.5	43.9	42.6	0.0
Kansas City	6,380	900	5,480	0	0	14.1	85.9	0.0	0.0
Knoxville	3,400	1,580	1,640	0	180	46.5	48.2	0.0	5.3
Las Vegas	1,420	140	1,240	40	0	9.9	87.3	2.8	0.0
Lexington-Fayette	3,460	1,520	1,940	0	0	43.9	56.1	0.0	0.0
Little Rock	3,140	400	2,560	60	120	12.7	81.5	1.9	3.8
Long Beach	4,920	1,660	1,740	1,480	40	33.7	35.4	30.1	0.8
Los Angeles	45,240	2,520	23,520	18,220	980	5.6	52.0	40.3	2.2
Louisville	10,720	3,180	7,540	0	0	29.7	70.3	0.0	0.0
Madison	760	220	340	200	0	28.9	44.7	26.3	0.0
Memphis	24,700	740	23,480	480	0	3.0	95.1	1.9	0.0
Miami	6,800	0	3,960	2,840	0	0.0	58.2	41.8	0.0
Milwaukee	19,160	3,740	13,960	1,040	420	19.5	72.9	5.4	2.2
Minneapolis	5,220	1,860	1,740	200	1,420	35.6	33.3	3.8	27.2
Mobile	3,800	100	3,560	140	0	2.6	93.7	3.7	0.0
Nashville-Davidson	6,100	600	4,900	600	0	9.8	80.3	9.8	0.0
New Orleans	27,420	580	26,200	520	120	2.1	95.6	1.9	0.4

New York	293,540	18,620	110,000	163,220	1,700	6.3	37.5	55.6	0.6
Newark	28,760	860	19,080	8,760	60	3.0	66.3	30.5	0.2
Norfolk	7,700	680	6,880	140	0	8.8	89.4	1.8	0.0
Oakland	8,060	260	6,720	680	400	3.2	83.4	8.4	5.0
Oklahoma City	4,360	1,240	2,740	380	0	28.4	62.8	8.7	0.0
Omaha	1,900	800	1,100	0	0	42.1	57.9	0.0	0.0
Philadelphia	69,620	7,940	52,580	8,640	460	11.4	75.5	12.4	0.7
Phoenix	6,140	1,420	1,580	2,980	160	23.1	25.7	48.5	2.6
Pittsburgh	8,720	2,360	6,100	260	0	27.1	70.0	3.0	0.0
Portland	3,040	1,240	1,460	340	0	40.8	48.0	11.2	0.0
Providence	4,900	2,360	1,400	780	360	48.2	28.6	15.9	7.3
Raleigh	1,020	120	840	60	0	11.8	82.4	5.9	0.0
Richmond	7,660	700	6,960	0	0	9.1	90.9	0.0	0.0
Riverside	1,660	740	120	640	160	44.6	7.2	38.6	9.6
Rochester	7,780	1,700	5,100	980	0	21.9	65.6	12.6	0.0
Sacramento	5,780	1,940	2,240	1,380	220	33.6	38.8	23.9	3.8
Salt Lake City	900	320	120	400	60	35.6	13.3	44.4	6.7
San Antonio	15,820	700	2,120	12,880	120	4.4	13.4	81.4	0.8
San Diego	6,240	840	1,620	3,380	400	13.5	26.0	54.2	6.4
San Francisco	5,300	860	2,840	1,100	500	16.2	53.6	20.8	9.4
San Jose	5,160	700	1,180	3,060	220	13.6	22.9	59.3	4.3
Santa Ana	1,240	0	100	1,060	80	0.0	8.1	85.5	6.5
Seattle	2,840	1,060	1,420	80	280	37.3	50.0	2.8	9.9
Shreveport	7,500	200	6,600	700	0	2.7	88.0	9.3	0.0
Spokane	1,040	920	80	0	40	88.5	7.7	0.0	3.8
Springfield, Mass.	6,240	1,620	1,440	3,140	40	26.0	23.1	50.3	0.6
St. Louis	18,260	1,980	16,280	0	0	10.8	89.2	0.0	0.0
St. Paul	2,780	1,760	580	300	140	63.3	20.9	10.8	5.0
St. Petersburg	3,060	620	2,380	60	0	20.3	77.8	2.0	0.0
Stockton	3,680	760	820	2,100	0	20.7	22.3	57.1	0.0

continued

Appendix Table 3.A DISTRIBUTION OF SEVERELY DISTRESSED POPULATION BY RACE, 1980 (continued)

Central Cities	Total	White	Black	Hispanic	Others	% White	% Black	% Hispanic	% Others
Syracuse	4,980	2,360	2,340	80	200	47.4	47.0	1.6	4.0
Tacoma	2,780	1,360	620	160	640	48.9	22.3	5.8	23.0
Tampa	5,960	1,060	4,620	280	0	17.8	77.5	4.7	0.0
Toledo	7,420	2,680	4,240	500	0	36.1	57.1	6.7	0.0
Tucson	2,200	720	360	1,120	0	32.7	16.4	50.9	0.0
Tulsa	2,860	840	1,580	60	380	29.4	55.2	2.1	13.3
Virginia Beach	1,180	380	800	0	0	32.2	67.8	0.0	0.0
Washington, D.C.	20,700	220	19,960	340	180	1.1	96.4	1.6	0.9
Wichita	2,800	1,800	1,000	0	0	64.3	35.7	0.0	0.0
Worcester	4,260	2,420	200	1,520	120	56.8	4.7	35.7	2.8
Total Cities (95)	1,253,480	156,380	773,240	308,880	14,980	12.5	61.7	24.6	1.2

Sources: U.S. Bureau of the Census, Census of Population and Housing, 1970 and 1980, Public-Use Microdata Samples.

Appendix Table 3.B COMPARISON OF POPULATION COUNTS USING RICKETTS–SAWHILL AND PUMS MEASURES OF UNDERCLASS POPULATION

Central Cities	Ricketts and Sawhill					PUMS				
	All Races	White	Black	Others	Hispanic	All Races	White	Black	Others	Hispanic
Akron	5,265	1,950	3,189	11	101	5,760	3,040	2,660	0	60
Albuquerque	5,442	302	69	7	4,994	4,820	340	200	80	4,200
Anaheim	0	0	0	0	0	1,380	460	0	0	920
Anchorage	0	0	0	0	0	1,380	620	160	340	260
Atlanta	46,272	1,281	44,355	79	547	23,020	1,180	21,220	220	400
Austin	2,835	84	2,339	0	412	4,700	0	1,400	0	3,300
Baltimore	84,315	21,539	60,851	772	1,050	52,660	6,440	44,760	360	1,100
Baton Rouge	11,220	1,038	9,812	137	222	4,120	280	3,720	0	120
Birmingham	4,367	1,067	3,222	6	72	8,880	720	8,160	0	0
Boston	9,919	4,226	3,218	177	2,053	19,160	4,740	8,820	180	5,420
Buffalo	10,683	4,674	3,098	300	2,589	12,620	2,960	8,420	100	1,140
Charlotte	4,249	1,052	3,169	23	5	5,680	600	5,000	0	80
Chattanooga	6,409	952	5,348	41	68	4,980	940	3,980	60	0
Chicago	189,853	17,197	147,739	2,693	21,820	165,840	11,020	129,480	800	24,540
Cincinnati	27,411	10,771	16,158	169	236	15,520	3,840	11,400	100	180
Cleveland	16,391	4,392	11,163	78	735	26,880	5,380	19,100	180	2,220
Colorado Springs	0	0	0	0	0	0	0	0	0	0
Columbus, Ga.	12,714	3,982	8,629	26	77	4,100	680	3,420	0	0
Columbus, Oh.	41,014	17,184	22,986	245	494	16,080	7,360	8,200	120	400
Corpus Christi	2,946	134	2,172	0	640	0	0	0	.	
Dallas	18,924	598	16,858	612	820	17,300	2,700	12,300	0	2,300
Dayton	7,192	3,591	3,503	20	78	8,800	2,840	5,820	60	80
Denver	22,406	3,052	6,285	944	11,923	7,460	860	1,940	220	4,440
Des Moines	1,598	1,140	278	22	158	2,740	1,780	720	140	100
Detroit	159,804	35,013	116,253	1,464	6,792	78,200	9,960	65,080	740	2,420

continued

Appendix Table 3.B COMPARISON OF POPULATION COUNTS USING RICKETTS–SAWHILL AND PUMS MEASURES OF UNDERCLASS POPULATION (continued)

Central Cities	Ricketts and Sawhill					PUMS				
	All Races	White	Black	Others	Hispanic	All Races	White	Black	Others	Hispanic
El Paso	7,262	162	79	23	6,998	5,500	500	0	0	5,000
Flint	9,169	3,698	5,166	67	214	7,720	1,960	5,520	60	180
Fort Lauderdale	0	0	0	0	0	1,860	100	1,760	0	0
Fort Wayne	0	0	0	0	0	3,040	1,280	1,660	40	60
Fort Worth	2,558	82	2,241	13	222	4,560	540	2,800	0	1,220
Fresno	4,860	875	1,629	373	1,983	7,060	1,040	2,180	180	3,660
Gary	4,249	689	2,729	0	831	7,700	640	6,700	0	360
Grand Rapids	3,548	1,600	942	19	965	4,980	2,220	2,020	220	520
Greensboro	0	0	0	0	0	2,260	280	1,980	0	0
Honolulu	1,651	222	11	1,299	69	3,720	420	0	1,880	1,420
Houston	7,372	102	4,069	306	2,895	16,880	760	12,900	60	3,160
Indianapolis	19,584	5,496	13,679	223	186	14,700	1,600	12,700	0	400
Jackson	1,484	336	1,131	8	9	5,100	0	5,100	0	0
Jacksonville	17,020	5,465	11,257	50	243	9,200	1,000	8,200	0	0
Jersey City	2,994	207	2,778	0	9	14,020	1,920	6,100	0	6,000
Kansas City	8,906	524	8,146	13	214	7,340	1,280	6,060	0	0
Knoxville	4,896	4,107	635	96	58	4,060	2,060	1,820	180	0
Las Vegas	0	0	0	0	0	2,040	400	1,600	0	40
Lexington-Fayette	7,214	3,032	4,052	6	116	3,720	1,660	2,060	0	0
Little Rock	0	0	0	0	0	3,540	400	2,960	120	60
Long Beach	13,921	4,639	4,620	1,116	3,473	6,480	1,920	2,560	160	1,840
Los Angeles	93,894	6,516	55,074	2,307	29,747	62,320	4,400	32,100	1,560	24,260
Louisville	34,545	15,675	18,400	175	276	12,460	3,360	9,100	0	0
Madison	0	0	0	0	0	1,120	440	440	0	240
Memphis	10,466	501	9,856	0	109	28,920	1,080	27,120	120	600
Miami	13,355	255	12,187	9	873	8,780	0	4,860	0	3,920

Milwaukee	21,643	2,819	18,019	65	699	24,020	4,340	17,500	500	1,680
Minneapolis	11,466	5,364	4,595	1,182	240	6,640	2,460	2,200	1,780	200
Mobile	9,887	617	9,058	46	166	4,580	160	4,280	0	140
Montgomery	10,578	691	9,759	37	91	.	.	.	.	.
Nashville-Davidson	14,473	4,311	9,641	268	253	6,300	800	4,900	0	600
New Orleans	25,268	2,366	22,090	126	686	31,880	780	30,220	120	760
New York	420,722	36,567	167,168	6,371	209,021	348,540	23,240	131,640	2,000	191,660
Newark	68,726	3,359	55,860	326	9,007	33,780	1,040	22,940	60	9,740
Norfolk	8,358	141	8,064	42	111	8,880	860	7,880	0	140
Oakland	4,243	1,188	1,996	242	817	10,660	400	8,840	620	800
Oklahoma City	8,359	5,540	1,536	575	700	5,220	1,440	3,280	0	500
Omaha	3,683	356	3,154	148	25	3,700	800	2,900	0	0
Philadelphia	113,845	23,515	63,802	892	25,340	88,860	11,140	67,080	1,020	9,620
Phoenix	24,517	5,571	5,330	856	12,739	7,480	1,480	2,120	240	3,640
Pittsburgh	3,194	1,256	1,900	6	32	11,400	3,300	7,840	0	260
Portland	8,323	2,748	4,441	758	270	3,800	1,720	1,660	80	340
Providence	13,627	8,098	3,098	565	1,732	5,600	2,680	1,660	360	900
Raleigh	2,848	0	2,811	0	37	1,380	120	1,200	0	60
Richmond	13,853	498	13,059	102	194	9,140	900	8,240	0	0
Riverside	0	0	0	0	0	2,360	1,040	120	240	960
Rochester	21,667	7,000	12,041	150	2,457	9,520	1,960	6,300	0	1,260
Sacramento	21,311	10,716	4,207	1,193	5,134	8,140	2,400	3,060	360	2,320
Salt Lake City	84	84	0	0	0	1,100	380	120	60	540
San Antonio	31,429	1,126	10,609	80	19,582	19,180	780	2,340	180	15,880
San Diego	5,526	1,330	2,108	167	1,885	9,260	1,640	2,660	760	4,200
San Francisco	5,634	3,794	477	865	470	8,080	1,060	4,180	860	1,980
San Jose	0	0	0	0	0	8,220	1,340	1,400	440	5,040
Santa Ana	0	0	0	0	0	2,440	260	100	80	2,000
Seattle	1,261	690	139	408	24	3,940	1,380	2,120	360	80
Shreveport	12,994	115	12,523	8	326	7,800	200	6,900	0	700

continued

Appendix Table 3.B COMPARISON OF POPULATION COUNTS USING RICKETTS–SAWHILL AND PUMS MEASURES OF UNDERCLASS POPULATION (continued)

Central Cities	Ricketts and Sawhill					PUMS				
	All Races	White	Black	Others	Hispanic	All Races	White	Black	Others	Hispanic
Spokane	4,135	3,577	122	288	135	1,540	1,340	80	120	0
Springfield, Mass.	20,215	8,584	2,813	58	8,695	7,020	1,800	1,800	40	3,380
St Louis	38,698	5,497	32,486	153	512	22,680	2,920	19,600	160	0
St. Paul	0	0	0	0	0	3,820	2,400	720	340	360
St. Petersburg	7,619	473	7,031	14	101	3,600	760	2,780	0	60
Stockton	3,675	941	666	208	1,837	4,820	960	1,180	60	2,620
Syracuse	6,409	3,642	1,956	394	366	5,300	2,500	2,460	260	80
Tacoma	0	0	0	0	0	3,140	1,720	620	640	160
Tampa	6,176	1,084	4,365	72	650	7,600	1,380	5,940	0	280
Toledo	13,649	8,864	3,780	113	862	8,080	2,920	4,660	0	500
Tucson	1,687	224	133	16	1,314	2,840	780	360	0	1,700
Tulsa	0	0	0	0	0	3,400	900	1,980	460	60
Virginia Beach	0	0	0	0	0	1,260	460	800	0	0
Washington, D.C.	18,775	610	17,960	80	119	29,300	320	28,380	260	340
Wichita	0	0	0	0	0	3,100	2,100	1,000	0	0
Worcester	13,341	8,262	1,353	251	3,470	5,400	3,120	400	120	1,760

Sources: U.S. Bureau of the Census, Census of Population and Housing 1980: Summary Tape File 3A and Public-Use Microdata Samples.
Note: See text for explanation of Ricketts-Sawhill (1988) census tract measures and PUMS measures.

References

Auletta, Ken. 1982. *The Underclass*. New York: Random House.

Bane, Mary Jo, and David Ellwood. 1986. "Slipping Into and Out of Poverty: The Dynamics of Spells." *Journal of Human Resources* 21 (1, Winter): 1–23.

Bane, Mary Jo, and Paul Jargowsky. 1988. "Urban Poverty Areas: Basic Questions Concerning Prevalence, Growth and Dynamics." Center for Health and Human Resources Policy Discussion Paper Series, John F. Kennedy School of Government, Harvard University, Cambridge, Mass.

Bound, John, and Harry Holzer. 1991. "Urban Industrial Change, Low Skill Jobs, and Black and White Men's Earnings, 1970–1987." Department of Economics, Michigan State University. Photocopy.

Duncan, G. J., R. D. Coe, and M. S. Hill. 1984. *Years of Poverty, Years of Plenty* Ann Arbor: University of Michigan, Institute for Social Research.

Ellwood, David T. 1986. "The Spatial Mismatch Hypothesis: Are There Teenage Jobs Missing in the Ghetto?" In *The Black Youth Employment Crisis*, edited by R. B. Freeman and H. J. Holzer (147–85). Chicago: University of Chicago Press.

Farley, John E. 1987. "Disproportionate Black and Hispanic Unemployment in U.S. Metropolitan Areas." *American Journal of Economics and Sociology* 46 (2, Apr.): 129–50.

Gans, Herbert J. 1990. "Deconstructing the Underclass: The Term's Danger as a Planning Concept." *Journal of the American Planning Association* 56: 271–277.

Glasgow, David. 1980. *The Black Underclass: Poverty, Unemployment, and Entrapment of Ghetto Youth*. San Francisco: Jossey-Bass.

Gottschalk, P., and S. Danziger. 1986. Testimony on "Poverty, Hunger, and the Welfare System." *Hearing before the Select Committee on Hunger, House of Representatives*. 99th Cong., 2nd sess., ser. no. 23. Washington, D.C.: U.S. Government Printing Office, April.

Green, Richard P. 1988. "Changes in the Spatial Dispersion of Extreme Poverty Areas in Large American Cities." Paper presented at annual meeting of the Regional Science Association, Toronto, Canada, November.

Hess, G. Alfred, Jr. 1986. "Educational Triage in an Urban School Setting." *Metropolitan Education*, no. 2 (Fall): 39–52.

Holzer, Harry. 1989. "The Empirical Status of the Spatial Mismatch Hypothesis." Department of Economics, Michigan State University, East Lansing. Photocopy.

Hughes, Mark Alan. 1988. "The 'Underclass' Fallacy." Woodrow Wilson School of Public and International Affairs, Princeton University, Princeton, N.J. Photocopy.

————. 1989. "Misspeaking Truth to Power: A Geographical Perspective on the 'Underclass' Fallacy." *Economic Geography* 65: 187–207.

Jargowsky, Paul and Mary J. Bane. 1991. "Neighborhood Poverty: Basic Questions." In *The Urban Underclass*, edited by Christopher Jencks and Paul Peterson. Washington, D.C.: Brookings Institution.

Jencks, Christopher. 1989. "What Is the Underclass—And Is It Growing?" *Focus* 12 (1, Spring/Summer): 14–31.

Jencks, Christopher, and Susan E. Mayer. 1990. "Residential Segregation, Job Proximity, and Black Job Opportunity." In *Inner-City Poverty in the United States*, edited by Lawrence E. Lynn and Michael G. H. McGeary. Washington, D.C.: National Academy Press.

Jencks, Christopher, and Paul Peterson, eds. 1991. *The Urban Underclass*. Washington, D.C.: Brookings Institution.

Kasarda, John D. 1985. "Urban Change and Minority Opportunities." In *The New Urban Reality*, edited by Paul E. Peterson. Washington, D.C.: Brookings Institution.

————. 1989. "Urban Industrial Transition and the Underclass." *Annals of the American Academy of Political and Social Science* 501 (Jan.): 26–47.

————. 1990. "Structural Factors Affecting the Location and Timing of Urban Underclass Growth." *Urban Geography* 11(3): 234–64.

————. 1992. *Urban Underclass Database: An Overview and Machine-Readable File Documentation*. New York: Social Science Research Council.

Katz, Lawrence, and Kevin Murphy. 1990. "Changes in Relative Wages, 1963–1987: Supply and Demand Factors." National Bureau of Economic Research, April. Photocopy.

Katz, Michael. 1989. *The Undeserving Poor: From the War on Poverty to the War on Welfare*. New York: Pantheon Books.

Kornblum, William S. 1985. "Institution Building in the Urban High School." In *The Challenge of Social Control*, edited by G. Suttles and M. Zald (218–29). Norwood, N.J.: Ablex.

Levy, Frank. 1977. "How Big Is the American Underclass?" Research Paper. Washington, D.C.: Urban Institute. September.

Lieberson, Stanley. 1980. *A Piece of the Pie: Blacks and White Immigrants since 1880*. Berkeley, Calif.: University of California Press.

Martinez-Vazquez, Jorge, and Rubin Saposnik. 1990. "A Contagion Model of Underclass Neighborhoods." Georgia State University, Atlanta. Photocopy.

Massey, Douglas S., and Nancy A. Denton. 1987. "Trends in Residential Segregation of Blacks, Hispanics, and Asians: 1970–1980." *American Sociological Review* 52: 802–25.

Mincy, Ronald B. 1988. "Industrial Restructuring, Dynamic Events and the Racial Composition of Concentrated Poverty." Paper prepared for Planning Meeting of Social Science Research Council on Industrial Restructuring, Local Political Economies, and Communities and Neighborhoods, New York, September 21–23.

Mincy, Ronald, Isabel Sawhill, and Douglas Wolf. 1990. "The Underclass: Definition and Measurement." *Science* 248, no. 4954 (April 27).

Moss, Philip, and Chris Tilly. 1991. "Why Black Men Are Doing Worse in the Labor Market: A Review of Supply-Side and Demand-Side Explanations." Paper prepared for the Social Science Research Council, New York City.

Myrdal, Gunner. 1962. *Challenge to Affluence*. New York: Pantheon.

Nathan, Richard P. 1987. "Will the Underclass Always Be with Us?" *Society* 24: 57–62.

Price, Richard, and Edwin S. Mills. 1985. "Race and Residence in Earnings Determination." *Journal of Urban Economics* 17: 1–18.

Reischauer, Robert D. 1987. *The Geographic Concentration of Poverty: What Do We Know?* Washington, D.C.: Brookings Institution.

Ricketts, Erol. 1990. "Origin, Nature, Causes, and Dimensions of the Underclass." Rockefeller Foundation. Photocopy.

Ricketts, Erol, and Isabel Sawhill. 1988. "Defining and Measuring the Underclass." *Journal of Policy Analysis and Management* 7(2): 316–25.

Sjoquist, David. 1990. "Concepts, Measurements, and Analysis of the Underclass: A Review of the Literature." Georgia State University, Atlanta. Photocopy.

U.S. Bureau of the Census. 1983. *Census of Population and Housing, 1980: Public-Use Microdata Samples Technical Documentation, 1983*. Washington, D.C.: Author.

Vrooman, John, and Stuart Greenfield. 1980. "Are Blacks Making It in the Suburbs? Some New Evidence on Intrametropolitan Spatial Segmentation." *Journal of Urban Economics* 7: 155–67.

Wacquant, Loic J.D., and William Julius Wilson. 1989. "Poverty, Joblessness, and the Social Transformation of the Inner City." In *Welfare Policy for the 1990s*, edited by David Ellwood and Phoebe Cottingham. Cambridge, Mass.: Harvard University Press.

Welch, Finis. 1990. "The Employment of Black Men." *Journal of Labor Economics* 8 (1, pt. 2, Jan.), S26–S74.

Wilson, William Julius. 1987. *The Truly Disadvantaged: The Inner City, the Underclass, and Public Policy*. Chicago: University of Chicago Press.

Chapter Four

DRUG SELLING AND LICIT INCOME IN DISTRESSED NEIGHBORHOODS: THE ECONOMIC LIVES OF STREET-LEVEL DRUG USERS AND DEALERS

Jeffrey Fagan

Young people in inner cities became involved in drug selling in the 1980s in unprecedented numbers. Some of them were employed, skilled workers; others were unemployed or unskilled workers; and still others were already active in illegal enterprises before the expansion of drug markets. In neighborhoods with active drug markets, opportunities for drug selling may have attracted young workers away from lower paying jobs in the formal economy, provided work for young people detached from labor markets, or offered higher incomes or income supplements to workers already active in both the licit and illicit sectors of the informal economy. Whether these young drug sellers were primarily skilled workers diverted to the drug economy or individuals with only marginal attachment to the legal labor force is an important issue for theory and policy, as is the mediating effect that neighborhood structure has on the functioning of local drug markets.

The economic and social restructuring of urban areas since the 1960s created new incentives for inner-city residents to participate in the informal economy. The informal economy grew disproportionately in neighborhoods with high concentrations of poor, minority populations (Sassen-Koob 1989). Traditionally, drug selling has been an important part of the informal economy in urban areas in the United States (Hunt 1990; Stepick 1989) and in other countries (Jimenez 1989; Lanzetta, Castano, and Soto 1989). Besides the motivation to reap profits, the decline of legitimate economic opportunities among inner-

The author is grateful to Bruce Johnson, Eloise Dunlap, and Ko-lin Chin for their contributions to this research. The data were collected under a grant from the National Institute of Justice. Robert MacCoun, Joan Moore, and the editors provided helpful comments on an earlier version of the manuscript.

city residents strengthened incentives to sell drugs (Bourgois 1989; Freeman 1992; Hochschild 1989; Johnson, Williams, Dei, and Sanabria 1990; Moss and Tilly 1991; Padilla 1991; Taylor 1990).

In New York City, crack distribution became a major part of the informal economy, where the unemployed could achieve economic returns well beyond the returns available from low-wage jobs (cf., Bourgois 1989; Hamid 1990; *New York Times* 1989a,b; Williams 1989). The introduction of this new and powerful cocaine product, and its popularity among a cohort of adults with high base rates of drug use, created new demand that exceeded the capacity of established distribution systems.[1] In turn, the expansion of the drug economy increased the opportunities for street-level drug selling through improved access to supplies, the creation of entry-level roles in drug distribution that required only a small capital investment, and the establishment of "controlled" selling territories with more stable incomes (Hamid 1990; Johnson, Williams, et al. 1990; Williams 1989).

The growth of the drug market has had important effects both on inner-city neighborhoods and on the economic lives of market participants. However, these impacts have proved difficult to pin down. Few studies have estimated actual returns from drug selling or the changes in labor force participation that result from entry into the drug economy (see Reuter, MacCoun, and Murphy 1990, for a review). The effects of drug selling on reservation wages (the minimum wage at which residents will accept legal work) or on participation in other criminal activity are also unclear. These are critical questions for public policy. The profitability of drug dealing obviously affects the feasibility of different strategies for steering inner-city youth back to the legal labor market, and our understanding of the role of drugs in the inner city will be quite different if drug dealing is largely restricted to a special segment of the population than if it is commonly mixed with legal labor across a broad spectrum of the labor force.

Participants in the drug economy are known to be a diverse population, including those with ties to the formal economy (Reuter et al. 1990) and others with lengthy careers in informal and illicit economic activities (Fagan and Chin 1990; Padilla 1992). Rates of drug selling vary by sample. Fagan (1990) found that among 1,206 inner-city youths in three cities, 8.9 percent of males and 4.4 percent of females in 1985 had sold drugs in the past year. But over 25 percent of gang members (both male and female) sold drugs. Case and Katz (1990) reported that

---

1. For a brief review of the natural history and psychopharmacology of crack, see: Chin and Fagan 1990; Fagan and Chin 1990; Inciardi 1987; Reinarman and Levine 1989; Siegel 1987.

12 percent of the African-American males in Boston in 1989 sold drugs in the previous year, compared to 18 percent of the white youths. Reuter et al. (1990) estimated that one in six African-American males in a 1967 Washington, D.C., birth cohort were arrested for drug selling between the ages of 18 and 20 years; actual participation rates for drug selling were likely to be far greater.

Estimates of drug income also vary widely by sample, and depend on whether researchers examine gross or net incomes. Reuter et al. (1990) estimated an hourly wage of $30, but the monthly net income was estimated at $2,015 after adjusting for variable hours. Moreover, selling was episodic, complicating efforts to establish a market wage equivalent. Taylor (1990) reported far higher incomes for young men in Detroit drug-selling organizations, but noted a wide variation in wages, depending upon position in the organization.[2] Bourgois (1989) did not offer a wage estimate, but noted that on a net basis street-level sellers earn little more than typical hourly wages in their most recent legal jobs (about $10 per hour). Williams (1989) estimated incomes ranging from $15,000 to over $100,000 annually, but both variation by rank within groups and variable participation made it difficult to develop standardized earnings estimates. Freeman (1992) also declines to provide a precise wage estimate. But he notes that 1990 data on disadvantaged youths in Boston show that formal-sector wages are not high enough to make it economically worthwhile for drug sellers to take up legal work, even if jobs are available.

In short, it remains uncertain to what extent drug selling has siphoned human capital from licit labor markets; or whether the drug economy is a segmented and economically isolated milieu with little overlap with the formal economy; or if drug selling is complementary with licit work. Moreover, there has been little investigation of how drug markets vary between neighborhoods according to residents' social and economic conditions. This chapter examines such issues for drug sellers and users in two New York City neighborhoods that have experienced increasing poverty and social distress.

EROSION OF SOCIAL AND ECONOMIC CONTROLS ON DRUG SELLING

The succession of drug "epidemics" over the last 20 years has mirrored a process of neighborhood disintegration and economic desta-

---

2. Taylor (1990) noted that although resembling youth gangs in composition and structure, the relationships within these groups are determined solely by shared economic interests. He referred to these groups as "post-gangs."

bilization, both in New York City and other inner cities (see, for example: Shannon 1986, regarding Racine, Wisconsin; Taylor, Taub, and Peterson 1986 and Wilson 1987, regarding Chicago; Hagedorn, with Macon 1988, regarding Milwaukee; and Sullivan 1989, 1991, regarding New York City). The drug crises have occurred in a context of rapidly changing neighborhoods where the formal and informal social controls that limited crime and governed drug use have been weakened.

Until the 1980s, new drugs eventually were integrated into neighborhood cultures.[3] Earlier drug distribution patterns in New York City tended to be smaller in economic scale or concentrated within neighborhoods. Before cocaine became widely available, hard drug distribution was centralized, with a smaller street-level heroin network of users responsible for retail sales (Goldstein et al. 1984; Johnson et al. 1985). As cocaine became widely available, competition erupted in distribution systems. The sudden change from a restricted and controlled drug market in the 1970s to a deregulated market for crack spawned intense competition for territory and market share. First with cocaine hydrochloride (HCL) and then crack, new businesses entered the market, bringing with them three important differences from the earlier social organization of drug selling.

First, compared to marijuana sales, proceeds from these drug sales were not widely retained in the neighborhoods. Marijuana money typically turned over several times at the local level before centralizing with one person or group. Neighborhood social and economic capital often was created, and with this process came the reinforcement of social and economic controls for appropriate use. With crack, however, intense market competition in an illicit commodity gave rise to violence as the mechanism to regulate drug selling. In addition, drug income was not reinvested as extensively in local businesses, but was quickly transferred to individuals elsewhere in the city or outside the country.

Second, the decline of legitimate economic opportunities in inner cities (Sassen-Koob 1989; Wacquant and Wilson 1989) and the growth of new street-level drug markets provided both incentive and opportunity for newcomers to participate in drug selling. Crack appeared predominantly in urban neighborhoods that had experienced profound social and economic deterioration Belenko, Fagan, and Chin

---

3. Hamid (1990) discussed the integration of marijuana into the culture of Caribbean neighborhoods in Brooklyn as a peaceful and unifying affair where dollars were reinvested in the community and ceremonial uses of the substance conveyed its social meaning.

1991). The 1970s were a decade of labor surpluses in inner cities, created by the outmigration of jobs to the suburbs and other regions of the country. Kasarda (chapter 3, this volume) shows that between 1970 and 1980, the number of blue-collar and clerical jobs in New York City declined by over 350,000. Traditionally, African-Americans had relied heavily on blue-collar jobs in manufacturing for economic sustenance and social mobility (Farley and Allen 1987). Since the 1970s, Puerto Ricans and other Latin American and East Asian immigrants have "colonized" these jobs (Tienda 1989a), but they also have come under labor market pressure from the loss of formal-sector employment in the inner city.[4] Thus, the economic restructuring of New York and other American cities resulted in large-scale exclusion of their nonwhite residents from constricting labor markets that also were transforming from manufacturing to services, and shifting spatially from the inner city to the surrounding suburbs (Hochschild 1989). Similar processes, compounded by language and other cultural barriers, created severe economic dislocations for Puerto Ricans, in turn creating conditions of severe impoverishment (Farley 1987; Kasarda 1991; Tienda 1989b). Cocaine and crack distribution thus represented new economic opportunities in neighborhoods where legitimate economic activity had been lost.

Third, the violence associated with crack set it apart. This violence resulted from several parallel processes: competition between sellers over territory (Goldstein et al. 1987, 1989), regulation of employees in new selling organizations (Cooper 1987; Johnson, Hamid, and Sanabria 1990; Williams 1989), the greater urge for crack or money to buy it among habitual users (Reinarman, Waldorf, and Murphy 1989; Hamid 1990), and for a small group, its psychoactive effects (Reinarman et al. 1989; Washton and Gold 1987).[5] Crack distribution attracted workers already skilled in violence and other crimes. The self- and social selection of violent persons to the crack marketplace has helped shape its social organization and neighborhood impacts. Neighborhood structures weakened by high residential mobility and loss of economic opportunities were unable to integrate and control either

---

4. This does not include the low-wage reindustrialization of New York through immigrant (often undocumented) Asian and Latin American labor (sweat shops); see Sassen-Koob 1991, regarding New York.

5. The different generations of drug markets themselves reflected differences in the types of drugs and their psychoactive effects: compared to heroin and marijuana street sales, cocaine and crack markets were more volatile owing to a high rate of transactions and the short half-life of the high these drugs produced (Bourgois 1989; Hamid 1990; Johnson, Williams, et al. 1990).

the volatile drug market or the violent crimes associated with it (Sampson 1986). The social processes that regulate behaviors changed as informal controls broke down in areas where drugs were distributed at the street level (Sampson 1987; Skogan 1990).

OBJECTIVES AND METHODS

This chapter examines the economic and social organization of street-level drug selling in Washington Heights and Central Harlem, two New York City poverty areas that have experienced different degrees of structural change since 1970. The contrast of these neighborhoods permits an analysis of the effects of neighborhood change and neighborhood structure on participation in drug selling and its consequences for residents who are active in the local drug industry (McGahey 1986).

The critical questions for this research involve whether the growth of drug markets in an era of declining licit economic activity led to the siphoning of well-educated and employed people into the informal and illicit drug economy, and spurred entry into other criminal activity. We examine these questions by focusing on two neighborhoods that differed not only in their drug economies but in their ethnic composition, in poverty concentration, and degree of isolation from the rest of the urban region. By comparing the two neighborhoods, we can assess not only the effects of drug involvement on the economic lives of people in poor areas but also the mediating effects of the areas themselves.

Sample Design

Both Washington Heights and Central Harlem have high concentrations of crack use and selling.[6] Samples of users and sellers were recruited through chain referral or "snowball" sampling procedures (Biernacki and Waldorf 1981; Watters and Biernacki 1989), techniques appropriate for "hidden" populations whose population parameters are not well known, whose probability of being represented in official records is uncertain, and whose behaviors are not amenable to social surveys applied to the general population.

---

6. See Belenko, Fagan, and Chin (1991) for an analysis of arrest patterns for crack offenses in New York City.

Since drug use and distribution are not normally distributed among the general population, samples were recruited in each neighborhood from populations with known concentrations of these behaviors: arrestees for drug possession and/or sales, residents who matched the arrested populations but who have avoided legal or social intervention for drug use or selling, incarcerated prisoners, probationers and parolees, and participants in residential drug treatment programs. Table 4.1 shows the proportion of the sample from each neighborhood in each of these categories. The full sample contained a total of 1,003 respondents.

Within each group, samples were constructed to represent different patterns of drug involvement: crack users or sellers, cocaine HCL[7] users or sellers who were not involved with crack, heroin users or sellers, polydrug (primarily marijuana) users, and infrequent or nonusers. Table 4.1 shows that the sample proportions were similar in the two study neighborhoods. Since the research was part of a larger study of crack, crack users and sellers were oversampled. Overall, crack users or sellers (N = 623) comprised 62 percent of the sample. Cocaine and heroin users comprised 14 percent and 9.5 percent, respectively; the remainder were polydrug users, and infrequent users or non-users.

Table 4.1 PERCENTAGE DISTRIBUTION OF RESPONDENTS' LEGAL STATUS AND SELF-REPORTED PRIMARY DRUG INVOLVEMENT BY NEW YORK CITY NEIGHBORHOOD

	Central Harlem	Washington Heights
N	452	551
Legal Status at Interview:		
Not in legal or treatment systems	57.6	61.5
Arrestees, not detained	11.2	9.1
Residential treatment	13.2	6.8
In jail	12.2	15.2
Probation or parole	5.8	7.4
Primary Drug Involvement:		
Crack	61.6	62.5
Cocaine HCL	13.2	15.9
Heroin	11.6	7.4
Marijuana	9.9	9.3
Nonusers	3.7	4.9

---

7. Cocaine hydrochloride in its powdered form.

Social and demographic characteristics of the sample are shown by neighborhood in Appendix 4.A. More than two-thirds were males in each neighborhood. Ethnicity reflected the aggregate characteristics of the neighborhoods, although Latinos were overrepresented in the Central Harlem sample and underrepresented for Washington Heights. Respondents were younger in Washington Heights, with more than 40 percent between 19 and 26 years of age. Fewer than half in each neighborhood were high school graduates, and fewer than 20 percent had ever attended college. About one-fourth lived with a spouse (or intimate partner) and/or their child. Most lived either alone or with other relatives or family members.

Although the sample was not designed to be representative of the general populations of the neighborhoods, it is representative of drug arrestees in New York City during the peak years of the crack crisis (Johnson, Hamid, and Sanabria 1990). It is uncertain how well the sample represents the drug-using or drug-dealing populations within each neighborhood, since the population parameters of these groups by neighborhood are not known. As neighborhoods, Central Harlem and Washington Heights are representative of two basic types of neighborhood change occurring in New York City. However, although generalizations to the populations involved in drug markets in each specific neighborhood are appropriate, caution should be exercised in broadening the findings beyond the specific neighborhoods investigated.

Sample Recruitment

Arrestees who were awaiting initial court appearances were recruited from the Manhattan central booking facility. They were identified from special charge flags for crack and cocaine recorded by arresting officers on booking slips.[8] Residential neighborhood was determined from the addresses (and the corresponding zip codes) provided by arrestees to the interviewers. Referrals for interview were made by pretrial services interviewers during routine jail screening of arrestees to determine eligibility for release on their own recognizance. Arrestees who indicated willingness to participate in a research study were given cards that told them where and how to arrange for an interview. Those detained were interviewed in the detention facility.

---

8. The arrest flags have been used by the New York City Police Department since 1986 to identify crack offenses, since charge categories do not distinguish various types of controlled substances.

Other subjects were recruited through chain referral procedures. Noncrack drug arrestees were selected from the same booking facility. Nonarrested neighborhood participants were matched to the arrested samples on age, gender, and ethnicity. Other sample members were drawn from participants in two residential treatment programs in Manhattan. Several types of chain referral methods were used. Arrestees were asked to nominate a potential respondent who "is like you, from your neighborhood and about your age, but who has avoided arrest." Interviewers then sought out the nominees, or they were referred to the field office by friends. Chains also were developed among drug users and sellers who were known to the interviewers through neighborhood contacts.

Residential treatment clients were recruited from their programs based on nominations of crack and other drug users by administrators and clinical staff. Treatment residents who had been in the program for at least one month and who met screening criteria for each drug user type were asked to participate in the study. Incarcerated drug offenders were recruited from felony drug offenders in New York State prisons, pretrial detainees in the Rikers Island detention facility in New York City, and sentenced misdemeanor drug offenders at Rikers Island. Prison inmates and detainees were identified from criminal history and drug-related information they provided at reception interviews, and were called out of population for interviews.

A brief (10-item) screening interview was used to classify respondents' drug use or selling patterns and to validate their reports. Respondents were classified by their primary drug involvement if they used (or sold) that drug on more than 50 occasions in their lifetime, and if they had not used (or sold) another substance more than that amount. Multiple drug users were classified according to the most frequent drug used or sold in the past year. Interviews were conducted with $N = 1{,}003$ respondents over an 18-month period from March 1988 to September 1989.

Interview Procedures

Interviews were conducted in a variety of settings where the participants could not be overheard by anyone else and where the identity of the respondent was unknown to anyone in the immediate setting. Prison and detention interviews were conducted in empty classrooms, usually on weekends. Interviews with arrestees and street samples were conducted in a storefront location, libraries, coffee shops, or other neutral, public locales. Urine specimens were requested as a validation of drug use for the neighborhood groups. Interviews lasted from one to two hours, with a short break after the first hour.

Interview stipends of $25 were provided, plus $5 for the urine specimen and smaller fees for referrals of potential interviewees and location information for possible follow-up. Respondents also were given two subway tokens and a pack of cigarettes. Treatment respondents were not given the stipend; it was donated to the treatment program. They also were not asked for urine specimens, since they had been in treatment for one month or longer and their abstinence was presumed. Jail and prison inmates were not asked for urine samples, nor were they offered stipends, owing to institutional rules.

Interview items were read aloud. Cards with the response sets were shown to respondents and the choices read aloud so that literacy problems were minimized. The interviews were conducted in both English and Spanish.

Variables

Interview protocols included four domains of information: initiation into substance use or selling; lifetime and annual involvement with both substances and nondrug crimes; the social processes of substance use or selling; and income sources and expenditures from both legitimate and illegal activities. A calendar was used to record time spent in treatment or detoxification programs, jails or prisons, or other institutions. For initiation, respondents were asked to describe processes of initiation into their primary drug: how, where, and with whom did they initially use (or sell) the substance; how much money did they spend; and the time between the first and second use and regular use (if any). Their expectations and reactions to the substance were recorded through multiple response items.

Criminal career parameters were recorded through self-reports of lifetime estimates and annual frequencies of drug use, drug selling, and nondrug crimes from 1984 to the present. Specific estimates were recorded for several types of drugs used or sold, as well as for a list of 20 nondrug crimes. Items were worded in common language (e.g., "beat someone so badly they needed to see a doctor). A categorical scale was used to record frequencies of specific behaviors, and midpoint means were used to calculate rates. This method was chosen in lieu of self-reports of actual numbers of crimes, to minimize distortion from the skewed distribution of responses for the small percentage of high-rate users or offenders. The response set represented an exponential scale of frequency, with nine categories ranging from "one or two times" to "more than 10,000."

The social organization of drug use and selling included several types of information. Respondents were asked whether they had sold drugs as part of an organization, and to describe their organization using dimensions developed by Fagan (1989) and Johnson, Hamid, and Sanabria (1990) in studies of drug selling among youth gangs. Items asked for respondents' participation in specific roles in drug selling, roles that were evident in their selling organization, and social processes that existed within their group. For example, respondents were asked if their group had specific prohibitions against drug use or sanctions for rules violations. "Systemic violence" (Goldstein 1985, 1989) associated with drug dealing was operationally defined through eight items covering specific types of violence. Respondents were asked whether they had experienced each of these violent events "regularly" in the course of their selling activity.

The economic lives of respondents were captured through questions on income and expenditures. Monthly dollar amounts were reported using a categorical scale of dollar ranges, ranging from one ("less than $100 per month") to nine ($10,000 or more). This option was chosen over actual dollar reports to minimize distortion of dollar estimates and possible recall problems among long-term substance users.[9] Dollar estimates were recorded for both legitimate and illegitimate sources of income, and for expenditures both for living costs and for drugs.

THE STUDY NEIGHBORHOODS

Washington Heights and Central Harlem both experienced rapid and profound social structural changes in the decade preceding the crack crisis. Both neighborhoods reflect concentrations of the urban "underclass," regardless of whether the definition is based on individual-level indicators of poverty (Jencks 1989) or location-based aggregate measures (Jargowsky and Bane 1990; Ricketts and Sawhill, 1988). Although both neighborhoods contained then and now a disproportion-

---

9. However, the use of these categories also may risk upward response bias. Respondents may feel that the existence of the larger categories suggests that someone is making that much money. In a domain where one's illicit income can serve as a status marker, this might promote exaggeration.

ate share of severely distressed households, table 4.2 shows that the neighborhoods are changing in markedly different ways.

Central Harlem in 1980 remained a homogeneously African-American community that had become much poorer in the preceding decade. Over one-third of its population was lost during the 1970s, whereas the percentage of families with incomes below poverty levels grew to over one in three. When adjusted for inflation, median income for families decreased by almost 25 percent over the decade; the decline was nearly 50 percent for unrelated individuals. More than one in five families (22.5 percent) were receiving public assistance[10] in 1980. In almost all of the 29 census tracts, more than 20 percent of the population had incomes below the poverty line, a common threshold for designation as a poverty tract.[11] Using the more conservative threshold of 40 percent of the population below the poverty line (Jargowsky and Bane 1990), nine census tracts could be classified as extreme poverty areas.

Central Harlem also experienced large demographic shifts during the 1970s. The percentage of married couples declined significantly in this period, but the percentage of single-parent families (primarily female-headed households) grew by only 4 percent. These trends reflect the flight from Central Harlem of working- and middle-class African-American families whose incomes were above poverty levels. The greatest growth was among poor, single individuals.

In Washington Heights, the white population of the neighborhood declined precipitously over the decade: nearly three in four residents in 1970 were white, compared to 27.7 percent in 1980 (table 4.2).[12] Departed white residents were replaced by Hispanics, who accounted for over half the 1980 population. The growth in the Spanish-speaking population (23.5 percentage points) and in foreign-born residents (12 percentage points) suggests that the neighborhood had become a reception area for immigrant Hispanics. The percentage of households headed by married couples declined by 17.1 percentage points, whereas single-parent households with children grew 12.7 percentage points.

Family income in 1980 was below poverty for nearly one in four families in Washington Heights. Median incomes, adjusted for infla-

---

10. Public assistance includes Aid to Families with Dependent Children (AFDC) and Home Relief (New York City Human Resources Administration).

11. Community Planning District 10, New York City Department of City Planning.

12. However, Census data for 1970 failed to accurately distinguish whites from Hispanics.

tion, were almost 25 percent lower in 1980 than in 1970 for families, and about 15 percent lower for unrelated individuals. In 1980 the poverty share of the population exceeded 20 percent in over half (*N* = 17) of the 30 census tracts in the area.[13] One in six residents received public assistance.

Table 4.3 provides another perspective on the growing concentration of poverty in the two neighborhoods. It compares the number of census tracts in each neighborhood that met each of three poverty definitions: at least 20 percent of the population below poverty, at least 40 percent of the population below poverty, and tracts defined as "underclass" using an aggregate, location-based definition from Ricketts and Sawhill (1988). For all three measures, the concentration of poverty increased sharply during the 1970s in both neighborhoods. However, the percentage of tracts in poverty in 1980 suggests that poverty concentration was more severe in Central Harlem. Central Harlem also had less diversity of education level and lower average income.

The concept of underclass reflects more than poverty dimensions. Some definitions include behavioral characteristics such as births out of wedlock and teenage births (Ricketts and Sawhill 1988; Kasarda, chapter 3, this volume). Table 4.4 shows recent natality and infant mortality data for 1988, which further illustrate the contrasts between Central Harlem and Washington Heights. Both out-of-wedlock and teenage births occurred at much higher rates in Central Harlem; infants born there were more likely to have low birthweights, and infant mortality per 1,000 live births was over 150 percent higher there than in Washington Heights.

The contrasts in the neighborhoods reveal two faces of poverty. Whereas Central Harlem is a severely distressed area, Washington Heights' composition is changing rapidly. Central Harlem remains homogeneously poor, with a declining population of families and low rates of labor force participation. Washington Heights faces the challenges of immigrant communities. African-Americans and Latinos have replaced non-Hispanic whites at a time when the employment base has been radically transformed. This has left large proportions of minority immigrants (or migrants from other parts of the United States) without formal-sector jobs, forcing them to engage in licit or illicit activities within the informal economy, or to use entrepreneurial skills to develop small businesses. Nevertheless, the outlook in

---

13. Community Planning District 10, New York City Department of City Planning.

Table 4.2 NEW YORK CITY NEIGHBORHOOD SOCIAL, STRUCTURAL, AND ECONOMIC PROFILES, 1970–80

	Washington Heights			Central Harlem		
	1970	1980	% Change	1970	1980	% Change
Population	180,710	179,941	−0.4	159,336	105,794	−33.6
Age (%)						
1–4 years	6.3	9.5	3.2	7.6	6.8	−1.1
5–17 years	15.9	15.7	−0.2	21.8	16.7	5.1
18–24 years	10.3	12.4	2.1	9.9	10.8	0.9
25–44 years	25.0	28.8	3.8	25.7	24.6	−1.1
45–64 years	25.1	18.9	−6.2	24.2	24.9	0.7
65 years and over	17.4	14.7	−2.7	10.8	16.2	5.4
Family Composition (%)						
Husband-wife[a]	76.8	59.5	−17.3	56.7	40.6	−16.1
Other without children	13.6	18.2	4.6	15.8	27.8	12.0
Other with children	9.6	22.3	12.7	27.5	31.6	4.1
Ethnicity (%)						
White	73.6	27.7	−45.9	2.0	0.6	−1.4
African-American	15.4	14.3	−1.1	94.6	94.1	0.5
Other	1.8	1.8	0	0.3	0.5	−0.2
Hispanic	b	54.2	—	b	4.4	—
Puerto Rican	9.2	c	—	3.1	c	—
Asian	b	1.8	—	b	0.2	—
American Indian	b	0.2	—	b	0.2	—
Spanish Language (%)[d]	30.7	54.2	23.5	5.0	4.4	−0.6
Foreign-Born (%)	36.6	48.0	12.0	3.2	6.5	3.3

Education Completed (%)[e]						
Not high school graduate	55.0	51.3	-3.7	67.8	57.2	-10.6
High school graduate	27.5	25.3	-2.2	24.7	28.8	4.1
Some college	7.7	10.6	2.9	4.6	8.8	4.2
College graduate	9.8	12.8	3.0	2.9	5.2	2.3
Income—Families (%)[f]						
Below $10,000	60.0	39.7	-20.3	79.0	65.6	-13.5
% below poverty	9.0	23.9	14.9	22.9	34.5	11.6
Median ($)	8,879	12,477	40.5	6,137	9,185	49.7
Median ($ 1980)[g]	16,614	12,477	-24.9	11,483	9,185	-20.0
Income—Unrelated Individuals						
Percentage below poverty	26.4	—	—	34.5	—	—
Median ($)	6,882	6,180	-9.8	5,499	3,813	-29.7

Notes: Dashes (—) denote not applicable.

a. With or without children.
b. Included in "Other" in 1970.
c. Included in Hispanic in 1980.
d. Of any race in 1970.
e. Persons over 24 years of age.
f. Income for 1969, 1979.
g. Median income for 1970 is converted to 1980 levels using gross national product Implicit Price Deflator for Personal Consumption Expenditures for the United States, 1970–79 (U.S. Bureau of Labor Statistics, Tuesday Spot Market Price Indexes and Prices, Washington, D.C.).

Table 4.3 CONCENTRATION OF POVERTY WITHIN NEW YORK CITY
NEIGHBORHOOD CENSUS TRACTS, 1970–80, BY NUMBER AND
PERCENTAGE OF TRACTS, PERCENTAGE CHANGE

	1970		1980		% Change
	N	%	N	%	1970–80[a]
Central Harlem					
Number of census tracts	70	(100)	71	(100)	
Areas with 20% below poverty	31	(44)	49	(69)	56.8
Areas with 40% below poverty	3	(4)	23	(32)	700.0
Underclass	4	(6)	9	(13)	116.7
Washington Heights					
Number of census tracts	107	(100)	111	(100)[b]	
Areas with 20% below poverty	30	(28)	61	(55)	96.4
Areas with 40% below poverty	2	(2)	21	(19)	850.0
Underclass	0	(0)	8	(7)	[c]
New York City					
Number of census tracts	2,156	(100)	2,203	(100)	
Areas with 20% below poverty	457	(21)	791	(36)	71.4
Areas with 40% below poverty	73	(3)	311	(14)	366.7
Underclass	27	(1)	140	(6)	500.0

a. Percentage changes computed on yearly percentage, not counts of census tracts.
b. Nine tracts had no population and were removed from the analysis.
c. Percentage change is infinite.
Source: John D. Kasarda, 1992, Urban Underclass Database (Chapel Hill, N.C.: University of North Carolina).

Table 4.4 NATALITY AND MORTALITY INDICES BY NEW YORK CITY
NEIGHBORHOOD, 1988

	Central Harlem	Washington Heights
Births per 1,000 population	20.6	24.2
Teen births (%)	16.3	9.8
Low birthweight (%)	21.2	8.4
Out of wedlock (%)	81.2	46.6
Infant mortality rate[a]	21.1	8.3

a. Per 1,000 live births.
Source: New York City Community District Vital Statistics Data Book, 1988, New York City Department of Health.

Washington Heights seems more promising. The percentage of families and college-educated residents is far higher, and the percentage of families living in poverty is lower. The promising childbirth statistics illustrate the relative health of Washington Heights residents. These factors comprise important parts of the fabric of informal social control in neighborhoods, and the beginning of the process of accumulating *social capital* (Coleman 1987; Coleman and Hoffers 1987). Whether these resources offer adequate incentives for potential drug sellers to remain in the licit economy is analyzed next.

RESULTS

Social Organization of Drug Selling and Violence

Street-level drug selling has been implicated in violence and victimization of both sellers and nonsellers (Fagan and Chin 1990; Goldstein 1989; Hamid 1990; Johnson, Hamid, and Sanabria 1990; Johnson, Williams, et al. 1990). And, among the range of street-level selling patterns, groups with more articulated structures and organizational characteristics have been associated with higher levels of violence, both within and outside the context of drug selling (Fagan 1989; Fagan and Chin, 1990).

Accordingly, Table 4.5 compares the structures of drug-selling organizations in the study neighborhoods for both males and females, and respondents' involvement in several forms of systemic violence associated with drug selling.[14] Respondents were asked to describe their organizations, and then to state whether they were "regularly" involved in any of eight specific types of violent events.[15]

Participation in drug selling was greater for both males and females in Washington Heights: nearly two-thirds of the Washington Heights males (65.9 percent) and 43.7 percent of the females participated in drug selling (table 4.5). In Central Harlem, half of the males (49.8 percent) and one in four females (27.5 percent) participated in drug selling. Over one in three males in Washington Heights was involved in a drug-selling organization, more than twice as many as the proportion of females.

Male sellers in Washington Heights more often reported that their groups had specific organizational features (table 4.5). However, selling groups were mostly informal and loosely organized. Few sellers reported that their organizations had specific names, and very few

---

14. Female participation in drug-selling organizations has rarely been studied despite the recent growth in street-level selling organizations for cocaine distribution.

15. Confidentiality procedures precluded asking about specific organizations, so comparison of responses from different members of the same organization was not possible.

Table 4.5 SOCIAL ORGANIZATION OF DRUG SELLING BY NEW YORK CITY
NEIGHBORHOOD

	Central Harlem		Washington Heights	
	Male	Female	Male	Female
N	303	153	389	158
% Involved: Drug selling	49.8	27.5	65.9	43.7
% Involved: Group selling	23.8	15.0	36.5	16.5
Structural Characteristics of Selling Group: "Does your crew have . . ." (%)				
A name?	8.6	5.2	12.3	1.9
A leadership structure?	19.8	10.5	30.1	13.9
Rules and norms?	20.8	9.2	29.3	13.3
Rules against drug use?	16.8	7.2	24.2	7.0
Specific territory?	20.1	9.8	32.1	8.9
Kids younger than 16 selling?	6.6	2.0	10.8	3.2
Violence Associated with Drug Selling: "Have you regularly . . ." (%)				
Had fights with rival dealers?	15.8	3.3	25.8	11.3
Assaulted buyers to collect debts?	16.2	5.9	22.7	6.0
Had fights over bad drugs?	17.8	8.6	24.1	10.0
Robbed drug dealers?	11.4	6.6	21.4	10.0
Robbed drug buyers?	10.8	6.6	12.3	8.7
Had disputes over paraphernalia?	26.6	25.0	22.5	24.0
Fought over the quality of drugs?	12.1	7.9	15.9	10.0
Been victimized while dealing?	18.2	10.5	21.6	3.9

said that they employed young people below 16 years of age.[16] In no
category did more than one-third of the group sellers in Washington
Heights report the presence of one of the features of organized selling;
in Central Harlem, fewer than 21 percent reported the presence of any
one of the dimensions of organization. Drug-selling organizations evidently are haphazard, ad hoc groups who may more accurately represent a decentralized distribution system than a coherent, formal, or
lasting organization. Even when such groups or crews do form, the
organizations are more likely to be temporary (Williams 1989) or to
have shifting membership at the lower ranks (Johnson, Hamid, and
Sanabria 1990). It is rare that these economic arrangements develop
into more lasting structures that resemble incipient organized crime
groups.

---

16. Adolescents are used to carrying drugs and money while avoiding the risk of adult
prosecution in New York State, where 16 years is the age of majority for criminal court.

Violence in drug selling was associated with the extent of the formal organization of the selling group. Both male and female sellers in Washington Heights more often reported "regular" participation in systemic violence than their counterparts in Central Harlem (table 4.5). The reported rates of participation in systemic violence suggest that about a quarter of the Washington Heights males were regularly involved. Violence was uncommon for female sellers in either neighborhood, but more frequent for females in Washington Heights.

There was no significant association between respondents' roles in drug-selling groups (seller, crew boss, lookout) and systemic violence (data not shown). When asked which of several roles they had held within such groups, most respondents indicated multiple roles, suggesting both mobility within groups and participation in multiple groups over time.

The association between drug selling and nondrug crime suggests that participation in systemic violence is part of a pattern of generalized crime. Systemic violence can be viewed as a regulatory process or a strategy for organizational maintenance in an economic activity that falls outside legal or formal economic control (Fagan and Chin 1990). If these behaviors are context-specific and limited to the unique arena of drug selling, we would expect no association between drug selling and other crimes. However, it appears that processes of self- and social selection result in the participation of generally violent and criminally active people in drug selling. Table 4.6 shows the average annual offending rates (lambda) over the three-year period for both males and females for nine types of criminal behavior. Rates have been adjusted for time at risk (on the street).[17]

For most crime types in table 4.6, group sellers were more active criminally in the three-year period than independent sellers or nonsellers, and male sellers were more active than female sellers. Consistent with their reports of higher rates of systemic violence, male group sellers in Washington Heights were more active in violent crimes. Offending rates for male group sellers in Central Harlem were greater for burglary, shoplifting, and petty larceny, but Washington Heights group sellers were more active in violent activities, such as robbery, assault, and fighting. Robbery rates, for example, averaged almost 25 crimes per year for those who committed any crimes. For nearly all crime types, lone sellers in Washington Heights were more active

---

17. Annual offending rates were calculated for each crime after adjusting for time on the street. Using monthly calendars, percentages of the year not at risk (on the street) were computed and the rates adjusted accordingly.

Table 4.6 ANNUAL OFFENDING RATES FOR NONDRUG CRIMES BY SELLING
STATUS, BY NEW YORK CITY NEIGHBORHOOD, 1986–88

Cells:
  Male rate
  Female rate

	Central Harlem			Washington Heights		
	Nonsellers	Lone Sellers	Group Sellers	Nonsellers	Lone Sellers	Group Sellers
Robbery	4.8	7.1	10.6	25.8	20.7	24.7
	3.4	2.4	8.7	12.3	5.5	4.8
Burglary	3.0	4.4	10.9	11.9	15.6	4.4
	0.5	0.3	0	3.4	0.4	0.5
Assault	1.2	2.5	6.0	0.7	10.3	10.4
	0.1	3.7	0.2	0.1	0.2	4.0
Shoplifting	31.6	23.2	58.3	25.1	28.1	32.5
	22.4	10.3	71.2	28.1	14.7	15.4
Grand larceny	13.6	17.2	26.8	23.7	20.1	31.7
	15.5	2.2	3.4	8.5	14.1	4.7
Fighting	4.0	3.1	13.5	10.7	13.0	20.1
	0.3	5.2	8.2	0.5	27.3	4.8
Petty larceny	6.4	1.7	27.4	12.7	11.5	20.6
	6.4	3.4	11.0	8.7	9.7	3.7
Prostitution/	8.2	12.6	12.3	5.7	14.3	14.3
pimping	89.3	74.6	73.4	81.2	59.9	38.0
Fencing stolen	4.9	9.1	22.2	27.4	15.4	31.8
goods	2.2	3.1	50.5	3.6	13.3	4.6

Note: Rates are annualized frequencies (lambdas) for active offenders: those reporting
at least one event during the three-year period, controlling for time on the street.

criminally than lone sellers in Central Harlem. Evidently, violence is
not specific to the context of drug selling. In Washington Heights,
where systemic violence related to drug distribution was greater and
where the social organization of drug selling was more formal, there
also was greater participation of drug sellers in violence outside the
milieu of drug selling.

Only for prostitution were female crime rates consistently higher
than rates for males. For women, one of the most dramatic impacts of
initiation into crack has been entry into prostitution (Chin and Fagan

1990). However, females in Washington Heights were less actively engaged in prostitution, especially among group sellers where incomes are higher. Complex issues surround the growth in prostitution and female participation in drug selling. First, the increasing number of female-headed households placed new demands on women to generate income. Second, the depletion of males in the 25- to 44-year age range removed some of the barriers to female participation in street-level drug selling in what was historically a male scene. Third, the demand for money to buy drugs followed the introduction and successful marketing of crack and was intensified by crack's short-lived high that compelled users to make numerous small purchases. Other factors may be implicated in the growth of prostitution, such as the coercive and violent milieu in which crack is bought and sold (Bourgois 1989; Fagan and Chin 1990; Johnson, Williams, et al. 1990), or the commodification of sex that evidently has accompanied the introduction of crack (Bourgois, 1989; Hamid, 1990).

Labor Force Participation and Income from Drug Selling

Table 4.7 compares self-reported monthly income from drug selling and work by respondents' work status. Respondents were asked to report their average monthly income in the year following their initial involvement with crack (or another primary drug). The amount earned from work and drug selling was calculated as a percentage of *total* reported income. The drug incomes reported are *gross* incomes—that is, costs of drug acquisition have not been subtracted.

The first row in each cell in table 4.7 shows the extent of labor force participation in each group, including both licit informal work and formal (taxed) wages. About one in four people were working at the time of the interview in each area. Working respondents were less likely to sell drugs in Central Harlem than in Washington Heights, especially as a part of group selling.

Income from drug selling is shown in the second row of table 4.7, and as a percentage of total income in the third row in each cell. Some "nonsellers" were actually infrequent sellers and received income from drug sales, since the standard for classification as a seller was "more than 50 times lifetime." Income from work is shown in the third row. Respondents who were unemployed or unable to work in the formal sector often still reported work income. They were involved in a wide range of informal and off-book economic activities, from babysitting to unskilled manual labor. In Washington Heights, informal work arrangements among "unemployed" or "unable to work"

Table 4.7 INCOME DISTRIBUTION BY DRUG-SELLING PARTICIPATION AND
EMPLOYMENT STATUS, BY NEW YORK CITY NEIGHBORHOOD
(monthly income)

```
Cells:
  Column % of respondents
  $ Income—drug sales
  % Income—drug sales
  $ Income—work
  % Income—work
```

	Central Harlem			Washington Heights		
	Nonsellers	Lone Sellers	Group Sellers	Nonsellers	Lone Sellers	Group Sellers
Working or in school	27.2%	23.2%	17.9%	29.9%	26.9%	31.9%
	$258	$2,015	$3,135	$50	$3,363	$4,819
	5.4%	85.6%	76.9%	4.5%	59.2%	74.4%
	$718	$635	$149	$658	$557	$742
	63.6%	39.2%	7.0%	63.0%	24.5%	19.6%
Unable to work/OLF[a]	23.0%	19.2%	18.9%	17.2%	22.8%	6.3%
	$88	$2,534	$1,986	$134	$4,576	$1,040
	5.5%	72.2%	59.7%	12.6%	74.5%	94.4%
	$297	$164	$108	$585	$427	$286
	31.0%	12.3%	15.0%	27.8%	16.89%	21.2%
Unemployed/ public assistance	49.8%	57.6%	63.2%	52.9%	50.3%	61.9%
	$328	$2,159	$3,087	$334	$2,863	$4,113
	10.2%	79.6%	64.0%	6.2%	64.48%	70.6%
	$282	$320	$316	$565	$606	$278
	29.6%	20.9%	12.1%	28.8%	25.7%	9.1%
N	261	99	95	221	145	160

a. OLF—out of the labor force.

nonsellers and independent sellers generated income comparable to
the work income earned by those engaged in formal-sector employment.

Several conclusions stand out from table 4.7. Most fundamentally,
the earnings from drug selling exceed by a wide margin the earnings
from legitimate work—whether the comparison is between the total
incomes of sellers and nonsellers or between the legitimate work earnings
and the drug earnings of sellers who also have formal-sector jobs.
In fact, for sellers, the share of income from working is so low that it

raises questions about the motivations of drug sellers for labor force participation.[18]

Impact of Drug Selling on Legal Income and Work Participation

The income potential from drug selling may be sufficiently high to discourage some people from participating in legal activities, whether in the formal or informal economies. Indeed, some economists have speculated that drug selling diverts young men (and, evidently, women) from the formal-sector labor supply in inner cities. To evaluate these issues, income and expense patterns for residents in the two neighborhoods were compared for the year before and after their involvement in their primary drug. Table 4.8 shows the income distribution by source for each neighborhood by selling status, and table 4.9 shows the respective patterns of expenditures for drugs and necessities.

Total income rose for all groups after initiation into crack (or another primary drug). Income levels were higher overall in Washington Heights, and the increases also were greater. In both Central Harlem and Washington Heights, overall income rose dramatically for drug sellers after initial involvement in their primary drug. For example, total self-reported monthly income for group sellers in Washington Heights rose from $3,859 to $5,934, an increase of 53.8 percent (table 4.8). In Central Harlem, the increase for the same group was 36 percent. The share of income from drug selling likewise increased.

Incomes also rose for nonsellers, but to a lesser extent, and in this case from increased earnings from nondrug crimes. In both neighborhoods, crime income for nonsellers more than doubled after involvement with this primary drug. This may be due to users' needs to generate money to support their increased drug consumption, or may simply reflect greater opportunities for crime once there is deeper involvement in the drug culture. Income from crime also rose for three of the four classes of drug sellers, but its percentage contribution to

---

18. The high returns from drug selling suggest that there is no apparent reason for drug sellers to work at all. Reuter et al. (1990) and others have suggested that drug sellers may remain in the licit work force to expand their contacts for drug selling. They also may use licit work as an income cushion against the uncertainties of the drug market. Legitimate work may be an escape route for leaving drug selling should the risks begin to outweigh the returns. Respondents also may view their time in drug selling as a temporary occupation, fully intending to abandon it and return to legitimate work after achieving some monetary goal (see Williams 1989, for example).

Table 4.8 MONTHLY INCOME DISTRIBUTION BEFORE AND AFTER DRUG INVOLVEMENT BY SELLING STATUS AND NEW YORK CITY NEIGHBORHOOD

Cells:	
$ Before	% Income
$ After	% Income

	Central Harlem						Washington Heights					
	Nonsellers		Independent Sellers		Group Sellers		Nonsellers		Independent Sellers		Group Sellers	
Drug sales	350	27.3	1,108	53.0	1,760	59.4	389	21.7	1,879	56.5	2,116	54.8
	253	18.5	2,196	67.9	2,887	71.7	217	9.5	3,454	69.3	4,276	71.0
Work	502	39.2	566	27.1	454	15.3	667	37.2	637	19.1	614	15.9
	404	29.6	360	11.1	247	6.1	594	26.0	469	9.0	417	7.0
Public	79	6.2	63	3.0	53	1.8	62	3.5	31	.9	27	.7
transfers	99	7.2	65	2.0	74	1.8	83	3.6	47	.9	22	.3
Crimes	143	11.2	84	4.0	385	13.0	476	26.6	389	11.7	722	18.7
	311	22.8	327	10.1	531	13.2	1,020	44.8	479	9.6	593	10.5
Total	1,281	100	2,089	100	2,960	100	1,789	100	3,326	100	3,859	100
	1,366	100	3,236	100	4,026	100	2,279	100	4,983	100	5,934	100

Table 4.9 MONTHLY EXPENSE DISTRIBUTION BEFORE AND AFTER DRUG INVOLVEMENT BY SELLING STATUS AND NEW YORK CITY NEIGHBORHOOD

Cells:	
$ Before	% Expense
$ After	% Expense

	Central Harlem						Washington Heights					
	Nonsellers		Independent Sellers		Group Sellers		Nonsellers		Independent Sellers		Group Sellers	
Shelter	113	10.6	227	15.3	123	5.1	149	11.5	293	12.3	176	7.3
	125	10.6	134	5.5	108	4.5	166	9.2	459	12.3	198	4.7
Food	89	8.7	117	7.9	181	7.5	98	7.6	168	7.1	215	9.0
	76	6.5	121	5.0	142	5.7	76	4.2	156	4.2	206	4.9
Clothing	129	12.1	205	13.8	497	20.5	157	12.1	408	17.1	735	30.7
	90	7.6	125	5.1	249	10.3	86	4.8	427	11.4	786	18.8
Drugs	323	30.4	458	30.8	580	23.9	385	29.7	965	25.8	583	24.3
	690	58.6	1,557	64.1	1,528	63.5	1,198	66.7	2,237	59.8	2,026	48.5
Child care	32	3.0	53	3.6	259	18.7	55	4.2	227	9.5	237	9.9
	28	2.4	238	9.8	128	5.3	63	3.5	473	12.6	336	8.0
Total	1,064	100	1,486	100	2,427	100	1,296	100	2,381	100	2,396	100
	1,178	100	2,429	100	2,407	100	1,796	100	3,740	100	4,178	100

overall income actually declined, owing to the much larger increases in drug income.

Both actual income and share of total income from legitimate work (formal and informal) declined for both sellers and nonsellers in each neighborhood after initiation into the primary drug. It is uncertain whether the decline in work income resulted from declining interest in work, an increase in reservation wages, or from less time being available for work after drug and criminal activities. Nonetheless, one clear consequence of involvement in crack was a decline in income from licit work and, as shown in Table 4.11, a decline in the total time allocated to licit work.

Respondents' expenditures increased with income. However, expenditures on the budget categories reported in table 4.9 did not keep pace with income gains, often resulting in large "excess" incomes. For example, a comparison of tables 4.8 and 4.9 shows that earnings exceeded listed expenses by 18 percent for group sellers in Central Harlem before crack involvement, but by 40 percent afterward. Other types of respondents showed comparably large sums of "unaccounted for" income after primary drug involvement.[19]

What becomes of this money? It is neither saved nor invested in certificates of deposit or other assets designed to yield long-term gains. Even where there is a future monetary goal for earned drug income, these goals are compromised in the day-to-day realities of survival for people in socially disorganized and economically distressed neighborhoods. Ethnographic accounts suggest that excess earnings are dispersed through family and social networks (Dunlap, chapter 6, this volume; Hamid, chapter 7, this volume), as well as through consumption and conspicuous spending. Money is given away to family members in the form of food or purchases of household goods, or as gifts of cash, jewelry, or clothing to loved ones or girlfriends/boyfriends, or is used for big purchases, like cars. Older matriarchs of intergenerational families often are the recipients of special largesse, both in recognition of past support and for preservation of a home location for organizing family logistics and emergency care.

---

19. There may be some error in respondents' estimates of their earnings and expenses. During peak periods of drug use, a great deal of money is exchanged, and accurate recall may be compromised by the consistent state of being high during these times and the spike in income and expenses. Yet, the stability of estimates within subjects when compared to monthly estimates of drug use suggests some confidence in the estimates. One other source of bias may result from selection of respondents who do not use their newfound wealth to leave the neighborhood. The sampling strategy limited respondents to those who elected to remain in the neighborhoods.

The primary increase in recorded expenditures was for drugs. Drug consumption patterns, shown in Appendix 4.B, are high for all groups. Appendix C shows changes in patterns of monthly expenditures for the year preceding and following involvement in crack. Crack generally was added to existing consumption patterns rather than used to replace other drugs (Chin and Fagan, 1990, data not shown). Increases in drug spending upon initiation into the primary drug ranged from 24 percent (for Washington Heights sellers) to nearly 40 percent for group sellers in Central Harlem.

However, the data do not resolve questions of temporal order. The increase in drug expenditures and incomes may reflect increased selling specifically to finance higher levels of personal consumption, or may reflect the independent generation of higher incomes that are then spent on drugs. Collins et al. (1985), in a study of arrestees, found that increased income facilitated increased drug consumption; in some cases an increase in crime income led directly to initiation into cocaine use. Finally, part of the increased drug spending reported by sellers may reflect money spent purchasing drug inventories for resale, not personal consumption.

Interpreting Income Changes for Drug Sellers and Drug Users

Income levels rose sharply in each study neighborhood after initiation into the primary drug, with the increases attributable principally to income earned from drug sales. However, questions remain about which people respond most strongly to the income-earning opportunities of the drug market, and whether work in drug selling substitutes for work in legitimate activities or other types of criminal activity. A regression model was used to analyze the contributions of human capital and drug and crime involvement to monthly income for the year following initiation into crack or another primary drug.[20] Log transformations of monthly gross income before and after crack involvement were performed to adjust for highly skewed distributions. Independent variables were human capital (education, licit labor force participation) and drug-crime involvement (participation in selling,

---

20. Since crack initiation in this sample was limited to the three-year period 1986–88, I did not deflate for inflation. However, for the small number of initiates to other drugs in the years preceding 1986, the failure to convert to real dollar incomes may be a source of error. The sample included 667 crack initiates and 149 cocaine HCL users who initiated their use or selling after 1982. Most of the remainder, heroin and polydrug users, initiated their drug involvement before 1980; their income reports may be systemically underestimated due to differences between nominal and real dollar incomes.

income from crime). Drug expenses were also included as a control variable to determine whether new incomes were driven by drug consumption. Additional control variables included prior income and demographic variables.

Explanatory variables were entered in blocks to test specific effects. The change in explained variance takes into account factors previously introduced; the coefficients are presented for the saturated model, while the R^2 increments assess the contributions of each block. Separate models for each neighborhood show contrasts in the factors contributing to total income. The results are shown in Table 4.10.

The models explained approximately 60 percent to 70 percent of the variance, but prior income accounted for most of the explanatory power of the model in each neighborhood. That is, current income was explained largely by income prior to initiation into crack or other drugs. Evidently, those already successful tended to remain so after becoming involved in crack or other drugs. However, the relationship between precrack income and postcrack (or other principal drug) income was stronger in Washington Heights. Demographic variables were largely unrelated to current income after controlling for previous income. Human capital did not systematically explain increases in incomes—that is, there is no evidence that better-educated individuals were more likely to raise their incomes from previous levels after initiation into crack or another principal drug.

The effects of illicit work and income on total income differ by neighborhood. Involvement in drug selling was unrelated to income in Central Harlem, but was a strong and significant predictor of income in Washington Heights. Central Harlem remained in the 1980s a poor neighborhood that was cut off from the rest of the city; this limited the size of the drug market. The stronger local economy and economic status of Washington Heights provided local buyers with relatively more money for drug purchases (see table 4.2). Also, the more organized drug-selling scene in that neighborhood (New York Times 1989c,d) and its strategic location for drug buyers from other neighborhoods (Sullivan 1991) contributed to an active drug market with a higher volume of transactions. With a more active drug market, it is not surprising that average incomes from drug selling were higher.

Working may present an opportunity cost for drug sellers in Central Harlem, and time spent at lower-wage licit work is time not available for the more lucrative returns of drug selling. But drug sellers simply may not be very good at legitimate work, resulting in a negative association between work and drug income (the major factor of total

Table 4.10 ORDINARY LEAST SQUARES REGRESSION ON TOTAL INCOME AFTER INITIATION INTO PRINCIPAL DRUG (Logged)

	Central Harlem			Washington Heights		
	Unstandardized Regression Coefficient	Standardized Regression Coefficient	R^2	Unstandardized Regression Coefficient	Standardized Regression Coefficient	R^2
Constant	4.40***			2.70		
Demographics			.030			.001
Male	.25	.05		−.28	−.05	
African-American	.16	.03		−.02	−.004	
Age	−.007	−.03		−.02	−.06*	
Prior Income			.461			.543
Total prior income ($)	.36	.37***		.70	.67***	
Labor Market Skills			.017			.004
Education	.06	.02		.02	.006	
Labor force participation	−.01	−.08**		−.008	−.04	
Current Drug-Crime Involvement			.185			.054
Involved in selling	.09	.02		.44	.08**	
Drug expenses ($)	.0002	.23***		.0002	.21***	
Income—crime (%)	−.02	−.47***		−.0009	−.07*	
Model Statistics						
F	107.74***			85.91***		
Adjusted R^2	.687			.596		

Notes: Unstandardized and standardized coefficients for saturated model, significance of T, and R^2 change for each block. Variables are entered in blocks as shown. Coefficients and R^2 change are adjusted for previously entered blocks. P(t): one asterisk (*) equals $p < .05$; two asterisks (**) equals $p < .01$; three asterisks (***) equals $p < .001$.

income). Either interpretation suggests that drug selling is an activity not well integrated with legitimate work.

Reliance on nondrug crime as an income source was negatively associated with total income in both neighborhoods. This was especially evident for Central Harlem residents (the standardized coefficient was -.47). Evidently, crime doesn't pay (as well) in that neighborhood; sellers were better off concentrating on drug transactions. In Washington Heights, drug sellers may prefer to avoid the less lucrative and (perhaps) riskier work in robbery and other crimes, so long as they can earn better incomes selling drugs.

The coefficients for drug expenses suggest that incomes rise concurrently with drug consumption. The patterns of income and expenses in tables 4.8 and 4.9 show that sellers are devoting a larger share of income to drug consumption than they did before their involvement with their primary drug. The direction of causation, however, is ambiguous: either more income is generated to support drug consumption, or increased income provides opportunities to spend more on drug consumption (i.e., there is a high income elasticity of spending on drugs). To further complicate the interpretation, a significant part of reported drug expenses may reflect "business" purchases for resale; in that case, the strong positive association could reflect the simple fact that the sellers with the highest gross incomes from drug distribution also have to spend the most on buying drugs for resale. However, Fagan and Chin (1990) found that sellers use the drugs that they sell, and that the recent portrayal of highly disciplined, abstinent young drug sellers is largely unfounded.

Effects of Drug Involvement on Labor Force Participation

The effects of the drug trade on labor force participation have been the subject of much speculation. Low-wage expectations for long-term legal employment may induce young men to turn their backs on low-paying legal jobs for the higher payoffs from drug selling (*Wall Street Journal* 1989). Organized drug selling also may be seen as a substitute form of business training that instills entrepreneurial skills. Adolescents who otherwise would be considered surplus labor are taught how to conduct business—how to buy wholesale and sell retail, keep books, pay bills, manage inventory and cash flow, calculate profit margins, and deal with competitors and unpredictable customers (see, also, Padilla 1992).[21]

---

21. Drug selling should not be thought of as full-time, 40-hour-per-week work. Reuter

Tobit analyses were constructed to determine the impact of drug selling on the respondents' degree of participation in legal work in the two neighborhoods. The dependent variable was the percentage of months of labor force participation (in formal or informal work) during the 36-month window, adjusted for the number of months on the street. Predictors were human capital and illegal work variables (criminal income, drug selling). Drug expenses were again included to test the possibility that drug use was removing workers from the labor market independent of their drug-selling activity. The results are shown in table 4.11.

Overall, legal labor market participation can be seen in table 4.11 to compete with both of its alternatives—drug selling and criminal activity. Involvement in these other activities results in less legal labor. The trade-off between drug selling and legal work is especially strong in Washington Heights. In fact, Washington Heights gives evidence of a more clearly defined local labor market along all dimensions. There is a very strong, positive relationship between years of education and the extent of legal labor force participation, indicating that drug opportunities have not preempted the work commitment of the more highly skilled. Legal labor force participation rates in Washington Heights are significantly greater for males and are lower for African-Americans. In Central Harlem, the direction of influence of all variables was the same, but several of the effects were less pronounced. In particular, the negative effect of drug selling on legal work was not statistically significant, leaving open the possibility that in Central Harlem drug sellers are recruited largely from a universe of nonworkers who otherwise might not be in the labor force at all or would be engaged in other types of crime.

In Washington Heights, the likelihood of legal work again increased with education. Drug selling was negatively associated with licit work, but drug spending was not. Thus, drug selling did appear to take workers away from the labor force, for reasons unrelated to drug

---

et al. (1990) reported that sellers typically worked three to four hours per day, and that only 37 percent sold drugs on a full-time basis. Thus, their earning estimate of $30 per hour is based only on hours worked. Although more lucrative than most blue-collar jobs, drug selling may not generate significantly more income than full-time licit work, unless other activities (like crime) can fill in the spare hours. Bourgois (1989) found that the hourly wage from drug selling, about $10–$12 per hour, was no greater than wages from licit work, and concluded that drug selling lacked tangible benefits over work. But drug sellers said that control over working hours and conditions was a significant, incalculable benefit. Bourgois provides detailed accounts of the decisions to leave licit work for drug selling. Young males weighed the nonmonetary costs in legal jobs (e.g., racial antagonism, low prestige) against hourly wages, and concluded that drug selling was preferable, despite the lack of earnings advantage.

Table 4.11 TOBIT MODEL FOR LABOR FORCE PARTICIPATION (Logged)

	Central Harlem			Washington Heights		
	Estimate	Standard Error	Probability of Chi-Square	Estimate	Standard Error	Probability of Chi-Square
Intercept	−11.66	5.31	.026	−8.16	4.62	.077
Demographics						
Male	5.57	2.13	.009	5.16	1.86	.006
African-American	−1.53	2.10	.047	−3.60	1.63	.027
Age	−0.09	0.12	.442	−0.15	0.11	.185
Labor Market Skills						
Education	5.12	1.10	.000	5.72	0.91	.000
Current Drug-Crime Involvement						
Involved in selling	−3.77	2.03	.063	−6.35	0.74	.000
Drug expenses ($)	−0.002	0.0007	.003	−0.0004	0.0003	.899
Income—crime ($)	−0.004	0.001	.003	−0.0009	0.0004	.026
Censored cases	206			213		
Noncensored cases	244			318		
Log likelihood	−1,193.7			−1,519.3		

use. However, working still appealed to the more highly educated. Drug selling apparently attracts workers with less human capital, people who might not otherwise fare particularly well in the formal economy.

CONCLUSIONS

Expansion of the drug economy through the marketing of crack created economic opportunities that were well exploited by the men and women of both Central Harlem and Washington Heights. In our sample, earnings from drug selling far exceeded earnings from legitimate work. Nonetheless, the extent to which drug selling draws well-educated or skilled workers away from legitimate work can be exaggerated (Chin and Fagan 1990; Fagan and Chin 1990, 1991). The people who benefited most from the growth of the drug economy had limited employment prospects in the formal economy prior to their involvement with crack or other drugs. They were unemployed; engaged in haphazard, informal sector work; or working for low wages prior to their entry into the drug economy. Many had a history of other criminal involvement. Their skills and mastery of illicit economic activities positioned them to make the most of the lucrative opportunities created by the expansion of drug markets, and contrasted with their limited alternative opportunities in the formal labor market.

The Paradox of Neighborhood Distress

There was a paradoxical relationship between the social and economic health of the study neighborhoods and the social organization and economics of drug selling. Although Washington Heights was less socially and economically distressed, there was greater economic impact from drug selling and more formally organized and violent drug selling activity. Incomes for both independent and group sellers were greater in Washington Heights. The drug-selling groups were more formally structured. Rates of nondrug crime also were greater in Washington Heights, particularly violent crimes.

The more active and violent drug market in Washington Heights may reflect the relatively better socioeconomic situation in the neighborhood. Washington Heights is a heterogeneous neighborhood, rich with ethnic diversity and immigrant cultures. It also is a retail drug market that serves both a local and a metropolitan clientele. The drug market in Washington Heights benefited from the neighborhood's proximity to major highways and bridges, allowing white clientele to make purchases and to quickly leave the neighborhood and city. The enormous profits of the drug trade spread to a broadly based network of working people, both white collar and blue collar.

Washington Heights sellers were active and profitable within a somewhat more upscale and diversified market. In turn, the higher profits created more extreme risks from drug selling, and contributed to more tightly defined selling territories and more tightly controlled selling organizations. For workers who lacked labor market skills and motivation, and thus had few alternative sources of income, the stakes involved in drug selling were extremely high, which contributed to the intensity of competition and conflict.

The experience of Washington Heights suggests that simply improving the social circumstances of a neighborhood may not eliminate drug markets or soften their organization. When demand for drugs is high and spans neighborhood boundaries, a less distressed neighborhood actually may have more talent (human capital) and entrepreneurial enthusiasm to populate an informal industry such as drug selling. Areas such as Central Harlem, which are socially and economically isolated, with a population that is severely distressed and shrinking, may find it more difficult to sustain a drug market that delivers substantial income gains for participants.

In Washington Heights, filling the market niche for drug products is a logical entrepreneurial response, particularly when the historical avenues to labor market participation have been truncated by the restructuring of the city and regional economy. The factors that determine the profitability and social organization of a drug market are extremely complicated. Drug sellers are suppliers of important goods and services to residents of more affluent areas (Sullivan 1991), and the vitality of a drug market in a neighborhood is bound up with the relationships within poor neighborhoods and between these areas and other parts of the city. To the extent that selling is spatially concentrated in a few areas, the interdependence of those areas with the larger city will sustain a drug market regardless of efforts to improve the material circumstances of neighborhood residents.

Higher Reservation Wages and Skills Mismatch

It is tempting to say that drug selling and associated criminal activity will raise the reservation wage of inner-city residents. However, it is difficult to calculate a reservation wage when so few local residents participate in the formal economy and when income from legal work (whether formal or informal) is so low. Since most respondents had little human capital to bring to the market place, they were unlikely to command a wage much higher than the legal minimum. The low rates of legal labor force participation imply that the local (legal) labor market did not clear at this wage rate, but whether this is due to high reservation wages by potential workers or an unwillingness of employers to hire neighborhood residents even at the minimum wage is unclear. Moreover, labor force participation rates already were low before the introduction of crack, implying that the reservation wage of inner-city residents may be high relative to formal-sector wages even when the income alternatives are "ordinary" crime or informal work.

For the people in this study, concentrated at the tail of the distribution of drug use, drug selling, and crime, there are few alternatives to drug selling that would not compromise their economic well being. For most residents, the realistic legal choices outside of the drug world appear to be a haphazard set of informal and illicit activities, occasional low-paying formal-sector jobs, public transfers, and barter exchanges.

There are other incentives to participate in drug selling. The social isolation of poor neighborhoods skews social norms, and allows the rapid spread of deviant norms and values within a closed social system. The social status of drug selling increases when few alternative success models are available, and when drug income is the primary route to gaining both material symbols of wealth and social standing in the neighborhood. Some turn to the drug industry to achieve the benefits of self-determination and economic independence, or to escape the petty humiliations and harassment faced by nonwhites in the market for unskilled labor (Bourgois 1989).

The data here are not sufficient to conclude that drug selling raises the reservation wage of many inner-city residents. What is more likely is that drug selling has an impact upon the conception of work, and the social evaluation of alternative economic opportunities. A "reservation wage" implies a more active trade-off of income opportunities than probably exists for the men and women in this study, most of whom are only marginally attached to the labor force. Their understanding of economics may reflect the polar extremes of drug income versus public transfers or low-paying informal jobs. Normal labor market considerations suggest that an active drug market will continue to attract people from the same corps of unskilled workers that currently populate this sector. Nor do the risks of drug selling—injury, death, incarceration—serve as effective deterrents to participation (Reuter et al. 1990). The risks are addressed by those who elect to participate in the drug-selling milieu: people experienced in violence and criminal activity.

Disruption of Traditional Job Networks

In the past, manufacturing jobs provided entry positions for African-Americans and Latinos on career ladders that had stable if unspectacular earning potential (Farley and Allen 1987), usually with the expectation of predictable annual increases and a cushion of health and other benefits. Manufacturing job opportunities have declined steadily in cities for 25 years (Kasarda, chapter 3, this volume). More recently, the public sector and jobs fueled by public spending (e.g., health care, social services) served similar mobility functions for non-whites entering the labor market. These jobs also have become marginal as municipal and state fiscal crises worsen. The shrinking of job opportunities has been accompanied by a changing composition of residents, which leaves inner-city neighborhoods without middle-class and strong working-class households.

Traditionally, informal social networks provided access for each succeeding generation to enter the labor market by providing information and personal contacts for young men to take advantage of job openings or union membership (see Sullivan 1989 and Anderson 1990, for rich descriptions of how such networks operated). The acute social distress in inner cities has disrupted these networks, both by the shrinking of manufacturing jobs and the changing composition of residents. As middle- and working-class minority families leave neighborhoods for better living arrangements, they take with them the social capital of their complex relationships with members of the younger generation, for whom they might have provided job information as well as role modeling and mentoring.

Without a diversity of job networks, the economic and social significance of the drug market increases. The drug market appears to be an extreme form of labor market segmentation, with vast opportunities for youth to enter into income generation in a diversity of roles, without going outside the neighborhood. Participants in drug selling are well matched both spatially and in the necessary skills for the drug economy, while lacking the skills, human capital, and job access necessary for success in the formal economy. Restoration of intergenerational job networks, as well as the creation of better-paying and accessible job opportunities, will be necessary to make formal-sector jobs a realistic alternative to drug activity.

Institutionalization of the Drug Economy

Drug selling has become institutionalized in neighborhoods like these two communities, giving rise to secondary economic markets that benefit many community residents. Such markets include the pool of casual labor that provides support services for drug selling (lookouts, renting storefronts or apartments) and the vast new market for sex. Drug purchases by white- and blue-collar customers bring cash into the community, and the funds are then distributed within the neighborhood through the secondary economy. Although most of the cash may concentrate among the upper echelons of the drug distribution system, there are obvious benefits to those in the retail network.

This development has important implications for efforts to reduce drug activity. Since neighborhood residents benefit from the secondary economic demand generated by drug selling, this undercuts efforts at formal and informal social control. Residents are likely to be less willing to disrupt drug selling when they directly benefit from it. Moreover, there are fears as to what will happen to the neighborhood if the circulation of drug money is interrupted. Until the risks of living in a drug-selling milieu are felt keenly by large numbers of residents, it may be unreasonable to ask people to act against their economic self-interest by suppressing drug activity.

Expansion of the Prostitution Industry

Prostitution was the only *new* career choice to follow crack initiation, primarily among women users and to a lesser extent among women sellers. Annual prostitution rates accelerated for those already involved (Chin and Fagan 1990). One result was the creation of excess supply in the market for sex, driving down prices (Bourgois 1989). The implications for AIDS transmission, victimization from violence, and family disruption are obvious. Why did crack have this profound impact on women?

Bourgois (1989) and Inciardi (1989) have both described the frequent sexual exploitation of women in crack houses and other crack scenes. Hypersexuality apparently accompanies crack use, at least for a time (Anderson 1990; Hamid 1990), creating a vast new market for sex, though under exploitative and humiliating circumstances. At the same time, women seeking cash to buy drugs are faced with limited choices. Their participation in nondrug crimes generally was limited to "hanging paper" (writing bad checks) and other hustles such as credit card fraud rather than violent income-generating crimes like robbery (Johnson et al. 1985). Their opportunities in drug selling also are limited. Women were a small part of the selling scene in the western U.S. described by Adler (1985). Bourgois (1989) reported that few women held important selling positions, and rarely held them for longer than six months. The crew described by Williams (1989) also was dominated by men. Compared to other drug markets, the market for crack is a coercive context, marked by high levels of violence where men hold both physical and economic power.

With limited access to the higher levels of income from crack selling, and consigned by traditional gender inequalities to lower wage-earning positions in the formal economy, women used their bodies as the primary income-generating resource available to them. Women exploited this resource that was exclusively theirs, a form of monopoly capitalism, even while being exploited. The lower rates of participation in prostitution by women sellers suggests that when this income source is available, it mitigates reliance on prostitution to generate income for drugs or other needs. Exploitation of women in such contexts reflects their secondary status in both the formal and underground economies. Often, the physical and verbal abuse and sexual exploitation is gratuitous, as described by Bourgois (1989). Women both are excluded from drug selling and, given the frequent victimization of sellers, may choose not to participate in it. The sexual exploitation of women in this context is, sadly, not surprising.

Importance of Economic Self-Sufficiency

The local drug economy seems to be a function of political decisions and economic forces that go well beyond the borders of a single neighborhood. The fate of neighborhood drug economies may depend on reversing several long-term trends. Most important is the restoration of legitimate, well-paying economic opportunities for inner-city residents. It is unlikely that the manufacturing base that sustained these neighborhoods before 1970 will be restored. A diversified local economy may, however, be developed through investments and incentives to locate businesses in the area and to maximize the recirculation of revenues among residents. This may launch other processes that can begin to replenish social capital among neighborhood residents by restoring intergenerational relationships, collective supervision of youths, and reinforcement of behavioral norms. Renewed efforts to increase the job skills and human capital of residents are also critical to increasing their salience within the formal and licit informal economies, and are likely to soften the demand for drugs that fuels the drug market. As this study demonstrates, human capital is highly associated with legal labor force participation, even among those attached to the drug community.

Epilogue: The Changing Social Context of Drug Use

Drug crises in the United States historically have been influenced by the social and economic contexts in which they unfold. The cocaine and crack crises were overlapping drug eras that emerged in the late 1970s and continued through the late 1980s. This era was marked by the confluence of several significant economic and social trends: a rapid decline in the wholesale price of cocaine amidst demand that peaked in 1985; the decline of the manufacturing sector and of licit jobs available to blue-collar and unskilled workers in inner cities; the intensification of poverty among minorities; the breakdown of neighborhood social networks; and the further widening of the income gap between whites and nonwhites, especially African-Americans.

Drug use rates were high in this era, as well. By 1980, over half of young adults (below 30 years of age) had had experience with illicit drug use. They were trained on how to smoke drugs, and could readily find sellers of illegal drugs. These young people entered the years of peak illicit drug use at a time when cocaine became widely available and economically accessible. Accordingly, this most recent drug crisis may reflect the unique social experiences and economic environment of the cohort that "came of age" during the era. This cohort fueled the demand for cocaine, while the expansion of drug markets created work and income opportunities that filled the void created by the decline of legal jobs available to young people in inner cities. The cocaine crises of the 1980s would not have been possible without these population and economic dynamics.

As the cohort that fueled the cocaine market ages, the demand for cocaine appears to be declining. There are few new initiates into cocaine use (Hamid, chapter 7, this volume). Young people turned away from heroin beginning in 1973, and it appears that young people now are turning away from crack or cocaine use after witnessing the crises of the 1980s.

We must carefully consider these interacting forces in fashioning policy responses to drug crises. It is unlikely that new drugs will be as widely accepted as was cocaine; therefore, drug selling is likely to decline as a viable economic alternative for unemployed young people. Moreover, drug selling is a regional economic activity that depends on consumers that cross neighborhood boundaries. Thus, declines in middle-class cocaine use will translate into diminished demand for drug sales in the inner city. If formal labor markets continue to decline or remain inaccessible for inner-city youths, however, residents' involvement in illegal work will continue—if not in selling drugs, then in meeting international demand for other illegal goods or services. The lessons of the crack crises should be drawn less from the pharmacology and behavioral dynamics of drug use than from the economic and social contexts that made possible the development of violent drug markets and the participation of large numbers of disenfranchised youths.

Appendix 4.A SAMPLE CHARACTERISTICS BY NEW YORK CITY
NEIGHBORHOOD

	Central Harlem (%)	Washington Heights (%)
N	452	551
Primary Drug Involvement		
Crack	61.5	62.6
Cocaine HCL	13.3	15.8
Heroin	11.7	7.3
Polydrug	9.5	9.6
Nonusers	4.0	4.7
Ethnicity***		
African-American	69.5	54.3
Non-American, African	1.5	3.4
White	6.0	8.5
Puerto Rican	17.0	23.4
Other Spanish-speaking	5.8	10.0
Other	0.2	0.4
Sex		
Male	66.2	71.3
Female	33.8	28.7
Age***		
Less than 19 years old	10.9	10.7
19–26 years	25.2	40.7
27–35 years	41.2	34.4
Over 35 years	22.7	14.2
Employment Status***		
Working	24.6	29.0
Unable to work/OLF[a]	21.2	19.3
Unemployed	54.2	51.7
Educational Attainment***		
8th grade or less	4.2	8.5
9th to 11th grade	37.6	44.8
High school graduate or GED	39.8	30.1
Some college	15.3	14.3
College graduate	3.1	1.6
Living Arrangement***		
Alone	17.3	14.3
Other relatives or family	36.3	41.7
Spouse/child	26.8	26.0
Friends	9.7	4.5
Group situation	6.0	9.3
Streets	3.8	0.5
Public facility	0.2	3.6

Note: Statistics (p [chi-square]): one asterisk (*) equals $p = .05$; two asterisks (**) equals $p = .01$; three asterisks (***) equals $p = .001$.
a. OLF—out of the labor force.

Appendix 4.B ANNUAL DRUG USE RATES BY SELLING AND WORK STATUS, 1986–88, BY NEW YORK CITY NEIGHBORHOOD

Cells:
  % use drugs
  % regular user[a]
  % hard drugs[b]
  % regular hard use
  % use needles

	Central Harlem			Washington Heights		
	Nonsellers	Lone Sellers	Group Sellers	Nonsellers	Lone Sellers	Group Sellers
	84.5	69.6	88.2	68.2	61.5	86.3
	83.1	69.6	88.2	65.2	64.1	84.3
Working	57.7	52.2	82.4	60.6	51.3	74.5
	52.1	52.2	82.4	57.6	48.7	66.7
	14.1	17.4	11.8	9.1	15.4	5.9
	95.0	94.7	94.4	94.7	90.9	100
Unable to	93.3	94.7	94.4	94.7	84.8	100
work/out of	90.0	94.7	83.3	89.5	81.8	60.0
labor force	86.7	94.7	83.3	89.5	78.8	60.0
	28.3	36.8	22.2	13.2	21.2	10.0
	94.6	93.0	95.0	89.7	86.3	88.9
	93.1	93.0	96.7	88.0	83.6	86.9
Unemployed	90.0	91.2	91.7	88.9	75.3	79.8
	86.2	89.5	91.7	84.6	71.2	78.8
	30.0	15.8	33.3	30.8	12.3	20.2

a. Use of marijuana, cocaine, heroin, or crack at least once a month.
b. Use of cocaine, heroin, or crack at least once a month.

Appendix 4.C MONTHLY EXPENSES FOR THE YEAR PRECEDING AND
FOLLOWING INITIATION INTO CRACK, BY NEW YORK CITY
NEIGHBORHOOD

Cells:	
$ Expense Before	% Total
$ Expense After	% Total

	Central Harlem				Washington Heights			
	Males		Females		Males		Females	
Shelter	160	11.6	101	13.4	203	12.8	187	18.1
	138	10.9	93	9.4	280	12.8	198	10.5
Food	122	9.5	99	15.4	121	10.5	112	13.1
	108	7.7	81	8.3	155	6.8	108	6.8
Clothing	243	17.9	180	20.4	486	20.4	204	23.0
	150	17.9	93	20.4	478	20.9	240	23.0
Drugs	494	25.7	231	19.3	631	23.6	556	21.9
	1,209	59.5	753	54.0	1,724	55.9	1,824	56.7
Child care	106	4.6	39	4.3	149	4.9	182	6.6
	125	4.1	37	2.7	226	5.0	349	6.2
Total	1,693	100	939	100	2,167	100	1,428	100
	1,998	100	1,245	100	3,083	100	2,940	100

References

Adler, P. A. 1985. *Wheeling and Dealing: An Ethnography of an Upper-Level Dealing and Smuggling Community*. New York: Columbia University Press.

Anderson, E. 1990. *Streetwise: Race, Class, and Change in an Urban Community*. Chicago: University of Chicago Press.

Belenko, S., J. Fagan, and K. Chin. 1991. "Criminal Justice Responses to Crack. *Journal of Research in Crime and Delinquency* 28 (1): 55-74.

Biernacki, P., and D. Waldorf. 1981."Snowball Sampling: Problems and Techniques of Chain Referral Sampling." *Sociological Methods and Research* 10: 141–63.

Bourgois, P. 1989. "In Search of Horatio Alger: Culture and Ideology in the Crack Economy." *Contemporary Drug Problems* 16 (4): 619–50.

Case, A., and L. F. Katz. 1990. "The Company You Keep: The Effect of Family and Neighborhood on Disadvantaged Youths." Cambridge: Harvard University, Kennedy School of Government. Photocopy.

Chin, K., and J. Fagan. 1990. "The Impact of Initiation into Crack on Crime and Drug Use." Paper presented at annual meeting of the American Society of Criminology, Baltimore, Md. November.

Coleman, J. S. 1987. "Social Capital in the Creation of Human Capital." *American Journal of Sociology* 94 (Suppl.): S95–S120.

Coleman, J. S., and T. Hoffers. 1987. *Public and Private High Schools: The Impact of Communities*. New York: Basic Books.

Collins, J. J., R. L. Hubbard, and J. V. Rachal. 1985. "Expensive Drug Use and Illegal Income: A Test of Explanatory Hypotheses." *Criminology* 23 (4): 743–64.

Cooper, B. M. 1987. "Motor City Breakdown." *Village Voice*, December 1: 23–35.

Dunlap, E., B. D. Johnson, W. Hopkins, I. Sobel, D. Randolph, E. Quinones, and K. Chin. 1989. "Studying Crack Users and Their Criminal Careers: The Scientific and Artistic Aspects of Locating Hard-to-Reach Subjects and Interviewing Them about Sensitive Topics." *Contemporary Drug Problems* 17 (1): 121–44.

Fagan, J. 1989. "The Social Organization of Drug Use and Drug Dealing among Urban Gangs." *Criminology* 27: 633–69.

————. 1990. "Social Processes of Drug Use and Delinquency among Gang Youths." In *Gangs in America*, edited by R. Huff. Newbury Park, Calif.: Sage Publications.

Fagan, J., and K. Chin. 1990. "Violence as Regulation and Social Control in the Distribution of Crack." In *Drugs and Violence*, edited by M. de la Rosa, E. Lambert, and B. Gropper. Research Monograph 103, National Institute on Drug Abuse. Rockville, Md.: U.S. Public Health Service.

————. 1991. "Social Processes of Initiation into Crack Use and Dealing." *Journal of Drug Issues* 21 (2): 313–43.

Farley, J. E. 1987. "Disproportionate Black and Hispanic Unemployment in U.S. Metropolitan Areas." *American Journal of Economics and Sociology* 46 (2): 129–50.

Farley, R., and W. R. Allen. 1987. *The Color Line and the Quality of Life in America.* New York: Russell Sage Foundation.

Freeman, R. B. 1992. "Crime and the Economic Status of Disadvantaged Young Men." In *Urban Labor Markets and Labor Mobility,* edited by George E. Peterson and Wayne P. Vroman. Washington, D.C.: Urban Institute.

Goldstein, P. J. 1985. "The Drugs-Violence Nexus: A Tri-partite Conceptual Framework." *Journal of Drug Issues* 15: 493–506.

————. 1989. "Drugs and Violent Crime." In *Pathways to Criminal Violence,* edited by N. A. Weiner and M. E. Wolfgang (16–48). Newbury Park, Calif.: Sage Publications.

Goldstein, P. J., D. S. Lipton, E. Preble, I. Sobel, T. Miller, W. Abbott, W. Paige, and F. Soto. 1984. "The Marketing of Street Heroin in New York City." *Journal of Drug Issues* 14: 553–66.

Goldstein, P. J., D. S. Lipton, B. J. Spunt, P. A. Belluci, T. Miller, N. Cortez, M. Khan, and A. Kale. 1987. *Drug Related Involvement in Violent Episodes.* Final Report, Grants DA-03182 and DA-04017, National Institute of Drug Abuse. New York: Narcotic and Drug Research.

Goldstein, P. J., H. H. Brownstein, P. Ryan, and P. A. Belluci. 1989. "Crack and Homicide in New York City, 1989: A Conceptually Based Event Analysis." *Contemporary Drug Problems* 16 (4): 651–87.

Hagedorn, J., with P. Macon. 1988. *People and Folks: Gangs, Crime, and the Underclass in a Rustbelt City.* Chicago: Lake View Press.

Hamid, A. 1989. "Incubation Times and Subsequent Use: A Comparison between Marihuana and Crack Use among Caribbean Users on the Islands and in Brooklyn." Paper presented at annual meeting of the American Ethnological Society, Santa Fe.

————. 1990. "The Political Economy of Crack-Related Violence." *Contemporary Drug Problems* 17 (1): 31–78.

Hochschild, J. L. 1989. "Equal Opportunity and the Estranged Poor." *Annals of the American Academy of Political and Social Science* 501: 143–55.

Hunt, D. 1990. "Drugs and Consensual Crimes: Drug Dealing and Prostitution." In *Drugs and Crime,* Vol. 13 of *Crime and Justice: An Annual Review of Research,* edited by James Q. Wilson and Michael Tonry. Chicago: University of Chicago Press.

Inciardi, J. A. 1987. Beyond Cocaine: "Basuco, Crack, and Other Coca Products." *Contemporary Drug Problems* 14 (3): 461–92.

————. 1989. "Trading Sex for Crack among Juvenile Drug Users." *Contemporary Drug Problems* 16(4): 680–700.

Jargowsky, P., and M. J. Bane. 1990. "Ghetto Poverty: Basic Questions." In *Inner City Poverty in the United States,* edited by L. E. Lynn and M. G. H. McGeary. Washington, D.C.: National Academy Press.

Jencks, C. 1989. "What Is the Underclass—And Is It Growing?" *Focus* 12 (1, Spring/Summer): 14–31.

Jiminez, J. Blanes. 1989. "Cocaine, Informality, and the Urban Economy in La Paz, Bolivia." In *The Informal Economy: Studies in Advanced and Less Developed Countries,* edited by Alejandro Portes, Manuel Castells, and Lauren Benton. Baltimore: Johns Hopkins University Press.

Johnson, B. D., A. Hamid, and H. Sanabria. 1990. "Emerging Models of Crack Distribution." In *Drugs and Crime: A Reader,* edited by T. Mieczkowski. Boston: Allyn and Bacon.

Johnson, B. D., T. Williams, K. Dei, and H. Sanabria. 1990. "Drug Abuse and the Inner City: Impacts of Hard Drug Use and Sales on Low Income Communities." In *Drugs and Crime,* Vol. 13 of *Crime and Justice: An Annual Review of Research,* edited by James Q. Wilson and Michael Tonry. Chicago: University of Chicago Press.

Johnson, B. D., P. J. Goldstein, E. Preble, J. Schmeidler, D. Lipton, B. Spunt, and T. Miller. 1985. *Taking Care of Business: The Economics of Crime by Heroin Abusers.* Lexington, Mass.: Lexington Books.

Kasarda, J. D. 1991. "The Severely Distressed in Economically Transforming Cities." Paper presented at the Conference on Labor Markets and Urban Mobility, Urban Institute, Washington, D.C., March.

Lanzetta, M., G. M. de Pardo, M. Castano, and A. T. Soto. 1989. "The Articulation of Formal and Informal Sectors in the Economy of Bogota, Colombia." In *The Informal Economy: Studies in Advanced and Less Developed Countries,* edited by Alejandro Portes, Manuel Castells, and Lauren Benton. Baltimore: Johns Hopkins University Press.

McGahey, R. 1986. "Economic Conditions, Neighborhood Organization, and Urban Crime." In *Communities and Crime,* edited by Albert J. Reiss, Jr., and Michael Tonry (231–70). Chicago: University of Chicago Press.

Moss, P., and C. Tilly. 1991. "Why Black Men Are Doing Worse in the Labor Market: A Review of Supply-Side and Demand-Side Explanations." Paper prepared for the Social Science Research Council, Committee on Research on the Urban Underclass, Subcommittee on Joblessness and the Underclass. New York: Social Science Research Council. Photocopy.

New York Times. 1989a. "Report from the Field on an Endless War." March 12, Sec. 4: 1.

————. 1989b. "Crack: A Disaster of Historic Dimensions, Still Growing." March 28: A20.

————. 1989c. "Selling Milk, Bread, and Cocaine in New York." March 30: A1.

————. 1989d. "Even with TNT, New York City Can't Destroy Drug Bazaars." June 1: A1.

Padilla, F. 1992. *The Gang as an American Enterprise.* New Brunswick, N.J.: Rutgers University Press.

Reinarman, C., D. Waldorf, and S. Murphy. 1989. "The Call of the Pipe: Freebasing and Crack Use as Norm-bound Episodic Compulsion." Paper presented at annual meeting of the American Society of Criminology, Reno, November.

Reinarman, C., and H. Levine. 1989. "Crack in Context: Politics and Media in America's Latest Drug Scare. *Contemporary Drug Problems* 16 (4): 535–78.

Reuter, P., R. MacCoun, and P. Murphy. 1990. "Money from Crime." Report R-3894. Santa Monica, Calif.: Rand Corporation.

Ricketts, E., and I. Sawhill. 1988. "Defining and Measuring the Underclass." *Journal of Policy Analysis and Management* 7 (2): 316–325.

Sampson, R. J. 1986. "Crime in Cities: The Effects of Formal and Informal Social Control." In *Communities and Crime*, edited by Albert J. Reiss, Jr., and Michael Tonry (271–310). Chicago: University of Chicago Press.

————. 1987. "Urban Black Violence: The Effect of Male Joblessness and Family Disruption." *American Journal of Sociology* 93 (2): 348–82.

Sassen-Koob, S. 1989. "New York City's Informal Economy." In *The Informal Economy: Studies in Advanced and Less Developed Countries*, edited by Alejandro Portes, Manuel Castells, and Lauren A. Benton (60–77). Baltimore: Johns Hopkins University Press.

————. 1991. "The Informal Economy." In *The Dual City: Restructuring New York*, edited by John H. Mollenkopf and Manuel Castells. New York: Russell Sage (published as S. Sassen).

Shannon, L. W. 1986. "Ecological Effects of the Hardening of the Inner City." In *Metropolitan Crime Patterns*, edited by Robert M. Figlio, Simon Hakim, and George F. Rengert (27–54). Monsey, N.Y.: Willow Tree Press.

Siegel, R. K. 1987. "Cocaine Smoking: Nature and Extent of Coca Paste and Cocaine Freebase Abuse." In *Cocaine: A Clinician's Handbook*, edited by Arnold M. Washton and Mark Gold (175–91). New York: Guilford Press.

Skogan, W. 1990. *Disorder and Decline.* New York: Free Press.

Spitz, H. I., and J. S. Rosecan. 1987. "Cocaine Reconceptualized: Historical Overview." In *Cocaine Abuse: New Directions in Treatment and Research*, edited by H. I. Spitz and J. S. Rosecan (5–18). New York: Brunner-Mazel.

Stepick, A. 1989. "Miami's Two Informal Sectors." In *The Informal Economy: Studies in Advanced and Less Developed Countries*, edited by Alejandro Portes, Manuel Castells, and Lauren Benton. Baltimore: Johns Hopkins University Press.

Sullivan, M. 1989. *Getting Paid: Youth Crime and Unemployment in the Inner City.* New York: Cornell University Press.

————. 1991. "Crime and the Social Fabric." In *The Dual City: Restructuring New York*, edited by John H. Mollenkopf and Manuel Castells. New York: Russell Sage.

Taylor, C. 1990. *Dangerous Society.* East Lansing: Michigan State University Press.

Taylor, D. G., R. P. Taub, and B. L. Peterson. 1986. "Crime, Community Organization, and Causes of Neighborhood Decline." In *Metropolitan Crime Patterns,* edited by Robert M. Figlio, Simon Hakim, and George F. Rengert. Monsey, N.Y.: Willow Tree Press.

Tienda, M. 1989a. "Neighborhood Effects and the Formation of the Underclass." Paper presented at annual meeting of the American Sociological Association, San Francisco, August.

_____. 1989b. "Puerto Ricans and the Underclass Debate." *Annals of the American Academy of Political and Social Science* 501: 105–19.

Wacquant, L. D., and W. J. Wilson. 1989. "The Costs of Racial and Class Exclusion in the Inner City." *Annals of the American Academy of Political and Social Science* 501: 8–25.

Wall Street Journal. 1989. "In the War on Drugs, Toughest Foe May Be the Alienated Youth," by Jane Mayer. September 8: 1.

Washton, A., and M. Gold. 1987. "Recent Trends in Cocaine Abuse As Seen from the '800-Cocaine Hotline.' " In *Cocaine: A Clinician's Handbook,* edited by Arnold M. Washton and Mark Gold (10–22). New York: Guilford Press.

Watters, J., and P. Biernacki. 1989. "Targeted Sampling: Options for the Study of Hidden Populations." *Social Problems* 6: 416–30.

Williams, T. 1989. *The Cocaine Kids.* New York: Addison-Wesley.

Wilson, W. J. 1987. *The Truly Disadvantaged.* Chicago: University of Chicago Press.

Chapter Five

THE STORY OF JOHN TURNER

Elijah Anderson

This is an ethnographic case study of the life of one struggling young black man of the Philadelphia inner city. Following in the tradition of Dollard (1932), Shaw (1930), Becker (1970), and others who used individuals' "own stories," as sociological data, this study seeks to represent cultural issues pertinent to an understanding of the black urban poor through the consideration of one individual's experience.

I met John Turner (a pseudonym), a 21-year-old black man, a week before Thanksgiving, in 1985. It was about two-thirty in the afternoon, and I was in a carry-out restaurant I regularly patronize. I had noticed this person behind the counter, in the kitchen, sweeping the floor, and busing tables, but I had not thought much about him. On this particular day, he stopped me, excused himself, and asked if he might have a word with me. I was surprised, but I said, "Sure. What do you want to talk about?" As he began relating what was on his mind, I saw that his story was relevant to more general social issues with which I am seriously concerned, and I asked his permission to tape the conversation. He consented.

John Turner was in "deep trouble" with the law. He was scheduled to appear for a court hearing in less than a week on charges that he had violated probation. He was very upset and was considering leaving town for Mobile, Alabama, where many of his "people" [relatives] lived. He said he would almost rather do this than appear "before the judge again," because he was sure the judge would send him away to prison for five years. I tried to advise him of the possible consequences of not appearing before the judge, saying he would be a fugitive from justice, in which case he would probably be hunted by the authorities; in any case, he would feel hunted. I pressed him to continue with his story.

The writing of this chapter was funded in part by the Academy of Sciences Committee on the Status of Black Americans. To protect their identity, none of the individuals in this account, except the author, are referred to by their real names.

John began with the history leading up to his predicament. He said that about two years previous, he was seeing a young woman who lived outside his own neighborhood, in a territory of a rival group of boys. Philadelphia is said to be a "city of neighborhoods," but more than this, the young men of many individual streets organize informally bounded areas into territories. Then they guard the territories, defending them against the intrusions and whims of outsiders (see Short and Strodtbeck, 1965; Short 1968; Suttles, 1972). These territories can become extensive, involving numerous other boys who then form larger corporate units that lend a certain structure to the general neighborhoods. Each neighborhood unit is responsible for the public behavior occurring within its boundaries. Members of the unit police the streets, harassing outsiders and strangers. It is not uncommon for a young man to walk up to a complete stranger, particularly a young male, and inquire about his business on the street or about who gave him permission to use these particular streets. If there is no acceptable answer, there may be a fight. The behavior of these young men has an impact on the crime rate of the respective areas; at times they commit the crime, at other times they discourage it. If they like a neighbor, they may protect him from assault; if they dislike him, they may rob his house or indicate to others that his house or car is fair game. In the area of John's home, the groups tend not to be formal, but are simply small groups of neighborhood boys who take a real interest in protecting and defending what they consider to be their turf (Anderson 1990; 1991).

Local male groups claim responsibility over the women in the area, especially if they are young. These women are seen as their possessions, at times to be argued over and even fought over. When a young man from outside attempts "to go with" or date a young woman of the neighborhood, he must usually answer to the boys' group, negotiating for their permission first. Otherwise, members of the group, including some of the women themselves, may consider it wrong to date an outsider. Women who deviate from these expectations may be subjected to social control in the form of harassment by both young men and young women. The young men come to see themselves as the women's protectors, if not their heroes.

As indicated above, it so happened that John Turner was seeing a young woman in a neighborhood adjacent to his own. The woman was being harassed by some of the young men and women of her neighborhood, and over a number of days they had been "bothering her." The young people would gather around her house, sit and stand outside, tease her and call her names. Upset, she would call John and inform him of the situation; and he would feel compelled to respond in some way. Sometimes he would go to her.

John is a high school graduate, a former halfback for the football team, and he has "done a lil' boxing." He is about 5'9" tall and weighs about 165 pounds; he is built like a prize high school football running back. He likes to dress in fashionable navy blue or dark green FILA athletic suits, designer jeans, T-shirts, jackets, and expensive, clean white "sneaks." In this uniform, he is a striking figure on the streets. At 21 years of age, John was the father of four children out of wedlock. He had two sons who were born a few months apart by different women, one daughter by the mother of one of the sons, and another son by a third woman.

John said of his own parents' relationship:

> He [father] left seven years ago, and he don't have much to do with us. That's between my mom and dad. That's them. I'm grown, now, and I try to help my mom as much as I can, 'cause I'm all she got. I'm her oldest son. My brother is just a baby. He got epilepsy. And my sister, she a woman, and she can only be so strong.

John had a reputation as a "runner [gang leader],"for "running" his own neighborhood with the help of his boys, although, at the time I met him, he claimed he had "left that life alone." As proof of his ganging days, he had a four-inch knife scar on the back of his neck, a gash left by a gunshot wound on his leg, and numerous scars on his hands and knuckles, indicating the many incidents of street violence of which he has been a willing or unwilling party. He spoke of occasions on which he had fought three and four men at a time and won.

At about eight o'clock on the night in question, his girlfriend, Audrey, who lived with her mother in the adjacent gang territory, called John and said she was being harassed by some of the young men and women of the neighborhood. John, being "a man," told her not to worry, that he would come over and see about it. Because the young men of the neighborhood had fought with him before, and with his experience of the streets, John knew there was a good chance for trouble that night. He wanted to take a measure of protection; he did "not want to be hurt again or killed by these guys." So before leaving he put his mother's derringer pistol in his pocket. He did "not want to hurt anybody, but just wanted to scare them if I had to."

At about nine o'clock that night, on the way to the home of his girlfriend, John spied a commotion on the street: police cars with flashers working, policemen and people standing around. Almost a block away, he began to tense up and instinctively ditched the pistol under a parked car.

Confronted with this situation, he expected to be stopped and frisked, and indeed he was. He cooperated. When the police demanded identification, he dutifully gave it. They asked his destination and he told them. But then a woman who had seen John throw something away spoke up: "Officer, that young man threw something under the car back there." The policemen searched under the car and found the pistol. "Is this yours?" they asked him. "Yeah," he said, "it's mine." He told the policemen that he feared he would be attacked by a group in that neighborhood, young men who had stabbed him in the neck before. He explained that he was not "out to hurt nobody, but just wanted to scare them if I had to." John figured that if he cooperated, if he were "a man about it and told the truth that they'd maybe let me go." But he also felt he had little choice; since the pistol belonged to his mother, he thought they could trace it to him anyway. "So I told the truth."

But instead of releasing him, the police arrested John, even though they "understood" he was telling the truth, that his story was plausible. It was not that unusual for a young black man in that neighborhood to carry a pistol around "for protection." John says they were impressed by his cooperation with them and by his politeness. They had determined that he wasn't the person they were looking for, but because he had broken the law, they said, "We have to arrest you." At his court hearing, the policemen appeared and even spoke on John's behalf, saying to the judge, "He's a good young man. He did what he was told, and didn't act smart."

But the judge gave John five years' probation and a $500 fine. John gave me the following account:

> I went to court by myself, with the public defender. They didn't even tell me that I had to get a public defender. When I went there, the public defender was there. He was lookin' for me. When the case came and he seen me get up, he said, "Oh, you Mr. Turner." He rushed me, rushed me through. I didn't know anything about this. This was my first time ever being locked up. I don't have a juvenile record. [This was] just like taking somebody out of college and throwing them in jail and expect for them to know what to do. I didn't know what to do, man. I didn't know I had to get a public defender. I didn't know these procedures to go through. I never been on probation, I never had to report to nobody. This is new to me, man. I could see it if I was an everyday criminal doing this as a everyday thing, but you just can't

take somebody off the street and label them and put them in an environment that they don't even know anything about. Understand what I'm saying? And you know what? I woulda' did better working by myself. He [public defender] just came at me with bullshit. And he didn't do no good but made things worse for me. He tried to get me to lie to the judge. When I told him I wanted to plead guilty, he said, "They ain't got nothing against you, they can't say it [the pistol] was yours, tell him it wasn't yours." I said to him, "Man, I'm not going in there lying. 'Cause if he find out I'm lying, I might get worse treatment than I'm gettin' now." So I told the truth. My grandmother always told me, "Tell the truth and shame the devil." Know what? I shoulda told a lie! 'Cause then I wouldn't had no probation. They couldn't a pinned it on me, 'cause he didn't have no proof. But nowadays, you tell the truth, it's just as worse if you had hung yourself, and I told the truth. I found out that my mom bought the gun in Virginia and didn't register it, so they couldn't a traced it back to nobody. They asked for the receipt for the gun, but my mom said, "Let them go on and keep the gun." They gave me a green sheet for me to come back and get the gun. My mom bring the receipt with the numbers on it and everything. My mom have it at home, now. My mom say, "I think it's best for them to keep the gun. Then there won't be no more trouble."

During the hearing John protested the sentence, saying that he had three children to support. (At that point in his life, John had only three children. By the time I met him, he had a fourth, a premature daughter who had just been born, and now he has several more.) The judge said in reply, "What am I to do? Lots of criminals have children." And John responded, raising his voice, "You're wrong, judge. I'm not a criminal! I'm not a criminal."

John was then assigned a black female probation officer who was about 27 years of age. John says that because he was unemployed at this time, he was unable to pay his fine on time, yet the probation officer held him accountable for this. Concerned about John's fine, his mother, who worked at a major pharmaceutical company based in the Philadelphia area, became involved and got him "on at her job" as a "lab technician, handling urine samples. It was the best job I ever had in my life. I was making $16,000 a year, which is pretty good for a young black man."

As he began working and bringing home a steady income, John was able to purchase and operate an automobile, date young women, and to operate more completely as a popular person within his own peer group. But during this time, his relationship with his probation officer began to sour. He claims they had something of an informal relationship, whereby if he could not appear at her office, then he would call.

She would also call him to set up meetings at his home, but when she would arrive, he might be outside in front of his house, or at times she would miss him altogether. This would go into her report along with something like "found in the street," John said.

One evening, approximately a year after his initial encounter with the law, John was stopped for a traffic violation. The policeman ran a computer check on him and found there was a "detainer" on John, that he was wanted by the police. Evidently he had not paid his fine. So the policeman arrested him, took him to jail, and booked him. By his own account, John remained in jail for approximately two weeks without notification of his family. This was during Thanksgiving of 1984, which John says was "very sad around my house since I wasn't there."

Finally he had a hearing before the judge who had originally sentenced him. The judge asked him if he was presently employed, to which he answered yes. The judge wanted to know the name of his employer and John gave the name of the pharmaceutical company. To this the judge responded, "Then you must make a good salary. Your fine is $1,300, and you must spend 13 weekends in jail." John said his probation officer did not speak up for him and remained silent during the whole proceeding. Someone from John's corporation, an observer, was in the courtroom during the proceedings, and this person told John he should appeal the judgment because he lacked counsel or a legal representative and thus was not adequately represented. John said he followed this person's suggestion, but "nothing ever came of it."

In the course of all this, his employer said he must quit his job "temporarily," until his legal difficulties were resolved. Thus, he quit his job and spent his weekends in jail, but after serving his time there was no job waiting for him and he was left unemployed. John then began looking for a job unsuccessfully for many weeks. The various places where he inquired told him they needed no help or that they would call him. As his best efforts repeatedly proved unsuccessful, he became increasingly demoralized.

Finally, after much looking, John found a job as a busboy at an Italian restaurant at the minimum wage. His duties included busing tables, mopping floors, peeling potatoes, and general "prep work" for the restaurant. In this job John was paid about $100 per week. His work shift was from 3 P.M. to 10 P.M. seven days a week. Further, his pay was reportedly irregular; his employer at times paid him on Monday, then on Friday, or he gave him $50 on Friday, then another $50 on Monday; he found that he sometimes had to argue with his boss for his pay. Also, on this job he had to endure the insults of his Italian co-workers. John said:

> These people right off the boat have no respect for blacks. They would call me nigger right on the job. They were always messing with me. Now, the boss was a good man. He liked me, and we got along, but the rest of 'em didn't give a care about me, and would call me out of my name.

John is the type of person who is used to settling and resolving disputes physically, and when the other person is "wrong," he must be made to answer to "justice." Once one of the young white men of the restaurant was riding him, so John invited him outside to "settle it in the parking lot." When they went to the lot, John began to talk and when this did not "work," he punched the other employee in the face and "busted his lip." The next day, reportedly, the boss very reluctantly told John not to take off his coat, that he was fired. John then was unemployed for a few days before the boss called him back, mainly because he was such a "good worker." But John felt that in general the people of the restaurant were prejudiced against him.

This perception made his work there very stressful, for while he wanted to lash out at people he defined as adversaries, he also had to keep the job for his family, including his mother, his sister, his epileptic brother, his girlfriend, and his children. He also needed money to pay on his fine, which he claims he was unable always to do on time, and (as indicated above) this led to other difficulties with his probation officer. Feeling trapped in his job, John didn't know what to do; he simply endured.

Because of his problems in paying his fine, John told me he had to go before the judge again, a judge who had the reputation, even among the police, "for hanging young black males." John was all but certain that the judge would send him away for five years. In an earlier encounter, he had seen the judge and the public defender "laugh at me. They don't mean me no good." At this point John had very little faith in the criminal justice system, particularly as it applied to black males.

By the time I met John Turner, he had stepped into the family role of his absent father, but he also wanted to view himself as a responsible father to his own four children and their mothers. It was just before our meeting, a little more than a week before Thanksgiving, that John's girlfriend had given birth to a premature baby girl, making him the father of four children. With the prospect of a jail term looming, he said:

I got to help out at home as much as I can. My mom, she don't have a
boyfriend, she don't have a fiance. I'm all she got. I'm her oldest male
child, and she depends on me. I'm her backbone. . . . Now, I don't mind
going to jail. I mean, I can take it. I'm a man. I'm not scared of jail. It's
my family. They need me. I make just $400 a month, and I use it to
help make ends meet for my family. I bring home every penny I can. I
can't go to jail. But I just don't know what to do now.

Intrigued by his story and wanting to render whatever assistance I
could, I offered to contact an attorney for John, while advising him
that if he fled he would be a fugitive.

I then contacted an attorney I knew, Leonard Segal, a partner in a
prestigious Center-City Philadelphia law firm, and told him about
John. I gave him John's telephone number, and he called John. After
hearing John's story, Segal told John, "Don't you worry about a thing.
You're not going anywhere. I'll take the case." Then John said, "How
much is it gon' cost me?" "Absolutely nothing," Segal replied. John
was somewhat skeptical but very happy about the prospect of real
legal assistance.

Because the case came before Segal on short notice, with two days
before the hearing, Segal had a schedule conflict and had to be out of
town on the day of the hearing. He told John that he should look out
for a female public defender whom Segal knew; that this person was
to represent John. He reassured John that he would be on the case,
but John was clearly worried and nervous. The story of John's life thus
far seemed to be about people letting him down. Thus, in this situation he expected to be let down again.

Early on Wednesday morning, the day of the hearing, John called
me to convey this discouraging news. In addition, he informed me
that Segal had asked him if he had any money, feeling that meant
Segal would want to be paid after all. I assured him that this was not
the case, that Segal probably wanted to know if he had money with
which to pay the fine, if necessary. John seemed to relax with that
explanation.

However, he needed my support and was obviously worried that
even I might not show up at the hearing as I had promised. I reassured
him, "Don't worry. I'll be there. Listen, no matter what happens, I'll
stay on the case, even if you do have to go away [his euphemism for
going to jail]."

Because of heavy traffic, I arrived at City Hall, where the hearing
was to be held, at 9:05, five minutes after the hearing was to have
begun. I rushed up the stairs to the courtroom. As I approached the
courtroom, I saw John, his mother, and others standing outside. John's

mother was about 45 years old, but she seemed tired this morning and looked much older. She was dressed in a dark green dress. Her lips were painted dark red, and her fingernails matched. She smelled of perfume.

I could see John's eyes brighten as he moved toward me. He seemed to come to life. He smiled, "Hey, Eli," and he shook my hand. I returned his greeting. John was dressed in an old parka, a "gangster cap," and boots. While I didn't think about this much at the time, his manner of dress was in the back of my mind. I wondered why he had not come to court dressed in more formal attire, and a few days later I asked him about this. His reply was, "The judge might've thought I had some money or something so I just cooled it."

As I approached, John said to his mother, "Hey, Mom, this is the professor." She looked at me with a half smile and extended her hand, "Hi, Eli. Thank you so much for what you're doing for John. His father has not done right by these kids, and I'm all alone. Thank you so much for helping us out." John's mother was somewhat familiar with me, acting as though she had known me for a long time. But she was genuinely appreciative.

After a while, I asked John about the public defender. "He's in there," he said, pointing toward the courtroom door. I had expected a female because of Leonard Segal's instructions, so I was surprised to find that John's counsel was a man. As I walked into the courtroom, John followed and pointed out a 35-year-old white man dressed in a dark gray pin-striped suit, sitting in the front of the courtroom. By now, we were standing around in the back of the room talking. The proceedings had not yet begun, and there were many other cases to be heard. There must have been about 40 people in the room. Soon the lawyer got up and started toward us.

Dressed in a brown tweed jacket with a tie, I introduced myself: "I'm Professor Elijah Anderson of the University of Pennsylvania and I'm here on behalf of John Turner. I'm very much concerned that we do all we can for him." He said, "I'm George Bramson, and I'm associated with Leonard Segal's law firm. I arrived at the office this morning and saw this piece of paper that said 'Get over to City Hall and see about John Turner.' So I'm here."

I was very happy to see the lawyer there. But he gave the impression that he felt he had better things to do than spend his morning defending John Turner. After talking with him for a few minutes, it became clear that he was very pressed for time. He kept looking at his watch and he mentioned he had a deposition to take at 10:30. It was now 9:30, and I became concerned that he might not have time to see

John's case through this morning. Moreover, I gained the distinct impression that Bramson was not comfortable defending John Turner.

As Bramson and I talked, the others demurred, leaving for seats nearer the front of the room. Bramson and I spoke about "the situation" of the courtroom and the likes of the people here. I got the impression that Bramson was very ready to assume that everything was all John's fault. He didn't say it, but he strongly implied that John was irresponsible and he expected me to agree with him, which I did not. But I didn't say so because I felt John's case was compromised enough; the last thing I wanted to do was to alienate the attorney. Bramson said, "It seems that John doesn't listen to people, and he's failed a number of times to fulfill his probationary obligations." My view of John was more sympathetic. I felt he was a somewhat confused young black man in trouble, and to some extent a victim of his circumstances. Although not entirely blameless, he was a person who needed a chance and a helping hand of support; he was like a fly stuck on flypaper, and the more he struggled to get off, the more stuck he seemed to become. But the lawyer's view seemed hardened.

Finally I said, "Do you think the judge will lock him up?" "Well, I don't know. A lot of it's up to his probation officer," he said, nodding toward the front of the room. I looked at her and asked, "Have you tried to talk with her?" "Yeah, and she's really against him," he said. "Think it'll do any good if I speak with her?" I asked. "You can try, see what happens," he said.

With that I went up to her. She was sitting on the front bench on the righthand side; Bramson had been sitting at the left front. As I approached, she was reading a newspaper. I looked down at her and said, "Excuse me, may I have a word with you?" I introduced myself and she offered a friendly smile and extended her hand, which I shook. "I'm here on behalf of John Turner, and I'm trying to do all I can for him. Can we talk?" I proposed. But with the mention of John Turner's name her expression changed completely as she coolly shook her head from side to side, and returned to her paper. Barely glancing at me, she said, "It's out of my hands now. It's up to the judge." She didn't look up again. I left and returned to Bramson. He said, "Well, you know, a lot depends on her. My plan is simply to argue for a continuance so that when Leonard Segal returns he can take it from there." That left me wondering what would happen and fearing the worst. We waited.

At 9:30 the judge had yet to arrive. Then we got word that he would be delayed and another judge would sit in his place. Bramson was cheered by this, for there was a good chance that the new judge would not be as arbitrary as the original "hanging judge." Meanwhile, a number of other cases went before ours. And we waited. Bramson mentioned that there was a good chance we would be able to get a continuance, if not some resolution of the matter. The large courtroom was abuzz with people. We sat off to the side of the room, reading newspapers, drinking coffee, and making small but quiet talk.

I looked around at the people sitting in the courtroom. On the other side of the room from us was John's probation officer, expressing surprising distance from John and his mother. Near the bench sat a young black man in handcuffs with two white sheriff deputies on either side of him. I wondered what he was here for. I saw middle-aged black women sitting around the room, possibly the mothers, aunts, and other relatives of the accused persons. I decided to go for a cup of coffee. In the hallway another young black man, his hands cuffed behind him, was being led by two white deputies. The picture had an eerily racial connotation, pointing to whites as the privileged and righteous and blacks, particularly young males, as unprivileged and wrong. Returning with my coffee, I spotted yet another young black man in handcuffs being marched down the corridor by two white deputies. I took my seat next to John. He looked worried. His mother looked worried. I wondered whether John would soon be in handcuffs between two white deputies.

Finally, at 10:30, the acting judge called John Turner. I asked Bramson if I should approach the bench with them. He said, "No, but give me your title again," and he made a mental note of my title and affiliation. "Sit tight, and I'll use you as a character reference in my appeal." Bramson, John, and his mother approached the bench. From the other side of the room, John's probation officer rose and moved toward the bench.

Bramson presented John Turner's case, asking for a continuance of the case until a time when Leonard Segal could take it. The judge looked over at the probation officer and said, "And what do you think of that, Ms. Johnson?" She replied, "No! No, your honor. This is his fifth time for messing up. No." (Actually this was his third time before the judge.) She was adamant. The judge concurred: "We'll have to wait for Judge Hoffman. He'll be in later this morning." Those gathered before the judge dispersed. Bramson approached me, saying, "Holy cow, you may as well get ready to spend the whole morning here." He was perturbed, for it meant missing his scheduled business for the morning. Yet he felt constrained to be there since his boss, Segal, had directed him to come. He left to make phone calls to rearrange his day. I was very grateful he planned to remain. I made my own phone calls. Then we waited and waited, watching other cases pass.

Finally Judge Hoffman himself arrived, and right away he began living up to his reputation for highly unconventional behavior on the bench. For instance, on this day, right before John's case, he called one man who was at home in his sickbed and accused him of being absent from court only because of the upcoming Thanksgiving holiday. He made a big show of this, and spectators in the courtroom were laughing at his antics. Bramson chuckled but also shook his head in apparent rejection of such behavior in a judge.

Finally the judge called John Turner. Again Bramson, John, and his mother rose and walked to the bench. The probation officer joined them. The performance this time was completely unexpected. The judge seemed very respectful to John's mother. "What a lovely mother you have, Mr. Turner," he said, nodding appreciatively. The lawyer, Bramson, made his appeal, but the judge rejected it out of hand, saying it was unnecessary. He said, "Young man, I'm going to give you a new probation officer. Now, I want you to report to your probation officer weekly and pay your fine on time. You must pay $100 per month. Now, if you don't do this, you're going to have to see me again. I don't want that to happen. You do as you are told, and everything will be fine," he lectured. The judge seemed nice and very different from what I had been led to expect. "All right, you may go now," he said, banging his gavel.

I wondered about the meaning of all of this. My feeling is that if John had had an ordinary public defender, the case probably would have been handled more unsympathetically than it was. In the present context, the judge may have been impressed, and to some degree sanctioned, by the lawyer from a prestigious Center City Philadelphia firm. A closely related issue is that of moral authority. Young black men caught up in the criminal justice system tend to have little, and those representing them may even feel compromised, morally if not politically, in the quest for effectiveness on behalf of their clients. Faced by a regular public defender, the judge may have felt in fuller control of the situation because public defenders negotiating the local court system may be constrained, and even controlled, by a powerful judge. In this situation, social stigma may amount to a legal disadvantage (Gottman 1963).

When the hearing was over, at 12:30, John's mother, Bramson, John, a few others, and I all felt very relieved at the outcome. We met in the corridor, and the lawyer began to lecture John, reiterating some of what the judge had said. John listened attentively and nodded his head in agreement. His mother was also attentive. We then thanked the attorney, said our goodbyes, and dispersed.

John returned to work at the Italian restaurant/carry-out, and his employer welcomed him. In many ways John was a very good worker, reliable, punctual, and honest. On occasion, to keep up with him, I would visit the carry-out and observe him there, mopping floors, busing tables, or preparing food. He would give me the latest on his situation, telling me about his desire "to do better in life" and saying how grateful he was that I had helped him out in his time of need. I was moved when he told me he had prayed and thanked God that I had come into his life and helped him. He said, "I didn't think people did that anymore."

As time passed, John appeared to be getting on fine, except he seemed always to be working. His fine was $100 per month, and his salary was not much more than $400. With this money, he was expected to help his mother, which he was very proud to do, and contribute to the support of his four children by three different women, which he did in the form of irregular small payments to their mothers. His employment at the restaurant did not include benefits of any kind. And John said he worried a great deal about what would happen if one of his children had an accident or came down with a serious illness. Because he made an effort to support his children financially, he conceived of himself as a responsible father; he simply wished to make more money.

Hence, John began actively looking for a better job, searching seriously but to no avail. In time, he concluded, "It's hard out here for a young black male. I'm telling you." Repeatedly, prospective employers would allow him to put in an application but would never call (Kirschman and Neckerman 1991). As this was happening, John was facing increasing tensions with his fellow employees. He complained that they would sometimes pick on him and taunt him "because they know I can't fight back. I need this job and they know it. They know I won't hit back, we do argue a lot." Although John had problems with his co-workers, he got along well with his boss, the proprietor of the restaurant, who said of him: "Yeah, John is a good worker. He's all right. He's just young and he has something of a temper. But he's a good worker. He always comes on time. He listens to me. I like him. He's a good boy" (see Anderson 1980.)

Seeing that John was having such a difficult time, I thought I would look into the matter and see if I could help him find a better employment situation. I contacted Curtis Hardy, a 60-year-old black union steward at a hospital in West Philadelphia whom I had known for about five years. Curtis is married and has three children, two of whom have graduated from college. Arriving in Philadelphia from North Carolina some 25 years ago, Curtis now lives in Germantown, a racially and class mixed area of the city. After rising to union steward he has a real sense of accomplishment on his job. For him, the work ethic is very important, and he has placed great emphasis on it in raising his children.

Approaching Curtis about John's situation, I told him I knew a young black man who badly needed a job. I mentioned John's difficulties and said I thought he needed a break. But Curtis seemed hesitant. He said, "I been burned too many times now." I persisted, trying to make a case for John. I told him John was 21 years old, was supporting four children out-of-wedlock, was well built physically, and was a good worker. I told Curtis that the new job might be a real turning point in John's life. Instead of $3.50 per hour, he would be earning $8.50, and he would experience a kind of job security he had never had before, not to mention excellent dental and health benefits for his children. After a while, Curtis was still skeptical but relented and said, "All right, tell him to go to the union hall on Tuesday and look for Joe Harris. Say I sent him. And tell him not to mess me up."

I was very pleased, but I noted Curtis's reluctance and his concern about being "messed up." Could such concerns be important in some way to the noted lack of networking among black people today? What did he mean by having "been burned too many times?" It was clear that I was asking him to vouch for someone he believed to be at risk.

It may be that black people who sponsor someone like John Turner are concerned on at least two levels. On the one hand, because of the peculiar history of race in our society, they may sense their hold on their own position to be somewhat tenuous. They themselves have had to wage a serious and often fruitless campaign for the full trust of employers and fellow workers. If one is to be sponsored on the job, one must be fully trustworthy. On the other hand, there is the twin concern that another black person might easily "make you look bad." Curtis, as a union steward, was not concerned so much with losing his job. But he was concerned about being "messed up," which for him has much to do with looking bad to oneself or others, particularly relatively powerful whites on the job. In response to these insecurities, black men such as Curtis tend to husband their resources and are usually extremely careful when recommending other blacks for jobs.

John was thrilled to hear about the prospect of getting a good job. He was eager to go to the union hall, even though it was across town and he lacked transportation. He was punctual. He spoke with Harris, as Curtis had instructed, and was quickly signed up. It was now a matter of a wait of possibly two weeks (at the most) before he would be hired, and he would definitely be hired; Curtis had said so and John had faith in my word.

But a week later, I went by the restaurant/carry-out where John worked and asked for him. His co-workers said, "He's in jail." I was shocked. "What happened?" I asked. "Oh, he beat up his girlfriend," one man told me. John had been calling his employer, trying to get bail money, but to no avail. I didn't know what to think. After a few days, I phoned John's home in hopes of getting information about him. To my surprise, John himself answered the phone. I said, "John! I heard you were in jail. What happened?" "I was in jail," he said. "I just got out." "What happened?" John told me:

> Well, see, this girl, the girl who's the mother of my one son, Teddy. See, I drove my girlfriend's car by her house with my other son (by another woman) with me. I parked the car down the street from her house and everything. So, I took John, Jr. (his son) up to the house to see his brother, and we talk for awhile. But when I got ready to leave, she and her girlfriend followed me to the car. I got in the car and put John in. Then she threw a brick through the window. Glass was flying every-where. My little son coulda got cut by it. So, I got out of the car and went around and slapped the shit out of her. She knew better than that. I didn't really beat her, I just slapped her. Then she went home and told her momma that I beat her up in front of her girlfriend. So then her momma got all hot and called the cops, and they came and got me. They locked me up for four days, Eli. It's a trip, Eli, you got to see that place. We got to talk about it. There were like 16 guys in one cell, all black guys. It's a shame, man. I ain't no criminal, I don't belong there. It's terrible. I think I got this bad cold from being in there. (He was currently suffering from the flu.) But then my mother talked with her mother, told her what really happened, and then her mother under-stood. So, she talked her daughter into dropping the charges. So they let me out. But I'm out now, Eli. I'll tell you about it. Oh, Eli, the hospi-tal called me. I'm supposed to start work on Monday.

I congratulated him on the prospect of his new job, but I began to be a bit apprehensive, having second thoughts about John and all I was trying to do for him.

Within a week, John was hired as a janitor at the hospital. He was an enthusiastic worker at his new job. Curtis liked him and began taking him under his wing, showing him the ropes and introducing him to the work culture. John told me that when he first met John, Curtis had lectured and warned him:

Now whatever you do, don't mess up. Good jobs are hard to come by, and you know this is a good job. You must keep your nose clean, do as you're told, come to work on time, and everything will be all right. You'll be on probation for the first 30 days, and if everything checks out, you'll be in the union. You'll be set. Do what your supervisor says, but the main thing is to do your work. If you have any problem whatsoever, come and see me. Your professor's got a lot of faith in you, boy. He thinks a lot of you. Now, don't mess him up. Don't mess him up.

After two weeks at his new job, John was a big success. When I asked Curtis for a report, it was glowing: "Yeah, he doing alright. He's a good worker, works a lot of overtime. He's always on time, do as he's told. Uh-huh, he's a good worker."

After five weeks on the job, John had a stellar work record, a fact of which he was very proud. He passed his period of probation and was admitted to the union. Getting into the union was an important milestone in John's life; he had often spoken of how good his life would be when he got into the union. "The union" had some sort of mystical appeal to John; he had never been a member of one, and he associated it with real power, independence, and job security.

I didn't see John for almost three weeks after that, and I assumed things were going well in his life. But then one night at 10:00 I received a telephone call from him. I was immediately concerned because he normally went to work from 4:00 P.M. until midnight.

"Hey, John, what's up?" I asked.

"I'm in trouble."

"What happened?"

"They tryin' to put me in jail."

"Who? What?" I asked, trying to catch up with him.

"I got home a couple days ago, and my mother hands me this piece of paper saying I have to report at 3:30 that day at the courthouse, so I did."

"What's the charge?" I asked.

"I didn't pay my fine. The judge wouldn't listen to me. And my probation officer acted like he didn't know me," John replied.

"Well, have you been making your meetings with your probation officer?" I continued.

"Yeah, I been making every meeting, once a week."

I suggested we get together and talk at the Broadway Restaurant, located in the heart of the black community. We met there. John showed up with Lionel, his half-brother whom he had found out about from his father only two years before. I had met Lionel about four months earlier.

We sat down and began talking. John was very depressed. He seemed not to understand the charges against him. He repeated the story about his mother's presenting him with the court order, the way the judge treated him unsympathetically, the way his new probation officer (a person with whom he thought he had a good relationship) was indifferent to him in front of the judge.

"Cause I didn't pay my fine, the judge said to me 11 to 23 months in jail," said John.

"Oh, no!"

"I begged him not to do it, that I would try to come up with the money, some way. Then he came down to six months in jail. He said that by not paying the fine that I was "playing with the court." I told him that I was trying to take care of my family and my kids. I told him I just didn't have the money. So he told me six months and gave me two days to report for incarceration. He said the best thing I could do now was to come back with some money, and if I do that then I might not have to go to jail. Man, I don't want to go to jail."

"Have you been paying on your fine at all?" I asked.

"Yeah, I paid $50, but me and my probation officer made a deal. He told me that I could pay what I could pay, and they couldn't send me away as long as I didn't have the money to pay," said John.

"But, John, you're making $8.50 an hour, you work at least 40 hours a week plus overtime. You mean you couldn't pay some of your fine?" I was incredulous.

"Well, I'm trying to help my mother out. I'm trying to give money to my kids. And I been putting some money away in case something happens. My kids. I'm saving money for their college education," said John.

"Well, John," I said, "if you don't pay your fine, you could go to jail. And if you're in jail, you won't be around to help your kids out. These people [the courts] mean business. They're serious."

John simply held his head in his hands and looked tired and sad. Lionel then backed me up, saying, "Man, why didn't you pay your fine? I don't want to see you go away. But there ain't no justice downtown, not for no black man. You got to do what they say. You shoulda paid it."

Looking forlorn, John said, "I took him [the judge] $200, and I told him I would try to get the other $1,100. It's the money for my kids' college education, but I'll take it out [of the bank]. And he [the judge] told me that if I pay my fine, then maybe I won't have to go to jail. So I'm gon' get the money. Eli, I don't want to go to jail. I got a real chance, now. The best job I ever had, and don't wanta blow it." We soon left the restaurant, and I drove Lionel and John to their respective homes.

One important consideration here is the manner in which money is spent by a person in John's circumstances. Money seems to disappear. With money, John becomes an important figure to his friends and family members. He helped his mother with her household bills. He took his girlfriend out, he bought shoes for his children, he loaned money to his friends; he simply ran through a significant portion of it. The more money John made, the more places he had to spend it. At the same time, he tried to hoard it or put a portion he thought he could afford away. And instead of paying his fine, John was saving this portion of his money at the local credit union; he had accumulated at least $1,300 there. Defending his behavior, he said he wanted to have money "in case something happens" to his children. If John, Jr. "hurts himself and has to go to the hospital, I want to be able to pay them *cash* money." When I asked about his medical benefits at work, he said, "They just began after I got into the union [a month after he began working]."

John, as I mentioned before, has considered himself the man of the house since his father left home seven years before I met him. In taking over his father's role, John presents himself as very responsible. He feels obligated to help his mother and siblings and to give his mother a portion of his money. When he has more, she gets more. A similar principle operates where his children are concerned. To meet this responsibility, he takes cash to his various "girlfriends" who are mothers of his children. When he buys shoes for his children it is an action wrought with symbolic meaning, in a small measure fulfilling his role as father and provider.

The next day, John took the $1,100 to City Hall. His understanding was that if he brought the money down, he would not have to go to jail. But in reality, the judge had only said he would consider his case with new information. There was no guarantee, but a paid fine was to be a positive development. However, after paying the money, he was locked up, placed in jail for six months. He called me that evening and said, "I'm in jail. I need a lawyer." He said the judge said he now needed a "private attorney" to "file a petition for early parole" and the judge would consider it.

As I thought of John's predicament, I wondered about his relationship with his probation officer. Shouldn't the probation officer have been monitoring the situation more closely? John and the probation officer seemed to have something of an informal, if not arbitrary, relationship. His probation officer was now a 30-year-old black male who seemed, at least initially, to be supportive. John could call him, and they could talk. And John said he met him at all the appointed times. But when the problem of not having paid the money arose before the judge, the probation officer became very firm and formal. John said that at the hearing the probation officer ignored him and "acted like he didn't know me." The probation officer failed to speak up for John and in general behaved in a manner contradictory to their relationship, or at least to the one John thought they had.

Could it be that the probation officer was trying to protect himself because of his sense that such "informality" with a client might compromise his own position of employment? On the one hand, it would seem that this informality would be supportive of certain humane goals of probation and would allow the probation officer to press John on the matter of his fine. On the other hand, this relationship could be considered irregular by "the system" and thus could result in disciplinary action for the probation officer. People like John—low-income black males in trouble—generally have a very low status in the minds of those staffing the system. Black probation officers, in particular, may feel that it is especially important to distance themselves from such persons, who are defined as outcasts. In a significant way, the problem could be that John's probation officer was only a class removed from him. He was familiar with the likes of John and had little time for "people like that." Equally important, he knew where such people fit and what they mean in the culture of the local court system. When confronted by this system, the probation officer was likely to look out for himself first. A person, color notwithstanding, far removed from John's world may be able to be supportive of him. But a black person very near him in the class structure may feel quite threatened by him. This scenario becomes all the more complicated because of the probation officer's desire to be of assistance to a "John." Yet he found this desire difficult to realize and was left being inconsistently formal and informal. In a tight situation such as that of the courtroom, his primary concern was with his own employment situation; he protected himself first.

The probation officer's concurrent desire to help John was indicated to me in a telephone conversation I had with him. After learning my identity, he was very interested and helpful. He gave me various pieces of information on the deal made between John and the judge and attempted to "collude" with me against the judge. Knowing that I was working to help John retain his job, the probation officer advised me:

I want you to know this: when John Turner was released to make arrangements with his employer for his stay in jail, he didn't tell them he
was being incarcerated. He told them he was going to have an opera-
tion, and so he was going to be out for two weeks. So you shouldn't go
back and tell his employer that he's in jail.

In this way, he tried to be helpful and ended by saying, "If there is
anything else I can do, let me know." I took him up on this and later,
after John was released from jail, I sought a second interview with
him. The following interview with the probation officer supports and
expands the foregoing analysis:

When I first met John Turner he lied to me. He told me he was in to see
me a week earlier and that we had discussed something. I caught him
in a lie. He turned me off right then and there. From then on, I did not
feel like going out of my way for him, and I will and do go out of my
way for some others. I supervise 150 people, and he is only one case. I
told him that if he didn't pay his fine that he was going to be incarcerated. No, I didn't hold hands with him and try to walk him through the
system. There are guys I will do that for—they're older, they're the
ones who respond. The younger guys are arrogant, and they think the
world owes them something. The older ones know better, and I feel
better about helping them.
    And the thing is, this guy knew that he was wrong. He knew about
this judge's reputation. He even told me about the judge; he said the
judge is crazy. So he knew better. He's a self-directive person, arrogant
and manipulative. He thinks it's all his show. He felt he was justified in
carrying the weapon, since he'd been attacked by those guys, and that
he shouldn't have to pay the fine. He wanted to get by, that's all. He had
a lot of opportunities to pay. I mean he could have paid something, $10,
something symbolic. But he didn't pay anything. And when you see
him, he's wearing gold chains and nice clothes, so he can't say he
didn't have the money. Since he came before the judge all those times
and still had not paid his fine, the judge just got fed up. He felt John Turner
was not taking him seriously, especially when he came up with $1,300
overnight. When he locked him up, the judge felt he had the last laugh.
    Toward the end, we became friends. We talked more, and once I
walked his girlfriend to the train to show her how to get out of town.
We talked, and he wanted to have dinner, but I said no. I didn't think
we should stretch it out. But we reached an understanding; he knew he
was going to jail. To people like him, though, jail is no big deal. They
go to jail, sit around and play cards; they don't mind so much. They're
not afraid of jail, and that worries me. Going to jail for them is not the
same as it is for me, or for you. I got a nephew in prison right now, and
he tells me about the life there. Alcoholics sitting around getting high
in jail; they make their own stuff right in jail. He wanted me to bring

him drugs, can you believe that? I still live in the black community. I want to get away from all riff-raff, but I'm just not able to afford one of those big mortgages yet, ha-ha. I've got 17 nephews and nieces, because I got so many brothers and sisters. And I try to look out for them. But frankly, I'm afraid of some of these younger guys, what they'll do to people like me and you. They don't care, don't worry about jail. They'll take you out of here.

After three months of incarceration, John, with the help of another private attorney I found for him, was allowed to leave prison on a work-release program and he returned to his job at the hospital.

Over the next year, I periodically talked to Curtis to see how John was doing. He would tell me that John was doing all right, coming to work, doing his job. But at a certain point I found out from John that Curtis and his boys were giving him (John) a hard time on the job. This was interesting because so many of the men who worked as janitors were solid, working-class black men who were imbued with the work ethic, went to church, were family men, and they were reacting to the insertion into their group of a person who threatened their values. In a sense, John Turner was an interloper, and because of this, and because he was considerably younger than the other men, he was someone to be socialized, to be "brought along" and shown the error of his ways. These men had great misgivings about John's many women, his babies, his cavalier attitude toward taking care of them. And John continued in this behavior and by now had several more children. In fact, a boy such as John can take a certain amount of pride in having babies. It suggests virility, manliness. According to the street, you are quite a man. But in terms of certain other working-class values, you are irresponsible, and Curtis and his men prided themselves on being responsible, even to the point of being conservatively responsible. So when they see the problems of the street—the drugs, the crime, the violence, and so on—they are ready to blame the people who engage in these behaviors.

Thus, when given the opportunity, these people will often attempt to reform the John Turners of the world. They do this not in a violent way but often in ways that can wound emotionally. The men John worked with would joke with him, make fun of him, kid him about his women and children, all in an attempt to shame him into behaving in the right way, to "bring him along." And Curtis, even though he was trying to be the "old head" and help him, began to "put his business in the street." For example, the men would be standing around getting ready to go to work and women would walk by. The men would make appreciative murmurs about them among themselves, and one day Curtis said to John so that everyone around could hear, "You'd better keep that thing in your pants. You can't take care of the ones you've got now." All the guys started laughing at that, but John felt very bad; he felt his business had been put in the street. This kind of thing continued to happen from time to time, and eventually John got tired of it.

At the same time, the streets were beckoning. John wanted to make more money. He wanted to be a hustler: He had already been a gang member, so the transition to street life was paved for him. And he wanted to show the guys at work that he didn't have to put up with their taunts. So one day he quit. He gave no notice; he simply didn't show up for work. After that I lost contact with him for over a year, but I did talk to Curtis and some of the other men, and this story came out. They did not admit to their part in so many words (they claimed he didn't want to work), but in conversation it came out that they had been ribbing him, trying to socialize him, trying to defend themselves from the likes of him.

In addition, the mothers of John's children had begun making demands on him. When he acquired a steady income and excellent benefits, several of them tried to legalize their claim on him or, as people in the community call it, they "went downtown and got papers on him." This played a part in souring him on his job. Another factor was that his mother, to whom he was so tied, had left Philadelphia and gone South, and he needed to be able to visit her. So he summarily quit his job, and I lost touch with him.

About a year later, however, I ran into him on the street. We shook hands, he said how happy he was to see me and that we had to get together because he had so much to tell me about what had been happening with him. So we arranged to meet at a restaurant. At that meeting we started out talking about various things, and 10 minutes into the conversation he revealed that he had dealt drugs but that he had given it up. I asked him, "When did you quit?" "Two weeks ago," he said. I was rather taken aback by his lifestyle, and began to wonder what was going on. I did not, however, act shocked or offended, because that would have scared him off (although I did wonder what he thought of me, the proper, decent professor, listening to this account of the low life), and he went on to tell me about the life of a drug dealer. He described crackhouses; lives destroyed by drugs; people selling everything, including food stamps for their children, to buy drugs; crack whores who spend their days prostituting themselves for a high; people ringing his doorbell at all hours of the day and night, desperate for crack; the large amount of money he made; the cars he bought; the valuable things people gave him for a $10 capsule of crack; the way he was the king of the neighborhood. At the same time, he suggested that he was a humane dealer and in fact was often helpful to victims of addiction. He told me of one woman who gave one of the boys who worked for him all her food stamps for some drugs, and when he found out about it, he searched her out and returned half of them so she could feed her child. He said the drug dealing couldn't really "take" with him because he didn't have the heart for it. To be a successful drug dealer "you have to be cold and hard and uncaring," and he could not be that way.

So John was ambivalent about this life, which I guess was why I was attracted to him. He seemed to care about the right things, yet he was trapped in his environment to the extent that he was somehow drawn back to it even when provided the opportunity to escape. When I was first getting to know him, these glimmers of hope, of corrigibility, that he displayed now and then spurred me to want to help him out. I felt that if he only had a break, he could make it. But over time, as I got to know him better and better, much of that feeling began to dissipate because he never seemed fully committed to improving himself. Having been given several opportunities, the responsibility was more and more on him to help himself; yet, he did not respond to these opportunities. This caused me to be less and less interested in helping him; I became increasingly disappointed by his behavior, but I still had hope for him.

An interesting aspect of this situation is the way in which John saw me. Compared to the ways of the streets, I played the role of a chump. Because I befriended him, I'm naive. But he was ambivalent about this because even though I am a university professor—I've made it— I could still talk his language and so I had a connection to his background. I was thus a puzzle to him, but he was ready to resolve this puzzle in a way that would benefit him. Even though he saw me as naive, he knew that I was also very helpful to him. To keep me interested in helping him, he had to paint himself in the right way. So, for example, he pointedly talked about going to church, about wanting to be a hard worker, about taking care of his family, about saving his money for his children's college education. All these statements, so he thought, would resonate with me and connect him, in my mind, with the "great middle-class tradition." Some of this talk was, I believe, sincere, but some of it was probably game-playing, calculated to shape my opinion of him and maintain my interest in helping him.

We spent a long time talking. He told me about his life over the past year, about going down South to stay with his mother, working at a construction job there, trying to help his mother out, and then about coming back to Philadelphia and working as a drug dealer, and why he gave up selling drugs. Part of the reason he stopped, he said, was that he saw death. So many of his friends had been killed or were under pressure from people in the neighborhood. He was also bothered by people coming to his house at all hours and by what drugs had done to decent people he had known growing up. He talked about girls he had known as a teenager who had been very picky about the boys they allowed near them, but who now would have sex with anyone just for a high. I think a part of him was genuinely confused and even demoralized by the things he saw going on around him, and he saw his role as a drug dealer as somehow incompatible with certain elements of decency that he genuinely aspired to. So even though he was caught up in this life, and liked to present himself as a tough young man, it was clear that he was mentally torn. Even as we were sitting in the restaurant, he waved to a friend of his who drove by in a Bronco, someone who was probably a drug dealer. His ambivalence cuts both ways and this makes it hard to trust him.

John, after all, was a gang "runner" or leader and his ties to the former gang members remain very strong. He was in many fights with them, which solidified the loyalty among them and also instilled bravado in him as an important aspect of his identity. These boys had no doubt also become drug dealers, and they considered him one of them. Because of these connections, I was incredulous that John could get out of the drug trade just like that. When he said, "I quit two weeks ago," I was highly suspicious. My sense is that it is very difficult to get out of the drug business once you get into it.

At any rate, as we were leaving the restaurant, John asked if I could lend him $5. Now this was after telling me how much money he made selling drugs, how many articles of leather clothing people have given him, how much jewelry. So what did this mean? If he really had no money, maybe he really did quit. Something must have scared him, or intimidated or provoked him to the point that he decided he had to get out. I gave him the $5, but that was not all he wanted. He also wanted his old job back. He wanted me to go see Curtis and convince him to give him his job back. I said I would do what I could, but I had no intention of appealing to Curtis again. I thought that since I had given him the $5, I wouldn't see him again for a long time.

However, a week later he called me. "What happened? What did you do? How did it work out?" he wanted to know. I replied, "I haven't found anything yet, but I'll keep trying." I was trying to stall him. Then one weekend I was out of town, and when I returned on Saturday night, my wife told me that John Turner had come to our house with his girlfriend. She wouldn't let him in but told him that I was in my office. So he called my office—over and over. My answering machine had one desperate inquiry after another on it: "Where are you? Where are you, man? I need a job." As my wife was telling me this, he called the house. He needed a ride from another section of the city to his sister's, with whom he was now living. Over the protestations of my wife, I agreed to go pick him up because I had by now come to realize that I had to sever my contact with him, and in order to do that I had to come up with a way to keep him from contacting me.

I drove to the corner at which we had agreed to meet, and John was waiting for me along with his girlfriend. They got in the car and I drove them home, stopping for gas on the way. Now John wanted $10. I gave it to him but with the even stronger conviction that I had to end our relationship. So I asked him if he had ever thought about joining the army. "Can you do that?" was his response. In his mind, I was almost a magician. I can make impossible things happen. So I told him to meet me at my office at 10:00 Monday morning and we would go down to the army recruiter together. He agreed to that and then before we got to his sister's house he asked me out of the blue if I had an extra suit. This totally surprised me, and I asked him what he needed the suit for. He said, "Well, I want to go to church on Sunday," invoking once again the respectability and decency that are supposed to keep me interested in helping him. Yet I think there was a part of him that really did want to reform. I don't think it was totally a matter of manipulation. I said, "No, I don't have a suit," and he let it drop. I dropped him off at his sister's house, which is in a dangerous neighborhood in which people get shot every day, locked my car doors, and left. The next day I looked over the want ads in the newspaper, and I noticed that many restaurants were changing their kitchen staffs. I became encouraged that even if the army did not work out, there were job prospects for John.

On Monday morning John showed up at my office punctually at 10:00. It was a rainy morning, and we got into a cab and went down to the army recruitment office in Center City Philadelphia. We went in and I introduced myself and John to the black sergeant who was the recruiter on duty. I was dressed in a sports jacket, and I explained that this was a young man who was interested in going into the army. And the first question from the recruitment officer to John was, "Are you on probation?" John of course had to say yes, to which the recruiter replied:

> When you get that cleared up, we can talk. We can't talk until you deal with that. You could go to the judge, go to your probation officer, and try to work out a deal. If the judge says O.K., then maybe we can do

something. We do do that. We let people go into the army to get their lives straightened up.

John could only say O.K. to that and we left with the feeling that we had struck out.

We then went to the probation office, which is only a few doors away. We went up to the sixth floor and tried to find John's probation officer. Her desk mate was there, but she was not. The desk mate said she was at the bank. This was 10:30 on a Monday morning, and this woman was at the bank on personal business. We waited for her to return for quite a while, but then John became impatient, and I was becoming more anxious to resolve this whole situation. Finally, we left and switched to Plan B, which was to investigate the want ads I had found the previous day.

As we were walking down the street on our way to the first of the restaurants, John began to question my position. He asked me if I thought "all that professor shit" works. "What do you think?" I answered. He was not at all sure. "If you had been a white professor, do you think it would have worked?" he wanted to know. He thought that professors have influence with recruitment officers, and if I had been a "real" professor I probably could have convinced the sergeant to accept him, thus reflecting his understanding of bureaucracy. He finally said, "It don't work, man. I think you're naive." This was really a major development in our relationship because he had never called me that before. We talked about this for awhile until we reached the restaurant district, John all the time giving me static about my failure to get him into the army: "You didn't do it. You couldn't do it." I finally got fed up with this and took John into the first restaurant we came to.

We walked in and asked for the manager. I explained that John was looking for a job, had restaurant experience, and was a good worker, and the manager, after looking us up and down, sent us back to the kitchen to talk to Al. Al asked some of the same questions the manager asked, then excused himself to confer with the manager. When he returned, he looked at John and said, "When can you start?" We were both very happy with this development, but John was ecstatic. He had a look of anticipation fulfilled on his face. We didn't even discuss the wage. This was a former drug dealer who was willing to work at anything, in part because he really did want something other than the tough, hard life of the drug dealer. At that point I left him to go back to my office, but I asked him to call me later.

John didn't call, but at 4:00 in the afternoon, he came by. He walked into my office and gave me a huge bear hug, and his first words were,

"I got it, man, I got it! How'd you do that? How'd you do that?" This was again the magician thing, as though I had done something magical by getting him this job. All I had really done was talk to the manager sensibly. But my very presence and the way that I spoke may have been what he was looking for. It might have helped him to trust the job application. John and I then went out to a restaurant to talk over the events of the day. John reiterated his disappointment with the army recruiter for not helping him out and his conviction that, had I been a white professor, he would have been more forthcoming. But he thanked me profusely for not giving up on him after that failure and for coming through at the restaurant.

I then asked him to tell me what had led to his quitting his job at the hospital, because I had never heard his side of the story. John explained that the men there were always "on my case," that they would tease him about his girlfriends and his children and also about his position as a "halfway man," since during part of his tenure there he was still partially incarcerated, spending his nights in jail but allowed out to work during the day. He talked about how the men embarrassed him in front of the girlfriends who came to see him, as well as in front of other workers who had not previously known of his background. He claimed that they spread his reputation as a stud around the entire organization, and also that their talk was for the most part motivated by jealousy of his success with women. He also brought me up to date on his women and children. He had had one girlfriend who used him to get pregnant twice and then forbade him to see her or the children. He explained how lonely he had been after his mother left, how difficult Thanksgiving had been without her, how he had enjoyed being down South with her. But he had had to come back because of the terms of his probation and because of "my children. I'm not the type of man to walk out on kids. They mine, I'm gonna stand by and take care of 'em as a man. I'm gonna do my part." He reiterated his disgust at what drugs have done to the black community in general as well as to various individual people in his life.

After telling me all this, John again asked me for money—$150 this time. After reflection and a little resistance I gave it to him, fully expecting never to see it again but also never expecting to see him again. His code of honor would forbid him to contact me again without paying me back, and my experience with him had taught me that he was unlikely ever to have the money. This was how I was finally able to sever our relationship. I had continued to help John even after it had become apparent that he was using me, because I wanted to see how he responded to various situations. At this point, however, I felt

I had developed a rather complete picture of him, in addition to which I was beginning to feel uneasy about our association. Consistent with my expectations, I have indeed not seen him since, but I have heard of him. The street life which he found so compelling seems to have brought him to a corner in Baltimore. There he had an altercation with somebody over something, perhaps a misunderstood drug deal, and he wound up being shot in the gut. On the streets it is said that as a result of that shooting, he is "carrying around a bag" and will be for the rest of his life. He is now about 27.

An important lesson to be learned from John's story is that of the basic incompatibility between "the street" and the more conventional world of legitimate jobs and stable families. When the street and the conventional world collided for John, the street prevailed in part because he lacked the personal resources to negotiate the occupational structure then available to him. At the point in his life, when the wider system became receptive to him in the form of a well-paying job, it was too late. The draw of the street was too powerful, and he was overcome by its force.

John—as are so many young black men caught up in similar circumstances—appeared to be in a state of drift when I met him. He was adrift between the street and the wider, more conventional society. But given the way he had been raised—learning at an early age to be streetwise and to survive by the laws of the street—the street had a profound advantage in vying for his heart and mind. Moreover, the various pieces of human capital he had accumulated over the years were more easily negotiable on the streets. In other words, the streets proved much more receptive to him than did the wider, more legitimate society, and this receptivity encouraged John to invest his personal resources in what could be described as an oppositional culture, which in many ways is a response to a feeling of rejection by the conventional society. John became fixated on this oppositional culture, rejecting the means for achieving status sanctioned by the wider society while accepting the dominant culture's goals of material success—money, gold, clothes, sneakers, cars, etc. (See Fordham and Ogbu 1986.)

Too often the wider system of legitimate employment is closed off to young men like John, by prejudice, by lack of preparation, or by the absence of real job opportunities (Wilson 1987; Kirschenman and Neckerman 1991; Anderson 1980). Yet they are able to observe others—usually whites—enjoying the fruits of the system, and through this experience they often become profoundly alienated. The boys often develop a contempt for the society they perceive to have contempt for them. In these circumstances a racist reality looms large in their

minds. Feeling that their opportunities for conventional advancement
are blocked, young men like John Turner are drawn to an alternate
means of gaining the things they see that others have (Cloward and
Ohlin 1960; Merton 1968). After growing up buffeted between an
unreceptive conventional world and the street, they drift (Matza
1964). Here they are easily drawn into the receptive street culture,
where a cunning intelligence mixed with a profound street wisdom
and physical prowess are highly valued. With these resources, they
negotiate and compete fiercely for very scarce coin: respect and
wealth.

This street-oriented subculture is often violent. A primary value is
physicality and a willingness to resolve disputes through violence.
Authority is asserted through conflict; shouts, bites, punches, knife
cuts, and gunshots are traded here. It is very important to be bad, to
be mean in the idiomatic sense, because to be mean is also to be cool.
It is extremely important not to be "square" or approximate through
behavior or sympathy the wider conventional society. These values
come together to make up the personal framework of the individual.

One way to achieve esteem or status in one's local community is to
exhibit superior physical prowess. As a predatory influence, the street
culture constitutes an enormous problem for the rest of the inner-city
population. Young people who are not strongly anchored in the conventional world are at risk of being preyed upon. Given the drugs,
poverty, unemployment, lack of opportunity and other social problems
besetting the community, well-meaning parents find it difficult to
anchor their children in conventional values.

In fact, in underclass communities, conventionality and the street
culture wage a constant battle for the hearts and minds of the younger
residents, and this dichotomy has become an organizing social principle. The residents generally divide their neighbors into those who
are "decent" and those whom they associate with the street (Anderson
1991). The culture of decency is characterized by close and extended
families, a low-income financial stability, deep religious values, a
work ethic and desire to "get ahead", and strong disapproval of drugs
and teenage pregnancy. The street represents hipness, an emphasis
on achieving and maintaining status based on one's person (not on
one's achievements as in the dominant culture), and a contempt for
conventional values and behaviors, which are easily discredited because of their association with whites; these can include doing well
in school, being civil to whites, and speaking standard English.

This oppositional culture is so alluring in large part because the
conventional culture is viewed as profoundly unreceptive by many
blacks in the inner cities. Youths observe the would-be legitimate role

models around them, and many find them unworthy of emulation. Legal hard work appears not to have paid off for the old, and they see the relatively few hardworking people of the neighborhood struggling to survive. From their elders and peers they hear repeated tales of racist treatment; and by now most have experienced it firsthand. At the same time, through street-oriented role models, a thriving underground economy beckons to them, in which enormous sums are promised, along with a certain thrill, power, and prestige. Streetwise and impoverished young men easily find places in the drug trade.

In the past, manufacturing jobs provided opportunities for young men like John and at the same time supported the values of decency and conventionality by having them pay off. The loss of these jobs has damaged the financial health of the inner city and undermined the quality of available role models. One important casualty has been the relationship between "old heads" and young boys (Anderson 1990). The old head was a man of stable means whose acknowledged role in the community was to teach and support boys and young men in their late teens and early 20s, in effect to socialize them to meet their responsibilities regarding work, family life, the law, and common decency. But as meaningful employment has become increasingly scarce and the expansion of the drug culture offers opportunities for quick money, the old head has been losing prestige and authority. In his place, a new role model is emerging. The embodiment of the street, he is young, often a product of a street gang, and indifferent at best to the law and traditional values. If he works at the low-paying jobs available to him, he does so grudgingly. More likely, he is involved, part time or full time, in the drug trade or some other area of the underground economy. He derides conventional family life: he has a string of women but feels little obligation toward them and the children he has fathered. His displays of self-aggrandizement through fancy clothes and impressive cars make their mark on young men like John.

By enforcing conformity to external displays of "manhood", the oppositional culture ravages the individuality of those who fall victim to it, eroding their sense of personal identity and thus of personal responsibility as well. Many of Cleckley's (1955) symptoms of psychopathology can be seen in John: "superficial charm and 'good' intelligence, unreliability, untruthfulness and insincerity, lack of remorse and shame, poor judgment and failure to learn by experience, lack of feeling for other people." When discussing his situation from a distance John showed quite a bit of insight, but once he found himself back in it, he was unable to make a positive adaptation of his insight. John's very identity was derived from the oppositional culture, and ultimately it immobilized him in the face of opportunity.

This reality has serious implications for society as a whole and for social policy. The progressive nature of the impact of the street points to a need both for very early intervention, in programs such as Head Start, before the oppositional culture has a chance even to begin developing in the child, and for continuing intervention with preadolescents and adolescents. It is extremely important, in particular, to give maturing boys (and girls, too, for that matter) job training and education in the practicalities of operating in the world of work. This training must then be rewarded with real jobs. The system must be more receptive to the John Turners of the world. The creditable promise of a job gives these young men a realistic outlook on life and a positive sense of the future, and at the same time builds hope and social peace. It is important for the wider society to understand that much of the behavior of John and others like him must be seen as adaptive. He is adapting to his situation of deprivation as it appears to him. Although his definition may be at odds with wider cultural definitions, it is real to him. And if he defines it as real, it is real in its consequences (Thomas 1951; Merton 1968).

The question of outlook is extremely important here. John envisioned a good life but was unable to accept the changes in behavior necessary to achieve it. In fact, the street life competed quite effectively with his vision of the good life. My experience with John suggests that simply providing opportunities for members of the underclass is not enough. They must also be provided with jobs that have income and prestige, and an attitude that allows them to invest their considerable personal resources in those jobs. Only then can they leave behind the attitudes and behavior that block their advancement in the mainstream but that also give them security in negotiating within their world. The reality is that these young men are being written off by mainstream society, they know it, and the world is the poorer for their loss.

References

Anderson, Elijah. 1980. "Some observations on Black Youth Employment." In *Youth Employment and Public Policy*, edited by B. Anderson and Isabel Sawhill. Englewood Cliffs: Prentice Hall.

————. 1989. "Sex Codes and Family Life among Poor Inner-City Youths." *Annals of the American Academy of Political and Social Science* 501 (Jan.).

————. 1990. *Streetwise: Race, Class, and Change in an Urban Community.* Chicago: University of Chicago Press.

————. 1991. "Neighborhood Effects on Teenage Pregnancy." In *The Urban Underclass,* edited by Paul Peterson and Christopher Jenks. Washington, D.C.: Brookings Institution.

Becker, Howard S. 1966. "Introduction" to *The Jack-Roller: A Delinquent Boy's Own Story,* by Clifford R. Shaw. Chicago: University of Chicago Press.

————. 1970. *Sociological Work.* Chicago: Aldine.

————. 1973. *The Outsiders.* New York: Free Press.

Cleckley, Hervey. 1955. *The Mask of Sanity,* 3rd ed. St. Louis: C.V. Mosby.

Cloward, Richard A., and Lloyd E. Ohlin. 1960. *Delinquency and Opportunity.* Glencoe, Ill.: Free Press.

Cohen, Albert K. 1955. *Delinquent Boys.* New York: Free Press.

Dembo, Richard. 1988. "Delinquency among Black Male Youth." In *Young, Black, and Male in America,* edited by Jewelle Taylor Gibbs (129–65). Dover, Mass.: Auburn House.

Dollard, John. 1932. *Criteria for the Life History.* New Haven, Conn.: Yale University Press.

Fordham, Signthia, and John Ogbu. 1986. "Black Students' School Success: Coping with the Burden of 'Acting White.' " *Urban Review* 18(2): 177ff.

Gibbs, Jewelle Taylor, ed. 1988. *Young, Black, and Male in America: An Endangered Species.* Dover, Mass.: Auburn House.

Goffman, Erving. 1959. *The Presentation of Self in Everyday Life.* New York: Doubleday/Anchor Books.

————. 1963. *Stigma: Notes on the Management of Spoiled Identity.* New York: Simon and Schuster/Touchstone Books.

Gurr, Ted Robert, ed. 1989. *Violence in America.* Vol. 1 of *The History of Crime.* Newbury Park, Calif.: Sage Publications.

Hirschi, Travis. 1969. *Causes of Delinquency.* Berkeley, Calif.: University of California Press.

Horowitz, Ruth. 1983. *Honor and the American Dream: Culture and Identity in a Chicano Community.* New Brunswick, N.J.: Rutgers University Press.

Jankowsky, Martin Sanchez. 1991. *Islands in the Street.* Berkeley, Calif.: University of California Press.

Kelly, Delos H., ed. 1990. *Criminal Behavior: Text and Readings in Criminology,* 2nd ed. New York: St. Martin's Press.

Kirschenman, John and Kathy Neckerman. 1991. " 'We'd like to Hire Them Out . . .' Race in the Minds of Employers." In *The Urban Underclass,* edited by Paul Peterson and Christopher Jencks. Washington, D.C.: Brookings Institution.

Matza, David. 1964. *Delinquency and Drift.* New York: John Wiley and Sons.

Merton, Robert K. 1968. "The Self-Fulfilling Prophecy" and "Social Structure and Anomie." In *Social Theory and Social Structure,* by Robert K. Merton. New York: Macmillan.

Miller, Walter B. 1990. "Lower Class Culture as a Generating Milieu of Gang Delinquency." In *Criminal Behavior,* 2nd. ed., edited by Delos H. Kelly (213–26). New York: St. Martin's Press.

Regoli, Robert M., and John D. Hewitt. 1991. *Delinquency in Society: A Child-Centered Approach.* New York: McGraw-Hill.

Scheff, Thomas J. 1984. *Being Mentally Ill: A Sociological Theory,* 2nd ed. New York: Aldine.

Shaw, Clifford R. [1930] 1966. *The Jack-Roller: A Delinquent Boy's Own Story.* Chicago: University of Chicago Press.

Short, James F. Jr. and Fred L. Strodtbeck. 1965. *Group Process and Gang Delinquency.* Chicago: University of Chicago Press.

———. 1968. "Why Gangs Fight." In *Gang Delinquency and Delinquent Subcultures,* edited by James E. Short, Jr. (246–56). New York: Harper and Row.

Suttles, Gerald D. 1972. *The Social Construction of Communities.* Chicago: University of Chicago Press.

Sykes, Gresham M., and David Matza. 1990. "Techniques of Neutralization: A Theory of Delinquency." In *Criminal Behavior,* 2nd ed., edited by Delos H. Kelly (207–12). New York: St. Martin's Press.

Thrasher, Frederic M. [1927] 1963. *The Gang.* Chicago: University of Chicago Press.

Thomas, William I. 1951. *The Unadjusted Girl.* Boston: Little, Brown.

Wilson, William J. 1970. *The Truly Disadvantaged.* Chicago: University of Chicago Press.

Wolfgang, Marvin E., Leonard Savitz, and Norman Johnston. 1970. *The Sociology of Crime and Delinquency,* 2nd ed. New York: John Wiley and Sons.

Chapter Six

THE IMPACT OF DRUGS ON FAMILY LIFE AND KIN NETWORKS IN THE INNER-CITY AFRICAN-AMERICAN SINGLE-PARENT HOUSEHOLD

Eloise Dunlap

For many children of the inner city, life's basic outcomes are determined at a very early age. Born into drug-dependent families, they inherit a lifestyle that swiftly forecloses alternative opportunities. This chapter examines how high-risk behaviors such as drug involvement are transmitted across generations within the family. It examines six case studies of single-parent, drug-dependent, inner-city African-American families. Although the extended kin network, an African-American cultural characteristic, helps support individual households in times of stress, the drug epidemic is pulling family structure apart. In some instances, the extended family becomes the mechanism by which drug abuse and other dysfunctional behaviors are transmitted to the young.

The stability of a family depends on the degree to which it can meet both the instrumental and expressive needs of its members. Single-parent households with strong kin networks to support them tend to be more stable than those lacking such networks, because they have more than one adult to call upon in times of stress. The absence of kin support exacerbates the isolation of single-parent inner-city households.

None of the household-families presented here would ordinarily be considered "stable." However, they represent different degrees of instability. The first set of families meets virtually none of the needs of their children. The second set of families meets instrumental needs and at least some of the expressive needs, but they are also transmitting highly destructive behavior patterns. The two sets of cases illustrate a continuum—a process of household disintegration in which

The research reported in this paper was funded by the National Institute on Drug Abuse (NIDA).

the children of less-unstable families go on to form households that are completely unstable.

METHODOLOGY

The experiences presented in this chapter are derived from two ethnographic studies conducted in New York City. (Johnson 1991; Ratner 1992). The studies are based largely on the symbolic interactionism paradigm (see Blumer 1969). This stance examines the individual and collective activities of people who are engaged in social interaction. The human groups involved may be as small as a family or as large as a nation. The people described here were chosen as representative of significant numbers of families that have been and are being torn apart by drug/crack addiction. Although the cases are interpreted as "ideal types," the individuals and families are real. (Note that to protect their identity, none of the individuals in the case studies are referred to by their real names.)

Researchers who work in inner-city social settings need to be sensitive to the fact that their findings may be used by others to make judgments and decisions, often of a policy nature, about a much wider group. The findings here could be misinterpreted or used to justify long-held prejudices about African-Americans by other Americans. This study, however, focuses on only one segment of African-American family life and cannot be generalized to all or even most black families and communities. The cases serve, rather, as a window through which some of the destruction occurring in drug-abusing inner-city black families can be seen.

AFRICAN-AMERICAN FAMILY STRUCTURE

The traditional definition of *family* does not reflect the reality of African-American families living in the United States (Hodkin 1983; Lane 1980; Wilson 1986). *Family* is defined in much of the theoretical, empirical, and clinical literature as the nuclear family, with other family structures treated more or less as variations of this norm (Foster 1983; Gilby and Pederson 1982; Schneider 1980). Some social scientists recognize, however, that diverse family forms have always coexisted with one another in a way that is similar to the coexistence of

diverse ethnic cultures in American society. The operational definition of *family* used in this chapter includes diverse forms of familial
organization embedded in extended family networks.

The importance of the extended family to African-Americans has
long been acknowledged (Foster 1983; Hale 1982; Wilson 1986). It is
a coping mechanism with historical roots. Research by Gutman (1976)
and Pleck (1973) demonstrated how African-Americans wove together
a culture in which many households appeared as nuclear in structure,
but in which the extended family/kin network was very important to
the survival of the family unit. During slavery, African family and
kinship patterns were devastated. Slaves established "fictive" kin networks by investing nonkin (i.e., those not related by blood) with symbolic kin status (Gutman 1976; Wilson 1989). Emerging from slavery,
multigenerational linkages among slave families were accompanied
by a conception of family and kin obligations of mutual support and
assistance that were as important as the blood relationships.

This extended-family organization persists today in African-American communities owing to the high incidence of poverty, unemployment, out-of-wedlock births, marital separation, and divorce. The extended family plays a central role in helping a family adjust to these
stresses. According to Wilson (1989): "Family resources depend on
the ability of family members to contribute tangible help such as
material support, income, child care, and assistance in performing
household tasks, and nontangible help such as expressive interaction,
emotional support, counseling, instruction, and social regulation."

Culturally based social studies have consistently shown that the
extended family helps to sustain black family life (Hale 1982; Wilson
1984). The economic and social constraints on African-American families have produced varied patterns of adaptive behavior (illegitimacy,
separation, doubling-up of families in single households, etc.), which
have been labeled by some observers as pathological or impoverished.
When viewed from a culturally sensitive perspective, however, the
strengths of black families can be delineated.

> In every Negro neighborhood of any size in the country, a wide variety
> of family structures will be represented. This range and variety does
> not suggest . . . that the Negro family is falling apart, but rather that
> these families are fully capable of surviving by adapting to the histori-
> cal and contemporary social and economic conditions facing the Negro
> people. How does a people survive in the face of oppression and
> sharply restricted economic and social support? There are, of course,
> numerous ways. But surely one of them is to adapt the most basic of its
> institutions, the family, to meet the often conflicting demands placed

on it. In this context, then, the Negro family has proved to be an amazingly resilient institution. (Billingsley 1968)

Although the extended family may not be unique to the black community, it is a long-standing cultural pattern that is particularly critical for women and children in times of difficulty.

FAMILY STABILITY: INSTRUMENTAL AND EXPRESSIVE FUNCTIONS

Traditional measures of family instability (e.g. illegitimacy, divorce, separation, female head of household, etc.) do not go far in helping us understand the detrimental impact of drugs on inner-city black families. In examining the actual functioning of families, and taking into account the reality of extended family networks, stability is better measured by the degree to which families are able to fulfill both the expressive and instrumental needs of their members, especially the children.

Billingsley (1968) stipulated that some family functions are basically instrumental, as when adults maintain the physical and social integrity of the family unit by providing income, food, shelter, clothing, and health care. Society places certain responsibilities on adults in families. They are expected to provide economically for the basic needs of their members. Billingsley also added the instrumental function of loyalty—members of the family are expected to remain with the family and to not leave prematurely, "except for a good cause." Death is the only recognizable good cause for senior members; junior members are expected to remain closely attached to the family until they get married. One critical measurement of family stability is the fulfillment of these instrumental needs.

The expressive function develops the "sense of belonging, of self-worth, self-awareness, and dignity" (Billingsley 1968). In addition this function includes the provision of companionship and of propagating various forms of love and affection. Thus, family relationships, interaction patterns, and parent-child relationships are important when considering family stability. Both the instrumental and expressive functions of the family are highly interrelated and can serve as objective measures of stability in family life.

All families have difficulty remaining intact, growing and developing without a sound economic footing. Yet, many black men have been unable to count on earning a living wage for themselves and their families. Too often money earned at low-wage jobs is insufficient to enable them to maintain their self-respect as providers of food, shelter, and other family needs (Madhubuti 1990). The major reason low-income black men separate from the family is their inability to secure and retain employment that pays respectable wages (Ploski and Williams 1983). Lack of employment or of income opportunity triggers a chain effect, ultimately creating a traumatic breakup of households. The male feels inadequate or useless; the female may see the male as another burden. Thus, the black family is often "broken" owing to the lack of a male householder. But frequently the single-parent female's love for children under her care, and her dependability in maintaining the family unit, can provide a stable family environment. The black family may also have strong kinship bonds and flexibility in family roles. Although the children's father may be absent, the extended family or kinship networks may provide the instrumental and expressive needs of the unit: financial assistance, emotional support, child care, clothing and furniture, and other material needs. Help provided through the kinship network enables some families to maintain a degree of stability through all the changes that affect them.

DRUGS AND THEIR IMPACT ON BLACK FAMILY LIFE

Since the 1960s, successive drug eras (Johnson and Manwar 1991) have had a negative impact on black family life. Jaynes and Williams (1989) demonstrated that husband-wife families constituted the overwhelming majority of black families until the 1960s, at which time the proportion of black families headed by women doubled. The explosion in inner-city heroin use and addiction, starting in 1965, especially among black and Hispanic males, contributed strongly to the dissolution of the nuclear family. Members of the heroin generation had an average of two to three children. They were infrequently married and rarely lived with or contributed to their families. Many of these children did not know who their fathers were. If the child knew the father's identity, contact with him was rare and his economic contributions to the family were nonexistent or minimal (Deren 1986). When mothers became hard-drug users, their children were generally raised by grandparents, kin, or the foster-care system (Sowder, Carnes, and Sherman 1981). Nichtern found that children in foster-care institutions had eating and/or sleeping problems, developmental lags (such as difficulties in bowel control and speech), learning problems, difficulties in their relationships with adults and peers, and were withdrawn (Nichtern 1973). Children of heroin-using parents lived in multi-problem families. There were more behavioral difficulties reported by teachers, more children repeating grade levels, and many absences (Sowder and Burt 1980). These children were also more likely to commit delinquent acts, and the acts were more likely to be serious ones. In addition, the children were more likely to become drug abusers and to enter drug treatment programs.

In the mid-1970s the heroin epidemic began to ease, and cocaine snorting became popular among nonheroin drug users in inner cities. By 1980–82 freebasing emerged (Speigal 1982). An explosion of crack use began in 1984–85. From 1986 to the present, crack came to dominate the illicit drug markets in most inner-city neighborhoods. During each of these drug eras, women were a prominent minority in the drug-abusing and drug-selling population. The majority of drug-dependent women were parents (Eldred and Washington 1976; Gerstein, Judd, and Rovner 1979; Gomberg 1979; Moise, Reed, and Ryan 1982). Since 1981, there has been a steady increase in births to substance-abusing women. Close to half-a-million children in New York State aged 17 and under are the offspring of substance abusers. The infant mortality rate for mothers who were substance users is about three times higher than the citywide (New York City) rate (Deren, Frank, and Schmeidler 1988).

Much research has indicated a relationship between parent and child substance abuse. Investigations and documentation of generational continuity in alcohol consumption strongly suggest that alcoholism is an intergenerational phenomenon (Rutgers University 1983). Significant relationships have been found between parents' and students' use of the same drug (Smart and Fejer 1972). Offspring are significantly more likely to use drugs and/or alcohol if parents are users or if the child perceives that the parents are users (Fawzy, Coombs, and Gerber 1983). In addition, research has confirmed that children who lack love, warmth, and closeness and exhibit signs of hostility show increased levels of substance use, delinquency, and dysfunctional coping strategies (Johnson and Pandina 1991). Further, older siblings act as role models by reinforcing certain attitude and behavior patterns and by providing advice and information. Siblings also may play an important role in influencing substance abuse.

The way behaviors are transmitted across generations is often indirect. Johnson and Pandina (1991), in examining the influence of family environment on adolescent alcohol and drug use, found that parental alcohol use was an important determinant of a child's alcohol or drug use. The parent's alcohol consumption itself contributed little to the child's behavioral problems. Rather, alcohol use was associated with a nonwarm and hostile parental relationship, which increased the likelihood of a child's use of alcohol or drugs. The study, however, is representative of white middle-class adolescents and did not consider whether family patterns operate in the same way for economically deprived inner-city adolescents. Other factors such as interpersonal or intrapersonal influences were not examined.

CASE STUDIES

In the case studies presented here, extended families act as a source of emotional and economic support, but when drugs are present, they also become the source of drug use and the vehicle for cross-generational transmission of drug behavior.

Unstable Households—Maureen, Priscilla, Fay

Almost total family instability is shown in the living situations of the individuals in the first three case studies included here. Maureen, Priscilla, and Fay have completely abandoned their families of procreation. The instrumental and expressive needs of their children have been grossly neglected. Instrumental functions of loyalty and economic support have been dropped for a life of drug abuse and consumption. Since instrumental functions are not performed, it is difficult for any of the expressive functions to occur. Although the extended family provides some resources, drug abuse among these women's parents and family has undermined the kin network. Family patterns perpetuate and facilitate the transmission of drug abuse to the next generation.

MAUREEN

Maureen was born in New York City in 1968 and grew up in the inner city. In her family of origin, she is one of four children—two girls and two boys. She was raised in a single-parent household where her two oldest siblings have the same father, but Maureen and her youngest brother each have different fathers. Maureen's mother thus has four children by three different men. At the time we met (1990), Maureen was 22 years old. While growing up, Maureen's constant companions were her first cousins, the offspring of Jeannie, a sister of Maureen's mother. Both mothers consumed drugs together. Jeannie introduced Maureen's mother to crack use (then known as freebase).

Maureen's drug-use career began at an early age and her introduction to drug use was through family members. Maureen's cousins smoked marijuana:

> I was about 11 years old and I would hang around my cousins all the time. They was older than me. We'd be smoking cigarettes and a lot of times they had joints. They always gave me a hit off their joint. Most of the time I'd take cigarettes from my mother's pack of cigarettes. She never knew it.

By 1983, at the age of 15, Maureen began to consume beer and alcohol on a regular basis. While growing up she related that she had seen "everybody" drinking beer and "wanted to know what it tasted like." In the 10th grade and 16 years old, Maureen dropped out of high school because of pregnancy. After giving birth to a son, she worked briefly as a file clerk in a doctor's office (about three months) but was unable to continue this job owing to stresses in her household. This is the only job she has ever held. By 1985, Maureen was 17 years old and had begun consuming cocaine, as well as alcohol and marijuana.

In Maureen's case one can see how a kin network encouraged cross-generational drug use, and how this contributed to the instability of her household. As stated, Maureen was raised in a single-parent household. Her stepfather lived with the family on and off, owing to his frequent contact with the criminal justice system.

> My stepfather treated us good, he never molested me or nothin' or my sisters. He and my mother fussed, but he never beat on her. He was on dope but I never knew it. . . . He started shootin' up and leavin' his works and blood all over the place. I'd go to the bathroom and blood'd be everywhere. But my mother didn't shoot nothin', she smoked weed, snorted a little coke, you know how it is, and they both smoked crack.

Maureen was introduced to drugs even before she was 11 years old. Her mother worked at various menial jobs, but mostly raised the family on welfare. While growing up, Maureen remembers her mother smoking marijuana and snorting cocaine. As her mother progressed deeper into drug use—smoking crack—the stability of the family deteriorated. Food, shelter, and clothing were minimally provided for. As a young adolescent, Maureen and her mother had an open relationship. Maureen was able to talk to her mother about the stepfather leaving his drug paraphernalia around the house, and her mother was able to stop this behavior. At this stage, Maureen could go to her and communicate her distress.

Once Maureen's mother began to smoke crack, however, instrumental and expressive needs of the family became neglected.

> We was with my mother over her girlfriend's house when Aunt Jeannie came by and she had some coke. She cooked it up and told Ma and Ruth to try it. After that things started goin' crazier. I had to take care of my oldest sister's two sons, my son, and my younger brother. I had to do everything. Most of the time we didn't have nothin' to eat. We stayed hungry all the time. When I washed clothes I'd find vials in her [mother's] pockets. . . . I 'member comin' home one day and she'd been smokin' for awhile then, but the house was full of people smokin' all over the place. I went to go to my bedroom and close the door and it was full too. I said to her, 'What's happenin'? I just turned round and left. I was tired, the house was dirty with vials on the floor and the table and I'd just had my son. . . . I just wanted to get away. . . . At first I had smoked some crack to kill my appetite, to keep me from bein' hungry. . . . I just felt like I couldn't take it no more so I took my son to my sister and left. . . . I went on a binge and smoked for three months. Nobody knew where I was, but I was out smoking crack and gettin' money anyway I could get it.

Once she became heavily involved in smoking crack herself, Maureen took her son back to her mother and sister. Maureen now (1990) lives with various "friends," and most of her activities consist of smoking crack or pursuing the means to get more crack.

Although Maureen's mother's drug use created the conditions to introduce Maureen to drugs, her mother's household is more stable than Maureen's, in that her mother has always kept an apartment. Her mother provided shelter for the family. Maureen does not provide this for her son. Attempting to provide shelter for her son, off and on, she stayed at various welfare hotels until she eventually left her son with her mother. In taking the grandson to raise, Maureen's mother displays her loyalty to the family. Just as Maureen was raised in a drug environment, her son's environment is also permeated with drugs. She tries to buy clothes and food for her son, but most of the time Maureen spends her total income on crack. Maureen's mother is now the model through which her grandson will learn about drug use.

Priscilla

Priscilla, like Maureen, does not maintain a permanent residence. She also does not contribute to the well-being of her child through the provision of food, clothing, shelter, or regular interaction. Priscilla's family of orientation was a single-parent household heavily involved in substance abuse. Due to her mother's neglect of her children as well as her use of alcohol and other narcotic substances, Priscilla's family life was permeated with psychological and physical abuse. Priscilla told her mother about being raped from the age of 8 (by several male family members and her mother's boyfriends) to the age of 15 (she had just been raped by her mother's boyfriend). Yet, the mother did not believe her and accused her of "flirting" with her friends. At no point in her life did Priscilla have trusting and positive relations with either her mother or father.

Like Maureen, Priscilla was born in New York and has lived in the inner city all her life. At the time of this study, she was 22 years old. She left high school before completion.

> I didn't have nobody to take care of me when I was in school. Most of the time my mother didn't come home. I'd try to keep myself up and put my clothes on and go to school, but a lot of times I'd be dirty and my clothes be wrinkled. I'd get up late and be late for school a lot of times and most of the time my mother didn't do nothin', so when I was in the ninth grade I just stopped goin' to school and ran away from home. I slept in hallways and over some of my friends' house. Some times people'd feed me and help me out a little. I 'member my Aunt tried to help me. She tried to teach me things like tellin' me what to do. I felt good 'cause it made me feel like somebody cared for me 'cause my mother was gone most of the time and she treated me like she didn't give a damn what happened to me.

Priscilla went to live with her father.

> Well, you know, I was havin' a lot of problems with my mother and I ran away and slept around for awhile, then I went to live with my father. He was livin' with his girlfriend and she had a daughter around my age and I got scared of what he was doin'. He was havin' sex with her [the daughter] and I was scared to go to sleep. The whole time I was there I didn't have no peace 'cause I was scared he would do the same thing to me too.

Priscilla's father was also heavily involved in alcohol and drug abuse. Due to her home environment, she began to experiment with marijuana at the age of 10. At 12, she began to drink alcohol. By the time she was 17, she had begun to snort cocaine that she got from a boyfriend she met through her cousin. Priscilla added crack to her drug consumption career at the age of 19.

Priscilla grew up in an unstable household. Minimal food, clothes, and shelter were barely provided for her. At the age of 14, Priscilla became pregnant. She moved back in with her mother and became more involved in drug use. Priscilla's child ultimately was taken by the father's parents. What Maureen's mother did for her daughter, Priscilla's boyfriend's parents are doing for her child. Grandparents are providing the instrumental and expressive support.

FAY

Fay is mostly homeless and rarely sees her children. In fact, she does not know where four of her eight children have been relocated. Fay's family demonstrates another dimension of family destruction. Her case displays how extended family networks are unable to provide and care for the large number of children that many crack-using women are having. The increasing number of children also lessens the extended family's effectiveness as a stabilizing mechanism.

Fay is a 34-year-old mother. Her oldest child is 15 years old and her youngest child is 4 months old. Her four oldest children (all by the same father) live with her stepparents. These four were awarded to her stepparents by the courts. Her last four children (each has a different father) were "crack babies" and have been placed in foster homes. Like Maureen and Priscilla, Fay too dropped out of high school. Fay has a learning disability, which further hindered her from keeping up with the coursework.

> I left school in the 10th grade 'cause I have a learning disability. I was always in classes that had a lot of kids in 'em; my last class had over 32 students. We never had enough teachers and I couldn't learn a lot 'cause they went too fast for me, so when I got in the 10th grade I just got tired of goin' there and I never went back again. I always wanted to go back to school to get my diploma, but my learnin' disability and me havin' another baby always stopped me. . . . I never knew my father, but my sister told me 'bout my mother. I was two years old when she died, so I don't 'member her too much. We [all her siblings] have the same mother but we don't have the same father. My oldest sister know who her father is but she don't see him. We had it hard when I was a kid. Mama Doris treated us like her natural children though. We didn't have much though 'cause my parents couldn't 'ford much but they were good to us, they treated us like we was their real children. . . . I wanted a lot of things but they couldn't afford it.

Fay comes from a family of 10 children, all of whom were raised by fictive parents. Because Fay's older siblings often talked about their mother's substance use, Fay knew that her mother was a heavy substance user. Fay was introduced to substance abuse in her household.

Her main exposure to drug abuse came from her older siblings, all of whom are currently either alcohol, heroin, cocaine, or crack users.

> We got along good together, all'uh us was friends and stuck up for each other. We went to parties together, played games together, we went to school together and we helped each other best we could with school-work. We girls was suppose to do the housework and laundry and shopping and stuff like that. We couldn't go outdoors though, we had to stay in the house 'til my parents came home . . . they both worked. We used to sneak out sometime you know. . . . I was about 14 years old and [this man] was nice to me, he was about 35 years old and I'd go to his room. I liked him but my mother found out 'cause his ex-wife and my mother was friends. She saw me goin' to his place and she told my mother. I always liked older men. . . . But we all did our part, we was taught the oldest one suppose to teach the next one to you so we all worked. . . .

Eventually, Fay left home and began living with the father of one of her children. He began to influence her further in drug consumption. She had already smoked marijuana and snorted cocaine with her elder siblings at parties. She began to experiment with these drugs at age 20. Because she was considered mentally slow, she was having relations with various older males in her neighborhood. She did not begin to have babies until she was 19. After having four babies, she moved in with the fifth child's father.

> We was both workin' and I could smoke 'cause he had the money. I was workin' part time at the cleaners and I mainly supported my habit through this and I got help from my son's father . . . but we was livin' together and he showed me a lot. He was on the needle but he showed me how to snort heroin and we used coke. . . . We was together for five years. . . . He started smokin' crack and I had the baby by him and we bought some coke and he cooked it up and showed me how to smoke it. It make me feel good . . . it was like a feeling of excitement, made me feel new and aware of myself and surroundings, I felt like I was on top of everything until I came down. He smoked everyday but I didn't at first. I just smoked 'bout once every two months, then I started smokin' everyday too. I stayed with him for over five years but we started stealin' from each other and fightin' over you know the drugs and everything. We wasn't payin' nothin' so we got put out and I left him and went back home.

Living in her stepparents' household were various siblings and their offspring and Fay's children. Fay's sisters and brothers, however, are also drug abusers. Fay's stepparents—even though fictive—give another view of the family as an important mechanism of support to single parents. They provided as much help to their stepchildren as they were capable of doing. Fay, as well as many of her siblings, are now allowed to "wash up" and "change clothes" at her stepparents' apartment. In this way they are continuing their support of their stepchildren. They have been able to take in four of Fay's children, as well as other children belonging to drug-using parents. They did not, however, have room for Fay's last four children. These four were taken from Fay and placed in foster homes. At the time that I met Fay, her last child had recently been taken from her by the courts, and she had been declared an "unfit" mother.

> You know like they took 'em but my last one was a boy. I don't know where he is now. I heard he was in a foster but the woman that was takin' care of him at first passed away; now I don't know where he is. He is four months old now, I went to see him, but now I don't know where he is. My godmother she took some you know. She adopted them legally because they say I'm an unfit mother, but she couldn't take this last one 'cause you know I wasn't around her at that time. . . . You know I just kept getting caught 'cause I didn't use nothin', but see I ain't no unfit mother. . . . See I'm different, I'm not like a lot of these women out here they be takin' their children with them and smokin' but see I ain't like that. I know someone, I got someone to take care of my children since I can't, so I ain't no unfit mother 'cause my children bein' taken care of. See I'm different from them.

Fay rationalizes that her children are being provided for by her stepparents and that therefore she is a "good" parent. Fay expresses confidence in strong family ties and family cohesiveness in coming to the aid of members in times of crisis. But she absolves herself of any responsibility for her offspring, and she continues to have babies and look for her family to take them even when there is no room in her stepparents' home. One sees here another dimension of family breakdown. Fay's stepparents are not heavy substance abusers, but their household is permeated with their stepchildren who use drugs/alcohol, and the stepchildren's offspring are being exposed to and socialized into drug consumption through the adults' involvement with substance abuse. The extended family is becoming overwhelmed by the sheer number of children being brought to it for support.

Less-Unstable Households—Vivian, Sarah, Island

The households in the next three case-studies have more resources, which contributes to more stability. Vivian, Sarah, and Island maintain their own apartments, they feed and clothe their offspring or the children in their care, and they have a more direct and constant relationship with their children. But whereas Maureen, Priscilla, and Fay do not consume drugs in their children's presence, and thus do not directly influence their children's future drug use, Vivian and Sarah freely use drugs around their children. Island drinks moderately and does not use drugs, but her household provides numerous other adult models of drug use.

VIVIAN

Although Vivian does not consider her apartment a crackhouse, she has a continuous flow of "friends" and relatives who freely use drugs and alcohol around her children. Many times children from the neighborhood can be found at her apartment with the adults, and parents come by with their offspring. Vivian keeps her apartment relatively clean. Although she has four children ages 16, 14, 10, and 7 years old, she likes to see "everything in place." Her children are generally well kept. Vivian is also particular about her appearance. Although she is a single parent, she provides the instrumental needs of her family.

Vivian was born in 1958 in the South, but was raised in New York City, where her family of origin moved when she was very young. Shortly after moving North, her father died, leaving her mother to raise 10 children alone.

> My mother had it very hard after my father passed. We would sneak out while she was watchin' television. . . . She had a hard time with us; she couldn't control us 'cause it was so many of us. So we stayed in the street all the time. I always got along with my brothers, and I used to like to follow behind what they was doin'. That's how I started, they'd give me some of whatever they had. . . . I think if my father was still alive we wouldn't of did a lot of things, but my mother she just couldn't keep up with all of us.

At age 10, Vivian began to experiment with alcohol that she acquired from her mother's supply of beer. By the time she was 15 she had begun to snort heroin. This was in 1973, at the height of the heroin era. When Vivian reached 16 years of age, she dropped out of school to have her first child. At this time she was smoking marijuana and still snorting heroin. At age 18, Vivian was pregnant with another child and had added a variety of drugs to her consumption list. She was sniffing Carbona (cleaning fluid), had used LSD on many occasions, had begun snorting cocaine, and was still snorting heroin. At 19, she started injecting cocaine and heroin. As she approached age 28, crack was being widely used and she added crack consumption.

While growing up, Vivian's siblings were, and are, heavily involved in drug use and/or selling. One of her brothers is a drug dealer, and her ex-husband is a drug dealer who has AIDS. Just as she was exposed to substance use through her household members (the mother drank alcohol and her older brothers experimented with drugs and shared them with her), her children are being exposed to and socialized into drug use/selling early in their lives through their household. Field observations of this household illustrate how the transmission of drug behaviors takes place:

> Much of the time her children are home alone with other children of family and friends. Adults and children constantly visit her apartment. Adults freely use drugs and alcohol while the children are present. Adults and children interact on various levels. When the adults want to hear "their music" the children change the tape. Generally, the children are playing tapes and dancing on and off. Children as young as 10 years old are allowed to "pour" drinks for the adults. This is accepted, though some disapproval is shown through comments such as "you too young to drink now so don't take long bringing me my drink" and "you better not drink none either." Adolescents, around the age of 14 or 15, discreetly pour themselves a drink. This is generally done when the adults are not paying attention to what the children are doing. . . . Adults and children come in and out of the apartment. . . . Vivian's ex-husband comes by. He is a crack dealer. He talked of having sold $900 worth of crack today. He has AIDS. The adults are drinking wine and using drugs while the children move in and out of the apartment. It is as if everyone is having a party, an air of festivity without any food, just the drugs and liquor and music.

A style of thinking, communicating, and behaving is being passed on as the children partake in family life. This family life focuses on substance abuse as a norm. This makes it difficult for the growing child to define self beyond the drug culture. Vivian's children are growing up in a family in which their mother consumes drugs, their father uses and sells drugs, and their aunts and uncles also use/sell drugs. Drug involvement permeates family interaction and lifestyle.

The process is like a downward spiral in family life. Vivian's household is categorized as "less unstable" because she provides the instrumental and expressive needs of her family. She maintains an apartment, feeds and clothes her children, and interacts with them. Since she has not abandoned her children, she is considered loyal to the unit. But her social interactions are detrimental to the children. As her children grow older and form families of their own, Vivian will not be able to serve as a stable resource to them. She may give help to her offspring, but the help is not conducive to family stability. For example, Vivian may be able to take in her grandchildren to raise, but like Maureen's mother, she will transmit to them the norms and behavior of drug culture.

Sarah

Sarah also exposes her children to drug use. Her apartment is a crackhouse. Individuals pay a fee of $2 to get into Sarah's apartment to smoke crack. They also have to give a portion of their drug to Sarah. In addition, Sarah rents out the bedrooms in her apartment for sexual activities.

Sarah is 28 years old and has two sons, ages 4 and 10. Her children were introduced to drug activity at a young age through the household. They are exposed to the daily traffic of individuals, many of whom are strangers to the children, invading their home with drugs. Most of the time, Sarah's children are ignored. Sarah feels exceptionally uncomfortable about the lifestyle she is displaying to her children; she therefore sends her children outside frequently. It is common to see her children outside playing late at night or simply roaming the streets. People, objects, and events are all transient for the children. It appears almost impossible for her children to get a sense of place in the world through family life because of this. Television sets disappear and have to be replaced. Many times it is months before the television reappears. Meals have no set time, order, or place. The guilt of having turned her apartment into a crackhouse pushes Sarah to try to make Sundays a day in which she cooks a meal for her family and spends the day with her children. This, of course, is an ideal, for she is rarely able to carry it out. Although she does cook for her children, the meals are erratic and she inevitably ends up letting individuals into her apartment to consume drugs (crack) even on Sundays.

In addition to transient objects and events, interpersonal contact is whimsical. Sarah's guilt hinders her interaction with her children. At times she is intensely involved with her children and at other times she is in her own world. Sarah shifts from intense involvement to total disengagement. Rather than telling her children what to do and giving them guidelines and rules, she responds most of the time to her children's behavior. For example, Sarah will compliment her oldest son for taking care of the younger one and being like a "grown man," but a few minutes later she will be scolding him for being in the house while she has company.

Sarah comes from a strong extended family network. She grew up in a two-parent household in the suburbs of New York City. Both parents worked and raised six children, of which Sarah was the youngest. Her parents frequently worked long hours and left their children home alone. They were not allowed outside when the parents were absent, so most of their time was spent in the house. Sarah received her general equivalency diploma (GED) from a special training school. While growing up she encountered problems with teachers in school. She wanted to drop out of school, but her parents enrolled her in a special training school. Due to her parents' care and support, Sarah was able to complete high school and to obtain better employment than the other women in this study.

At age 12, Sarah began to smoke marijuana. Sarah's oldest brother introduced the younger siblings to drug use.

> We would get high together. . . . We all used to get high together and nobody really knew what was happening. I was 12 when I smoked my first joint. We would watch while George cooked the coke. . . . My oldest brother showed us how to use it. He is in jail now for robbing to get money, but when I first started smoking me and my brothers and sisters we all chipped in and bought the coke and George would cook it up.
> . . . When I was at home me and my brothers and sisters got high every day except Sunday. I started smoking freebase about 1981. My brother he had brought it home to us and showed us how to do it. I was working as a teller and had money all the time then. . . . On Sundays I worked at the numbers spot but I used to dibble and dab in the money, so I lost that when my boss found out.

At age 18, Sarah had her first child. Her husband attempted to dissociate her from her siblings owing to their drug consumption. This was the stimulus for the dissolution of her marriage. Sarah's siblings not only introduced her to drug use, but they also provided her with an ideology, a way of rationalizing her drug behavior.

> I always knew what I was doin' when I took my first hit. I was lucky because I had someone to teach me. . . . My brothers taught me a lot, I love them very much. . . . They taught me how to deal in the street. They always said you have to accept what you do, you know, you can't never have feelings of being sorry when you spend all your money. See you don't sit and cry about it because you knew what you were doin' when you spent that first dollar. I ain't sorry and I don't cry over it. . . . Why cry when you know you are going to do it again tomorrow?

Sarah admired her brothers. Through them she learned how to prepare and use drugs, and the appropriate attitude. Norms, values, expectations, and behaviors were defined and modeled for her through her family kin network. As stated, her relationship with her brothers was also a source of tension in her relationship with her spouse. After the breakup of her marriage, Sarah's parents stepped in and helped her maintain her present household. They make sure her rent is paid, the children have food and clothes, and that Sarah has a telephone.

Sarah provides the expressive and instrumental needs for her family. She interacts with her children, but at the same time this interaction socializes the children into the drug culture in their home environment. Sarah almost certainly will be a less-dependable resource for her children, as they grow older, than her parents have been for her.

ISLAND

Island is a 60-year old female who is the head of her household. She grew up in New York but was born in the Virgin Islands. The family/kin network that she now nurtures are her fictive kinspeople. She was raised by her stepmother and her stepmother's kin network. While growing up she suffered many hardships, but remained faithful to her fictive relatives. She has no contact with her biological relatives and has never known them. Upon birth she was given to her father by her mother. When Island was about 5 years old her father passed away and she was left with her father's wife. Before the death of her father, her stepmother promised him that she would bring Island to the United States and raise her. Similar to most of the other women in this study, Island did not complete high school. She left school in the 11th grade to care for her ailing stepmother. She married at the age of 18 but did not have the first of her two children until five years after her marriage. She was married to an ex-convict who drank heavily and physically abused her and their children. She was forced to leave her husband when her children were very young because her husband raped their daughter, who was then six years old. Shortly after Island separated from her husband, he passed away. Her household became the place of refuge for her entire family kin network.

Island's household is where many of her drug-using relatives' children have been placed by the foster care system. Through her own initiative, Island has taken in and raised many of her relatives' children. Most of the time Island's house is full of family members' children. Most of her relatives lead lives that render them transient and undependable.

Island has been living in her present apartment for over 15 years. She feeds and clothes the children of her family network and maintains constant interaction with them. Island, however, does not use any drug. She drinks moderately. Seldom does she go out to a "party" or other special occasion and have more than a few drinks. Island's son, however, is a "freelance" crack dealer and virtually all her siblings are alcohol users. Her siblings' offspring, including her children, are drug users. Loyalty to family, although fictive, is highlighted. Island's house at any point in time is full of the offspring of various drug-using family members:

> I raised my children. I raised my sister's nine. I raised my brother's 2. And I raised all of my nieces and nephews, I done raised 89 kids. . . . See my sister, she had 2 boys, one baby from one brother, another baby from another brother. . . . And one father was light skinned and one was dark. . . . The light-skinned one told her, take that black baby out of my face, that's not my baby. So I took him home. She had 1 baby from my husband. . . . All her children got different fathers. . . . She got 7. She had 12 in all . . . but 5 died. . . . And she had abortions. Baby must have been what about six, seven months when she gave herself abortion. Took him downstairs and burned him in the furnace. . . . His father made headlines . . . he beat up the police. . . . I raised all her kids. . . . How I got them, she had gave this lady a girl abortion. And the afterbirth killed the girl and the girl told who gave it to her and they came and got her. She went to jail so I had to take care of her kids . . . she did five years. . . . I took care of my brother's 2 children when my brother's wife killed her father. . . . Um, he wanted to beat the mother. He went after the mother and the daughter took an ice pick and stabbed him. . . . And she stayed in jail three years and I raised Deborah and Ronald. . . . Then my sister-in-law got sick and she had 7. I took care of them. Then I had another sister-in-law she got sick and she had some. And I took care of them. . . . And then my sister-in-law, when she died I took Bob and then her kids. I took my niece's 2 kids, then another niece's kids. I had 5 more of my nieces' kids. . . . [I raised them] by myself.

The children growing up in Island's house live in a world in which nothing is permanent. They are moved frequently from foster care institutions to Island's household, to their parents, and back again to Island. This is a vicious circle in which they revolve until they are young adults and can fend for themselves. Interpersonal contact with their parents is arbitrary and impermanent. The frequent movement from one family member's care to another demonstrates the unstable world they become accustomed to at an early age. This also exposes them to multiple erratic nurturing figures.

Island's daughter Sonya (37 years old) and her son Ross (35 years old) help in the care of the children who come into the household. Ross is a freelance crack dealer and Sonya is an ex-heroin addict who smokes crack and is a prostitute. Most of the time Sonya is in her own world. Her attitude toward the children is one of annoyance. She responds to the children's behavior rather than setting guidelines and rules. The children have to watch her carefully because she shifts from one mood to another frequently. Her involvement can be aggressive but rarely nurturing:

> At about this time a baby began to cry and Sonya went and rolled a stroller out of the closet. I learned that the little girl was about 18 months old. I am told that she becomes very afraid when she is around males. When a male enters the room she goes into a crying fit. When she did this Sonya rolled the stroller into the closet and let her cry until she went to sleep. She felt that the baby was tired anyway and needed the rest. The mother [Island] is keeping the child for her friend who lives upstairs on the floor above them. . . . I see that the child is treated indifferently. Sonya takes her out of the stroller by one arm and puts her on the floor. The little girl goes over to where Sonya's mother is sitting and stays near her. The mother never recognizes the child. . . . In a few minutes he [Ross] came into the living room, picked the baby girl out of the stroller, and changed her diaper. He then put her on the floor to play and this started a conversation about the baby and the dog who continued to run from her. No one pays her any attention.

The children currently in Island's care, ages five, seven, and nine, receive similar treatment. Much of the time the television set gets most of the attention. When they come home from school, the children are more or less ignored unless they do something that solicits correction. No one checks or cares whether homework is given or worked on. There is no inquiry about the school day or about anything that happened that day with the child. The children are very careful not to annoy the adults. Food is cooked and left on the stove for each individual to make a plate when hungry. Too much food eaten by any one person is enough to cause a family feud. Thus, the feature of family and home environment for the children coming through Island's household is impermanence and unpredictability. The motivating factor behind most of the behavior is drug use. The result of these factors is evident in what has happened to most of the children that have been raised in Island's household:

> Well, they say you could have the strength, you ask the Lord to give you strength and he give it to you. . . . Arthur . . . 16 years I had him. Arthur had got in trouble by following somebody selling drugs. . . . Norman, you see Norman was put away. Norman's mother, when Norman was about six years old, was drinking wine. And when he do something she skin his meat [penis] back and forth. . . . Yeah, and pull in and kinda punch him. . . . And he got tired of it and he left. He ran away and the police find him one morning sleeping on the car. That's

how I got him. He got mixed up with the wrong crowd and went out there and robbed a cab and that's why he's back in jail. And Barbara, just got out there and she started doing what her mother did. Smoking reefers and what not and using that stuff. . . . Loretta was a drug addict all her life, all her days. . . . Well most of them are out there in the street. Barbara, she's in jail and Norman in jail. BoBo he somewhere in Brooklyn. Roy and Karema is back with their mother. The other ones are out there in the street with drugs and what not. . . . I don't want no drug addict around me. I'm tired of that. That's why I wanted to get away. Sonya and Ross and I want to get away. I can't get no rest.

Although Island does not consume drugs herself, her son sells drugs (angel dust, heroin, and at present, crack). Much of what has happened to the children who have lived with her has been influenced by her son and daughter who reside with her. Although most of these children have been introduced to drugs through their own parents, in Island's household they are furthermore exposed to drugs, causing further problems. When Island talks of Arthur being in jail for "following somebody selling drugs," the "somebody" she refers to is her son, Ross. Norman, Wilford, and Arthur are only a few of Island's family/kin members who have been raised by her and have sold drugs for Ross. Before his present jail charges, Norman was on probation for selling drugs.

Island's household is more stable than most of the members of her kin network, yet it is by no means free from the effects of drugs. The children coming into her household are further exposed to the economic realities of drug use. The young men have inadequate education and no skills to get jobs, so their only alternative is to sell drugs for their uncle. As Island talked of being tired of drugs and drug-using members, she related the desire to get away, to flee all the confusion, just her with her daughter Sonya and her son Ross. But Sonya is a crack user and a prostitute, and Ross is a freelance crack dealer. In this we see the dilemma of many families: their powerlessness to prevent the destruction of their households or family kin network.

The motivating factor behind most of the behavior in Island's family kin network is substance abuse. Her kinship network displays another dimension of family instability: Island's sister-in-law kills her father to protect her mother, goes to jail, and thus Island raises her children. Contact with the criminal justice system, unemployment, family desertion, lack of health care, violence in relationships, and confusion over self-identity (as evidenced by the dispute over the "shade" of color of a child) are some of the many issues that surface in this family. At the same time, one sees in Island the degree of stability that an

extended family can give to the family/kin network. With each trag-
edy, Island is a "saving force" for the children.

The predominance of drugs and their role in undermining the stability of many inner city families is seen in another dimension as
Island talks about her siblings' and other relatives' substance abuse
and family relations:

> Yeah, all of them [her siblings] drink. I got one sister . . . you go over
> there and she just tell you she giving you some more and then she'll
> give you a Mickey [Finn]. . . . That's the way she do. . . . She call that
> socialize, you know, put a Mickey in your drink she thinks that fun.
> . . . Well, her daughter did [take drugs]. . . . My other sister got four
> girls. One of her girls don't, uh, take drugs. But Lucy, Henrietta, Lance
> did [use drugs]. Susan don't do it. Now she [the sister] got one son in
> jail for murder. He killed a man on Belview Street and Denver Boule-
> vard. He stabbed him 17 times. . . . He said his mother is next when he
> come home. . . . He told his stepfather that he had stabbed a man and
> when he went to get a bottle for his mother she called the police on
> him, she told him take your last drink. And he said for her doing that
> he gonna get her when he come home. . . . Andrew was in the street.
> Dorsey's in the street. Henrietta in the street. Danny do [use drugs].
> Doris do [use drugs]. She, she got AIDS. . . . She's a prostitute crack-
> head, dopehead. Anything you wanna name she is one. . . . Dorsey he
> gets the doctors and gets the crack. . . . Go and get the doctors and get
> the scrit [prescriptions] and sell the pill to get crack. . . . The baby boy
> he got stepchildren. He think he better than anybody else so I don't
> mingle with him. . . . He think he better . . . 'cuz he's a big time crack
> dealer. Dope seller on Eva St. . . . He don't mingle with us.

Here is presented another illustration of parents and offspring participating in substance abuse. Along with the issues of generational
transmission of drug use, and parent-offspring joint participation in
substance consumption, is the issue of trust among family members.
People learn to love and trust in Island's household. But, when children grow up in households where the basic element of trust is dis-
torted, their outside interaction will be destructive. In Island's family,
the sister "tricks" people by putting Mickeys in their drinks. When
her son kills someone, she neither discusses it with him nor advises
him to turn himself in, but calls the police while he has gone to the
store to buy her a bottle of liquor.

Substance abuse can be grounded in family experiences in a variety
of ways, not just in the structural aspect of the family. Such findings
are consistent with the theoretical model that relates drug abuse to
environmental stress (Duncan 1974, 1975); and with the view that
substance abuse may be a mechanism whereby individuals cope with

a stressful family and social environment (Duncan 1974, 1975; Khant-zian, Mack, and Schatzberg 1974; Randall 1971).

Although Island acts as a shield against much of the brutality and chaos in the life of children belonging to various family kin members, she further reinforces the drug environment for these children. Virtually all the children she has raised now use or sell drugs, are in prison or on probation, or in the street.

CONCLUSION

In each of the cases included here, drug abuse and sales within the larger family kin network exercise a tremendous influence on life within the single-parent household. The abuse of drugs, particularly of crack, in the black community is having a devastating effect on families. Families that previously would have been viewed as stable by supplying instrumental needs (even if at a subpoverty or minimal level) and emotional support from the kinship unit (although single-parent units) are drastically affected by the crack epidemic. African-American females who traditionally have played a vital role in keeping families intact are being psychologically, emotionally, and financially overwhelmed. Provision of food, clothes, and shelter becomes secondary to the needs of addicted mothers to acquire crack. In many instances, these woman were, and their children are, grossly neglected. Many women experienced physical and psychological violence very early in their lives; the consequences are evident in their neglect and mistreatment of their own children. Nurturance, the expression of warmth and positive feelings among family members and a common element in many precrack single parent households, is disappearing.

At the same time, kinship support systems, both real and fictive, are being overwhelmed by the sheer numbers of children that must be cared for by the more stable households. Island estimates that 89 children from her extended family or neighborhood have lived with her for significant periods of time. Fay's stepparents provided support for her, her siblings, her children, and others, but could not provide a home for Fay's last four "crack babies."

This chapter's discussion has only begun to touch on the issue of family stability. The family unit is deemed stable to the degree it is able to provide for instrumental and expressive needs. The first three cases demonstrate the total breakdown of the single-parent unit as measured by the inability of the parent to provide food, shelter, and clothing for her offspring. Although the parent may not have influenced the child's future substance use directly, the larger kin network in which the child was placed introduced the drug environment. The second set of cases illustrates more direct transmission of substance abuse behavior. That is, the parent introduces drug consumption by modeling such behavior for the child. The child may participate in this consumption through pouring drinks and interacting with adults while they are consuming drugs. Individuals may acquire an ideology or a perspective regarding their substance abuse through family members, and may also be introduced to other aspects of drugs such as dealing.

For these households, the family and home environment is impermanent and unpredictable. It is almost impossible for children growing up in these families to define themselves except in relation to the world of drugs that surrounds them. The wider kin network that might rescue them from a drug orientation only reinforces it and helps to isolate further the individual from "mainstream" influences.

References

Aldous, J. 1969. "Wives' Employment Status and Lower Class Men as Husband-Fathers: Support for the Moynihan Thesis." *Journal of Marriage and the Family* (Aug.): 469–76.

Bernard, J. 1966. *Marriage and Family among Negroes.* Englewood Cliffs, N.J.: Prentice-Hall.

Billingsley, A. 1968. *Black Families in White America.* New York: Simon & Schuster.

Blumer, H. 1969. *Symbolic Interactionism: Perspective and Method.* New Jersey: Prentice-Hall.

Deren, S. 1986. "Children of Substance Abusers: A Review of the Literature. *Journal of Substance Abuse Treatment* 3: 77–94.

Deren, S., B. Frank, and J. Schmeidler. 1988."Children of Substance Abusers in New York State: Trends and Estimates." Treatment Issue Report 67, New York State Division of Substance Abuse Services, Bureau of Research and Evaluation. New York: New York State Division of Substance Abuse Services, April.

Duncan, D.F. 1974. "Reinforcement of Non-Narcotic Drug Dependence." *Clinical Toxicology Bulletin* 4(2): 69–75.

————. 1975. "The Acquisition, Maintenance, and Treatment of Polydrug Dependence: A Public Health Model." *Journal of Psychedelic Drugs* 7: 209–13.

Dunlap, E. Forthcoming. "Inner-city Crisis and Drug Dealing: Portrait of a Drug Dealer and His Household." In *Crisis and Resistance: Social Relations and Economic Restructuring in the City*, edited by Suzanne MacGregor. London: University of Minnesota and Edinburgh Press.

Eldred, C., and M. Washington. 1976. "Interpersonal Relationships in Heroin Use by Men and Women and Their Role in Treatment Outcome." *Interpersonal Journal of the Addictions* 11(1): 117–30.

Fawzy, F.I., R.H. Coombs, and B. Gerber. 1983. "Generational Continuity in the Use of Substances: The Impact of Parental Substance Use on Adolescent Substance Use." *Addictive Behaviors* 8: 109–14.

Foster, H. J. 1983. "African Patterns in Afro-American Family." *Journal of Black Studies* 14: 201–32.

Frazier, E. F. 1939. *The Negro Family in the United States*. Chicago: University of Chicago Press.

Gerstein, D. R., L. L. Judd, and S. A. Rovner. 1979. "Career Dynamics of Female Addicts." *American Journal of Drug and Alcohol Abuse* 6: 1–23.

Gilby, R. L., and D. R. Pederson. 1982. "The Development of the Child's Concept of the Family." *Canadian Journal of Behavioral Science* 14: 110–21.

Gomberg, E. 1979. "Problems with Alcohol and Other Drugs." In *Gender and Disordered Behavior*, edited by E. Gomberg and V. Franks. New York: Brunner/Mazel.

Gutman, H. G. 1976. *The Black Family in Slavery and Freedom: 1750–1925*. New York: Random House.

Hale, J. 1982. *Black Children: Their Roots, Culture, and Learning Styles*. Provo, Utah: Brigham Young University Press.

Hill, R. 1971. *The Strengths of Black Families*. New York: National Urban League.

————. 1972. *The Strengths of Black Families*. New York: Emerson-Hall.

Hodkin, B. 1983. "The Concept of Family: Building an Empirical Base." Paper presented at the annual meeting of the Canadian Psychological Association, Winnepeg. June.

Jaynes, G.D., and R.M. Williams, eds. 1989. *Blacks and American Society*. Washington, D.C.: National Academy Press.

Johnson, B. D. 1991. *Natural History of Crack Distribution/Abuse*. Grant Proposal to National Institute on Drug Abuse.

Johnson, B. D., and A. Manwar. 1991. "Towards a Paradigm of Drug Eras: Previous Drug Eras Help to Model the Crack Epidemic in New York City during the 1990s." Paper presented at the Cocaine/Crack Research Working Group, New York. November.

Johnson, B. D., T. Williams, K. Dei, and H. Sanabria. 1990. "Drug Abuse in the Inner City: Impact on Hard Drug Users and the Community." In

Drugs and Crime, edited by M. Tonry and J. Q. Wilson, (313–71). Chicago: University of Chicago Press.

Johnston, L. D., P. M. O'Malley, and J. G. Bachman. 1991. "Drug Use Trends among High School Students." Press Release. Rockville, Md.: National Institute on Drug Abuse.

Johnson, V., and R. J. Pandina. 1991. "Effects of the Family Environment on Adolescent Substance Use, Delinquency, and Coping Styles." *American Journal of Drug Alcohol Abuse* 17(1): 71–88.

Khantzian, E. J., J. F. Mack, and A. F. Schatzberg. 1974. "Heroin Use as an Attempt to Cope: Clinical Observations." *American Journal of Psychiatry*, 131: 160–64.

Ladner, J. 1971. *Tomorrow's Tomorrow: The Black Woman*. Garden City, N.J.: Doubleday.

Lane, W. 1980. "Classical Moral Paradigms and the Meaning of Kinship: A Philosophical Examination." *Dialectical Anthropology* 5: 193–214.

Langner, T. S., J. C. Gersten, E. Greene, J. Eisenberg, and E. McCarthy. 1974. "Treatment of Psychological Disorders among Urban Children." *Journal of Consulting and Clinical Psychology* 42(2):170–79.

Liebow, E. 1966. *Tally's Corner*. Boston: Little-Brown.

Madhubuti, H.R. 1990. *Black Men: Obsolete, Single, Dangerous? The Afrikan American Family in Transition*. Chicago: Third World Press.

Moise, R., B. G. Reed, and V. S. Ryan. 1982. "Issues in the Treatment of Heroin Addicted Women: A Comparison of Men and Women Entering Two Types of Drug Abuse Programs." *International Journal of the Addictions*, 17(1): 109–39.

Moynihan, D. 1965. "Tangle of Pathology." In *The Black Family: Essays and Studies*, edited by R. Staples (3–13). Belmont, Calif.: Wadsworth.

Myrdal, G. 1964. *An American Dilemma*. New York: Pantheon.

Nichtern, S. 1973. "The Children of Drug Users." *Journal of the American Academy of Child Psychiatry* 12: 24–31.

Nobles, W. 1974. "Africanity: Its Role in Black Families." *Black Scholar* 9: 10–17.

————. 1985. *Africanity and the Black Family: The Development of a Theoretical Model*. Oakland, Calif.: Institute for the Advanced Study of Black Family Life and Culture.

Pleck, E. 1973. *The American Family in Social-Historical Perspective*, edited by Michael Gordon. New York: St. Martin Press.

Ploski, H. A., and J. Williams, eds. 1983. *The Negro Almanac. A Reference Work on the Afro-American*, 4th ed. New York: Wiley-Interscience Publication.

Rainwater, L. 1970. *Behind Ghetto Walls: Black Families in a Federal Slum*. Chicago: Aldine.

Ratner, Michelle (ed.). 1992. *Crack Pipe as Pimp: An Eight City Study of the Sex-for-Crack Phenomena*. New York: Lexington Books (forthcoming).

Randall, B.P. 1971. "Short-Term Group Therapy with the Adolescent Drug Offender." *Perspectives in Psychiatric Care* 9: 123–28.

Rodman, H. 1963. "The Lower Class Value Stretch." *Social Forces* 42 (Dec.): 205–15.

Rutgers University. 1983. "Children of Alcoholics." In *Alcohol Bibliography Series*. Piscataway, N.J.: Center of Alcohol Studies Library.

Scazoni, J. 1971. *The Black Family in Modern Society.* Boston, Mass.: Allyn and Bacon.

Schneider, D. M. 1980. *American Kinship: A Cultural Account.* Englewood Cliffs, N.J.: Prentice-Hall.

Speigal, J. 1982. "An Ecological Model of Ethnic Families." *Ethnicity and Family Therapy,* edited by G.J. Pearce and J. Giordano (31–51). New York: Guilford Press.

Smart, R. G., and D. Fejer. 1972. "Drug Use among Adolescents and Their Parents: Closing the Generation Gap in Mood Modification." *Journal of Abnormal Psychology* (79): 153–60.

Sowder, B., and M. R. Burt. 1980. "Children of Heroin Addicts: An Assessment of Health, Learning, Behavioral, and Adjustment Problems." New York: Praeger.

Sowder, B., Y. M. Carnes, and S. N. Sherman. 1981. "Children of Addicts in Surrogate Care." Services Research Branch, National Institute on Drug Abuse. Institute for Human Resources Research. April. Photocopy.

Weber, M. 1958. *The Protestant Ethic and the Spirit of Capitalism.* New York: Free Press.

Willie, C. 1976. *A New Look at Black Families.* New Bayside, N.Y.: General Hall.

Wilson, M. N. 1984. "Mothers' and Grandmothers' Perception of Parental Behavior in Three-Generational Black Families." *Child Development* 55: 1333–39.

———. 1986. "The Extended Family: An Analytical Consideration." *Developmental Psychology* 22: 246–58.

———. 1989. "Child Development in the Context of the Black Extended Family." *American Psychologist* 44(2): 380–85.

Chapter Seven

DRUGS AND PATTERNS OF OPPORTUNITY IN THE INNER CITY: THE CASE OF MIDDLE-AGED, MIDDLE-INCOME COCAINE SMOKERS

Ansley Hamid

A remarkable property of crack, or smokable cocaine, is its appeal to an older generation living in low-income minority neighborhoods. The "War on Drugs" has generated widespread emotional support among Americans because they believe it is a crusade to save the very young from the temptations of drugs; typically, however, crack users are older persons. In my primary study sites in Harlem (Manhattan) and Flatbush (Brooklyn), New York City, crack users tend to be clustered in the 30-and-above age range, with only a few younger than 23. This finding also applies in other local communities (Curtis 1991). Moreover, crack consumption has invaded the middle class of the inner-city. Those arrested recently in New York for alleged use include a high school principal, school teachers, police officers, corrections officers, managerial staff in both public and private corporations, and other mature professionals or seasoned workers.

Youths, on the other hand, are now involved with crack mainly as distributors. Although some have experimented with crack, most have quickly discontinued it, even by seeking out treatment or professional support. Among youth groups, powerful norms appear to have arisen discouraging the use of "hard" drugs such as heroin and smokable cocaine (Hamid 1991). As a result, it is rare for a young man or woman in Harlem or Flatbush today to smoke cocaine. Beer, cigarettes, and

This research was supported by a grant from the National Institute on Drug Abuse, to study the "Natural History of Crack Distribution," and by the Harry Frank Guggenheim Foundation. Additional support was provided by Narcotic and Drug Research, Inc., and by the John Jay College of Criminal Justice of the City University of New York. The opinions in this paper do not necessarily represent the official positions of the United States Government, Narcotic and Drug Research, Inc., or John Jay College of Criminal Justice.

I acknowledge with appreciation the many contributions to this research and paper made by Eloise Dunlap, Earl Beddoe, Rick Curtis, Lisa Maher, and Bruce Johnson.

marijuana are their preferred drugs. The few who use cocaine intra-nasally call it "nitro," as if to deny that the substance is cocaine. Young males in this age group apparently find crack users (who may be older siblings or even parents) so repulsive that some have made a pastime of beating them up (Hemphill 1990).

This chapter considers some consequences of crack's popularity among older users. In particular, I discuss the role that crack use, in this segment of the population, has played in the social and economic decline of low-income, minority neighborhoods and in the loss of older role models who can link youths to the mainstream job market.

ECONOMIC AND SOCIAL DECLINE IN THE INNER CITY

The gross parameters of the decline of inner-city neighborhoods in New York City and in major cities across the United States have by now been well documented (Hughes 1988; Jencks and Peterson 1991; Kasarda, chapter 3, this volume; Moss and Tilly 1991; Myrdal 1962; Ricketts and Sawhill 1988; Wilson 1987). Since the 1960s, New York City has lost over 520,000 manufacturing jobs. In the same time period, the city lost over 50 percent of its low-income housing units. A consequence of male unemployment has been a decline in marriages and a rise in the number of female-headed households, while the loss of affordable housing has obliged households to suffer makeshift shelter and highly mobile lifestyles, or to "double up" and "treble up" in housing units meant for single families.

By the 1980s, these effects had become concentrated in areas similar to the study neighborhoods in Central Harlem and Flatbush. Both study sites were principal recipients of intra- and interneighborhood migration during that decade. When housing in nearby neighborhoods was destroyed through abandonment, arson, or accidental fires, residents fled to the study sites, crowding into the available housing.

By 1990, at least three generations often were co-resident in the same household, made even more crowded by the presence of nonrelated sharers or "paying guests." But the paths of the household members diverged greatly; the sense of a coherent unit with common purposes had vanished. A typical woman in her late 40s or early 50s may be a grandmother. Having recovered from alcohol (and sometimes heroin) use in the 1960s, she has now rediscovered church and is devoted to it. Meanwhile her children 23 years of age or older have been devastated by crack, and live in a circle distinct from and even predatory upon the mother's. Her grandchildren, from ages 12 to 23, resist crack and heroin use, have dropped out of school, are unemployed, and are parenting their own infants. Some sell drugs, and the few who are briefly successful at it may contribute economically to the household. Children under the age of 12 in the house may be the offspring of any of the preceding generations. Often neglected, they form cliques that roam at will from the television set to the streets.

My study neighborhoods are among the most socially distressed of New York City. They outrank other areas in the proportion of population living in poverty, dropout rates among children of school age, criminal offending (at any age and in every offense category), drug arrests, child abuse and neglect, poor health indicators, and substance abuse. New York Police Department (NYPD) precinct statistics show that within the patrol borough of Brooklyn South in 1989, the Flatbush study site ranked first in robbery, rape, burglary, and grand larceny complaints; second in assault complaints; and third in homicide and grand larceny auto complaints. It ranked second in the number of narcotics complaints and arrests; in Manhattan North, Central Harlem topped every list (NYPD precinct statistics, 1989). As the statistics worsened, the public began to consider these parts of the city "off-limits." Other citizens rarely set foot in the neighborhoods. Those who resided there rarely left the neighborhood for legal job opportunities or cultural enrichment.

PIVOTAL ROLE OF MIDDLE-AGED WORKERS

In the erosion of inner-city neighborhoods, the role of mature workers is pivotal. Mature workers have high societal value because they are expected to be mature parents and householders who teach work-related skills and attitudes in their families, and uphold orderliness and pride in the neighborhood. In America, they have been the backbone of strong unions, political clubs, churches, parent-teachers associations, and similar organizations. Older workers also play crucial roles in the upward mobility of youth. Many jobs become available to younger men through informal recruitment by older relatives and friends. Older workers, or "old heads," cultivate a coterie of young protegés, whom they train to be work-ready, then place in actual employment (Anderson 1990). The "old head" institution also strengthens community and cross-generational cohesion. One could surmise that the decline of the inner city could not have occurred had there been sufficient mature and stable workers who pulled their weight, invested their disposable incomes and energies wisely, and looked out for the young men and women coming up.

RESEARCH METHOD

Since 1978 I have been engaged in a number of anthropological research projects focusing on drug use and distribution in several sections of Brooklyn and Harlem. I lived in a Brooklyn study site continuously for five years and have been living in another in Central Harlem for the past seven years (since 1985). In these research projects, more than 200 study participants have been interviewed, tape-recorded, and observed in their neighborhood settings. I have also made additional observations in other neighborhoods where I have not resided.

In this fieldwork, I have been struck by the large number of middle-aged (30- to 50-year-old), middle-income ($30,000–$60,000 per annum) persons who have become crack users, and have lost considerable status or local standing as a result. The individuals portrayed in this chapter are typical of my sample of crack users. They are drawn principally from "freakhouses" (defined in the next section) in a six-block area of Central Harlem in which I have conducted intensive work since 1989. I have preserved the study participants' statements of their earnings and accounts of their job careers. Although in some cases these may be exaggerated, other evidence (for example, speech, dress, familiarity with things, persons, and places) identify all participants as having belonged to the $30,000-plus income bracket, and to have enjoyed relatively comfortable childhoods.

HOW SMOKABLE COCAINE ERODED MIDDLE-AGE AND MIDDLE-INCOME STATUS

What happened to the many Caribbean-Africans and African-Americans who remained resident in Flatbush and Central Harlem after they had gained jobs as professionals, corrections officers, policemen, junior executives, bank tellers, small businessmen and contractors, or skilled and unionized workers? Many of them had a rendezvous with smokable cocaine.

Cocaine smoking was diffused in New York City's lower-income minority neighborhoods in at least five successive stages. In the first stage (1979–81), the intranasal use of cocaine hydrochloride powder escalated in *"after-hours clubs."* Its distributors (who were often controlled smokers of freebase, the first form of smokable cocaine in the current "epidemic") experienced a sudden surge in prosperity and popularity. In the second stage (1982–85), *"freebase parlors"* were established in the homes/distribution outlets of these distributors, where freebase was isolated batch-by-batch from cocaine hydrochloride powder and served to a select company of experimenters. In the third stage (1986–87), as personal use destroyed the viability of early distributors, their (mostly nonusing) successors converted rental units specifically into businesses, or *"crackhouses,"* where preprepared, prepackaged freebase (now called "crack," and packaged in vials) was sold as well as consumed. The apartments of users were also important locales for group use and for initiating newcomers to the practice. Some were commandeered by distributors and turned into crackhouses. In the fourth stage (1987–90), indoor selling locations such as crackhouses were eclipsed by *"curbside distribution,"* where many competing distributors (usually as independent freelancers, or sometimes organized in "businesses," "gangs," and "posses") manned street corners to have the first shot at a steeply increased clientele. Use was often "curbside" too, particularly for the many users who had by then lost their apartments and had overstayed their welcome at friends' or relatives' homes. Since 1990, it appears that cocaine smoking has entered a fifth stage of "peaking" and decline. *"Freakhouses,"* or the apartments of users who still have them, have emerged as locales of use and as shelters for other homeless users, while an appreciably humbled distribution remains "curbside" ("Briefings" 1990; Treasler 1991; Hamid 1991).

In each of these five stages, the lead was taken by mature, middle-aged, seasoned workers, self-employed persons, or individuals who had distinguished themselves in successful, long-lived criminal careers such as pimping, numbers-running, racketeering, and the distribution of the other illegal drugs (heroin and marijuana). "After-hours clubs" created the demimonde where affluent persons from both legitimate and illegitimate enterprises met to show off and to have expensive fun. In "freebase parlors," only these individuals could afford the $50 (half-gram) batches of freebase that were being prepared continuously during "binges" that lasted 48 or 72 hours. Then in "crackhouses" or in their apartments, as cocaine prices fell until $5 bought as much as $50 did formerly, these same users introduced the practice to a more heterogeneous, poorer but mostly coeval, population of initiates. The stage of "curbside use and distribution" saw all these older persons on the street buying crack from teenaged, nonusing distributors, in some cases their own children. Today, "freakhouses" are often the apartments of elderly single males (60 years of age or older), who are the latest (and, it seems, the last) segment of the population to initiate cocaine smoking. Assured of their apartments through Social Security Insurance (SSI) payments, they attract a serfdom of other crack-using males and females who exchange tithes of sex, crack, and money in return for living space.

In the case studies presented here, persons over the age of 23 explain their crack use and its consequences. The narratives cover many themes—for instance, that "fast" money grows "faster" when cocaine distribution supplants marijuana, and yet the change is ruinous to distributor and consumer alike. Other cases explore the ways in which common complaints of middle age and middle income are given a new twist by crack: restlessness and a longing for unaccustomed excitement, rebelliousness against middle-class norms and values, the challenge of unprecedented amounts of disposable income, and the emergence of criminal tendencies that had so far remained hidden.

RASTA MUSA'S[1] FREEBASE PARLOR: THE PITFALL OF "FAST" MONEY

Rasta Musa's career illustrates how a significant political and economic force in minority communities was fragmented following the onset of smokable cocaine. Spearheaded by middle-aged Caribbean-African marijuana distributors who had prospered in some 15 years of successful marijuana distribution, the Rastafari movement initiated an influential program, utilizing exclusively indigenous capital and resources, for Caribbean cultural and economic development. At the same time it mobilized Caribbean immigrant populations in New York City to compete more effectively in the city's fiercely ethnic politics and commerce (Hamid 1980). Rastafarians constituted a "development elite" in New York as in the Caribbean.

The following account of one prominent Rastafarian's participation and downfall in the evolving New York drug scene records how co-

---

1. To protect their identities, none of the individuals in this chapter's case studies is referred to by his/her real name.

caine and crack distribution came to supplant other drugs. It also notes the strong resistance to cocaine that Rastafarians exerted, before eventually succumbing to both its use and distribution.

Middle-Aged, Mid-Level Marijuana Distributor

Musa was 35 years of age when he settled in Flatbush, Brooklyn, in 1971. It was rumored that he was well-educated, widely traveled, and had held a government position in Trinidad, his home country. In New York, he had worked for a number of years at various low-paid, free-lance, literate jobs: as contributor to a pornography magazine, as an occasional columnist in a Caribbean magazine, and as a data processor for an advertising firm in Manhattan. Then, in 1976, while working on a reggae music project in Jamaica and New York with a video production company, one of his Euro-American co-workers introduced him to a Euro-American marijuana grower from Oregon. The grower assured Musa that he had hundreds of pounds of fresh high-grade sinsemilla ("without seed": intensively cultivated, high-potency marijuana). He offered sinsemilla to Musa at $1,200 a pound, which Musa knew he could sell in Brooklyn for $2,800. He asked the grower to entrust a pound to him and assured him that he would return with the money in about an hour. He returned, paid the grower $1,200 and kept $1,600 for himself. A few weeks later, the grower introduced Musa to several Euro-American suppliers of Colombian "commercial" (the staple of the booming street-level marijuana traffic, selling for $300–$500 per pound), who also stocked "exotics"—high-grade marijuanas, hashish, and hash oils from around the world.

Middling Prosperity

In this way Musa became established as a mid-level marijuana distributor, who "moved weight" (sold pounds or more) from importers and cultivators to street-level sellers. A few Rastafari "blocks" (distributing organizations selling marijuana from one or several street-level locations) depended on him to supply them. He sold 3 to 5 pounds of sinsemilla a week, making a $300 commission on each pound; and 20 or more pounds of "commercial" marijuana, at a profit of $50–$100 on the pound. He soon accumulated a substantial fortune, and bought property in relatives' names in Trinidad and California.

Middle-Age Political and Ideological Development And Commitment to Community

In 1974, Musa became an ardent Rastafari. He was among the first Caribbean-Africans from islands other than Jamaica to embrace the ideology and to wear dreadlocks (hair allowed to grow long and matted by shunning combs or brushes, as the Old Testament recommends). He had expert knowledge of the Scriptures and of the writings and world view of Marcus Mosiah Garvey, a Jamaican Pan-Africanist who had stimulated the spread of Rastafarianism in the 1930s on his home island, and is revered as a prophet of the religion. The Garveyite tenet that Musa heeded most exhorted Africans at home and throughout the diaspora to develop their independent economic institutions. In the 1920s, Garvey had raised subscriptions in the United States of $5 each for the organization he founded, the Universal Negro Improvement Association, and had invested in a shipping company, the Black Star Line, whose ships traded between West Africa, the Caribbean, and the United States. He also founded newspapers, restaurants, and other businesses. In Musa's mind, the "nickel bags" (small brown envelopes, stuffed with about four grams of "commercial" marijuana and selling for $5) that were packaged by his street-level distributors were subscriptions, identical to Garvey's, that he was asking from this generation of Africans.

Adapting Garvey's prescriptions, Musa encouraged mid-level Jamaican distributors like himself to stimulate cultivation in Jamaica. Rural Jamaicans were taught to grow, cure, and export sinsemilla to the United States in quantities sufficient to meet their demand. They were then independent of Euro-American or Hispanic importers of Colombian, Mexican, or Far Eastern product, as well as of domestic growers. On a smaller scale, Rastafarians eventually expanded marijuana production in Trinidad and introduced it to Grenada. Musa was thus an early founder of a movement that eventually "Caribbeanized" a sizable corner of New York's marijuana market.

In New York, Musa reinvested much of his marijuana revenues in conformity to Rastafari principles. He helped some co-religionists establish their own "gates" (street-level marijuana distributorships). He gave seed money to others for a health-food store and a vegetarian cookshop, and earned the affection of many Rastafari "daughters" (young women) for his financial support of their efforts in becoming seamstresses, making Rastafari artifacts, parenting, and education. Many mid-level Rastafari marijuana distributors followed his example.

Middle-Age Spirituality

Musa was recognized for his "good works." Personally, he lived an austere and even ascetic life, exercised regularly, and played ball in the park. He lived alone, had no car, dressed casually, and had a modest manner of speaking. His many co-religionists visited his home regularly but briefly. Apparently his affairs with women were respectful and discreet, and in the neighborhood he was mostly seen by himself. On Marcus Garvey's birthday, he welcomed guests to a vegetarian feast and an evening of drumming and Rastafari chants. The event became an institution in Rastafari Brooklyn and demonstrated the high esteem in which he was regarded.

How Interdiction Destroyed the Marijuana Economy and Promoted Cocaine

When cocaine for intranasal use was introduced to Musa in the late 1970s by a young Puerto Rican marijuana distributor, he refused it and explained that it was contrary to his religious beliefs. In the winter of 1981, however, his attitude changed. Vigorous street-level interruption of the marijuana traffic by law enforcement agencies, international seizures of large shipments, and successful crop eradication and substitution programs had made marijuana scarce. Musa had been spending much of his time at a candy store in Harlem, from which "nickel bags" of "commercial" and "dimes" of sinsemilla were sold by a co-religionist, Rafi.

Tired and dispirited one night, he was approached by two young Puerto Rican women of mixed African descent who were regular customers at the candy store. Although in the past he had politely ignored their smiles and other signs of favor toward him, this time he stepped out from behind the bulletproof partition and walked with them out of the store. The young women, sisters named Joanna and Nancy, confessed that they were very attracted by Musa's graying dreadlocks and his kindly manner. They wanted to know him better. They were strangers in the predominantly African-American neighborhood, and made their living through discreet prostitution. Musa accompanied them to their apartment on Adam Clayton Powell Boulevard, and, perhaps spurred on by the sisters' genuine friendliness, snorted some of the cocaine they offered him. The drug relieved the anxiety and fatigue that had overcome him. He stayed the night at the sisters'.

Subsequently, Musa was seen often in their company. In Brooklyn, he made inquiries and was soon introduced to a cocaine powder distributor from whom he bought "8ths" (3½ grams $275) several times a week. The marijuana traffic showed sudden bursts of activity that provided him with the money. He also discovered that many of the marijuana distributors he dealt with also used cocaine intranasally. When they visited, mounds of cocaine were shared and exchanged.

Overcoming Misgivings about Cocaine

Although the intranasal use of cocaine was becoming more prevalent among Rastafarians, they were still distrustful of the practice, which violated their religious beliefs. Marijuana use and distribution (as well as vegetarianism) were divinely justified. But where was the justification for cocaine? Rastafarians rationalized that it was a tonic with merely physical effects: it toned up the body, it stimulated and prolonged sex, and it induced wakefulness. It was an extraordinary food rather than a drug.

Learning to Smoke Cocaine from Colombians in Trinidad

Musa's doubts about cocaine were removed during a trip he made with Joanna and Nancy to Trinidad early in 1982. Marijuana had been impossible to find in New York, and he had needed a holiday as well as an opportunity to attend to business he maintained on the island. Both women traveled with several ounces of cocaine strapped to the insides of their thighs. In Trinidad, they went to Rafi's father's house in Central Trinidad. Rafi, the earlier-mentioned Rastafari marijuana distributor from Harlem, had also returned home and had started a very popular reggae discotheque that his father managed.

"Taking coals to Newcastle" is the quaint Anglo-Caribbean phrase Musa used to describe their import of cocaine into Trinidad. Several Colombian distributors were conspicuous in inner-city neighborhoods in Port-of-Spain and San Fernando, Trinidad's largest cities. Each had a few kilos of high-grade cocaine to sell, at prices well below those in New York. Rafi and Musa befriended one, Pablo, in Port-of-Spain and took him home to Central Trinidad.

Rafi's discotheque was a well-known drug distribution locale, and many intranasal users of cocaine in Trinidad, whose numbers were increasing, started going there to buy the drug. Pablo, the Colombian, produced five kilos, which were quickly sold. Pablo also taught Musa and Rafi how to smoke freebase. He had brought with him half a kilo of "basuca" (cocaine paste preceding crystallization), which he cooked into freebase with baking soda.

Eventually Musa returned to New York City with four kilos of cocaine from Pablo, strapped as before to Joanna and Nancy. One of his first duties upon returning was to send two "daughters" to Trinidad to pick up more cocaine. Through the use of women or families as couriers, Rafi was able to send frequent shipments of cocaine to New York City until late 1984.

Development of New York City Cocaine Market

Cocaine hydrochloride powder kept arriving from Trinidad regularly at prices several thousand dollars cheaper per kilo than New York's. To sell them, Musa and others to whom Rafi sent supplies worked around the clock. Quickly, an extensive network of mid-level cocaine distributors who bought several ounces at a time fell into place. Telephones rang constantly. Buyers drove up from Washington, D.C., and Maryland, who were willing to pay double the local prices.

Freebase Parlors

Musa's New York apartment was transformed into a freebase parlor as he sought customers for smaller quantities (half-grams at $50 each) of cocaine—or as they crowded to his door. He converted many Rastafarians to cocaine smoking, and through Joanna and Nancy, attracted a sizable Hispanic clientele for the first time in his drug distribution career. The scene was greatly enlivened by the arrival of a succession of entertainers from the Caribbean, who had bookings in America and Canada. Many were "freebasers" and claimed that cocaine strengthened their vocal chords.

How Cocaine Smoking Unraveled Fortune, Morality, and Politics

In the dense crowd at his apartment, and in the midst of continuous smoking and attending to business, it was a while before Musa realized that for him, a generous person, the cost of freebasing was prohibitively high. Personal use and gifts to his companions sharply reduced his cocaine profits. But he felt compelled to smoke freebase himself, and when there was company, was obliged to share it. He and others were puzzled by this compulsion. At first, they felt that it was caused by careless preparation of the drug, or its improper ingestion. They experimented with a variety of techniques—constructing pipes, measuring out exact amounts of the drug and baking soda, altering the cooking process, finding new heat sources—but to no avail. The compulsion to prepare and smoke freebase remained, and continued to siphon off business profits.

Escape to Ethiopia

In 1983, Rafi discontinued supplies of cocaine to several co-religionists in New York City who could not pay for consignments. Musa was one. To find cocaine to support his own need and for business, he was obliged to network among distributors for whom he had been formerly a major supplier. Many were receiving their own bulk shipments from the Caribbean or Florida. Personal use, however, prevented Musa from making any profits. Convinced that he had been a false prophet in advocating the use and distribution of cocaine, especially smokable cocaine, Musa reportedly tidied up what remained of his business interests in early 1984 and flew to Central Africa, where he now works on a farm managed by a Rastafari colleague.

BRUNO: CRACK SATISFIED A MID-LIFE QUEST FOR EXCITEMENT

Restlessness and a desire for novel sexual or other excitement appear to be common mid-life crises among Americans and result in a high divorce rate for married couples. Among African-Americans, the imbalanced male-female ratio aggravates the problem. Marriageable men are objects of keen competition when women greatly outnumber them. Some male African-Americans regard polygamy as "African culture," but its practice usually causes them considerable hardship. Bruno's story reveals the special appeal crack had for these restless hearts. As a well-paid worker, he could initially afford to yield to its temptations; yet it led to a bitter end.

After returning home from military service in Korea in 1978, Bruno was briefly unemployed before becoming a corrections officer in 1979. Energetic and ambitious, he rose in a couple of years through the ranks, earning, with overtime and other benefits, close to $50,000 per annum. He supplemented this income by helping out at a friend's auto repair shop and by exploiting other legal and illegal opportunities to earn cash. To qualify for further promotions, he became a zealous student at a college of criminal justice. Married to a junior bank executive, and the father of two children, he maintained a stylish apartment in a new housing project in Flatbush, Brooklyn.

Despite his good fortune, however, Bruno was discontented with his free time. Most of it was spent with his extended family. He had many cousins, with whom he and his wife drank inordinate amounts of alcohol in family gatherings lasting several days. Swayed by the large amounts of disposable income he carried about in wads of $100 and $50 bills, he yearned for more, or different, excitement. In 1981, a female co-worker introduced him to a circuit of "after-hours clubs," and after becoming a habitué, he began using cocaine intranasally and soon graduated to freebasing.

Bruno is remarkable for the rapidity with which he abandoned self-preparation of freebase for crack, after its introduction in 1984. He presents a problem for the student of drug-consumer behavior. Because initially he had the money, he could have avoided risk of arrest or robbery (or of receiving inferior product) by buying cocaine in bulk and using it in private settings. Instead, he preferred to buy and smoke crack in the highly exposed locales where it was sold. He survived many mishaps before 1986, when he lost his job as a result of a positive drug test. The following transcript reveals Bruno's perspectives on his addiction.

Can't Explain His Craving for Crack

And you know, to tell the truth, the high now, it's a fucked-up head, and I don't know why I keep doing it . . . but it's superaddictive and compulsive. You just want to keep doing it no matter what happens. I would beg Alice for money. Because at this point I cannot manage my money. My whole check goes to her account. I cannot make money at this point in my life . . . and it's really frustrating . . . a grown man, approximately 35 years old, has been around the world somewhat, and is somewhat educated, has seen career heights, and know better. I absolutely know better. It can't do me any good at all. It can only do me harm, and eventually, if one continues to do it, death is there. But is that a deterrent, actually? No, it's not.

A Lust for Extramarital Sex

I say to myself that it's the sex I want—but you see the funny thing about the whole situation is that I say that I'm going for sex and once I smoke, that's it. A lot of times I've had women take their clothes off and . . . you know . . . open up and stuff. Then I say, hold on a minute, let me get a hit. And then I say, take a few dollars, leave me the fuck alone. It's really weird.

Job Loss

That's the way I lost my job too. I was inebriated, I was walking down the street with a young lady and this guy says, "Yo, I know where to get this and that." So he took me to the place and I gave him some money. He brought back the stuff and then he said, "Let me check it out." Well, I let him have it and he bolted down the stairs with it, and I caught him. I ended up beating him near to death. Damn near to death. And that really scared me. It scared me because I was carrying a firearm, a legal weapon from my job (as corrections officer). He ran down into the subway station. Transit police pulled the file on me, wanted to shoot me, and if I didn't say certain things, they probably would have. I said he tried to rob me and he ended up getting arrested. But I had to take a urinalysis on my job and ended up being terminated when it came back positive. On this job, use, sales, distribution of drugs is illegal. You have to commit a criminal act to obtain them . . . so you're out.

WILLIAM: UNTYING QUEEN VICTORIA'S APRONSTRINGS AND "LEARNING THE STREET"

A continuing identity drama for middle-class African-Americans is the proper incorporation of the "street" into their lives. In seeking identity with African-American males who live in "dangerous" neighborhoods, must a young, middle-class African-American male carry a gun, have a rapsheet, or distribute drugs? Or is the adoption of styles of dance, speech, and dress adequate? A stream of African-American writing and film has explored this area. Crack also has had a part to play on this stage, as William's transcript demonstrates.

It is interesting that William reintroduces class distinctions in the course of cocaine smoking. He distances himself from the "freakhouse," "crackheads," and crack, preferring to smoke freebase in a smaller company of equals. In these respects, he is the opposite of Bruno. His preference probably reflects the current state of the crack market, which is in decline, and to which he made an exceptionally late entry.

Victorian Upbringing

First, I should tell you that my background is solidly Victorian, rigid, strict, and disciplined. Although I don't know my father, my mother was very keen about us getting an education, and that's how she raised us. She was a bookbinder: like my grandmother, she had tried housekeeping for the rich, white folks but couldn't take it. She was very militant that way.

My older sister, myself, and my younger sister were all sent to Roman Catholic School. I was sent to Resurrection, and it's strange that I'm now living next to St. Alphonso, because all these Catholic schools— you can include St. Charles—used to compete academically back in the fifties and sixties, when Catholic schools were the best schools to attend. I went to a public school for one year only, because my mother couldn't afford the fees, but I got expelled and then my lover sent me back to Catholic school. I graduated, and he even paid for the two years I spent at a community college studying for a liberal arts degree.

Testing the Middle-Class Limit: Homosexuality

I have told you that I was gay. I told my mother when I was 13, but shoot! I learned to have a good douche when I was 11! When I was 15, I had a relationship with a Postal Service employee, and went to live with him in Brooklyn. He paid for my tuition, my mother made sure he did. But then Uncle Sam took my lover away five years later, in Vietnam. In 1967. When he died, I got all his money and his wife couldn't understand it. But she was a lush, and would have gone through it. Instead, I used the money to set up trust funds for his two children, and I was left with $30,000.

Testing the Middle-Class Limit: "The Street"

Since my upbringing was so strict and Victorian, as I explained to you, I was very sheltered, and always wanted to find out other things. I learned other things from my next lover, who was a pimp. I learned the street, I learned its language, I learned how to hustle. He taught me a lot, before he was killed three years after we started going together, in 1972.

Testing the Middle-Class Limit: Drugs

I am a late bloomer when it comes to drugs. I began drinking when I was 19 and didn't begin using reefer [marijuana] until I was 24, in 1971. But I was part of those uproarious sixties, when everyone was like, yeah, let's try it out. In 1972, I began doing intranasal cocaine.

Friends introduced me to it. They took me down to the Club Baron on 137th, and we snorted and listened to Dizzy Gillespie. By God, I thought smoke was coming from his horn that night, because I was very much into jazz, and very much into vibes, or feelings. The coke was very mellow. You'd take a couple of lines, and you'd feel all the sensations of it over four to five hours. Then it would "drop." You'd feel it falling inside your throat, and that's your final proof that it was good coke. It's true that my expenses climbed from $25 to $100 to $200, but it really wasn't a problem. I had found myself a dealer and dealt with him. I feel if you can pay for your drugs—cigarettes, whatever—then you are entitled to them.

Testing the Middle-Class Limit: Crack

I started smoking crack only last year, on New Year's Day, 1990. I was going through some changes, I was kicking a whole lot of old garbage out of my life. And then I must have had a flashback to those old, glorious sixties, "let me find out." I started out with [crack] vials, but there was too much movement with that. People running in and out to buy it or use it. So then I discovered "cook-up" [self-preparation or freebase]. I'd buy $10 worth [of cocaine hydrochloride powder, for "cooking-up" into smokable cocaine] and settle in with that. Now I have it down to a science. Two or three friends together, about $100 of coke, $25 of that for sniffing, the rest cooked up pure for smoking.

Maintaining Class Distinctions in Crack Use

You see, the "dungeon" [Chuck's Place: a nearby "freakhouse," where many crack users live, and where there have been many recent quarrels] is too radical for me, yessuh! I can't go through all those trials and tribulations. Here, if I see you looking at the ground [crack users often search floors anxiously for crumbs of crack, while knowing there is none], you're out. I think that it's the agitation, the movement that causes worries and leads to compulsive use. When you enjoy the stuff in peace and calm, you can control yourself. If I had to work today at 4 P.M., I'd stop this by 1 P.M., if the drugs were good, or by 2-3 P.M., if they weren't very powerful. And then on the job, no drinking or drugs. It only happened once that I passed out on the job. Up at Montefiore Hospital, and it really was because I'd been out late the night before drinking wine.

Some Worker Characteristics of Middle-Aged, Middle-Income Cocaine Smokers

It's strange that you should be interested in job changes which have occurred as a result of crack. I keep telling you that your timing in coming here is exactly right! It was only last week that I was saying to three or four persons who were here [at William's, smoking cocaine] that we all had something in common. We were all over 35. We all came from very straitlaced backgrounds, family wise, and we all had better-paying jobs, as professionals or executives. But after 25, there had been rocky roads, and eventually some of us kept the jobs, but some just went out on the street, while others just couldn't give a shit, and settled for less-important jobs.

I started off working on 8th Avenue as a messenger for $50 a week, but soon gave it up. Next, I went to Boston, which I call my "finishing school." I joined Barney and Schulberg, a pharmaceuticals firm as stock clerk, but rapidly rose to a manager's position, earning $200 a week. I was very aggressive when it came to work, and when my sister's husband died, I came back here to be near them, and started in 1972 in a supervisor's position at World Industries, at $15,000 a year. But within two years, I had an executive position. By 1977, I had a home in Richmond, where my youngest sister was living, I had CDs and other investments.

Living with Crack after Losing Job

But in 1975, the company had brought in a white replacement, and as I was only the token nigger in the first place, I knew I was on my way out. I quit in 1977, and took away $50,000 in compensation.

I saw some rough times after that. I used to sit in bars a whole lot, I just couldn't understand what had happened to me. I learned to play the numbers. In 1977, I got this Certificate in Training as a home health aide, but although I worked, it didn't prevent me from being homeless for about a year, from 1982 to 1983. But then in 1985, I began specializing in AIDS cases. As I am homosexual, and as a lot of patients were rich, white homosexuals, it was one of our own looking after one of our own. What I do is work two days with my rich cases, who fly me to Key West and places like that, and then put in a day with a poor AIDS patient. That's how I justify it to myself.

REGGIE: CRACK MENDS A BROKEN HEART

As indicated earlier and as illustrated by the case of Bruno, marriage is a frequent casualty of mid-life upheavals. Couples cite growing apart, with divergent interests or careers, as a frequent source of conflict. Reggie's transcript shows how crack can be a catalyst. In Reggie's story, the "rocky roads" that William mentioned—of personal and career crises—converged in crack use, job loss, and loss of family and shelter.

Perfect Family Man

Although I had used heroin in Vietnam, I became a complete family man after marrying in 1977. My wife was the only woman I have ever loved, and I was very much into her and our children. We both came from good backgrounds, had had good educations, and were giving the same to our children. By 1986, I was earning $40,000 on the job at the hospital, I had a partnership with a friend in a garage, I did freelance photography, and we had homes here in New York and in North Carolina and two cars.

Suffering for the Past

My wife had been a heroin user too, and then she learned that she had AIDS and would die soon. She changed completely. I would come home and find the house dark, just the television on, and the kids were being neglected. What was most painful for me was that she shut me out of her illness. She knew she was going to die and she made it hard on all of us.

Wife's Infidelity

Finally I sat her down and explained to her that if she was going to die, she might as well make the best of it. Now why did I tell her that? A few weeks later, I came home early from work, and found the chain on the door. As I was fumbling to get it off, my wife comes running up, buttoning her blouse. She said that she had company, and that I should go away. I went in and found that she had a man in our bedroom. I tore the house up to prevent me tearing them up.

After that my wife kept disappearing more frequently, leaving me to look after four children. One of her boyfriends she used to go to for weeks was a man who had just got out of prison, and I used to think, "here you are leaving everything, to go to nothing." In 1987, she complained about me to the Family Court, and she got an Order Of Protection which prevented me from living at the apartment. She sent the children to live with my mother-in-law, and I found another apartment.

Crack Provides Solace and Sex

When all this started, my wife had said that she didn't mind if I had my fun. That's when I first smoked crack. This woman took me to a

place where everyone was a professional—policemen, corrections officers, bus dispatchers, about 10 of them—and they offered me a hit.
That first time wasn't very impressive, but when I tried it a couple of
weeks later, I really liked it. Since then, my smoking increased as time
went on. In 1988, I lost my job, and moved here in March 1990. Since
losing the job, I have earned my living as a jack-of-all-trades.

COCHISE: ALL THAT MONEY CONFUSED ME

Many seasoned workers in low-income, minority communities came
from poverty-stricken childhoods, and grew up managing without
cash. Although many learned rapidly how to invest disposable income
profitably, perhaps an equal number never did. In the following interview, Cochise describes his cocaine smoking as a response to large
amounts of disposable income, job-related stress, marital problems,
and alcoholism. He thanks crack for delivering him to less-well-paid,
less-stressful employment. Living in his tire-repair shop and attending
customers, he is the father of an 18-month daughter, whose mother is
a crack user in the neighborhood. He restricts his consumption, and
his wife's, to a few vials after work, but drinks beer throughout the
day.

A Native American Raised among African-Americans

My name is Cochise and I am 50 years old. I have lived in this part of
Harlem since I was 9—all my life you could say. I am a Native American, a Cherokee. My father was part Irish, and part Cherokee, and my
mother was all Cherokee. Both are still alive. My father has retired
from his job—he used to paint ships for the government—and lives in
Virginia, where I was born. My mother lives in New Jersey.

My real name is John Running Deer Byrnes. The names represent
both my Native American and Irish parents. My oldest son's mother is
an Apache, and I go every year with her to pow-wows. Some were held
at Fort Dix, in New Jersey; but the one I really want to attend is in the
Rockies, in California, where my people, the Cherokee, have their reservation. Those Native Americans can look at me and see that I am one
of them.

Although I was born in Virginia, I was raised in North Carolina.
When I was 9, I was sent to live with my aunt on _ th Avenue, where
she owned a bar. Her husband owned a fish store close by. After I quit
school in the 11th grade, I worked in her bar, and in several of the other
bars near here. I also worked as a laborer, a machine quiltmaker, a

printer, in a steel company making doors for apartments, in private sanitation, and at the Post Office. In 1958, I got married—in the same year that my oldest son was born to the Apache woman. My wife was African-American, and we had five kids. But in 1978, we got divorced.

Sudden Money and Fame

In 1970, I got a job at the Transit Authority, and eventually I became a troubleshooter earning between $1,000 and 1,500 a week. I used to repair machinery and special equipment, because I was good at mechanical things. I used to be sent out into dark tunnels to work for hours, and it was dangerous. I lost that job two years ago because of crack.

Family Background of Alcoholism

Well, you know my background. I am Native American. So that should tell you about my drinking. And Irish! When I was a kid—I remember I was still in a high chair—one of my parents gave me a glass of beer. They both drank a lot. So drinking was just part of my life. But I never really touched it until I was 17 or so. It was just a social thing at first. But then around 1975, when I was 35, I began having problems with it. I used to have blackouts, I couldn't remember how I drove from one place to another, or when I had gotten on a bus to go I don't know where. So I turned myself into a drug and alcohol hospital in Freeport, Long Island, for a 5-day detox. But it wasn't enough: I think you should be kept at least 60 days. I was back out drinking when I came back.

I started using crack in 1985. I just knew some people who were doing it and they said why don't you try it, so I did. I was really having a lot of trouble at home. I got married again in 1980, to an African-American woman from North Carolina, and she had two children. Around 1985, I was making a lot of money at the Transit Authority, and I had just bought a five-speed Toyota. My wife was getting angrier with me over all kinds of stuff and she tried to wreck the car several times. So I don't need aggravation, and we separated. And that's when I tried crack.

Embarrassment of Riches

It was the money too. Before I was making that much money, I was happier. All that money just gave me more headaches. How to spend it, who's going to steal it. And now that I have lost that job, and am only making what I make from tire repair, I am happier again. Not having all that money helped me control my crack use. I last used crack four days ago, and it's only at night after work that I smoke. Look at this. I have fixed your bike. That's an accomplishment. I feel good about it. I helped build the damn subways, but they didn't appreciate me for that. Gave me a hard time, wouldn't give me time off when my father was ill, stuff like that. Here, I am my own boss. I work well with the land-lord, and he trusts me to look out for the whole property, including the restaurant next door.

Four day ago, I smoked two $3 bottles [vials]. I smoke in abandoned buildings or hallways, or sometimes I come here. But my wife and my kid come first, way before any kind of drug.

SAM: CRACK MADE ME STEAL ON THE JOB AND MAKES ME VIOLENT

Crack can bring out underlying pathologies. Sam is among the young-est of the crack users to be found in the Central Harlem study neigh-borhood, and is a comparative newcomer to cocaine smoking. He is also the latest to have suffered job loss because of crack use. It appears that crack has unleashed a violence in Sam that had been latent since early childhood. In the following transcript, he describes the "violent role" he is beginning to play as a strategy to get more crack.

Solid, Lower-Middle-Class Background

My name is Sam and I am 24 years of age. I come from a good family who lives over in St. Nicholas projects. My father is 68 and a cabdriver, but he doesn't live with us anymore. My mother has been working for New York City Transit Authority for the longest while, and still works there today. My older brothers and a sister all completed school, work in good jobs, and have their own homes. I have my own room with color TV over at my mother's apartment, and that's where I live. It's just that I come over here and beam up, and then I just end up sleeping here. Sure, there's a lot of tension between my mom and me because of crack.

Dropping Out of School and Hanging Out

I went to school here in Central Harlem at P.S. 136, and then to Martin Luther King Junior High School. But I dropped out in grade 10, when I was 15, or in 1982. I had had a lot of problems at school, because I used to get into a lot of fights. I always get into a lot of fights because I have always had a very quick temper.

After I dropped out of school, I used to hang around the neighbor-hood with other kids from the projects. Then, about five years ago, when I was 18, I got a job in construction and worked at that until the beginning of this year when I got fired, because of crack. When I got the job, I also started using marijuana and beer.

Introduction to Crack

I only started using crack three years ago, in 1988. A young lady offered me some in a blunt [emptied out cigar, refilled with marijuana: the crack had been sprinkled into it]. They call those "wullas." But six months afterwards, I started taking the "stem," and that was when it was all over. Because when Scottie sends down that beam [makes circle with hands in an ensnaring motion] and beams you aboard the Enterprise, you have no choice. If you want to take care of any kind of business, you have to do it before you take that first "hit," because afterwards you can't take care of any sort of business. If you have money in your pocket, it burns a hole in your pocket until you buy drugs. Because then the monkey is on your back. No, it isn't a monkey really; more like a gorilla!

Stealing on the Job

I have gotten into so much shit in the last six months because of crack, it's unbelievable. What's frightening is every day I get into some shit because of crack. First, I started stealing on the job. This is a private construction company, and as I was the foreman, I had keys to the storeroom. I used to take one item or two at first, but then one night, I stole about $4,000–$5,000 worth of tools. I took out a whole duffel bag filled with hammers, spanners, jackhammers, carpenter tool belts, brand new heavy duty extension cords—all kinds of stuff. I sold it all for $125, bought crack with that, and got fired.

Diversifying Crime

Next, I got arrested twice for assault early in January. The first time I was mad at my girlfriend—at the time we had an apartment together on this block—and I picked her up and slammed her against a wall. Some neighbors called the police, and I got locked up for seven days for that. The next time I slugged her, and got locked up for a month. By the time I got out, we had lost the apartment, and I had to go back to my mother's apartment to live.

Crack Distribution

When I got out of jail, I started selling crack for someone around here. He used to give me a package of 100 $3-vials, and I kept $50 from the sales. He didn't know I was a user, so I used to spend the $50 with another distributor to buy crack for myself. Then one day I was really rollin.' I was pitching [was the actual seller, not a steerer or other staff], and I had made up a lot of money. I had so much money that I needed to turn it over and get more product. Of course, I hadn't been beaming up, otherwise I would have spent up all that money. In fact I was going to eat when I made a sale to an undercover TNT [Tactical Narcotics Team officer]. They busted me with eight vials and I got six months.

Need For Crack Triggers Violence

Now let me tell you about the violence. When I get that hit, I usually stay real quiet. Maybe I'll move around the room a bit. Maybe I'll want sex, it depends on the mood. But then I start needing more. And if someone comes in with some, I'll ask them for it. If they refuse, I pull this out [he pulls out a small razor]. Or otherwise, I'll beat them up. I've beaten up Reggie and Kathy here. Yesterday, a man came in here and shared his smoke, but he had two cameras he was trying to sell. So I cut his face with the razor—he had to get 30 stitches—stole the cameras, and sold them for $20.

No, I don't like the trouble my quick temper brings me. But I am always like that. I had fights in school, I had fights in prison. I don't like what happens to me. I've gotten stabbed, shot at—all kinds of things have happened to me because I go off.

POST-CRACK LOCAL LABOR MARKET

The aftermaths of these stories affirm a certain labor-market logic at work in them, rather than individuals merely undergoing contingent crises or tragic accidents. Having lost well-paid jobs, commanding positions in their families, grassroots political roles, and community respect, middle-aged, formerly middle-income crack users often end up being satisfied with low-paid, intermittent work in the immediate neighborhood. As a result, the shape of the local labor market has been altered. The bottom tier of "noncompeting" laborers (Doeringer and Piore 1968) has expanded at the same time that retrenchment has shrunk the ranks of better-paid workers in formal-sector employment.

For example, Bert, a 31-year-old Trinidadian African and former electronics technician, is adept at discovering or creating bottom-tier work. Within a small radius of his mother's home in Flatbush, he trims hedges, stacks garbage, carries loads, assists neighbors in home repairs, sweeps and cleans driveways and sidewalks, and washes cars. By working close by, he is able to smoke crack at home during the day when his mother is at work.

In Central Harlem, Reggie (see previous transcript) is involved in a staggering number of drug exchanges almost every day. His friend Chuck, who has made him second in command at his "freakhouse"/ apartment, explained that one of the valued qualities that recommended Reggie to the post was that "he is a hustler. If you need something for the apartment and you tell him about it, it is here. Look, right now he's with Sandy at the church [close by] hustling for some food." Chuck pointed to a discarded washing machine that Reggie had hauled back to the apartment and repaired. He was hoping to sell it for at least $50. Reggie later stated his belief that "New York is paved with gold: people throw away fantastic things, sometimes brand new, which you can scavenge and resell." In his transcript, he described himself as a "jack of all trades": fixing cars, doing carpentry, performing construction jobs. He has been seen in the neighborhood selling big, black plastic bags, probably "scammed" at a construction site. On another recent occasion he was selling gallon cans of paint. In several of these undertakings, labor was contributed by Chuck or other co-residents of the "freakhouse."

"Scrapping," or retrieving and selling scrap metal, is a growth industry for crack users. Scrap metal yards (where metal is weighed, bought, and sold) in Brooklyn are thriving, and several new yards have sprung up, near which crack distribution has immediately emerged. Although it is hard work, scrapping nevertheless brings in a regular daily income. Scrappers are routinely seen around the neighborhood pushing shopping carts filled with odd pieces of metal. They are good at spotting the valuable types (copper and aluminum, for example) and can wring profit out of sites (abandoned buildings or heaps of garbage) that appear valueless. Scrappers in Bushwick have mapped out territories so that each has his own route and storage places across the section that others do not molest.

Some labor entrepreneurs have learned that shelters for the homeless, where many crack users sleep and eat, provide pools of readily exploitable labor. They may be seen in the morning at some of the bigger shelters in Brooklyn, recruiting day laborers for such work as "picking" (sorting through and selecting valuables from discarded clothes or garbage), selling watches or other merchandise on sidewalks (under pain of arrest, a day in custody and forfeiture of merchandise), and demolition (removing debris, stairways, and fire escapes from abandoned buildings). Homeless persons who were also crack users were brought in by contractors from New York City to work as kitchen or maintenance help during the summer season, a practice revealed during the investigation of the recent murder of a New York City couple at one of several upstate resorts for the elderly.

Many crack users manage to secure regular, if low-paid employment, after they have lost better jobs. Both Cochise and William (see previous transcripts) have found jobs they like, as a tire repairman and a home health aide, respectively, and William expects to earn more in his specialty of working with AIDS cases after he qualifies as a Licensed Practical Nurse (LPN). Bruno (see previous transcript), however, may be more typical. After he lost his $50,000-per-annum job, he has held a series of jobs that never paid more than $19,000. He was dismissed from each in turn for theft or fraud. Between jobs, he spent several months in treatment. Currently unemployed, he is negotiating to spend the next two years in upstate New York in a therapeutic community.

FEMALE WORKER-USERS: SHASHI'S "MISSION"

Women also have had their work lives altered by crack dependence, though in different ways from men. In the study neighborhoods, female crack users were most likely to be heads of households supported by public transfer payments, such as Aid to Families with Dependent Children (AFDC). Whereas formerly they might have spent the two-week period between "welfare checks" at home, consuming beer, marijuana, and television soap operas, the burden of maintaining an increasingly expensive crack habit has forced them onto the street, to earn money from prostitution and other crime (Hamid 1991). Many of these women devote themselves to "hustling" and sex-for-crack exchanges—despite the risks of apprehension by the criminal justice system and the consequent loss of their children and welfare payments.

The "mission" is the street word (borrowed apparently from the "Star Trek" television series) used to describe the multiple, unique "jobs" that crack users perform to procure crack or cash. Shashi, a 26-year old African-American woman who has moved directly from 10 years of AFDC support, during which time she never worked, to postcrack duty as a sex-worker, describes a recent mission in the transcript following. The mission goes on for four days nonstop. Like others, Shashi intersperses "missions" with periods of abstinence, during which she receives treatment services and attends meetings of Alcoholics Anonymous. Although she does not describe the sexual services she provides explicitly, when new money suddenly appears in the transcript, it is the result of sexual exchange.

Getting the Urge to Use Crack

This mission started when I had gone out to a restaurant with somebody from the rooms [Alcoholics Anonymous]. We started talking about crack. He was saying how he don't get the urge to do it anymore. But I was rushing the motherfucker so I could leave and get high. I had $20 that I was going to spend on crack. . . . I went straight to the fourth floor apartment in 2025 and smoked that $20. After that, I left and went home 'cause I didn't have any more money on me.

Finding "Victims" and Crack: First Day

The next day I came back and did it again. This time, I had $50 that somebody had given me for Valentines Day. They had also bought me some perfume from Macy's, and I sold it. And the $50 went just like that. This time, I went to Martense to cop 'cause they got good stuff over there. Me and this cab driver went there and got a "dime" from the fourth floor, but he didn't like it. So, we went riding around and he said he knew where two other places were. We rode around all day in his yellow cab getting high. We were picking up people and smoking up the fare money. We did this all the way 'till the next day. Came the next day, we wound up at his house and still had the company cab.

Second Day

Later, we went out to cop again on Fulton Street. He gave me $40 and told me, he said, "Do you see that building right there?" The fucking building was condemned. When we left there, he copped some dope on Fulton Street and we went back to his house. He sniffed the dope, but I wasn't interested in that. We smoked and he started to take off his clothes again. He said, "You stay here while I go and get some more. I gotta pick up another fare." When he came back, he had stupid money and drugs. When we finished with that he drove me back.

Third Day

I went back to Martense and copped some more crack. I smoked a nickel in the hallway of a building a couple of doors away. When I left there, I went back to 2025—why that building I just don't know. It's an empty apartment where people would smoke. They got it boarded up now. Anyway, I smoked lovely in there by myself. When I smoked everything, I started trying to figure out where I could get more drugs. I need money now, so I started calling up all my old friends—the ones that still get high. I got a hold of one guy who lives on Ocean Parkway. He pays about $1,000 a month rent. I went over to his place. He gets too paranoid. He wanted to fuck, but he can't when he gets high. Anyway, we bought a fifty piece from an apartment on St. Pauls. When we got back to his place we cooked it up. He didn't trust me. He asked me if I had pockets in my clothes. "Ain't no pockets in my clothes." And he told me, "Don't touch the drugs." He was going to take a shower. I'm an addict. I took half of the motherfucker and put it in my shoe. I kept it so then when he came out of the shower, I had the stem and everything ready. I said, "You ready to take your hit now?" I got him off balance and he never noticed that anything was gone. Once we smoked that, he said that he didn't have any more money. So I thought, "As soon as you step off and go to the bathroom again, I'm in the drawer, looking for money." I need money. But that motherfucker was smart and didn't keep any money laying around. I told him, "Don't you want another hit? So, let's go get one." And that's when he pulled out the money. Stupid money, stupid money. But he got so paranoid from smoking, I had to leave. I couldn't take it. He would go out on his balcony to look and see if anyone was coming to get him. He'd go from one room to the other. He couldn't stay still. I had to leave. I couldn't even steal nothing from him because he had me getting paranoid.

Fourth Day

When I left, I still had that other hit in my shoe. I took a hit from it in the hallway of his building. After that, I went back to 2025 and found some empty capsules. I needed some money for cigarettes and beer, so I sold one nickel from the rock I had in my shoe. Then, I wanted to go somewhere to sit down and smoke. I went back upstairs to the fourth floor apartment in 2025 and started all over again. People was begging me for a hit, but I told 'em, 'I ain't got it.' I smoked what I had and then I left. I went to a friend's apartment in the Ebbetts Field Houses and chilled out for seven day after that. I didn't have no more money and I was tired after being on a mission for four days.

All in all, Shashi had worked 96 hours more or less continuously to earn approximately $250, all of which was spent on crack. She had run the gamut of risks—from jail to beating, and from loss of custody of her 10-year-old daughter to further estrangement from her kin and loss of welfare payments.

YOUNG NONUSING DISTRIBUTORS

In the drug market the most arduous and risky tasks of drug distribution fall to young males. Nonusing crack distributors rarely profit permanently from their work. Much of their income goes for conspicuous consumption in the form of clothing, gifts, and entertainment. At the end of brief spells of prosperity, many join their customers at the bottom tier of laborers in the local job market, or wind up imprisoned or dead. The ethos of community development for which Musa had been a spokesman and practitioner has not been repeated in the age of crack.

The following transcript of an 18-year-old male African-American describes the motivations and outlook of the typical young crack distributor, the extent of his engagement in the trade, and the nexus between drug dealing and other violent crime.

"Hanging Out"

When we are hanging out, how we dress is very important. Tonight I'll wear my eight-ball jacket, costing $250; pants worth $30—like Levis; a shirt for $40; $80 Timberland boots; and my gold jewelry—the ring and bracelet—cost $800. I'll wear one of those brim hats you see old men wearing. So I'll have about $1,200 on my body, or $12,000 between the group of us. I don't drink or smoke or do drugs: but the rest of the fellas will snort up about three $30 bags of "nitro" [intranasal cocaine] or $90's worth. They'll drink a lot of beer, mostly Heineken or Budweiser—say about 10 $1 bottles, or about $100 in all. And maybe they'll smoke about five "nickel bags" ($5) of reefer, or $25. That's in one night of hanging out, like tonight. We don't spend much on food, and maybe we'll rap to the girls who hang there and buy them beer.

So it's to buy clothes, jewelry, and sneakers that we try to make money mainly. I spent about $1,800 on myself alone at Christmas time. I bought my girlfriend a shearling coat for $140 and a ring for $79. Shearling coats are the rage this year, and they are robbing them off people's backs. I had just got a settlement since turning 18 for an accident I had when I was 14, so I had that cash just before Christmas. That's how my mother paid down on the house in Queens.

Selling Crack

Three of us sell crack while we hang out, and I suppose we are a sort of protection, since nobody will mess with us when we are all there. They are selling for another 26-year-old African-American in the neigh-

borhood, who gives them packages of 100 $2 vials—real tiny bottles!—
to sell, and pays them $100 a night, or by commission. I think they are
selling less and that there are fewer customers nowadays, and they are
bringing VCRs and stuff like that to pay with. In this neighborhood,
the Puerto Ricans control the bulk quantity while we sell it at the street
level. None of us uses crack. Snorting "nitro" is not as destructive as
smoking cocaine: it just gets you high.

I started selling crack when I was 13, in 1985. I was in Junior High
School and I remember I wanted a pair of sneakers and my mother gave
me $20, which wasn't enough. So I told an older guy I knew I would
sell the crack, and I got busted that same day. The judge let me off.
When I turned 16, I started out again as a lookout for a pal who had
just returned from jail, and took over his business when he went back
to jail. I'd buy about $400 worth of crack and repackage it. I'd make at
least double my money. I'd do it occasionally to buy clothes, or to help
out my mother. I'd tell her I got the money from my girlfriend, or from
gambling. When we hang out, we gamble a lot. We play a game with
dice called "silo." But nowadays, I'm trying to stay out of trouble to
graduate (he was also remaining in school and trying to graduate on
the advice of his attorney, who was representing him in a charge of
armed robbery).

Other Crime

The other way to make money is to rob people, although some of us do
get welfare. We do that when we are really broke. Then we look around
for somebody who might have money. A housewife or a worker, or
maybe even a crack dealer. Usually we hunt down Puerto Ricans. Then
we use our guns, because when people see a gun, they give up their
money.

Guns

Between us, we have 6 weapons: a .22 automatic, a .25 automatic, a .38
Special revolver, a Tech-9 and a 30/30 shotgun. I have the .25 and I
keep it mostly at home. I take it out with me, to school or when we are
hanging out, when I am expecting trouble. I will use it, to defend myself.

Anticipating A Short Life

I was planning on joining the army, but now the country is going to war
[December 1990], so I don't want to do that anymore. Maybe I'll go
back to school to study nursing. I'd like to get a job in construction. I
was good at taking and developing pictures too. I learned photography

while I was at the High School of Graphic Arts, at 50th Street. I hope I can live long, if I don't run into any problems.

CONCLUSION

This chapter has provided a glimpse of the transformation of labor markets and the loss of wealth and of income-generating potential triggered by cocaine use in the inner city. The middle-income, seasoned workers introduced here not only withdrew substantial wealth, vigor, and intelligence from the upkeep of families and neighborhoods, but also gave up useful, regular work in favor of long hours of occasional labor, with virtually no protection and at high risk of arrest, incarceration, and violent injury. Crack-dependent women, in contrast, generally increased their cash earnings, but only because they needed money to buy crack and only by means of theft and sale of sexual services. In the process, they walked away from family and kin networks, and incurred equally high risks. Even the young distributors who for a time earned good money had fatalistically short time horizons that inhibited wealth accumulation, either for themselves or for the neighborhood. There is no time for investment in income-generating assets or labor skills, and few chances to return to the mainstream labor market for youths who have been marked by arrest for drug distribution or armed robbery.

The crack epidemic, in sum, has helped to deplete human and physical wealth in the inner city. Crack revenues, reckoned in several billion dollars, have been rapidly removed from inner-city neighborhoods. For low-income, minority areas crack has been a social "vacuum cleaner" that collects wealth in whatever form it exists, exchanges it for drugs, then extracts it from the community.

References

Anderson, Elijah. 1990. *Streetwise*. Chicago: University of Chicago Press.
"Briefings: From Crack House to Freak House." 1990. *Science* 245 (Aug. 31): 982.

Curtis, Richard. 1991. "Highly Structured Crack Markets in New York City." Report to the Working Group on the Ecology of Crime and Drugs. New York: Social Science Research Council.

Doeringer, P. B., and Michael Piore. 1968. *Internal Labor Markets and Manpower Analysis.* Lexington, Mass.: D.C. Heath.

Hamid, Ansley. 1980. *A Precapitalist Mode of Production: Ganja and the Rastafarians in San Fernando, Trinidad.* Ann Arbor, Mich.: University Microfilms.

————. 1991. "The Decline of Crack Use in New York City: Drug Policy or Natural Controls?" *International Journal on Drug Policy*, 2(5): 26–28.

Hemphill, Clara. 1990. "Crack Use Is Declining." *Newsday.* Oct. 11: 3.

Hughes, Mark Allan. 1988. "The 'Underclass' Fallacy." Princeton University, Woodrow Wilson School of Public and International Affairs. Photocopy.

Jencks, Christopher, and Paul Peterson, eds. 1991. *The Urban Underclass.* Washington, D.C.: Brookings Institution.

Moss, Phillip, and Chris Tilly. 1991. "Why Black Men Are Doing Worse in the Labor Market: A Review of Supply-Side and Demand-Side Explanations." Social Science Research Council, New York, N.Y. Photocopy.

Myrdal, Gunnar. 1962. *Challenge to Affluence.* New York: Pantheon.

Ricketts, Erol, and Isabel Sawhill. 1988. "Defining and Measuring the Underclass." *Journal of Policy Analysis and Management* 7(2): 316–25.

Teasler, Joseph B. 1991. "Crack Dealer Feeds a Family and Habits of Fewer Uses." *New York Times.* May 16: A1, B4.

Wilson, William Julius. 1987. *The Truly Disadvantaged: The Inner City, the Underclass, and Public Policy.* Chicago: University of Chicago Press.

Chapter Eight

MOBILITY INTO AND OUT OF POOR URBAN NEIGHBORHOODS

Edward Gramlich, Deborah Laren, and Naomi Sealand

By now it has become well-known that the share of poor people living in poor urban areas grew between the 1970 and 1980 Censuses (Ricketts and Mincy, 1988, Jargowsky and Bane, 1991). The growing concentration of poor people in poor areas could be quite damaging to the long run income prospects of this population. In the common view, poor people could be trapped both in poverty and in their poor neighborhoods, where they suffer a lack of job opportunities, a lack of upper-class role models, excessive crime, and limited possibilities for real income growth. Perhaps worse, their children could be condemned to substandard schooling, much worse than that provided to others, making it all the more difficult for these individuals to rise above their surroundings.

Beyond these fears, relatively little is known about the poor urban census tracts. In a previous paper (Gramlich, Laren, Sealand 1992) we used newly-available geographical data from the University of Michigan's Panel Study of Income Dynamics (PSID) to demonstrate a very high degree of individual mobility into and out of poor urban areas, with as many as one-fifth of certain population groups entering and leaving these census tracts in a year. This high degree of individual mobility, commonly called churning, shows why it may be difficult to discern strong neighborhood effects on individuals (Jencks and Mayer 1990). At the same time, we also solved transition matrices to show how poor urban areas were gradually becoming poorer and blacker, and becoming the home for more black adults in families with children. Combining the micro and the macro information in such a way gave a more complete picture of the recent evolution of

This work was performed under a grant from the Russell Sage Foundation. Charles Brown, Gary Burtless, Paul Courant, Sheldon Danziger, Greg Duncan, Douglas Massey, Christopher Jencks, Jeffrey Lehman and the editors have made helpful comments.

poor urban areas than one would get from the census information alone.

This chapter extends these results in two ways. First, the previous results were done with 1980 transition matrices and geographical data. Geographical information for 1970 has now been added to the PSID. We have used this new information to conduct the same exercise with 1970 data, extrapolate forward, and check the projection method. The second extension involves income growth. Do those who exit poor urban areas have larger income gains than those who do not? We analyze income changes for stayers and leavers to try to answer this question.

POOR PEOPLE AND PLACES

To maintain consistency, we use the same basic definitions of poor people and poor urban areas as in the earlier paper. We are interested in adults of various income classes followed longitudinally in their working years. Hence we examine individuals aged 17-64, categorized by their permanent income status. Although we do not explicitly follow children in the study, we also categorize adults by whether they did or did not live in families with children. Since for most of the span of the PSID there were trivial numbers of Hispanics, Asians, and native Americans, we omit these groups altogether, and just focus on whites, blacks, and their sum.

As in the earlier paper, we have broadened the normal Current Population Survey (CPS) definition of income to include some transfers in-kind, the bonus value of food stamps, and to exclude federal income and payroll taxes. These alterations give a much better measure of true disposable income, especially for poor people, than the normal CPS figures. We then divide this disposable income by the family's poverty needs standard to adjust for family size and put the one-year family income figures on a needs-adjusted basis.

Since the family is the logical unit for computing income-needs status, it would be convenient to use it as the unit of analysis for longitudinal study. But there are so many, and varied, changes in family composition over time that it is impossible to follow families longitudinally without either restricting the sample to the odd subset of families without major compositional change, or using arbitrary rules to identify "the same family" over time. What we did instead is to follow individuals over time and to record each person's income status for a particular year as that of the entire family to which he or she belonged in that year. In those cases where individuals were changing family status in a way that their family income could not be measured, we simply kept the individuals in the sample without a designated income class.

Another measurement issue involves the time horizon. It is now routinely conceded that one year is too short to measure true income status—incomes vary greatly from year to year, and many of those observed with low incomes for one year are not "poor" in any meaningful sense. In the previous paper we dealt with this problem by assigning individuals on the basis of three- and seven-year centered averages of the family's income-needs ratio. The differences in results between the three- and seven-year results were relatively slight, so for this paper we just used centered three-year averages.[1]

Using these conventions, we define persistently poor people as all those individuals in families with a three-year centered average family income-needs ratio of 1.25 or below, amounting to 9 percent of the total nonaged adult population for which an income class is designated in 1970 and 7 percent in 1980. We define as "middle income" (not the usual sociological definition of the term) all those individuals in families with a three-year centered average family income-needs ratio of between 1.25 and 3.0, totaling 44 percent of the relevant population in 1970 and 37 percent in 1980. We define as "high income" (again, not the usual sociological definition of the term) all those individuals in families with centered average family income-needs ratio of at least 3.0, from 47 percent of the relevant population for the different averaging concepts in 1970 to 56 percent in 1980.

As for poor places, two approaches have been used. Wilson (1987) and Jargowsky and Bane (1991) have used the straightforward technique of simply categorizing census tracts on the basis of their poverty rates. Ricketts and Sawhill (1988) have tried to construct a more elaborate measure of what they call "underclass" census tracts. These are tracts that are more than one standard deviation above the national mean on four dimensions—receipt of welfare, male labor force nonparticipation, prevalence of single-headed families, and prevalence of high school dropouts. While there is a great deal of overlap in the

---

1. If an individual's income-needs information was missing for the middle year of the three-year average, the average was not computed and the individual was not assigned to an income group. If an individual's income-needs information was missing in any other year, we computed the average based on two years of data. In constructing these averages, we never mixed years in which an individual was in a family headed by a single person with years in which an individual was in a family headed by two persons.

census tracts classified as poor by these two approaches [see Kasarda, this volume], there is at least one problem with the Ricketts-Sawhill approach for our purposes. It classifies as nonpoor many very low income census tracts in southern states where public assistance guarantee levels are low. For this reason we used the more straightforward poverty rate approach.

Table 8.1 shows the distribution of individuals aged 17–64 (hereafter adults), classified by race and three-year average income-needs, across census tract types, for the early 1980s, approximately the midpoint of our analysis. The note to the table says that the unweighted PSID sample size is 46,937 person-years, or 9392 people. Which is the better measure of the true sample size depends on the serial correlation of individual behavior, involving a set of relationships we have not yet attempted to estimate.

The table shows that 4 percent of the weighted sample of adults lives in metropolitan census tracts with poverty rates of at least 30 percent (poor urban tracts); 19 percent of the weighted sample of adults live in metropolitan census tracts with poverty rates between 10 and 30 percent (middle-income tracts); and 51 percent of the weighted sample of adults live in metropolitan census tracts with poverty rates of 10 percent or less (high income tracts). The balance of the weighted sample of adults, 26 percent, lives in nonmetropolitan

Table 8.1 POPULATION DISTRIBUTION 1979–84

Hypothetical sample of 1,000 adults aged 17–64

Group	Poor	Middle	High	Nonmetropolitan	Total
Poor whites	2	10	8	17	37
Middle whites	6	54	120	103	283
High whites	4	62	320	101	487
Unassigned whites	1	15	39	19	74
Poor blacks	9	8	2	7	26
Middle blacks	13	20	6	14	53
High blacks	6	12	8	2	28
Unassigned blacks	3	5	2	2	12
Total	44	186	505	265	1,000

Notes: Metropolitan census tracts are defined as poor if their poverty rate is at least 30 percent, middle-income if their poverty rate is between 10 percent and 30 percent, and high-income if their poverty rate is 10 percent or below.

Individuals are defined as poor if they are in a family with a three-year average income-needs ratio of 1.25 or below, middle-income if in a family with a three-year average income-needs ratio between 1.25 and 3.0, high-income if in a family with a three-year average income-needs ratio of at least 3.0, and unassigned if family income could not be measured.

The unweighted sample size is 46,937 person-years or 9,392 people.

areas. These nonmetropolitan tracts and nontracted areas are sufficiently spread out that the normal influence of neighborhood on individuals could be expected to be much weaker, or at least much different, than in urban areas. Moreover, tracts could be identified for only a minority of the nonmetropolitan sample: the remaining people were either living in tracts we were unable to identify or in nontracted areas. For both reasons we have simply treated nonmetropolitan areas as a group and have not dealt with the internal migration among them.

Table 8.1 also shows how people of different incomes are distributed across these areas. As already mentioned, across all areas, poor adults comprise 7 percent of the sample ($[37 + 26]/[1,000 - 74 - 12]$); blacks comprise 12 percent of the sample ($[26 + 53 + 28 + 12]/1000$). But in poor urban tracts poor adults comprise 28 percent of the sample ($[2 + 9]/[44 - 1 - 3]$), blacks 70 percent of the sample ($[9 + 13 + 6 + 3]/44$). Both the poverty and black rates are much higher than for all other areas, including even nonmetropolitan areas. Of course, it is this concentration of poor people and blacks in poor urban tracts that forms the crux of the urban poverty problem.

MOBILITY: TRANSITION MATRICES

The tabulations so far have shown the population composition for different types of census tracts, but have not directly addressed the mobility issue. The most straightforward way to do this is by analyzing transition probabilities, as is done in table 8.2. This shows mobility patterns for persistently poor adults in families with children for the early 1980s. The top panel of the table, for whites (with an unweighted sample size of 583 person-years or 198 people), shows that a whopping 20 percent of poor white adults in families with children leave poor urban areas in one year. This is a remarkably high rate of emigration, and while there could be all kinds of subtle explanations, on its face it offers strong evidence against the entrapment hypothesis.

Other entries in the panel for whites show another high rate of exit (22 percent) from high-income areas. When poor people leave poor areas, they obviously move up, and when they leave high-income areas they obviously move down. But it is also noteworthy that when they leave middle-income areas, they are more likely to move up than down (compare .080 with .023). The rate of exit from nonmetropolitan areas is always quite low absolutely and relatively. Once people of any racial or income group get to nonmetropolitan areas, that is pretty much where they stay.

Table 8.2 TRANSITION MATRICES FOR PERSISTENTLY POOR ADULTS IN
FAMILIES WITH CHILDREN, 1979–84 (three-year average concept)

Whites (583 person-years, 198 people)

	Tract Type in Year $T+1$				
	Poor	Middle	High	Nonmetropolitan	Total
Tract Type in Year T:					
Poor	.804	.143	—	.053	1.000
Middle	.023	.882	.080	.015	1.000
High	—	.146	.784	.070	1.000
Nonmetropolitan	.003	.009	.008	.980	1.000

Blacks (2,472 person-years, 703 people)

	Tract Type in Year $T+1$				
	Poor	Middle	High	Nonmetropolitan	Total
Tract Type in Year T:					
Poor	.901	.087	.010	.002	1.000
Middle	.064	.891	.032	.013	1.000
High	.061	.212	.725	.002	1.000
Nonmetropolitan	.025	.010	.013	.952	1.000

These patterns differ in key respects for black adults in families
with children, as shown in the bottom panel of table 8.2. Now the exit
rate from poor urban areas is much lower (10 percent). This is still a
high enough rate of exit to shed doubt on the entrapment hypothesis,
but the fact that it is so much lower than for similarly situated whites
means that perhaps poor whites and blacks are not similarly situated
after all. The other side of the matrix is also inverted: now poor blacks
have a very high 28 percent rate of exit from high-income areas. And
those leaving middle-income areas are now much more likely to move
down than up (compare .032 with .064).

Transition matrices for all other groups—poor white and black
adults in families without children, middle- and high-income white
and black adults in families with and without children, and those for
whom we could not assign incomes—were also calculated, though
not shown.[2] Middle- and high-income whites are about as likely to
exit poor tracts as are poor whites, but are less likely to migrate to
poor tracts. Middle- and high-income blacks are, if anything, even less

---

2. All transitions matrices are available from the authors on request.

likely to leave poor areas than are poor blacks, though they are also less likely to fall back into poor areas when they leave middle-income areas.

IMPLICATIONS OF TRANSITION MATRICES

The statements up to now have focused on the implications of these transition matrices for individuals. It is also interesting to see what the matrices imply for the areas, as can be discerned by solving them out.

Focusing on poor metropolitan tracts, suppose the share of any income, racial, or family group living there in a particular base year is P, the same share living in middle-income tracts is M, and the share living everywhere else is $(1 - P - M)$. Using a_{ij} as the coefficients of the transition matrix, the share of this group living in poor metropolitan tracts in the next $(+1)$ period is:

$$P_{+1} = a_{11}P + a_{21}M + a_{31}(1 - P - M). \qquad (8.1)$$

A similar expression can be constructed for the share of the group living in middle- and high-income tracts next period, and the expressions can then be moved forward to compute the paths of P and M through time. They can also be solved simultaneously for steady state values of P and M, where $P = P+1$ and $M = M+1$. The solution is:

$$P = (a_{31} + ba_{32})/[1 - a_{11} + a_{31} - b(a_{12} - a_{32})] \qquad (8.2)$$

$$\text{where } b = (a_{21} - a_{31})/(1 - a_{22} + a_{32}).$$

The equation shows that the equilibrium share P depends positively on both the staying probability, a_{11}, and the entrance probabilities, a_{31}, a_{21}, and a_{32}.

One can then repeat the calculations 16 times—for each of the 8 racial and income groups for which initial conditions are shown in table 8.1, multiplied by two because each group was split into those in families with and without children.

Table 8.3 shows the result of an attempt to predict the demographic composition of poor urban areas in 1980, moving the 1970 figures forward in time with 1970 transition matrices.[3] These predictions worked well in some cases, not so well in others:

---

3. The 1970s transition matrices were actually computed for the years 1970–74 and the 1980s transition matrices for the years 1979–85. In extrapolating, we applied the 1970 transition matrices from 1970–75, the 1980 matrices from 1980 forward, and averages of the two matrices for 1975–80.

Table 8.3 1970–84 ACTUAL AND PREDICTED POPULATION COMPOSITION IN
POOR METROPOLITAN CENSUS TRACTS (three-year average concept)

Hypothetical sample of 1,000 adults aged 17–64 living in poor metropolitan census tracts, 1970

Group	Init. 70	Pred. 80	Act. 80	Resid.
Poor whites, children	20	60	20	−40
Poor whites, no children	19	34	48	14
Middle whites, children	109	62	95	33
Middle whites, no children	83	61	80	19
High whites, children	59	70	37	−33
High whites, no children	41	39	64	25
Unassigned whites, children	8	11	4	−7
Unassigned whites, no children	21	24	28	4
Poor blacks, children	126	119	150	31
Poor blacks, no children	91	91	143	52
Middle blacks, children	140	154	193	39
Middle blacks, no children	165	138	144	6
High blacks, children	29	39	47	8
High blacks, no children	28	26	60	34
Unassigned blacks, children	29	16	29	13
Unassigned blacks, no children	33	50	35	−15
Total	1,000	994	1,177	183
Poverty rate (%)	28.2	34.1	33.4	−0.7
Black rate (%)	64.1	63.7	68.1	4.4
Percentage of persistently poor in poor urban areas:				
Whites	3.1	7.5	5.1	−2.4
Blacks	26.2	25.4	35.3	9.9
Total	12.4	14.7	17.9	3.2
Percentage of adults in families with children in poor urban areas:				
Whites	1.6	1.6	1.2	−0.4
Blacks	20.7	21.0	26.1	5.1
Total	3.7	3.8	4.1	1.3

Notes: Init., initial; Pred., predicted; act., actual; resid., residual (see text for further explanation).

- The predictions anticipated a slight decline in the overall population of poor urban areas, instead of the rise that actually occurred. This error can be explained by an influx of some population groups, particularly poor blacks and middle-income blacks with children. This influx, in turn, can be explained by the fact that over the decade the boundaries of high poverty urban census tracts expanded to include new areas and these people.[4]

- The predictions correctly anticipated a slight rise in the poverty rate.
- The predictions forecast a stable number of blacks in poor urban areas. Again, the number grew because poor and middle class blacks were engulfed by the new boundary changes.
- The predictions anticipated a slight rise in the share of persistently poor living in poor urban areas. This rise occurred, but was again underestimated because of the poor blacks added by the boundary changes.
- The predictions anticipated a slight rise in the share of children living in poor urban areas. Again this rise was underpredicted, again because of the poor blacks with children added by the boundary changes.

To summarize, the predictions forecast a series of slight changes— a slight drop in the overall population of poor urban areas, slight rises in the share of persistently poor and children living there. The actual numbers showed larger changes than those predicted because poor and middle-income blacks with children were added to poor urban areas, largely because poverty rates in census tracts adjacent to those poor in 1970 rose enough to create new poor tracts in the 1980 Census. If this pattern repeats itself, any attempt to project forward from 1980 will also understate the poverty, blackness, and number of children being educated in poor urban areas.

With this background, the next step is to run the projections forward from 1980, this time using 1980 transition matrices and the steady state solution of the transition model to project the permanent composition of poor urban areas. These calculations are shown in table 8.4. The left column gives the initial 1980 population, rescaled so there are 1000 adults living in poor urban areas in 1980. The right column gives the steady state prediction, using equation 8.2 above.

Because the transition coefficients change slightly, the new projections show some similarities and some differences to the old. In the new projections:

- The aggregate population of poor urban areas drops slightly.

---

4. The latter assertion is based on separate comparisons of the 1980 population distribution for census tracts that were poor in 1970 and those that became poor by 1980.

Table 8.4 1979–84 AND EQUILIBRIUM POPULATION COMPOSITION IN POOR
METROPOLITAN CENSUS TRACTS (three-year average concept)

Hypothetical sample of 1,000 adults aged 17–64 living in poor metropolitan census
tracts, 1980

Group	Init. (3)	Eq. (3)
Poor whites, children	14	16
Poor whites, no children	27	36
Middle whites, children	59	35
Middle whites, no children	65	65
High whites, children	31	22
High whites, no children	70	39
Unassigned whites, children	4	6
Unassigned whites, no children	27	22
Poor blacks, children	100	91
Poor blacks, no children	109	108
Middle blacks, children	142	168
Middle blacks, no children	147	120
High blacks, children	55	80
High blacks, no children	89	53
Unassigned blacks, children	26	15
Unassigned blacks, no children	35	38
Total	1,000	914
Poverty rate (%)	27.5	27.5
Black rate (%)	70.3	73.6
Percentage of persistently poor in poor urban areas:		
Whites	5.1	6.5
Blacks	35.3	33.6
Total	17.9	18.0
Percentage of adults in families with children in poor urban areas:		
Whites	1.2	0.9
Blacks	26.1	28.6
Total	4.1	4.1

Notes: Init., initial; Eq., equilibrium (see text for further explanation).

- Instead of rising slightly, the poverty rate in poor urban areas is
  stable.
- Instead of being stable, the projected number of black people in
  poor urban areas rises slightly.
- The share of the persistently poor in poor urban areas rises slightly.
- The share of white children growing up in poor urban areas starts
  at a low 1 percent and falls.

- The share of black children growing up in poor urban areas starts at a high 26 percent and rises.

The 1970 projections forecast a slow rise in numbers of poor people in poor urban areas (which happened), and no rise in numbers of blacks (a rise occurred). Because these projections were on balance conservative in forecasting changes in poor urban areas, at least the qualitative directions of the 1980 projections should be realistic. But the possible change in designation of census tracts, whether now considered poor or nonpoor, lends an element of uncertainty to the projections.

Comparing these results to others in the literature for the decade of the 1970s, the share of the poor living in poor urban tracts seems to be gradually increasing, as Ricketts and Mincy (1988) also found. But the picture on Wilson's (1987) "disappearing black role model" hypothesis is more complicated. As Wilson found, many of the upper-income blacks are leaving poor urban areas—exit rates for these groups vary between 5 and 10 percent a year. For upper-income blacks in families without children these exit rates exceed entrance rates and the groups show net emigration. But exactly the reverse pattern is observed for upper-income blacks in families with children: now entrance rates exceed exit rates and the population of upper-income blacks with children in poor urban areas rises.

This points to what is perhaps the most disturbing trend of all, one that has up to now received very little attention. The numbers in the bottom of table 8.4 show a sharp divergence in racial patterns for children. Very few white adults in families with children live in poor urban census tracts, and this number seems to be dropping sharply. At the same time, more than one-quarter of black adults in families with children live in poor urban census tracts, and this number is rising. If it is true that public schooling is much worse in these poor urban areas, the implied racial disparity in the educational experience of children is definitely not good news for efforts to promote educational equality.

INCOME GAINS

The final step in the process involves income gains. Do those who exit poor urban areas do better than those who do not? One would think that other things being equal, a person residing in a poor urban

area would have a harder time making a decent income than one not
so located—there would be fewer jobs, fewer job contacts, fewer role
models, more crime. This section uses the PSID data to examine this
question.

The results here could be viewed as the outcome of a natural experiment. Starting with individuals residing in poor urban areas,
some stay and some move out. How do the income gains compare?
Or, starting with individuals residing in nonpoor urban areas, some
stay and some move to poor urban areas. How do these income gains
compare? Of course, viewing this as a natural experiment immediately makes clear a difficult problem. Rather than fixing the experi-
mental treatment exogenously and randomly, our movers and stayers
determine their status voluntarily. Hence any results here will over-
estimate the true impact of moving because of selection bias.

We made the comparison by examining the growth ratio

$$(Y/N)_f/(Y/N)_i, \tag{8.3}$$

where (Y/N) refers to the three-year average income-needs ratio for an
individual, the "f" subscript refers to the final three-year average for
the individual, and the "i" subscript refers to the initial three-year
average for the individual.

The comparison incorporates several changes from our earlier work:

- Since we were now looking for income changes, we did not divide
  the sample into income-needs classes. Doing so would lose our real
  success stories—those who moved from a low income-needs ratio
  to a high ratio.
- Since we cared mainly about income gains following entry into or
  exit from poor urban areas, we combined those living in middle or
  high-income urban areas, labelling the combined tracts "nonpoor"
  areas.
- Since the income gains of multiple movers are difficult to interpret,
  we omitted all multiple movers in conducting the tests.[5]
- Since mobility behavior in rural areas is difficult to characterize,
  we omitted from the comparisons all individuals who lived in
  nonmetropolitan areas at any time during the period.
- Since comparisons of the ratios would not be meaningful if the
  three-year income-needs ratios were measured for the same year,
  we only included individuals in the comparison when there was
  no overlap between the Y/N values. That is, the initial three-year

---

5. Only about 3 percent of adults in the sample moved more than once.

average was not computed from any Y/N values used in the final three-year average.

The results are given in table 8.5. Beginning with whites in the top panel, the 7 people who started in nonpoor urban areas and moved down into poor urban areas clearly fared worse than the many people who stayed in nonpoor urban areas. The growth ratio for the first group was only 0.911 while the ratio for the second group was 1.139. On the other side, the 19 people who moved up from poor urban areas also did fairly well (with a growth ratio equal to 1.133). The only problem of interpretation is what to make of the 30 individuals who started in poor urban areas and did not move to higher income tracts—their growth ratio was 1.487. Whether these results for whites are interpretable at all is difficult to tell—there is a selection bias problem, and many sample sizes are very small.

Matters are slightly clearer for blacks in the bottom panel of table 8.5. Of those who started in nonpoor areas, the 60 who moved down into poor urban areas clearly did worse than the 785 who stayed in nonpoor areas. Of those who started in poor areas, the 106 who moved up did better than the 464 who stayed.

In income terms, then, moving from nonpoor to poor urban census tracts was correlated with income losses for individuals of both races. Moving from poor to nonpoor urban census tracts was correlated with

Table 8.5 INCOME GAINS FOR THOSE LEAVING AND STAYING IN POOR AND NONPOOR METROPOLITAN CENSUS TRACTS, 1979–84 (final three-year income-needs average over initial three-year income-needs average)

Whites (2,114 people)				
Group	Number	Share	Growth Ratio	Std. Dev.
Stayed in poor area	30	.012	1.487	.798
Stayed in nonpoor area	2,058	.976	1.139	.460
Moved up	19	.009	1.133	.352
Moved down	7	.003	0.911	.406

Blacks (1,415 people)				
Group	Number	Share	Growth Ratio	Std. Dev.
Stayed in poor area	464	.288	1.011	.351
Stayed in nonpoor area	785	.616	1.077	.409
Moved up	106	.058	1.096	.360
Moved down	60	.038	1.019	.523

Notes: Those with missing income-needs (Y/N) data, multiple movers, and those ever residing in nonmetropolitan areas are excluded; shares, growth ratios, and standard deviations (Std. Dev.) are based on weighted data.

income gains for blacks but not whites, though the small sample sizes
lead to statistical doubts about the results for whites. And the whole
question of whether these correlations reflect causal influences remains to be explored.

IMPLICATIONS

Overall, there is both good and bad news in these results. The good
news is in the micro figures, specifically the reassuringly high exit
rates from poor urban areas for people of both races and the healthy
income gains for whites who remained in poor urban areas. The bad
news comes when one works out the full long run implications of all
exit and entrance probabilities for all groups. Then poor urban areas
are seen to be getting poorer and blacker—home to an ever larger
share of the persistently poor, home to an ever larger share of black
adults in families with children, and a harder place for blacks to make
good income gains.

These kinds of tabulations illustrate once again the importance of
what has come to be known as the churning phenomenon. As overall
entities, poor urban areas seem to be changing slowly over time, gradually becoming poorer and blacker. But this overall gradual change
masks much sharper changes for particular individuals, with as many
as one-fifth of certain groups leaving or joining these tracts in a particular year. In the past similar relationships have also been observed
for people's income, employment, and family status. Apparently when
it comes to the longitudinal status of an individual, nothing is very
stable—not income, employment, family status, or even place of residence.

These numbers raise a series of questions for researchers and policy-
makers alike. For researchers, the questions involve explaining the
transition probabilities and specifically the sharp racial differences.
Deeper questions involve whether there is a causal relationship, as
opposed to a statistical correlation, between an individual's place of
residence and income. For policy-makers the numbers raise the old
question of whether public policy should be focused on poor people
or poor places. The high emigration rates reported here would seem
to favor aiding people and not places, because people do not seem to
be very tied to places. But when one works out the deeper implications, such as the potentially adverse effects of this high degree of

mobility for public school education, even those conclusions might be questioned.

The one undisputed implication, however, is that it is clearly wrong to think that because poor urban areas change their shape slowly, particular individuals are trapped in these areas. Like molecules, individuals in these slowly changing areas are moving around quite rapidly.

References

Gramlich, Edward M., Deborah Laren, and Naomi Sealand. 1992. "Moving Into and Out of Poor Urban Areas." *Journal of Policy Analysis and Management* 11(2): 273–87.

Jargowsky, Paul A. and Mary Jo Bane. 1991. "Ghetto Poverty in the United States, 1970-80," in Christopher Jencks and Paul E. Peterson, *The Urban Underclass*. Washington, D.C.: The Brookings Institution.

Jencks, Christopher and Susan E. Mayer. 1990. "The Social Consequences of Growing Up in a Poor Neighborhood." In Lawrence E. Lynn, Jr. and Michael McGeary, *Inner City Poverty in the United States*. Washington, D.C.: National Academy Press.

Massey, Douglas S., Mitchell L. Eggers, and Nancy A. Denton. 1989. "Disentangling the Causes of Concentrated Poverty." University of Chicago. Photocopy.

Ricketts, Erol R. and Ronald Mincy. 1988. "Growth of the Underclass: 1970–80." Urban Institute. Photocopy.

Ricketts, Erol R. and Isabel V. Sawhill. 1988. "Defining and Measuring the Underclass." *Journal of Policy Analysis and Management* 7(2): 316–25.

Wilson, William Julius. 1987. *The Truly Disadvantaged: The Inner City, the Underclass, and Public Policy*. Chicago: University of Chicago Press.

Chapter Nine

SOCIAL ISOLATION AND THE UNDERCLASS

Roberto M. Fernandez and David Harris

In *The Truly Disadvantaged*, William Julius Wilson (1987) argues that there have been profound changes in the social structure of the urban ghetto over the last 25 years. Wilson asserts that the inner-city black communities of major metropolitan areas have been at the intersection of a number of large-scale social and economic processes, such as shifts in industrial composition, the suburbanization of jobs, and the exodus of the black middle class to the suburbs. According to Wilson, the net result of these changes is that inner-city black communities are in crisis and their residents are in serious danger of forming an "underclass" trapped in a permanent condition of emiseration.[1]

A crucial part of this argument is that the underclass is "socially isolated." Wilson (1987:61) contends that social isolation is a key theoretical concept that serves as an alternative to "culture of poverty" explanations of the maintenance and reproduction of the underclass. Social isolation serves as the critical link between the macro-level social and economic processes just mentioned and the behavior of poor people. Wilson (1987:60) defines social isolation as "the lack of contact or of sustained interaction with the individuals or institutions that represent mainstream society." Social isolation is, therefore,

The authors would like to thank William Julius Wilson and the other members of the Urban Family Life Project for making available the Urban Family Life Survey (UFLS) data. We are particularly grateful to Martha Van Haitsma for her help and advice regarding the UFLS data. Christopher Jencks and Tom Cook provided helpful suggestions on all phases of the project. Laura Juran and Judith Levine provided excellent research assistance. This research has been supported by a grant from the Social Science Research Council's program for Research on the Urban Underclass.

1. Although Wilson used the term "underclass" in *The Truly Disadvantaged*, he has since changed his mind about the utility of the term, arguing that it distracts us from the important research issues (Wilson 1991). Because this chapter is conceived as a test of a number of the ideas in *The Truly Disadvantaged*, we have chosen to use the term "underclass" in the same way that Wilson did in that work. Our empirical operationalization of this concept (explained in the text) is best described as "nonworking poor." We substitute this term for "underclass" when presenting this chapter's analyses, because the term "nonworking poor" accurately reflects our measurement.

clearly distinct from residential segregation, although the phenomena empirically covary and their effects may reinforce one another (c.f., Jencks 1988). In Wilson's view, social isolation exacerbates the effects of being concentrated in very poor areas because such isolation limits inner-city residents' opportunities only to those found in their socially disadvantaged neighborhoods. Cut off from mainstream society, underclass individuals lack exposure to conventional role models (such as stably employed adults) and to marriageable partners, as well as access to job networks.

Wilson is not alone in voicing concern for the social isolation of the ghetto poor. A number of the classic ethnographic studies of ghetto life, such as Rainwater's *Behind Ghetto Walls* (1970) or Liebow's *Tally's Corner* (1967) have poignantly described the isolating effects of extreme poverty. For these and other authors (e.g., Martineau 1977), concern about the social isolation of the poor is important in its own right. However, the concept of social isolation also plays a critical role in the large and growing literature on neighborhood effects on poverty (for a review, see Jencks and Mayer 1990). As Jencks and Mayer (1990) and Tienda (1989) have pointed out, the different theories of how neighborhoods affect individuals imply distinct patterns of interpersonal contact and isolation. For example, epidemics require contact between peers who are "infected" and those who are susceptible to the infection (Crane 1991a, 1991b), whereas socialization processes imply interaction with role models who are often adults. For all these reasons, the concept of social isolation bears crucial theoretical significance.

The question of the social isolation of the ghetto poor is also of vital importance for public policy. Wilson's (1987:157–59) universal reform package emphasizes social mobility precisely because it is a means of breaking down the social isolation of the inner city and the continued reproduction of the ghetto underclass. In the absence of plausible evidence for the social isolation hypothesis, however, policymakers are more likely to try to explain the persistence of the underclass by turning to "new-style workfare" policies that are based on the culture of poverty (Wilson 1987:159–63).

This chapter has two major goals. First, on a conceptual level, we seek to refine and further specify the concept of social isolation. In light of the centrality of the concept for Wilson's theory, in particular, and the neighborhood effects question more generally, we believe that such conceptual development is warranted. For this task, we draw upon theoretical constructs in the field of network analysis (for an excellent comprehensive review, see Burt 1980), especially the burgeoning literature on social support networks (for a review, see House, Umberson, and Landis 1988). As such, we distinguish multiple dimensions of social isolation that reflect different images of ghetto life.

Our second major goal is empirical. We test key propositions derived from Wilson's discussion of social isolation using data from the Urban Family Life Survey (UFLS, conducted by the National Opinion Research Center, University of Chicago) of poverty areas in Chicago. Much of Wilson's argument relates to changes over time in the structure of interpersonal relationships, such as those associated with the exodus of the black middle class from the inner city. Because of the cross-sectional nature of the UFLS, we are not able to address those arguments.[2] However, Wilson's model yields a number of cross-sectional predictions that are testable with the UFLS data.

Our strategy is first to focus on the theoretical linchpin of Wilson's model: the proposition that the underclass is socially isolated. To this end, we examine whether various dimensions of social isolation vary by socioeconomic class, and whether such variations are consistent with Wilson's hypothesis. Next, to assess the role that neighborhoods play in social isolation, we study whether individuals in poor areas are any more isolated than individuals in other areas of the city. Evidence that neighborhood patterns of isolation vary independently of individual social class would provide support for the notion that neighborhood effects operate to worsen conditions for the ghetto poor. We are particularly concerned with possible interactions between individual and neighborhood poverty on social isolation (i.e., whether the experience of poverty is any more isolating when it occurs in high-poverty areas). Finally, to make the analyses substantively interpretable, we analyze gender differences in the structure of social isolation. Sample-size restrictions have hindered our ability to make all the relevant comparisons by ethnic group. Consequently, this study focuses on the African-American population.[3]

It is important to be clear about the logical status of the empirical work we report. Regarding both class and neighborhood effects, we investigate whether simple bivariate relationships exist between class and neighborhood with various dimensions of social isolation. As

---

2. Such longitudinal evidence is very difficult to obtain. The only relevant data we have found is Anderson's (1991) ethnographic study, which discusses the flight of the black middle class from "Eastern City."

3. Our current work examines class and neighborhood patterns of social isolation for non-Hispanic whites, Puerto Ricans, and Mexican Americans, as well as non-Hispanic blacks.

such, we are attempting to estimate the upper bound of class and neighborhood effects on these conceptions of social isolation. It is possible that isolation does not have empirically discernible consequences on other variables of interest. Indeed, other work has addressed this question (e.g., Van Haitsma [1989], on social isolation and labor force attachment). However, class or neighborhood differences in these outcomes are not likely to be due to social isolation if there are no class or neighborhood differences in isolation.

In our view, class and neighborhood differences in social isolation form critical residues left by the social processes that are hypothesized to reproduce the underclass. If we cannot find the traces of these processes, then we would conclude that whatever those processes are, social isolation does not play a prominent role in them. However, other processes might leave the same traces of class and neighborhood differences in social isolation. Therefore, empirical support for the propositions we address here is *necessary*—but not sufficient—for Wilson's model to operate as he describes it. The strength of our approach is that we are looking closely with detailed measures at class and neighborhood patterns of isolation. This is especially important in an area of study where theory makes fine distinctions but measurement is still relatively poor. Therefore, our results should be of great interest to other researchers who have typically limited themselves to measuring only selected dimensions of isolation when studying behavioral outcomes. This chapter thus forms the necessary foundation for our future work, in which we will begin the arduous process of developing models to explain the various dimensions of isolation. By controlling alternative explanations that might account for class and neighborhood effects, that work should sharpen our estimates of the degree to which class and neighborhood account for the social isolation of the ghetto poor.

REFINING THE CONCEPT OF SOCIAL ISOLATION

As cited earlier, Wilson posits that members of the underclass suffer from a "lack of contact or of sustained interaction with the individuals and institutions that represent mainstream society" (Wilson 1987:60). To be empirically useful, this definition needs to be refined. What constitutes "mainstream society"? Who are the individuals and what are the institutions? In Wilson's discussions of both individuals and institutions, the important dimension of social isolation is the disjuncture between the interpersonal social networks of members of the underclass and the networks of others. He explicitly describes the individuals that the underclass is isolated from (1987:60):

> Unlike . . . the inner-city blacks of earlier years, the residents of highly concentrated poverty neighborhoods in the inner city today not only infrequently interact with those individuals or families who have a stable work history and have had little involvement with welfare or public assistance, they also seldom have sustained contact with friends or relatives in the more stable areas of the city or in the suburbs.

Therefore, for Wilson, "mainstream society" consists of individuals who are steadily employed, not involved in public assistance, and who reside in "stable areas." Regarding "stable areas," it is reasonable to infer from the context that Wilson means areas that are not blighted with urban problems such as crime, drugs, and unemployment. Clearly, in this context, social isolation means a lack of *personal contact* between members of the underclass and mainstream society.

The question remains as to what Wilson means by "institutions." From his discussion, Wilson seems to mean established behavioral patterns, as in the institution of work (1987:60–62). In this sense of the term, to say that the underclass is socially isolated means that they are not likely to be steadily employed, nor are they likely to know people who are steadily employed. Here, too, interpersonal contact is emphasized.

In other sections of *The Truly Disadvantaged* (1987:136–38), Wilson uses the term "institution" to describe neighborhood organizations, such as "churches, stores, schools, recreational facilities, etc." Although there is certainly a paucity of these institutions in underclass areas, it is *not* from these organizations that Wilson sees the underclass as being isolated, but from the *black middle and working class* that has left the inner city (137–38). The black middle and working class had formed a "social buffer" that helped to sustain these neighborhood organizations during economic downturns. Here, too, Wilson (1987:144) recognizes the impact of these institutions on interpersonal relations. Although the main effect of the scarcity of these institutions is to degrade the quality of life in these areas, the disappearance of these institutions is tragic because they had provided role models and were settings for contact between more affluent and poor blacks. With the demise of these institutions, such interclass contact was cut off.

Table 9.1 outlines a number of conceptions of what Wilson and others have referred to as social isolation. The first major dimension is isolation from institutions, conceived as a lack of participation in

Table 9.1 DIMENSIONS OF SOCIAL ISOLATION

I. Isolation from institutions—lack of participation in:
    A. Community organizations
    B. Political organizations
    C. School-related groups
    D. Social clubs
    E. Church-related groups

II. Personal network characteristics
    A. Structure
       1. Volume—number of nominations for minor (everyday) social support, major (emergency) support, and friends
       2. Range or breadth—number of distinct individuals named across all three networks
       3. "Multiplexity" or depth—number of people cited as multiple sources of support or friendship
    B. Composition
       1. Percentage with spouse or partner
       2. Percentage with no friends
       3. Percentage with kin in support network
       4. Percentage of friends "mainstream"
          (a) Percentage of friends employed
          (b) Percentage of friends on public aid
          (c) Average level of education of friends

local organizations. As just mentioned, participation in these organizations is important because they provide a context for interclass contact. The second major grouping of variables in table 9.1 derives from characteristics of the personal networks in which individuals are embedded. From the preceding discussion, it is clear that Wilson also conceives of social isolation as the lack of interpersonal contact between members of the underclass and others. The structure of personal relations has been studied extensively in the literature on "personal networks" (see McCallister and Fischer 1978), which uses a survey technique in which respondents provide information on their relationships to others (e.g., community studies by Fischer 1982; Fischer et al. 1977, and Wellman 1979; and national surveys by Burt 1984 and Marsden 1987). The method was also used in the Urban Family Life Survey, data from which form the bases of our empirical work in this chapter.

Table 9.1 distinguishes a number of characteristics of personal networks that are useful for testing Wilson's views on social isolation. At the most general level, the social isolation of the underclass depends on whether underclass individuals' networks are more insular than those of nonunderclass individuals. This involves examining at least two major dimensions of individuals' personal networks: structure and composition.

The first component of structure, related to the size of the network, is volume, understood simply as the number of contacts an individual's network provides. A number of researchers (e.g., Liebow 1967; Rainwater 1970; Schulz 1969) have argued that social relationships in extreme poverty areas are marked by ambivalence and distrust because of the often dangerous nature of the ghetto (e.g., Furstenberg 1989; Merry 1981). If these researchers are correct in stating that people in such areas often cut themselves off from others, then we would expect network volume to reflect strong class and neighborhood effects.

A second size-related structural component we distinguish is the range of people's network contacts: the number of distinct individuals who are included in the network (on the concept of range, see Burt 1983). Although related to volume, range captures the breadth of the contacts by eliminating from consideration redundant links to others. Distrust and ambivalence, if they are more prevalent among the underclass, would also be reflected in the range of personal networks.

The third structural feature of personal networks we consider is the degree of overlap among different network relations (i.e., "multiplexity"). In the Urban Family Life Survey, respondents were asked to provide information on three kinds of relations: friends, daily social support, and crisis support. The extent of overlap among these relations captures a potentially important aspect of network structure: the degree to which friendship and social supports are concentrated in a few people. As such, it reflects the *depth* or closeness of social relations. It might be that poor people have fewer such close relations. This would indicate another way in which poor people may be cut off from one another.

On the other hand, deep relations may not be all good. The concentration of social ties in few people may signal insularity. Following Granovetter's (1973) classic argument, strong ties are likely to be inbred, whereas weak ties are more likely to link people to disparate parts of the social structure. Therefore, in conceptualizing isolation, "shallow" ties may be more important than "deep" ties. A number of ethnographers have also argued that because poor people have few options in obtaining vital resources, they tend to overburden their social relations (Hannerz 1969; Rainwater 1970), creating uneasiness and resentment among neighbors and reinforcing the tendency to be distrustful of potentially exploitative relations. From this perspective, one might expect underclass individuals' social networks to be more concentrated than other individuals' networks.

The second major dimension of personal networks we distinguish is the social composition of the network. Not only the form of the social network may be affected by being nonworking poor but also the character of the people contained in the network. The first important dimension we examine here is whether the individual has a spouse or a stable intimate partner. Especially in light of Wilson's concerns about the paucity of marriageable partners in poverty areas, we expect underclass individuals to be less likely to be involved in stable, close personal relations with either spouses or intimate partners. The second facet of network composition is whether the individual has any friends at all. The question of distrust among the ghetto poor is even more apparent here than when considering network size. The kin composition of the network of support relationships is another dimension of possible isolation. Ethnographic accounts (Aschenbrenner 1975; Stack 1974) often emphasize that poor blacks rely on extended kin relations as a strategy for buffering themselves from the harsh effects of extreme poverty (see also Hays and Mindel 1973). Although Stack (1974) downplays the degree of separateness of black family life, she does think that poor blacks are hesitant to move out of their neighborhoods for fear of losing these relations. To the extent that the poor are limited to relying on relatives for social support, they might be cut off from others.

Perhaps the most important issue involving network composition for Wilson is his argument that the underclass is cut off from "mainstream society"—individuals who are steadily employed and not involved in public assistance. Status competition may lead working people to estrange themselves from the nonworking poor. An example of this process may be found in Anderson's (1976) ethnography of black street-corner men, which showed that the employed "regulars" consciously distanced themselves from the nonworking "hoodlums" and "wineheads." Similar arguments and evidence are presented in Anderson (1991:58–66). More general studies of homophily (e.g., Feld 1982, 1984; Laumann 1973) have consistently shown that individuals choose friends that resemble them. Therefore, we would expect that underclass individuals would be less likely to be friends with people who are highly educated or steadily employed, and more likely to be friends with people who are on public aid. The degree to which underclass individuals name "mainstream" friends is of significant interest, since this gives an indication of the extent to which the underclass is detached from mainstream role models.

We also examine homophily by neighborhood poverty level, controlling for the effects of individual poverty. Although studies of homophily have looked at the class patterns of friendship choices, to our knowledge, no studies have examined affiliation patterns by neighborhood poverty. This is important to study because the geographic definitions of the underclass (e.g., Bane and Jargowsky 1988; Ricketts and Mincy 1990; Ricketts and Sawhill 1988) assume that there are strong neighborhood patterns of social isolation. For these reasons, we study homophily patterns by both individual and neighborhood poverty.

DATA AND MEASURES

In this study, we test for class and neighborhood effects on these dimensions of social isolation using data from the Urban Family Life Survey. Conducted by the National Opinion Research Center during 1986 and 1987, the UFLS has a number of advantages for our purposes. First, it is a survey of poverty areas, and therefore underclass members are likely to be included. The sample design consists of a multistage, stratified probability sample of persons aged 18–44 who resided in poverty areas (defined as census tracts where 20 percent or more of the families had income below the federal poverty line) in Chicago.

Second, the survey collected network data that are critical for testing the social isolation hypothesis. Survey respondents were asked to provide information on three kinds of relations: friends, daily social support, and crisis support. Respondents were asked to name up to three friends (specified to be nonkin and nonspouse or partner), up to six people on whom the respondent could "depend . . . for everyday favors" (daily support), and up to six people who the respondent "could turn to for help in a major crisis" (support in crises). Counting the number of relations of all types in which the respondent is involved is a measure of the volume of contacts in the network.[4] Counting the number of people named at least once across all three relations is a measure of the range of the network. Network multiplexity, or the

---

4. In preliminary analyses, we have examined separate measures of network size for friends, daily social support, and emergency support. All of the substantive results we report for network volume are replicated across these three measures. In the interest of brevity, we report the results for the summary network volume measure here.

degree of overlap among the various networks, is measured as the number of times a person appears in more than one relation.

With regard to the network composition variables, respondents were asked to describe their relationships to the people named in the daily and crisis support networks. This information forms the basis of the "percentage of kin in support network" variable. Respondents were asked in a separate item if they were currently married or intimately involved with a partner. The "percentage mainstream" variables were derived from the friend network.[5] For each person named as a friend, respondents were asked to describe the person's gender, race/ethnicity, education, employment, marital status, and whether or not they were on public aid. We focus on three of these variables: percentage of friends employed, percentage of friends on public aid, and the average education level of friends.

To address whether there are neighborhood effects on social isolation, we used the 1980 poverty rate of the respondent's census tract at the time of the interview. We used the poverty rate as a summary measure for neighborhood effects both because of its face validity and the evidence in Jargowsky and Bane (1990, 1991) that areas identified by poverty rates of 40 percent and above correspond to ghettos in the minds of local officials. For the research reported here, we treat the poverty rate as a continuous variable. When we examined the data for nonlinearities in social isolation, we adopted the 40 percent poverty level as our criteria (see discussion upcoming). Although some changes in the areal distribution of poverty certainly occurred between 1980 and the fielding of the survey in 1987, no reliable alternatives existed until the 1990 Census data become available.

The central questions guiding this research require us to define individuals as to whether or not they are members of the underclass. There are many competing conceptions and definitions of the term. Among the most prominent are areal "confluence of social ills" definitions (Ricketts and Mincy 1990; Ricketts and Sawhill 1988), and definitions based on concentrated poverty (Massey, Eggers, and Denton 1989), persistence of poverty (Bane and Ellwood 1986), and weak labor force attachment (Tienda and Stier 1991; Van Haitsma 1989). Given the current lack of consensus and empirical ambiguities (Jencks

---

5. Nontrivial percentages of people named no friends (see the subsequent analyses in the text of "percentage with no friends"). This means that the friend composition data are subject to possible selection bias (Marsden and Hurlbert 1987). We consider the implications of this fact when we discuss the results for network composition later in the chapter.

1991), we use elements of several of these definitions when testing whether the underclass is socially isolated.

Table 9.2 lists the criteria we use to distinguish class. The crucial distinction in the class variable is between the nonworking poor and the working poor. As such, our definition shares elements of Van Haitsma's (1989) and of Tienda and Stier's (1991), as well as Wilson's (1987) emphasis on labor force attachment as a defining feature of the underclass. We define poverty as 125 percent of the official poverty line, for three reasons. First, although many statistics are reported using the federal poverty line, the government sometimes uses poverty levels above the official line to determine eligibility for poverty pro-

Table 9.2 DEFINIITONS OF CLASS

I. Nonworking Poor
    A. A respondent who lives with his or her current partner is considered nonworking poor if:
        1. The total household income is less than 125 percent of the official poverty line;
        2. The respondent does not work most or all of the time;
        3. The respondent is not currently in school; *and*
        4. The respondent's partner does not work most or all of the time.
    B. A respondent who does not live with his or her current partner or does not have a current partner is considered nonworking poor if:
        1. The total household income is less than 125 percent of the official poverty line;
        2. The respondent does not work most or all of the time; *and*
        3. The respondent is not currently in school.

II. Working Poor
    A. A respondent who lives with his or her current partner is considered working poor if:
        1. The total household income is less than 125 percent of the official poverty line; *and*
        2. The respondent works most or all of the time; *or*
        3. The respondent is currently in school; *or*
        4. The respondent's partner works most or all of the time.
    B. A respondent who does not live with his or her current partner or does not have a current partner is considered working poor if:
        1. The total household income is less than 125 percent of the official poverty line; *and*
        2. The respondent works most or all of the time; *or*
        3. The respondent is not currently in school.

III. Nonpoor
    A. Any respondent whose household income is greater than 125 percent of the poverty line is considered nonpoor.

grams (e.g., the cutoff for food stamps is 130 percent of the official poverty line). Second, there is important evidence based on the Gallup poll that the American public thinks that the official poverty line is too low (O'Hare et al. 1990), and they estimate that 125 percent of the official poverty line reflects the American public's sentiment of where the poverty line should be. Finally, using 125 percent of the official poverty line follows the precedent of a number of important empirical studies in this area (e.g., Bane and Ellwood 1986).

Table 9.3 shows the distribution of respondents across the various categories of class and census tract poverty area. Following Bane and Jargowsky's (1988) argument that 40 percent poverty appears to correspond to what most observers would consider underclass, we have defined high-poverty areas as those where 40 percent or more of families are below the federal poverty line (see also Jargowsky and Bane

Table 9.3 PERCENTAGE DISTRIBUTION OF CLASS BY RACE, AREA, AND GENDER (weighted percentages)

	Males			
	Nonworking Poor	Working Poor	Nonpoor	Unweighted Total N
Non-Hispanic black	20.9	28.1	51.0	404
High-poverty area	29.9	28.2	41.9	71
Low-poverty area	18.8	28.1	53.1	333
Hispanic	6.8	44.5	48.8	368
High-poverty area	1.9	54.3	43.8	26
Low-poverty area	7.1	43.8	49.1	342
Non-Hispanic white	5.4	12.5	82.0	122
High-poverty area	—	—	—	8
Low-poverty area	5.2	12.3	82.5	114
	Females			
Non-Hispanic black	35.2	29.5	35.3	752
High-poverty area	52.7	26.2	21.1	195
Low-poverty area	29.2	30.6	40.2	557
Hispanic	20.2	48.9	30.9	553
High-poverty area	34.8	39.7	25.5	37
Low-poverty area	19.5	49.4	31.1	516
Non-Hispanic white	24.4	23.2	52.4	236
High-poverty area	28.7	20.8	50.5	11
Low-poverty area	24.3	23.3	52.5	225

Note: Dashes (—) denote unweighted N < 10.

1990; Wacquant and Wilson 1989).[6] The racial distribution in our census tract study areas, as shown in table 9.3, further limits our inquiry. In particular, there are very few non-Hispanic whites and Hispanics in high-poverty areas. This fact alone has profound consequences for understanding the nature of neighborhood effects. Concentrated poverty means black poverty in these data; poverty concentration is intimately connected with racial segregation in Chicago. Small sample sizes have also curtailed our ability to distinguish between Mexican-Americans and Puerto Ricans, the two major Hispanic subgroups in Chicago. Thus, as stated earlier, this work focuses on non-Hispanic blacks.

ANALYSIS

Our strategy of analysis is to sort individuals into categories of nonworking poor, working poor, and nonpoor and to examine differences across a number of dimensions of social isolation. We next study the effects of neighborhood poverty on the various measures of social isolation after controlling for class differences. Evidence of such neighborhood effects would support Wilson's (1987) arguments about the reproduction of the underclass. Finally, we explore the issue of interaction effects between class and neighborhood characteristics. In particular, we look for evidence of isolation being even more extreme for the nonworking poor in poor areas than we would expect on the basis of class or area alone. To make the analyses substantively interpretable, we examine gender differences in the structure of social isolation.

---

6. For a number of subpopulations, the contrasts between the percentage of poor in the high- and low-poverty areas are quite small. For example, combining the percentages for the nonworking poor and the working poor for black males yields 58 percent in high-poverty areas and 47 percent in low-poverty areas. Although a number of factors might account for this relatively small spread (compositional changes since 1980, slight differences in the definitions of household composition, shifting patterns of segregation), the most important factor is likely to be that the poverty line for individuals in this study is set at 125 percent of the official poverty line, whereas the official poverty line is used in defining census tract poverty rates. This has the effect of increasing the poverty rate in areas officially defined as "low" poverty. This measurement difference is only relevant when, as in table 9.3, we set a poverty threshold for the areal data. In the substantive analyses that follow, we used census tract poverty as a continuous variable and do not impose such thresholds.

Class Differences in Social Isolation

Table 9.4 addresses the question of class effects on isolation from social institutions. The table shows the percentage of males and females attending meetings of local organizations. Although not all the patterns are statistically significant, the results show the nonworking poor participating the least in local organizations, whereas the nonpoor participate at the highest rates. The main exception is for school organizations for females, among whom there is no evidence of class differences in participation. In several cases for both sexes, there are significant differences in participation between the nonworking and working poor. These results tend to support the inference that the nonworking poor tend to be isolated from the local institutions that Wilson argues are so important for providing interclass contact.

Table 9.5 examines class differences in three structural aspects of people's personal networks. Among black males, we found no evidence of class effects on the volume, range, or "multiplexity" of their personal networks. Among black females, however, the poor and nonworking poor do appear to be isolated in these ways. Starting with network volume, we found large class differences that are consistent with the idea that the nonworking poor are the most isolated and that the nonpoor are the least socially isolated. The contrast between the nonworking poor and the nonpoor is highly significant, whereas the contrast between the nonworking poor and the working poor is also statistically reliable, albeit at a lower level of significance.

When we considered network range, we found a similar pattern in which nonworking poor have the narrowest range of contacts, whereas

Table 9.4 PERCENTAGE REGULARLY ATTENDING MEETINGS OF VARIOUS LOCAL ORGANIZATIONS BY CLASS AND GENDER FOR NON-HISPANIC BLACKS

	Community	Political	School	Social	Church	Unweighted Total N
Males:						
Nonworking poor	9.6	4.4	**3.7**	**5.9**	10.3**	74
Working poor	11.7	8.4	12.9	13.3**	16.8**	116
Nonpoor	13.8	5.5	12.2	21.3	27.4	215
Females:						
Nonworking poor	**12.5**	3.9*	31.1	5.2**	*27.3**	287
Working poor	19.2	5.4	31.6	6.9**	33.8**	209
Nonpoor	23.4	7.1	30.6	16.3	43.0	257

Notes: Percentages are weighted; two-tailed *t*-tests; * = p < .10; ** = p < .05; asterisks left show contrasts with working poor; asterisks right show contrasts with nonpoor.

Table 9.5 AVERAGE NUMBERS OF RELATIONS, DISTINCT INDIVIDUALS, AND
OVERLAPS ACROSS MINOR SUPPORT, MAJOR SUPPORT, AND
FRIENDSHIP NETWORKS BY CLASS AND GENDER FOR NON-HISPANIC
BLACKS

	Nmber of Relations	Number of Distinct Individuals	Number of Multiple Ties	Minimum Unweighted N
Males:				
Nonworking poor	5.95	4.91	.98	70
Working poor	5.81	4.66	1.06	104
Nonpoor	6.18	4.95	1.12	190
Females:				
Nonworking poor	*5.97**	4.69**	**1.14**	270
Working poor	6.44**	4.94**	1.42	196
Nonpoor	7.30	5.61	1.57	233

Notes: Percentages are weighted; two-tailed t-tests; * = $p < .10$; ** = $p < .05$; asterisks left show contrasts with working poor; asterisks right show contrasts with nonpoor.

the nonpoor have the broadest networks. For black women, poverty status seems to have the most important class effect on breadth of contacts, since only the contrasts with the nonpoor are significant. The results for "multiplexity" also show an orderly progression for both males and females. However, class differences are only significant for black females, and in this case, the disjuncture is found between the nonworking poor and the other groups.[7]

These results have several important implications. First, important gender differences exist in the structure of interpersonal relations among nonworking poor blacks. Not only are women more likely than men to be poor (see table 9.3), but poor women have more constricted networks than non-poor women. In contrast, black males' interpersonal networks do not reflect the isolating effects of poverty. Moreover, it is not simply poverty that isolates women; being nonworking poor further increases their isolation, at least along the lines of volume and multiplexity. This lends some credence to the imagery in Rainwater's *Behind Ghetto Walls* of AFDC (Aid to Families with Dependent Children) women being cut off from others, whereas nonworking poor men are less constrained in their associations.

Second, these results shed light on some of the questions raised by urban ethnographers about the nature of social relations in the ghetto.

---

7. It is important to note that the measures of breadth and depth show a modest correlation (about 0.16) for both males and females. All the results for network breadth reported here are unchanged if we control for depth. Similarly, the results for depth are unaffected by controlling for breadth.

The important factor affecting the breadth of relations is poverty, rather than nonworking poor status. Depth of relations, however, is affected more specifically by being nonworking poor. As discussed earlier, deep relations can be insular, so we might consider the fact that black nonworking poor women report shallower relations as good news. However, such shallow relations would be most effective with broad personal networks, not the narrow networks found here. For this reason, we lean toward the alternative interpretation of shallow networks as indicative of caution and ambivalence in interpersonal relations among the very poor. It is also worth noting that according to these results, poor women are not overburdening their relations, or, if they are, then nonpoor women are even more burdensome to their network contacts.

The social isolation of the nonworking poor should not only be reflected in the structure of people's networks but also in the composition of the network. Table 9.6 presents class differences for three network composition measures. For black women, the percentage with a spouse or close partner is significantly lower for the nonworking poor than other classes. This pattern also appears for black males. In all these cases, the major class break is between the nonworking poor and the working poor, indicating that the nonworking poor are more socially isolated along this dimension than other classes.[8] For

Table 9.6 AVERAGE PERCENTAGE WITH PARTNER, PERCENTAGE WITH NO
FRIENDS, AND PERCENTAGE WITH KIN IN SUPPORT NETWORK BY
CLASS AND GENDER FOR NON-HISPANIC BLACKS

	Percentage with Partner	N	Percentage with No Friends	N	Percentage with Kin Support	N
Males:						
Nonworking poor	**34.7**	59	20.1	72	**72.5*	66
Working poor	71.5	80	20.6	107	64.5	109
Nonpoor	72.7	173	16.3	201	66.0	204
Females:						
Nonworking poor	**47.3**	227	17.6**	279	63.4	272
Working poor	66.1	171	15.0**	202	64.9	199
Nonpoor	65.8	225	8.6	247	66.3	246

Notes: Percentages are weighted; two-tailed t-tests; * = $p < .10$; ** = $p < .05$; asterisks left show contrasts with working poor; asterisks right show contrasts with nonpoor.

---

8. If we use marriage rather than marriage or partner as the relation studied, we find similar class patterns, except that black females who are working poor show marriage rates that are intermediate between those of the nonworking poor and the nonpoor.

both sexes, the nonworking poor do not fare well in the markets for marriage or serious relationships.

The second column of table 9.6 shows the percentage of various class and gender groups who report having no friends. For women, the pattern of isolation follows the consistent pattern of the nonworking poor showing greatest isolation, with the nonpoor being the least isolated. The major break occurs with poverty status: both the nonworking and working poor are significantly more isolated than the nonpoor. Regardless of class, males are somewhat more likely to report having no friends than are females. However, there are no significant class differences among black males in the percentage reporting no friends.

It is worth noting that these results follow the same pattern as that for network range in table 9.5. As in table 9.5, we find an important gender difference in the class pattern of isolation: there are no class differences among males, but poverty serves to isolate females. At least part of the reason for poor black women's restricted range of contacts appears to be a lack of friends. Black men, however, do not show any evidence of having their friendships constrained by class.

The last column of table 9.6 investigates class differences in the percentage of kin found in the two social support networks.[9] There is a significant difference between the nonworking poor and the other classes in the extent to which black men rely on kin for social support. This is consistent with Stack's (1974) argument that relying on extended kin networks for help and support is a survival strategy. However, the fact that poor black women are no more likely to rely on kin for social support than nonpoor black women appears anomalous when one considers that much of the social support that Stack (1974) observed involved domestic exchanges by poor black women.

As mentioned earlier, an important theme in Wilson's argument is that the underclass is isolated from "mainstream" society. Table 9.7 addresses this question by asking from whom the nonworking poor are isolated. The table presents the average percentage employed, the percentage on public aid, and the average years of education for those named as friends.[10] All three variables show strong class effects in the

---

9. These and other results (reported later in the text) do not change if one examines the daily social support and emergency support networks separately.

10. These results are potentially affected by the restriction of the sample to those who named at least one friend. Marsden and Hurlbert (1987) suggested controlling the number of friends named to correct for possible selection bias. Table 9.7's results do not change when we control this variable.

Table 9.7 AVERAGE CHARACTERISTICS OF FRIENDS BY CLASS AND GENDER
FOR NON-HISPANIC BLACKS

	Percentage Employed	N	Percentage on Public Aid	N	Average Years of Education	N
Males:						
Nonworking poor	56.9**	53	**31.2**	53	11.64**	52
Working poor	63.0**	78	15.8**	76	11.60**	75
Nonpoor	76.0	166	4.0	165	12.44	161
Females:						
Nonworking poor	**44.2**	216	**44.7**	208	**11.77**	197
Working poor	56.5**	163	26.0**	157	12.13**	148
Nonpoor	75.9	221	11.8	217	12.76	203

Notes: Percentages are weighted; two-tailed t-tests; $* = p < .10$; $** = p < .05$; asterisks left show contrasts with working poor; asterisks right show contrasts with nonpoor.

expected directions. Nonworking poor tend to have fewer employed and highly educated friends, and tend to have more friends on public assistance than people in other classes. Moreover, the contrasts between the nonworking poor and the working poor are also significant for females. For both males and females, there are also strong effects of being working poor, so the class effects are not simply a result of nonworking poor people being themselves unemployed or on public aid. Poverty and a lack of steady employment act to significantly restrict contacts to people with nonmainstream characteristics.

Although there is clear evidence of class effects in table 9.7, it is useful to consider the level of contact with mainstream individuals among the nonworking poor. The means show that although the isolation of the nonworking poor from people with mainstream characteristics is far from complete, the degree of isolation is disturbingly high. A minority of women's friends are employed, and over 40 percent of minority women's friends are on public aid. The degree of contact between nonworking poor males and people who are employed is somewhat better, but a large proportion of minority males have no employed friends. In analyses not presented here, we determined that among nonworking poor black men who named at least one friend, over a fifth (22.4 percent) said that none of their friends are employed. Among nonworking poor black women, complete isolation from "mainstream" people is even greater: over a third (34.4 percent) said that none of their friends are employed. In addition, 28 percent of nonworking poor black females had friendship networks composed entirely of people on public aid.

These patterns are even more distressing when we consider that these figures are likely to *overstate* the degree of contact with mainstream individuals because of the selection bias inherent in these data. Those who are most isolated (i.e., those who do not name anyone as a friend) are not included here, and as table 9.6 shows, such isolates are disproportionately drawn from the nonworking poor.

Finally, whereas class segregation in these networks is quite strong, it is important to note that the evidence of racial segregation in these networks is even stronger. For both black males and females, the average percentage of friends who are black is 97 percent. Although the degree of racial isolation is extreme in these data, it should be emphasized here that this segregation occurs regardless of class. Among blacks, the average percentage of friends who are black varies between a low of 96 percent for the nonpoor and a high of 98 percent for the non-working poor.

Neighborhood Effects on Social Isolation

As we argued at the outset, the processes usually proposed to induce neighborhood effects often require certain groups to be isolated from one another. In this section, we look for evidence of areal differences in participation in local organizations and in the pattern and composition of individuals' social networks, controlling for the class differences documented in the previous section.

Table 9.8 presents the results of simple regressions designed to show the independent effects of class and neighborhood poverty level on meeting attendance.[11] The constant shows the rate of meeting attendance for the nonpoor living in census tracts with zero percent poverty composition. The coefficient for neighborhood poverty has been scaled to reflect a change from zero percent poverty to 100 percent poverty. To illustrate, in the second column for black males, controlling for class, there is a difference of 13.2 percent in the rate of attendance of political meetings between census tracts with zero percent and 100 percent poverty.

Comparing the results in tables 9.4 and 9.8, the class effects we found in table 9.4 tend to be preserved after controlling for tract pov-

---

11. Because the meeting attendance variables are dichotomous, regression analyses are not appropriate because they suffer from heteroskedastic errors. To address this issue, we have replicated all analyses of dichotomies using logistic regression. With a few exceptions discussed later in the text, none of the substantive results changed when we used this technique. For ease of presentation, we have chosen to report the regression results.

Table 9.8 NEIGHBORHOOD AND CLASS EFFECTS ON REGULAR MEETING
ATTENDANCE BY GENDER FOR NON-HISPANIC BLACKS

	Community	Political	School	Social	Church
Males:					
Constant	15.7	9.4	12.3	30.4	29.9
Neighborhood:					
Percent poverty in tract	−6.0	−13.2*	−2.8	−30.1**	−7.0
Class:					
Nonworking poor	−3.7	0.5	−7.5**	−13.1**	−16.8**
Working poor	−2.1	3.2	1.5	−7.5**	−11.4**
N	409	409	409	409	408
Females:					
Constant	22.3	5.2	35.7	15.3	51.6
Neighborhood:					
Percent poverty in tract	3.1	6.5	−17.0	3.7	−28.3**
Class:					
Nonworking poor	−11.0**	−3.9**	2.2	−11.6**	−13.0**
Working poor	−3.9	−1.9	1.6	−9.6**	−8.7**
N	763	763	761	762	763

Notes: Two-tailed t-tests; * $= p < .10$; ** $= p < .05$.

erty level. However, we found relatively little evidence of neighborhood effects in these data. Black males living in poorer areas are less
likely to participate in political and social groups than black males
living in more affluent areas, but the neighborhood effect is independent of class only for social groups. For black females, the only neighborhood effect evident is on participation in church groups: controlling for class, women in poor areas are less likely to attend church
meetings than women residing in other areas. All totaled, the evidence
of neighborhood effects on participation in local institutions is not
very strong.

The case for neighborhood effects on isolation is stronger in table
9.9, which addresses the question of whether there are neighborhood
effects on the structure of interpersonal networks. There is little evidence of neighborhood or class effects for males, but there is a consistent pattern of neighborhood and class effects in the volume,
breadth, and depth of social relations for black women. For black
women, the effect of neighborhood poverty is to increase social isolation. Since individual women's class is controlled in these comparisons, these neighborhood differences are not due simply to the fact
that nonworking poor respondents are more likely to live in poorer
areas. In fact, these analyses show that poor women in poor neighborhoods suffer from the independent isolating effects of both class

Table 9.9 NEIGHBORHOOD AND CLASS EFFECTS ON STRUCTURE OF PERSONAL
NETWORKS BY GENDER FOR NON-HISPANIC BLACKS

	Number of Relations	Number of Distinct Individuals	Number of Multiple Ties
Males:			
Constant	5.78	4.52	1.28
Neighborhood:			
Percent poverty in tract	1.49	1.55*	−.53
Class:			
Nonworking poor	−.34	−.12	−.13
Working poor	−.46	−.36	−.06
N	305	296	296
Females:			
Constant	7.92	6.02	1.84
Neighborhood:			
Percent poverty in tract	−2.09**	−1.41**	−.89**
Class:			
Nonworking poor	−1.10**	−.76**	−.34**
Working poor	−.81**	−.66**	−.12
N	615	595	595

Notes: Two-tailed t-tests; * = $p < .10$; ** = $p < .05$.

and neighborhood. This is in marked contrast to black men, whose patterns of relations are not significantly affected by either factor.

Table 9.10 considers neighborhood effects on three aspects of network composition. In general, the pattern of class effects we found in table 9.6 is reproduced here, implying that class differences in isolation are not explained by neighborhood poverty. However, we also find some evidence of independent effects of neighborhood poverty. For black males, neighborhood poverty is associated with lower chances of having a spouse or partner. (These results are similar if one uses percentage married.) No such effects appear for females; in fact, the insignificant effects are in the opposite direction. Turning to the second column, we find no evidence of significant neighborhood effects.

The last column of table 9.10 shows the percentage relying on kin for social support. Again similar to the results in table 9.6, nonworking poor black males are more likely to rely on kin for support than those in other classes. Residence in poor neighborhoods is associated with a lower degree of reliance on relatives for support. Although Stack (1974) has little to say about poverty areas per se, it is surprising to find this pattern if extended kin relations are buffering the effects of poverty. The pattern of neighborhood effects for black females is

Table 9.10 NEIGHBORHOOD AND CLASS EFFECTS ON COMPOSITION OF
PERSONAL NETWORKS BY GENDER FOR NON-HISPANIC BLACKS

	Percentage with Partner	Percentage with No Friends	Percentage with Kin Support
Males:			
Constant	86.4	10.5	72.4
Neighborhood:			
Percent poverty in tract	−46.0**	14.9	−22.4**
Class:			
Nonworking poor	−33.7**	4.2	10.2**
Working poor	−0.5	3.9	−0.7
N	309	376	296
Females:			
Constant	62.8	4.8	62.3
Neighborhood:			
Percent poverty in tract	8.3	12.1	13.4*
Class:			
Nonworking poor	−18.8**	7.2**	−4.3
Working poor	0.3	5.5**	−2.1
N	620	724	600

Notes: Two-tailed t-tests; * = p < .10; ** = p < .05.

much easier to reconcile with Stack (1974) than the pattern for black
males. For females, reliance on family increases with neighborhood
poverty, although this effect is not as statistically reliable as the corresponding coefficient for males.

Table 9.11 examines neighborhood effects on another aspect of network composition, that is, the percentage of friends employed, the
percentage of friends on public aid, and the average years of friends'
education. To control for possible selection biases due to the fact that
the most isolated individuals (those who named no friends) did not
respond to this question, we have controlled for the total number of
friends in this table (see Marsden and Hurlbert 1987). As for the other
dimensions of social isolation, the class differences evident when
neighborhood poverty was not controlled (see table 9.7) are consistently reproduced here. However, we also see some statistically significant effects of neighborhood poverty on the percentage of friends
who are "mainstream." With the exception of one insignificant effect
for black males, the poorer the neighborhood of residence, the less
likely that friends are employed or highly educated, and the more
likely they are to be on public aid. Therefore, for blacks it is not only
poverty and a lack of steady employment but also evidence of a sep-

Table 9.11 NEIGHBORHOOD AND CLASS EFFECTS ON CHARACTERISTICS OF
FRIENDS BY GENDER FOR NON-HISPANIC BLACKS

	Percentage Employed	Percentage on Public Aid	Average Years of Education
Males:			
Constant	94.2	−0.4	12.98
Neighborhood:			
Percent poverty in tract	−20.9	33.1**	−2.72**
Class:			
Nonworking poor	−18.8**	25.7**	−.58**
Working poor	−12.4**	11.1**	−.74**
Total number of friends	−5.5**	−2.3*	.10
N	294	291	275
Females:			
Constant	77.8	10.5	13.08
Neighborhood:			
Percent poverty in tract	−16.6*	38.3**	−1.24**
Class:			
Nonworking poor	−29.6**	27.6**	−.84**
Working poor	−19.1**	13.2**	−.59**
Total number of friends	1.2	−4.0**	.02
N	597	579	545

Notes: Two-tailed t-tests; $*$ = $p < .10$; $**$ = $p < .05$.

arate neighborhood-level process serve to isolate residents of poor areas.

Interaction Effects on Isolation

An important part of Wilson's (1987) argument about the underclass is that the ghetto poor have been at the intersection of two forces: increasing poverty and the deterioration and degradation of ghetto neighborhoods. Social isolation serves to worsen the effects of these two factors on life chances because it restricts inner-city residents' opportunities only to those found in their poor neighborhoods. This section asks how these two forces combine to produce social isolation. In particular, we examine the question of interaction effects, of whether the experience of poverty is any more isolating when it occurs in the context of poor neighborhoods.

If the experience of poverty is more isolating in the context of very poor neighborhoods, then we would expect to find stronger effects of neighborhood poverty among the poorest people. This is the pattern predicted by threshold models of poverty (e.g., Crane 1991a, 1991b). We searched for these nonlinearities in the effect of neighborhood by examining the effects of the census tract poverty rate separately for each class. More specifically, we fit three coefficients (splines) for the effect of tract-level poverty on social isolation, one for each class.[12] We predicted that the slope for neighborhood poverty would be steeper for nonworking poor than for the other two classes. If there are interactions between class and tract poverty, we expected to find the coefficients for poverty rate and isolation to vary by class. If poor neighborhoods aggravate the experience of poverty for the nonworking poor, then we expected to see a stronger effect of census tract poverty on isolation among the nonworking poor.

It is worth noting that this is somewhat different from the traditional approach for studying statistical interaction. Interactions of the type hypothesized here are usually assessed by fitting linear terms for the interacting variables, and then a term for the product of the two variables. The coefficient for the latter term is then interpreted as the bonus to the linear effects associated with combining the two variables. We explored this parameterization in preliminary analyses. However, this approach rarely showed significant results. In addition, small sample sizes would occasionally produce problems of multicollinearity. In substantive terms, these analyses generally showed that our samples were too small to detect interactions if they were occurring in these data. This is not surprising, since these are likely to be subtle effects, and huge sample sizes appear to be required to isolate them (e.g., Crane 1991a, 1991b).

Table 9.12 shows the results for the measures of institutional attachment. For both black males and females, the neighborhood patterns in table 9.8 tend to be mirrored in table 9.12. For example, for political groups among black males, greater neighborhood poverty was associated with decreasing participation in table 9.8, and in table 9.12, the same pattern of results appears. The splines, however, reveal that the effect of neighborhood poverty on participation is most important among the working poor.[13] The effects of neighborhood poverty rate within the other two classes are in the predicted direction, but they are much smaller and not statistically significant.

---

12. In preliminary analyses, we examined in detail the relationship between the various dimensions of isolation and the census tract poverty rate for evidence of thresholds. We looked for disjunctures in these relationships at 35 percent, 40 percent, and 60 percent poverty levels. None of these results were compelling. We think that our strategy of fitting separate effects for neighborhood poverty for each class is the best way to address the question of interaction effects using these data.

13. Here, too, the coefficients for area have been scaled to reflect a change from zero percent poverty to 100 percent poverty.

Table 9.12 NEIGHBORHOOD, CLASS, AND INTERACTION EFFECTS ON
ATTENDING MEETINGS FOR VARIOUS ORGANIZATIONS BY GENDER
FOR NON-HISPANIC BLACKS

	Community	Political	School	Social	Church
Males:					
Constant	18.7	6.9	16.3	38.7	32.4
Class:					
Nonworking poor	−5.6	0.8	−14.3*	−34.0**	−12.4
Working poor	−14.0	14.6**	−7.6	−15.6*	−32.6**
Splines:					
Nonworking poor	−8.9	−8.5	4.7	−3.5	−25.4
Working poor	22.3	−33.1**	13.5	−30.6	51.6*
Nonpoor	−16.4	−4.0	−16.5	−58.8**	−15.5
N	409	409	409	409	408
Females:					
Constant	25.3	−0.3	29.5	15.5	42.3
Class:					
Nonworking poor	−10.8	3.7	11.2	−8.8	−0.7
Working poor	−16.5*	5.2	8.9	−15.9**	4.3
Splines:					
Nonworking poor	−5.1	1.2	−23.9*	−3.8	−35.7**
Working poor	32.5*	0.5	−20.3	22.4	−40.0*
Nonpoor	−7.3	24.1*	4.3	2.9	3.2
N	763	763	761	762	763

Notes: Two-tailed *t*-tests; * = p < .10; ** = p < .05.

For social groups, the neighborhood effect in table 9.8 is also reflected in the spline for the nonpoor in table 9.12. Whereas the nonpoor in nonpoor areas have the highest rate of participation in social
groups (a rate of 38.7 percent, shown by the constant), the nonpoor's
participation attenuates dramatically as neighborhood poverty increases. This might be because the character of social groups in the
poorest areas is unlikely to be attractive to the nonpoor. It is worth
noting that the nonworking poor participate at such low levels (as
shown by their coefficient for class) that only a small additional decline in participation is associated with neighborhood poverty. This
latter effect is not statistically significant.[14] The last column for males

---

14. For a number of the group participation variables (e.g., political and social groups
for black males, and school groups for black females), the data show evidence of floor
effects. The rates of participation are very low for the nonworking poor (as shown by
the class coefficients), so it is difficult for neighborhood variation in poverty rates to
further depress participation. In proportional terms, small absolute decreases in participation associated with poorer neighborhoods should be weighed more heavily when
approaching the floor of zero participation. We addressed this issue by repeating all
these analyses using a technique that corrects for such floor (and ceiling) effects, logistic

in table 9.12 shows that among the nonworking poor, residents of poorer neighborhoods show an increased tendency to attend church meetings. The splines for the other two classes are negative, but not statistically reliable. These offset one another, accounting for why we did not find neighborhood effects for this variable in table 9.8.

The overall pattern for black men is inconsistent with the notion of interaction effects for the nonworking poor. None of the nonworking poor splines is statistically different from zero, but, more importantly, in no case are the splines for the nonworking poor largest in magnitude. In fact, only in the case of church groups is the spline for the nonworking poor of a reasonable size.

Turning to black women, we find some evidence of interaction effects for several variables. For both school and church groups, participation among the nonworking poor declines as neighborhood poverty increases. In both cases, the magnitudes of the effects are substantial, although they are not very different from the splines for the working poor. For these two variables, then, the isolating effects of poverty are made worse by the poverty of the neighborhood. The remaining two significant splines are inconsistent with this pattern, in that they are both positive. For community groups, among the working poor, residing in high poverty areas is associated with greater participation in community groups. We do not have an explanation for this effect. The spline for political groups, however, is very interesting. It shows evidence that nonpoor women are more likely to participate in politics as the poverty of the area increases. We think it quite plausible that nonpoor women in poor areas would be most likely to be drawn into politics. This might reflect the leadership roles that nonpoor women are more likely to adapt as neighborhood poverty increases.

Table 9.13 presents the analyses for network volume, breadth, and depth. For black women, the patterns of effects are relatively orderly. For all three variables, all the splines are negative, showing that isolation increases with neighborhood poverty. For two of the three isolation measures, the splines for the nonworking poor are significantly different from zero. This is independent of the deleterious effect of class, which shows that the nonworking poor are more socially iso-

---

regression. The results do not change when the dichotomous dependent variables (the group participation variables, current partner, and having no friends) are reanalyzed using logistic regression. With the two exceptions noted later in the text, the analyses we report always agree with the logistic regression results with regard to the statistical significance of effects. There are slight changes in the relative magnitude of the splines, but the order of importance of the effects never changes in the logistic regressions.

Table 9.13 NEIGHBORHOOD, CLASS, AND INTERACTION EFFECTS ON
STRUCTURE OF PERSONAL NETWORKS BY GENDER FOR NON-
HISPANIC BLACKS

	Number of Relations	Number of Distinct Individuals	Number of Multiple Ties
Males:			
Constant	5.74	4.20	1.44
Class:			
Nonworking poor	−.30	.89	−.81**
Working poor	−.30	−.35	.21
Splines:			
Nonworking poor	1.49	−.32	.88
Working poor	1.13	2.52	−1.89*
Nonpoor	1.63	2.65**	−1.09*
N	305	296	296
Females:			
Constant	7.99	6.05	1.74
Class:			
Nonworking poor	−1.24*	−.77	−.34**
Working poor	−.84	−.74	.26
Splines:			
Nonworking poor	−1.93**	−1.46*	−.65
Working poor	−2.23	−1.23	−1.78**
Nonpoor	−2.34	−1.50	−.56
N	615	595	595

Notes: Two-tailed t-tests; * = $p < .10$; ** = $p < .05$.

lated than the other classes. As such, these results echo those we found in table 9.9, where we did not address the interaction issue (recall that there were clear neighborhood effects for black women in table 9.9). We would be hard-pressed to argue that these results show any evidence of interaction effects, however. Although statistically insignificant, the splines for the other classes are quite similar to those for the nonworking poor. The relationship between neighborhood poverty and social isolation does not appear to vary by class. On the basis of the results in tables 9.9 and 9.13, we would argue that there is convincing evidence of neighborhood effects on volume, breadth, and depth of social contacts for black women, but little evidence of neighborhood-class interactions.

Black men are another story. The range of nonpoor black men's contacts appears to increase with the level of neighborhood poverty. In contrast, for the working poor and nonpoor, the depth of relations appears to decrease as neighborhood poverty increases. This pattern of increasing broad but shallow ties with neighborhood poverty would appear to be the most beneficial in structural terms, because weak ties are more likely to reach disparate parts of the social structure than strong ties. The question arises: to whom are those ties directed? We address that question next when considering the network composition variables.

Table 9.14 presents the results for whether respondents have a spouse or partner, whether their network consists of no friends, and the degree of reliance on kin for social support. The first column of the table reveals interesting gender differences. For males, the propensity to form intimate relations decreases with increasing neighborhood poverty for all three classes. The strongest and most statistically reliable effect is for the nonpoor, rather than the nonworking poor.[15] Here, too, these patterns are inconsistent with the notion of an inter-

Table 9.14 NEIGHBORHOOD, CLASS, AND INTERACTION EFFECTS ON COMPOSITION OF PERSONAL NETWORKS BY GENDER FOR NON-HISPANIC BLACKS

	Percentage with Partner	Percentage with No Friends	Percentage with Kin Support
Males:			
Constant	91.3	15.3	64.5
Class:			
Nonworking poor	−47.6**	5.7	35.7**
Working poor	−3.1	−22.7**	0.2
Splines:			
Nonworking poor	−22.1	−1.9	−69.6**
Working poor	−53.6	83.9**	−.9
Nonpoor	−63.1**	−1.8	4.8
N	309	376	296
Females:			
Constant	65.5	1.3	60.9
Class:			
Nonworking poor	−34.3**	16.8**	−6.1
Working poor	19.6*	0.8	6.8
Splines:			
Nonworking poor	40.3**	−3.1	21.4**
Working poor	−59.3**	37.0**	−9.5
Nonpoor	−0.8	23.9	18.2
N	620	724	600

Notes: Two-tailed t-tests; * = $p < .10$; ** = $p < .05$.

---

15. Note that the spline for working poor just misses being statistically significant here, but does appear significant when logisitic regression is used.

action between personal and neighborhood poverty. The pattern for women, however, is quite different. The splines show strong and statistically significant nonlinearities in the relationship between area poverty and the propensity to have an intimate partner. Although the working poor are more likely than the other classes to have a partner,[16] the effect of neighborhood is strongly negative for them. In contrast, although on average the nonworking poor are significantly less likely to be involved in intimate relations, the chances of having an intimate partner increase with the degree of neighborhood poverty.

In separate analyses, we found that this strong nonlinearity is not evident if marriage is used as the intimate relation: the chances of black nonworking poor and working poor women being married decrease as neighborhood poverty rates increase. The coefficient for the nonworking poor spline for marriage is negative, albeit statistically insignificant. Therefore, the strong nonlinearity found in the analyses for partners is due to the fact that nonworking poor black women's chances of being involved in common-law marriage arrangements increase as neighborhood poverty increases. Therefore, it appears that nonworking poor black women are adapting the terms of their intimate relations in which they are involved in response to neighborhood poverty concentration. If we consider that AFDC concentration is related to poverty concentration, this pattern might reflect efforts of women in poor neighborhoods to creatively circumvent AFDC requirements.

The second column of table 9.14 presents the splines predicting whether respondents named no one as a friend. Working poor black males are fairly gregarious on average, but they become increasingly isolated as neighborhood poverty increases. Here, too, this might be due to the character of potential friends in poor neighborhoods. For females, the working poor also appear more reluctant to name friends as neighborhood poverty increases. Although these results support the idea that the working poor are trying to achieve a degree of social distance from their neighbors, they do not support the idea that the nonworking poor are more isolated as a result of neighborhood poverty concentration. Even for black women, for whom we have found evidence of neighborhood effects on volume, breadth and depth of relations, we find no evidence of their being more cut off from others as a result of being nonworking poor in poorer areas.

---

16. The coefficient for working poor black women, which is significant at the 0.10 level in table 9.14, is not statistically significant when the analyses are replicated using logistic regression.

The last column of table 9.14 addresses neighborhood effects in the pattern of social support. Although we found in table 9.10 that neighborhood poverty affects the degree of reliance on kin for black males, the results in table 9.14 show that this pattern is true only for the nonworking poor. Although nonworking poor black males tend to rely heavily on kin for social support, they tend to do so less and less as their neighborhood's poverty concentration increases. Similar to the results in table 9.10, the results for females are in the opposite direction: nonworking poor black women increase their reliance on kin as neighborhood poverty concentration increases. This is consistent with Stack's (1974) argument about the importance of extended kin as a survival strategy. Kin help to shelter nonworking poor black women not from poverty per se but from the the the poor neighborhoods in which they reside. As noted earlier in the discussion of table 9.10, the extended kin network does not shelter nonworking poor black males from the street.

Table 9.15 investigates interaction effects on whether respondents' friends show "mainstream" characteristics. As in table 9.11, we control for the total number of friends named, in an effort to correct for possible selection bias. We find consistent evidence of class differences in friends' characteristics. These differences are all in the expected direction. However, the patterns for the splines show that relationships between neighborhood poverty and friends' attributes tend to vary together for all three classes, although the splines are not significantly different from zero for percent employed. This is consistent with the pattern of neighborhood effects we found in table 9.11, but shows little evidence of an interaction between individual poverty and neighborhood poverty.

DISCUSSION

On a conceptual level, this chapter has delineated a number of dimensions of the concept of social isolation that bear particular relevance to different theories of poverty. Reflecting Wilson's (1987) concerns, we have distinguished isolation from local institutions from a lack of interpersonal contact. Within the category of interpersonal contact, we distinguished between the structure and composition of networks. By focusing on the lack of social contact with "mainstream" individuals, Wilson emphasized the latter dimension of iso-

Table 9.15 NEIGHBORHOOD, CLASS, AND INTERACTION EFFECTS ON
CHARACTERISTICS OF FRIENDS BY GENDER FOR NON-HISPANIC
BLACKS

	Percentage Employed	Percentage on Public Aid	Average Years of Education
Males:			
Constant	97.4	1.8	13.04
Class:			
Nonworking poor	−25.6**	13.4*	−.69
Working poor	−17.4	19.2**	−.85*
Splines:			
Nonworking poor	−9.8	60.9**	−2.56**
Working poor	−13.9	−0.2	−2.54**
Nonpoor	−30.6	25.2*	−2.90**
Total number of friends	−5.7**	−2.3	9.3
N	294	291	275
Females:			
Constant	87.0	1.9	13.48
Class:			
Nonworking poor	−40.1**	38.4**	−1.40**
Working poor	−37.1**	28.2**	−1.12**
Splines:			
Nonworking poor	−13.7	33.5**	−.88*
Working poor	10.0	19.1	−.87
Nonpoor	−48.9	68.6**	−2.69**
Total number of friends	1.3	−4.1**	1.94
N	597	579	545

Notes: Two-tailed t-tests; * = $p < .10$; ** = $p < .05$.

lation. Other authors (Aschenbrenner 1975; Stack 1974) have been concerned with the kin composition of the social support network. Still others (e.g., Martineau 1977; Rainwater 1970; Schulz 1969) have discussed the structural dimensions of network volume, breadth, and depth.

We then performed simple descriptive analyses addressing the question of whether the underclass is socially isolated. The first two columns of table 9.16 summarize this evidence. We found considerable evidence that nonworking poor blacks are socially isolated along various dimensions, often more so than the working poor. We also found clear gender differences in the patterns of isolation. Nonworking poor black males and females were consistently less likely to participate in local institutions and to have mainstream friends than people in other

Table 9.16 SUMMARY OF EMPIRICAL RESULTS FOR VARIOUS DIMENSIONS OF SOCIAL ISOLATION OF NON-HISPANIC BLACKS, BY GENDER

	Class Effects?		Neighborhood Effects?		Interaction for Nonworking Poor?	
	Male	Female	Male	Female	Male	Female
I. Institutions						
A. Community	No	Yes	No	No	No	No
B. Political	No	Yes	Yes	No	No	No
C. School	Yes	No	No	No	No	Yes
D. Social	Yes	Yes	Yes	No	No	No
E. Church	No	Yes	No	Yes	No	Yes
II. Personal Network						
A. Structure:						
1. Volume	No	Yes	No	Yes	No	No
2. Breadth	No	Yes	No	Yes	No	No
3. Depth	No	Yes	No	Yes	No	No
B. Composition:						
1. Percentage with partner	Yes	Yes	Yes	No	No	Yes
2. Percentage with no friends	No	Yes	No	No	No	No
3. Percentage with kin support	Yes	No	Yes$^-$	Yes$^+$	Yes	No
4. Percentage of friends "mainstream"						
(a) Percentage with friends employed	Yes	Yes	No	Yes	No	No
(b) Percentage with friends on public aid	Yes	Yes	Yes	Yes	No	No
(c) Friends, average level of education	Yes	Yes	Yes	Yes	No	No

classes, but only women showed evidence of being cut off from people generally.

We next examined the role of neighborhood poverty in social isolation, independent of class (columns 3 and 4, table 9.16). For black males, we found only scattered evidence of neighborhood effects for participation in local organizations and the structure of interpersonal relations. For black women, we found little evidence of such effects for local institutions and several of the network composition variables. However, we did find strong evidence of neighborhood effects on the "mainstream" composition of the friendship network for black males and females. In addition, the volume, breadth, and depth of black females' networks are constricted by neighborhood poverty.

Finally, we searched the data for evidence of interactions between class and neighborhood poverty. As Jencks and Mayer (1990) have discussed, whether interaction effects are operating is of crucial policy significance. If the experience of poverty is more isolating in the context of very poor neighborhoods, then an argument can be made for policies that redistribute the poor among nonpoor neighborhoods. Of course, decreasing the level of poverty in those areas in which the poor are currently concentrated would occur at the cost of slightly increasing poverty in other currently less-poor areas. However, the social benefits of such a dispersal strategy should outweigh the costs if the increase in isolation in currently nonpoor areas is very slight while the decrease in isolation in the poorest areas is large. This is precisely what would be implied if there are strong positive interaction effects on isolation between individual and neighborhood poverty.

Although we found evidence of a few interaction effects, the evidence is not strong overall (see the last two columns of table 9.16). Nonworking poor black males appear to be especially likely to eschew kin-support relations as neighborhood poverty increases. Also, nonworking poor black women are more likely to engage in common-law relationships as neighborhood poverty increases. With these exceptions, the evidence for interaction effects is quite weak in these data.

We have purposely kept these descriptive analyses simple by introducing few controls. Nevertheless, we think the results of the analyses have several important theoretical and policy implications. First, with regard to both class and neighborhood effects, there are empirically discernible consequences on social isolation, but these effects vary considerably by gender and the particular dimension of isolation. This argues for a disaggregated approach to studying social isolation and its effects.

Second, because neighborhood effects on substantive outcomes such as school dropout and teenage pregnancy often rely on isolation as a mediating mechanism, the fact that we find some evidence that at least certain dimensions of social isolation are structured along neighborhood lines is encouraging for those researchers pursuing the issue of neighborhood effects on other outcomes. The fact that there are precious few interactions between class and neighborhood implies that the dispersal of poor people to other areas will involve a proportionate redistribution of isolation. For a number of dimensions of social isolation, this is not at all troubling. When the dimension of isolation being considered is the "mainstream" composition of the network of friends, dispersal of poor people would simply have the effect of bringing poor people into more contact with more affluent people, and vice versa. Since there are many more affluent people than poor people and, consequently, very few poor would have to reside in any one area, this breaking down of social segregation along economic lines does not strike us as being particularly objectionable—even for the affluent.

However, if the dimension of isolation being considered is breadth of relationships, then the attendant feelings of fear associated with living in poor, dangerous neighborhoods would also be spread through the population with the dispersal of poor people. Of course, this would only be true if the mixing of people were two-way (i.e., poor people being placed in more affluent areas, and the more affluent moving to poorer areas). If, as in the Gautreaux project (Rosenbaum and Popkin 1989), we do the former but not the latter, then it would be reasonable to expect a net decline in fear. On the other hand, gentrification of poor areas probably creates additional problems, such as feelings of resentment or relative deprivation among the poor currently living in those areas, so that an increase in fear is not the only cost affluent people are likely to bear when settling in poor areas.

In future work, we anticipate extending this study in two directions. First, we will examine ethnic variations in the structure of social isolation, and in particular, class and neighborhood patterns of isolation for Hispanics and whites. Second, we will determine whether the class and neighborhood effects we found here can be accounted for by other characteristics. Our preliminary analyses have shown that many of the results in this chapter are quite robust. Although the task of developing models will not be easy—given the subtle nature of some of the relationships between class, neighborhood, gender, and social isolation—that work should shed additional light on the social processes that encapsulate the ghetto poor.

References

Anderson, Elijah. 1976. *A Place on the Corner.* Chicago: University of Chicago Press.

————. 1991. *Streetwise: Race, Class, and Change in an Urban Community.* Chicago: University of Chicago Press.

Aschenbrenner, Joyce. 1975. *Lifelines: Black Families in Chicago.* New York: Holt, Rinehart and Winston.

Bane, Mary Jo, and David Ellwood. 1986. "Slipping into and out of Poverty: The Dynamics of Spells." *Journal of Human Resources* 21:1–23.

Bane, Mary Jo, and Paul Jargowsky. 1988. "Urban Poverty Areas: Basic Questions Concerning Prevalence, Growth, and Dynamics." Center for Health and Human Resources Policy Discussion Paper Series. Cambridge, Mass.: John F. Kennedy School of Government, Harvard University.

Burt, Ronald S. 1980. "Models of Network Structure." *Annual Review of Sociology* 6:79–141.

————. 1983. "Range." In *Applied Network Analysis,* edited by R.S. Burt and M. Minor (176–94). Beverly Hills, Calif.: Sage Publications.

————. 1984. "Network Items in the General Social Survey." *Social Networks* 6:293–339.

Campbell, Karen. 1988. "Gender Differences in Job-Related Networks." *Work and Occupations* 15:179–200.

Crane, Jonathan. 1991a. "Effects of Neighborhoods on Dropping Out of School and Teenage Childbearing." In *The Urban Underclass,* edited by Christopher S. Jencks and Paul E. Peterson (299–320). Washington, D.C.: Brookings Institution.

————. 1991b. "The Epidemic Theory of Ghettos and Neighborhood Effects on Dropping Out and Teenage Childbearing." *American Journal of Sociology* 96:1226–59.

Feld, Scott L. 1982. "Social Structural Determinants of Similiarity among Associates." *American Sociology Review* 47:797–801.

————. 1984. "The Structured Use of Personal Associates." *Social Forces* 62:641–52.

Fischer, Claude S. 1982. *To Dwell among Friends: Personal Networks in Town and City.* Chicago: University of Chicago Press.

Fischer, Claude S., et al. 1977. *Networks and Places: Social Relations in the Urban Setting.* New York: Free Press.

Furstenberg, Frank F., Jr. 1989. "How Families Manage Risk and Opportunity in Dangerous Neighborhoods." Department of Sociology, University of Pennsylvania. Photocopy.

Granovetter, Mark S. 1973. "The Strength of Weak Ties." *American Journal of Sociology* 78:1360–80.

Hannerz, Ulf. 1969. *Soulside: Inquiries into Ghetto Culture and Community.* New York: Columbia University Press.

Hays, William C., and Charles H. Mindel. 1973. "Extended Kin Relations in Black and White Families." *Journal of Marriage and the Family* 35:51–57.

House, J.S., D. Umberson, and K.R. Landis. 1988. "Structures and Processes of Social Support." *Annual Review of Sociology* 14:293–318.

Hurlbert, Jeanne S., and Alan C. Acock. 1990. "The Effects of Marital Status on the Form and Composition of Social Networks." *Social Science Quarterly* 71:163–74.

Jargowsky, Paul A. and Mary Jo Bane. 1990. "Ghetto Poverty: Basic Questions." In *Inner City Poverty in the United States*, edited by Lawrence E. Lynn, Jr., and Michael G. H. McGeary (16–67). Washington, D.C.; National Academy Press.

———. 1991. "Ghetto Poverty in the United States, 1970–1980." In *The Urban Underclass*, edited by Christopher S. Jencks and Paul E. Peterson (28–100). Washington, D.C.: Brookings Institution.

Jencks, Christopher S. 1988. "Deadly Neighborhoods." *New Republic*, June 13:23–32.

———. 1991. "Is the American Underclass Growing?" In *The Urban Underclass*, edited by Christopher S. Jencks and Paul E. Peterson (28–100). Washington, D.C.: Brookings Institution.

Jencks, Christopher S., and Susan E. Mayer. 1990. "The Social Consequences of Growing Up in a Poor Neighborhood." In *Inner-City Poverty in the United States*, edited by Lawrence Lynn (111–86). Washington, D.C.: National Academy Press.

Laumann, Edward O. 1973. *Bonds of Pluralism: The Form and Substance of Urban Social Networks*. New York: John Wiley and Sons.

Liebow, Elliot. 1967. *Tally's Corner: A Study of Negro Streetcorner Men*. Boston: Little, Brown.

Marsden, Peter V. 1987. "Core Discussion Networks of Americans." *American Sociological Review* 52:122–31.

Marsden, Peter V., and Jeanne Hurlbert. 1987. "Small Networks and Selectivity Bias in the Analysis of Survey Network Data." *Social Networks* 9:333–49.

Martineau, William H. 1977. "Informal Social Ties among Urban Black Americans." *Journal of Black Studies* 8:83–104.

Massey, Douglas S., Mitchell L. Eggers, and Nancy Denton. 1989. "Disentangling the Causes of Concentrated Poverty." Paper presented at a conference on William Julius Wilson's *The Truly Disadvantaged*, Northwestern University, Evanston, Ill., October.

McCallister, Lynne, and Claude S. Fischer. 1978. "A Procedure for Surveying Personal Networks." *Sociological Methods and Research* 7:131–48.

Merry, Sally Engle. 1981. *Urban Danger: Life in a Neighborhood of Strangers*. Philadelphia: Temple University Press.

O'Hare, William, Taynia Mann, Kathryn Porter, and Robert Greenstein. 1990. *Real Life Poverty in America: Where the American Public Would Set* the *Poverty Line.* Washington, D.C.: Center on Budget and Poverty Priorities.

Rainwater, Lee. 1970. *Behind Ghetto Walls.* Chicago: Aldine.

Ricketts, Erol, and Ronald Mincy. 1990. "Growth of the Underclass: 1970– 1980." *Journal of Human Resources* 25:137–45.

Ricketts, Erol, and Isabel Sawhill. 1988. "Defining and Measuring the Underclass." *Journal of Policy Analysis and Management* 7:316–25.

Rosenbaum, James E., and Susan Popkin. 1989. "Employment and Earnings of Low-Income Blacks Who Move to Middle-Class Suburbs." In *The Urban Underclass,* edited by Christopher S. Jencks and Paul E. Peterson (342–56). Washington, D.C.: Brookings Institution.

Schulz, D. 1969. *Coming up Black: Patterns of Ghetto Socialization.* Englewood Cliffs, N.J.: Prentice-Hall.

Stack, Carol B. 1974. *All Our Kin: Strategies for Survival in Black Communities.* New York: Harper and Row.

Tienda, Marta. 1989. "Poor People and Poor Places: Deciphering Neighborhood Effects on Behavioral Outcomes." Department of Sociology, University of Chicago. Photocopy.

Tienda, Marta, and Leif Jensen. 1988. "Poverty and Minorities: A Quarter Century Profile of Color and Socioeconomic Disadvantage." In *Divided Opportunities: Minorities, Poverty, and Social Policy,* edited by Gary Sandefur and Marta Tienda (23–62). New York: Plenum Press.

Tienda, Marta, and Haya Stier. 1991. "Joblessness and Shiftlessness: Labor Force Activity in Chicago's Ghetto Poverty Neighborhoods." In *The Urban Underclass,* edited by Christopher S. Jencks and Paul E. Peterson (135–54). Washington, D.C.: Brookings Institution.

Van Haitsma, Martha. 1989. "A Conceptual Definition of the Underclass." *Focus* 12 (1):27–31.

Wacquant, Loic J. D., and William Julius Wilson. 1989. "The Cost of Racial and Class Exclusion in the Inner City." *Annals of the American Academy of Political and Social Science* 105:8–25.

Wellman, Barry. 1979. "The Community Question: The Intimate Networks of East Yorkers." *American Journal of Sociology* 84:1201–31.

Wilson, William Julius. 1987. *The Truly Disadvantaged: The Inner City, the Underclass, and Public Policy.* Chicago: University of Chicago Press.

―――――. 1991. "Studying Inner-City Dislocations: The Challenge of Public Agenda Research." *American Sociological Review* 56:1–14.

Adele V. Harrell is a senior research analyst at The Urban Institute's State Policy Center. She chaired the Conference on Drugs, Crime and Social Distress: Barriers to Urban Opportunity, held in Philadelphia. She is currently conducting research on the link between neighborhood deterioration and crime which includes a review of model programs for prevention and early intervention in troubled areas. Her analysis of the relationship among indicators of community drug use, child abuse, drug-related emergency room admission, overdose deaths, and crime rates provides guidance in monitoring drug trends within cities.

George E. Peterson is a senior fellow at The Urban Institute and co-director of the Urban Opportunity Program. His research has dealt with the financing of state and local governments and the development of urban policy. He was a member of the National Urban Policy Committee of the National Academy of Sciences. Among his recent publications is *Reagan and the Cities* and he is the editor of two other volumes in the Urban Opportunity Series, *Urban Labor Markets and Job Opportunity*, with Wayne Vroman, and *Big-City Politics, Governance, and Fiscal Constraints*.

ABOUT THE CONTRIBUTORS

Elijah Anderson is the Charles and William L. Day Professor of the Social Sciences at the University of Pennsylvania, where he has been a faculty member since 1975. An expert on the sociology of black America, he is the author of the classic work, *A Place on the Corner: A Study of Black Street Corner Men* (University of Chicago Press, 1978), and numerous articles on the black experience. He is also author of the recently published ethnographic study, *Streetwise: Race, Class and Change in an Urban Community* (University of Chicago Press, 1990), for which he won the Robert E. Park Award, American Sociological Association.

Eloise Dunlap is a project director at National Development and Research Institutes where she conducts ethnographic research on crack sellers and drug abusers in New York City. Recent publications include *Personal Safety in Dangerous Places; Inner-city Crisis and Crack Dealing: Portrait of a Drug Dealer and his Household;* and *Exorcising Sex-for-Crack: An Ethnographic Perspective from Harlem.*

Jeffrey A. Fagan is an associate professor at the School of Criminal Justice at Rutgers University. His current research includes the economic lives of women drug sellers and users in New York City, the effects of criminal sanctions on drug offenders, and the social ecology of drug use and selling in inner cities. He is the author of "Intoxication and Aggression," a chapter in the Drugs and Crime volume for the Crime and Justice series, and *Drug Use and Delinquency among Inner City Youths,* coauthored with Joseph Weis. He is Chair of the Working Group on the Ecology of Crime and Drugs for the Committee for Research on the Urban Underclass. He also is editor of the *Journal of Research on Crime and Delinquency.*

Roberto M. Fernandez is associate professor in the Department of Sociology and a Faculty Fellow in the Center for Urban Affairs and Policy Research at Northwestern University. He was an instructor and assistant professor in the Department of Sociology at the University of Arizona from 1984–89. He has published extensively in the areas of race and ethnic relations and social networks and studies race and ethnic variations in spatial mismatches induced by the relocation of a manufacturing plant from the central business district to a suburb of a Midwestern city.

Edward M. Gramlich is director of the Institute of Public Policy Studies at the University of Michigan. He is also professor of economics and public policy, and a past chair of the economics department. He has also served as Acting and deputy Director of the Congressional Budget Office, Senior Fellow of the Brookings Institution, and director of the Policy Research Division at the Office of Economic Opportunity. He is the author of a textbook on benefit-cost analysis, a book on United States budget problems, and other books and articles on macroeconomics, public finance, poverty, and labor econmics.

Ansley Hamid is assistant professor of Anthropology at John Jay College of Criminal Justice, New York City. He has been doing ethnographic fieldwork in the areas of drug use, mis-use, and distribution in the Caribbean and in Caribbean communities in New York since 1976. He has also served as a social worker/crack specialist at treatment centers in Harlem. He has written several articles on marijuana and crack use and distribution, and he is currently preparing a manuscript on these topics.

David Harris is a National Science Foundation Fellow who has recently completed his first year in the University of Wisconsin-Madison's Ph.D. program in sociology. His research interests include racial and ethnic identity and social stratification. His most recent paper, "An Analysis of the 1990 Census Count of American Indians," was prepared for presentation at the 1992 Annual Meeting of the American Sociological Association.

John D. Kasarda is Kenan Professor of Business and Sociology and director of the Kenan Institute of Private Enterprise at the University of North Carolina at chapel Hill. He has produced more than 50 scholarly articles and eight books on urban development, employment, and underclass issues. He has also served as a consultant on national urban policy to the Carter, Reagan, and Bush administrations and has testified numerous times before U.S. Congressional committees on urban and employment issues.

Roger Lane is Benjamin R. Collins Professor of Social Sciences at Haverford College and author or editor of several books, mainly on crime, policing, and black history. *The Roots of Violence in Black Philadelphia* (1986) won the 1987 Bancroft Award in American History. His most recent book, *William Dorsey's Philadelphia and Ours: On the Past and Future of the Black City in America*, (1991) is the primary basis for the article included in this volume.

Deborah Laren is a senior research associate with the Panel Study on Income Dynamics at the Institute for Social Research at the University of Michigan. She has also been a research associate with the Institute of Public Policy and the Economics Department at the University of Michigan. He has authored a number of articles on poverty, income maintenance, and applied public finance.

Naomi Sealand is a research associate with the Panel Study of Income dynamics at the Institute for Social Research at the University of Michigan. She has authored articles on the impact of neighborhoods on child and adolescent behavior.